Speaker's Sourcebook II

Quotes, Stories, & Anecdotes for Every Occasion

Glenn Van Ekeren

PRENTICE HALL
Englewood Cliffs, New Jersey 07632

Prentice-Hall International (UK) Limited, *London*
Prentice-Hall of Australia Pty. Limited, *Sydney*
Prentice-Hall Canada, Inc., *Toronto*
Prentice-Hall Hispanoamericana, S.A., *Mexico*
Prentice-Hall of India Private Limited, *New Delhi*
Prentice-Hall of Japan, Inc., *Tokyo*
Simon & Schuster Asia Pte. Ltd., *Singapore*
Editora Prentice-Hall do Brasil, Ltda., *Rio de Janeiro*

©1994 *by*
PRENTICE-HALL, Inc.
Englewood Cliffs, NJ

10 9 8 7 6 5 4

Library of Congress Cataloging-in-Publication Data
Van Ekeren, Glenn.
    Speaker's sourcebook II / Glenn Van Ekeren.
        p. cm.
    Includes index.
    ISBN 0-13-825217-3—ISBN 0-13-825225-4 (pbk.)
    1. Quotations, English. I. Title. II. Title: Speaker's sourcebook two.
PN6081.V36 1994   93-8954
                                                              CIP

ISBN 0-13-825217-3

ISBN 0-13-825225-4 (pbk)

PRENTICE HALL
Career and Personal Development
Englewood Cliffs, NJ 07632
Simon & Schuster

Printed in the United States of America

DEDICATION

This book is dedicated to my wife Marty, whose constant support and loving encouragement provided the spark necessary to make this dream a reality. And to my children, Matthew and Katy. Thank you for believing in your dad.

ACKNOWLEDGMENTS

Few readers rush to read the acknowledgments. For the author, however, it is a valuable opportunity to express appreciation to some important people.

My deepest gratitude is extended to Lois Baartman for spearheading this project. Her willingness to oversee the process from rough notes to a final manuscript is sincerely appreciated.

Thank you, Nelvina Sterk, Judy Schemper, and Deb Ten Clay for your technical assistance and excitement about the book.

To my editor, Tom Power, thank you for your encouragement, patience, and belief in my ability to produce this second edition.

Listing all of the family, friends, co-workers, and professional acquaintances who continually influence my life is not possible. Suffice it to say the material in this edition would not be possible without them.

ABOUT THE AUTHOR

Since 1979, Glenn Van Ekeren has dedicated his professional speaking and workshop facilitating to help people and organizations maximize their potential.

As the Director of People Building Institute and Director of People Development at Village Northwest Unlimited, his efforts revolve around the belief that people can change the quality of their life and the world around them by becoming better tomorrow than they are today.

Glenn is the author of the original *Speaker's Sourcebook*, published through Prentice Hall. In addition, he revised *The Complete Speaker's and Toastmaster's Library* as well as *Braude's Treasury of Wit and Humor* for Prentice Hall. Glenn is the author of monographs on a variety of topics and writes the popular "Potential" newsletter.

Glenn, his wife Marty, and their two children, Matthew and Katy, live in Sheldon, Iowa.

CONTENTS

HOW THIS BOOK WILL ENRICH YOUR SPEECH-MAKING

Have you ever noticed how a spell-binding speech seems to flow effortlessly—almost spontaneously? The opening grabs your attention, the key points are captivating, and the closing comments prompt you to action. You are almost amazed at your own attention span, interest, involvement, and support of the speaker's message.

Such orations are the result of hours of research, preparation, and organization. Every point is intricately planned, written, and injected with supportive material to impact the listening audience. Top-notch speechmakers have learned to lace their speeches together to appear natural and simply delivered.

Speaker's Sourcebook II was designed to help you develop and deliver speeches that will impact your audiences. This reference offers a bountiful buffet of speech-making, speech-enhancing material. You can choose from a chronicle of inspirational anecdotes, thought-provoking quotes, life-enriching vignettes, and light-hearted stories that will nourish your information-hungry audience.

Speakers called upon to address managers can draw from the experience and expertise of practitioners who offer life-tested insight for excelling in management. Share with them the qualities, attitudes, and skills proven leaders exhibit. Scan the insights on creating a synergistic team that produces outstanding results. Drive home the importance of organizational and personal values, as well as the dynamic impact of empowerment and setting a positive example. Timely material on excellence, as well as customer service, will reinforce your delivery and credibility. Hundreds of leadership and organizational development pointmakers are at your fingertips.

Suppose your next audience is assembling to hear an inspirational keynote that will help them discover the characteristics and lifestyles of winners. Enlighten and entertain them with selections from achievement, desire, cultivating dreams, building self-confidence, perseverance, and success to name just a few. Help people tap into their potential, expand the limits of their capabilities, and improve attitudes.

Broaden people's awareness and ability to experience work fulfillment, implement time management principles, understand wealth, and achieve worry-free living. Help people cultivate a sense of humor, deal with problems, failure and mistakes, and formulate a plan for living life to the fullest.

An invaluable selection of material exists to help people understand the key ingredients for building and maintaining positive, uplifting relationships. In addition, your audience will benefit from the ideas for dealing with arguments, persuading others, and seeking to understand what is important to other people.

The next time you're asked to deliver a talk to school educators, glean insights, humor, and inspirational thoughts from the chapters on learning, education, and youth. Encourage, challenge and assist teachers to continue making a difference in people's lives with thoughts from the world's great educators and philosophers.

Tap into a reservoir of openers, one-liners, closures, and supportive material throughout the book. Locate the perfect story or quote to accent your message. Then, spend time considering how to best put it all together to capture the hearts and minds of your audience.

Speaker's Sourcebook II even appeals to the person who never plans to enter the world of public speaking. You can enjoy a quiet evening of reading at home, grab a few minutes during your workday, or set aside a time for personal reflection and use the material as a source of insight and inspiration. Draw upon the wisdom of others to encourage, enhance, and enrich your life. The stories of real people with real experiences come to life on these pages. You will feel as if you have shared in their lives and will come away touched by their experiences.

It is my hope that *Speaker's Sourcebook II* will be a timely and matchless resource for all who read it.

ABILITY

- Our strengths are our tools, our personal reality. Our weaknesses are only what we are not.

  Joe Batten

- To be granted some kind of usable talent and to be able to use it to the fullest extent of which you are capable—this, to me, is a kind of joy that is almost unequaled.

  Lawrence Welk

- Do not let what you cannot do interfere with what you can do.

  John Wooden

- The maturing of any complex talent requires a happy combination of motivation, character, and opportunity. Most talent remains undeveloped.

  John Gardner

- For better or worse, you must play your own little instrument in the orchestra of life.

  Dale Carnegie

- There is only one protection in good times and in bad, and it doesn't lie in technology alone, or even mainly. Play consistently to your strengths and invest consistently in them and you won't need to change your flavor.

  The Supermarketers

- To build on a person's strengths, that is, to enable him to do what he can do, will make him effective . . . to try to build on his weaknesses will be . . . frustrating and stultifying.

  Peter Drucker

- Ability is the art of getting credit for all the homeruns somebody else hits.

  Casey Stengel

1

PUTTING ABILITY IN PERSPECTIVE

Did you know that after Fred Astaire's first screen test, the MGM testing director dictated a memo that read: "Can't act! Slightly bald! Can dance a little!" That harsh evaluation, written in 1933, was hung over the fireplace in Fred Astaire's Beverly Hills home.

A football expert studied Vince Lombardi's coaching and made this observation: "He possesses minimal football knowledge. Lacks motivation." So much for experts!

Socrates was charged with being "an immoral corrupter of youth." His uncanny ability to challenge accepted standards through pointed questioning confused and angered even the most learned.

Book publishers gave Norman Vincent Peale less than promising feedback on his writing ability.

Einstein was criticized for not wearing socks or cutting his hair. One observer noted: "He could be mentally retarded."

Fortunately, these famous achievers were able to dig deep, put their abilities in perspective, and excel beyond their critics' expectations. Each person, in their own unique way, assessed their abilities and determined to use what they had.

•   •   •

I can't help but reflect on the biblical story of the talents. Now, a *talent* was an ancient unit of money, but it serves as a parallel to individual ability. The story opens with the master of a wealthy estate preparing for a journey into a far country. Prior to his departure, he entrusted a portion of his wealth to three of his servants. To one he gave five talents. To the second servant he gave two talents. The third servant received one talent. Each was instructed to use what they had been given.

About a year later, the master returned and called together his servants to see how they had done. The servant given five talents had invested wisely and now possessed ten talents. "Well done, thou good and faithful servant. Because you have been faithful with what you have, I will give you more."

The second servant had also used what had been given him and the master was likewise pleased with his efforts.

Can you imagine the feelings of the third servant? The master inquired how he had done. "You only gave me one talent," responded the servant, "and I was very careful not to misuse it. In fact, I put it in a safe place during your absence. Here it is as good as new."

To put it lightly, the master was furious. "Thou wicked and slothful servant! How dare you not wisely use what I gave you." He then took the talent and gave it to the servant who had ten.

The third servant was first in the chain of people in human history who cry out: "Somebody else gets all the breaks," or "The rich get richer and the poor get poorer." You've heard those rationalizations and probably several others.

Listen now to the unwritten message of the master. "Take what you have and use it. What you initially possessed will be multiplied." Storing our talents in a safe place or keeping them buried inside results in the loss of the very thing we tried to protect.

No matter what abilities you have, use them to their fullest. Invest them wisely in activities, projects, people, and life and you will find them multiplying. It's an irrevocable law: "What you sow, that will you also reap."

．　　．　　．

All people are created with the equal ability to become unequal. Let that statement soak in. All people are created with the equal ability to become unequal. Not everyone is equipped with the same talents, gifts, or abilities. Each of us is created in a unique way. Our personalities are as diverse as the universe itself. Yet there is one constant: We can, by using what we have to the fullest, stand out from the crowd.

Take Tom Dempsey. Tom was born without toes on his right foot. He grew up in a home environment with parents who did not place limitations on him because of a disability. He was taught to use what he had and not make excuses when life's challenges met him face to face. Tom Dempsey learned to capitalize on his physical attributes rather than minimize his abilities because of them.

Tom Dempsey eventually became a place kicker in the National Football League. While playing for the New Orleans Saints, he kicked a 63-yard field goal, one of the longest in NFL's history. He achieved an uncommon feat with a foot half the size of his other one.

Napoleon Bonaparte said, "People take only their needs into consideration; never their abilities." Not Tom Dempsey. He knew that by placing limitations on what he *could* do, focusing on his needs rather than abilities, he risked creating limits on what he *would* do.

"The distribution of talents in this world should not be our concern," says Alan Loy McGinnis. "Our responsibility is to take the talents we have and ardently parlay them to the highest possible achievement."

Thomas Edison was almost deaf. Yet he didn't spend his time attempting to learn how to hear. Instead he focused on his ability to think, organize, and create. His accomplishments speak well for his decision to build on the qualities he possessed. "If we did all the things we were capable of doing," reflected Edison, "we would literally astound ourselves." Have you astounded yourself recently?

A YOUTHFUL BEGINNING

Cyrus H.K. Curtis, the founder of Curtis Publishing Company, learned how to apply his abilities and tap the talents of others. At thirteen, he started his own four-page newspaper using a handpress he purchased for $3.00. Curtis attained a circulation of 100 copies a week of his *Young America* publication and then a fire destroyed his entire operation.

A few years passed and in 1870, he was offered an advertising position for a small paper in Boston. Curtis's tenacity and advertising flair led to substantial success, and the owner, recognizing his business aptitude, offered to sell him the paper for $250.00. Hesitant about the profit potential, Curtis turned down the offer. Interestingly enough, the owner finally gave Curtis the publication for nothing and for the next five years, he made little but learned a lot. He consequently gave up the publication and moved to Philadelphia, where he married.

It was his wife, Louisa, who prompted his first major publishing success. Curtis was spreading his wings with a new publication, *The Tribune and Farmer*. His wife read the so-called "Woman's Page" one day and let her husband know she wasn't impressed.

"Who writes that section?" she asked.

"I do," replied Curtis.

"It's absurd material," Louisa continued.

"Well," snapped Curtis, "you write then."

And she did. In fact, her page became the most popular section of the paper. Louisa's ideas and writing were so successful that the "Woman's Page" turned into several pages and was finally renamed *The Ladies' Home Journal*.

After generating a few profits, Curtis went on to buy a little weekly publication, *The Saturday Evening Post*.

From a failing Boston newspaper to the profitable *Ladies' Home Journal* and *Saturday Evening Post*, Curtis maintained faith in his own business and writing abilities. He was also smart enough to know when other people were more capable.

MORE THAN LUCK

To say "Babe" Didrickson Zaharias was an athletic phenomenon might be an understatement. Spectators marveled at her ability to run, jump, ride, and play basketball and baseball. She made quite a name for herself in the 1932 Olympic tryouts by winning five first places in track and field. She attained international acclaim during the Los Angeles Olympics that same year by placing second in the high jump, first in the women's 80-meter hurdles, and first in the javelin throw.

It would be safe to say that most people would be satisfied with such achievements. Not Babe. She took up the game of golf, searched out a quality instructor, studied the game, and worked to refine her swing. She analyzed the golf swing, broke it down into manageable parts, and mastered each component. Babe was known to spend hours on the practice tee, sometimes hitting a thousand range balls in an afternoon. At times, her hands would become so sore and raw, she could barely grip the club. Babe would stop long enough to tape them up and then continued her practice regimen. She was determined to master the fundamentals and perfect her swing. Her preparation, training, and just plain hard work paid off as she won the U.S. national woman's amateur and British woman's amateur championships.

Babe's later battle with cancer exemplified her courageous spirit to overcome the odds. She faced it with the same determination as she faced other life challenges. She was a winner in the hearts of an entire nation.

Were her achievements lucky? I don't think so. Could it be she was just a natural athlete? Unlikely. Babe Zaharias became a champion by living by this philosophy: In order to develop one's abilities, one must define and refine them.

• • •

As Paderewski played the piano before Queen Victoria, she listened with intent enthusiasm. When he had finished the queen commented, "Mr. Paderewski, you are a genius!" "Ah, your majesty," he responded, "perhaps. But before I was a genius, I was a drudge."

In music, sports, or any other endeavor, there is usually a fumbling beginning. Life's outstanding achievers like "Babe" and Paderewski understand the price to be paid for mastery. To be considered accomplished in any area is the result of taking even the smallest talent and practicing it into excellence.

FROM BUSBOY TO ENTREPRENEUR

Dave Thomas had a difficult childhood that gave him the determination to excel and succeed. He was adopted, but lost his mother when he was five. After her death, his adoptive father married three more times and moved the family frequently. At twelve years of age, Thomas got his first job and quit school after the tenth grade to work full-time in the restaurant business.

Thomas worked his way up from a busboy in a family restaurant to manager of four failing Kentucky Fried Chicken franchises. Kentucky Fried Chicken's late founder, Colonel Harland Sanders, became Thomas's mentor and taught him the ropes about promoting a business.

Dave was a fast learning student. Soon he had turned around the Kentucky Fried Chicken franchises and was given a stake in those businesses. The profits, which made him a millionaire by his thirty-fifth birthday, provided the starting capital for Thomas to open his first Wendy's, in 1969.

Although Thomas is the company's single largest owner, holding 8 percent of Wendy's stock, he has removed himself from most operational responsibilities. In his book, *Dave's Way* (Berkley Publishing, 1992), he admits to being a cheerleader and marketer but not effective with day-to-day details. He travels the country, in between doing commercials, to insure quality control and motivating Wendy's employees.

Dave Thomas assessed his abilities and placed himself in a position that would capitalize on his strengths. Doing what he knows best, Thomas is the inspiration behind Wendy's success.

LOOK BEFORE YOU LEAP

In one of Russell Myers' Broom Hilda comic strips, the little green witch is peering over the edge of a cliff. Across a deep canyon is Gaylord the Buzzard. Gaylord is beckoning to Broom Hilda, "Come over here with me!"

Broom Hilda considers Gaylord's challenge, then looks down at the canyon and replies, "I can't jump that far!" Gaylord responds, "You're defeating yourself with negative thinking. I'm writing a book on the power of positive thought, in which I can prove you can do anything if you have the correct attitude!"

Broom Hilda contemplates Gaylord's challenge as she surveys the giant chasm separating them. Gaylord gives his final pitch, "Tell yourself you can do it—and do it!" Broom Hilda feels a surge of self-confidence as she responds, "Okay—here I come!" She steps back, kicks up her leg, and takes a giant leap . . . down, down, down.

Gaylord calmly looks over the edge of the cliff and watches Broom Hilda falling, becoming a mere pencil dot in the canyon below. He turns, walks away, and comments to himself, "You know, I think I'll add a chapter on building up your leg muscles."

This section on expanding the limits of your abilities is not intended to communicate the message that anyone can do anything they set their mind to. Rather, people who invest their time developing their leg muscles (and other abilities) will exceed their previous limits. Believing you can do something is great, but combine it with developed abilities and new chasms will be mastered.

WHAT ARE YOU HIDING?

Leave the world of reality for a moment and suppose you have acquired substantial wealth. What would you do with the money? Perhaps you would decide to spend it on something you've always wanted. Sharing it with family or friends might sound like a possible option. Hiring a financial consultant to offer investment ideas is another possibility.

In answering that question, I wonder how many people would follow the path of W. C. Fields. Wanting to keep his wealth a secret, Fields reportedly tucked his money away in 200 different bank accounts throughout the United States and Europe. Fearing someone would find him out, he opened each account under an assumed name.

When W. C. Fields died, the executors of his estate encountered an overwhelming nightmare. They were able to trace only forty-five of the accounts, leaving a substantial amount of money uncovered. It is estimated that $600,000 or more was never found.

Let's talk about reality. You are wealthy. Your talents, skills, and abilities are intangible forms of wealth.

So, what are you doing with your wealth? Are you making wise investments, sharing your talents with others? Or are you hiding them for future use? Enrich your world and the world around you by uncovering those forgotten, hidden, or rusted abilities.

FIND YOUR FASTBALL

During the time this chapter was being written, our family journeyed to Minneapolis to enjoy a Minnesota Twins baseball game. The combination of sitting in the twenty-eighth row of the upper deck and slow action in the middle innings caused my mind to wander back to childhood days.

As a youngster growing up in South Dakota, I attached my baseball allegiance to the Twins. Rod Carew, Harmon Kilebrew, and Tony Oliva won my respect. However, this night my mind focused on the success of another Twin I admired. He developed a reputation as one of baseball's leading left-handed pitchers. Jim Kaat exemplified the success experienced by people who learn to capitalize on their strengths.

Leo Hauser, in *Five Steps to Success* (Hauser Productions, Wayzata, MN) tells this story about Jim Kaat. Kaat traces his success back to spring training in 1966. The Twins had acquired a new pitching coach, Johnny Sain, who silently watched his pitchers perform. Then, one by one, he called them in for a personal chat.

"Jim," said Sain, "I've been watching you pitch. Tell me, what are your four best pitches?"

Kaat, knowing his pitching ability well, responded: "My best pitch is my fastball. Then comes my curve. My slider and changeup are third and fourth."

"What pitch do you spend the most time practicing?" asked Sain.

"My slider and changeup," said Kaat. " If I can improve on those two pitches, I know I'll have a good season."

Sain looked at Kaat, pondered his comments, and then responded, "I see it a little differently, Jim, and want you to take a different approach. Work on your fastball. I know it's your favorite pitch so go out there in practice, warm-ups, and during games and concentrate on your fastball. Throw your fastball 80 to 90 percent of the time all year and you'll win a lot of ball games."

Kaat left Sain's office stunned. He had expected expert tips for improving his changeup or slider. At least Sain could have provided technical advice for smoothing out his curve ball. Telling him to do more of what he already did best didn't make much sense.

That season Jim Kaat threw fastball after fastball. Kaat said he thought his arm was going to fall off but he heeded the advice of his coach. That year, 1966, Jim Kaat won twenty-six games and went on to become pitcher of the year in the American League.

I had the privilege of seeing him win one of those games. And tonight, I wonder what advice these pitchers were given by their coaches.

Now I'm no pitching coach but it seems to me there are some parallel questions to ask in the game of life. Do you know what your fastball is? Have you identified your best pitch? Are you using it 80 to 90 percent of the time? How often do your God-given talents sit idle while you try to overcome limitations?

Find your fastball and build on it. Who knows, your slider and changeup may become unnecessary.

UNLEASH YOUR POWER

When the circus came to our small town in northwest Iowa, throngs of people gathered to watch the raising of the tent. My son, Matthew, was fascinated by the powerful elephant's ability to stretch the canvas into form.

That night, we attended the circus production under the big top. Matthew immediately noticed the elephants standing quietly while tied to a small wooden stake. "Daddy, how come the elephant doesn't pull the stake out of the ground and run away?" Matthew queried (I love those "teachable moments").

Maybe you have had the same question. While still young and powerless, an elephant is tied by a heavy chain to an immovable steel stake. The animal discovers that, no matter how hard he pulls, the chain will not break and the stake remains secure. Then, as the elephant grows, he continues to believe he cannot move as long as there is a stake in the ground beside him.

There are people conditioned to behave like these elephants. They are restricted in thought, action, and results. Therefore, they never stretch beyond their self-imposed limitations.

ACHIEVEMENT

- Nothing stops the man who desires to achieve. Every obstacle is simply a course to develop his achievement muscle. It's a strengthening of his powers of accomplishment.

  Eric Butterworth

- Plant the seeds of expectation in your mind; cultivate thoughts that anticipate achievement. Believe in yourself as being capable of overcoming all obstacles and weaknesses.

  Norman Vincent Peale

- It is time for us all to stand and cheer for the doer, the achiever—the one who recognizes the challenge and does something about it.

  Vince Lombardi

- One of the most difficult things everyone has to learn is that for your entire life you must keep fighting and adjusting if you hope to survive. No matter who you are or what your position you must keep fighting for whatever it is you desire to achieve.

  George Allen

- Productive achievement is a consequence and an expression of healthy self-esteem, not its cause.

  Nathaniel Branden

- If what you did yesterday seems big, you haven't done anything today.

  Lou Holtz

- Great things are not done by impulse but by a series of small things brought together.

  Vincent van Gogh

- The man who has accomplished all that he thinks worthwhile has begun to die.

  E. T. Trigg

- Accomplishment will prove to be a journey, not a destination.

  Dwight D. Eisenhower

- Accomplishment automatically results in change.

  Jim Tunney

- Nothing is so fatiguing as the eternal hanging on of an uncompleted task.

  William James

- If it were easy it would have been done before.

  Jeanne Yaeger

- Some people dream of worthy accomplishments, while others stay awake and do them.

  Anonymous

- Accomplishing the impossible means only that the boss will add it to your regular duties.

  Doug Larson

- Success and achievement are more important than one's financial statement. Life's measurement is not only quantitative but qualitative.

  Bill Byrne
  Habits of Wealth

PROVE IT!

A great story has made the rounds about a scrawny, seemingly undernourished old man who entered a restaurant and asked who he needed to see to get a job at a nearby lumberjack camp. "You won't need to go far," the restaurant owner replied as he pointed to a nearby booth. "The supervisor is having lunch right over there."

The jobseeker approached the supervisor and exclaimed, "I'm looking for a lumberjack job." The boss politely tried to talk him out of the idea. Surely this weak old man wouldn't be able to fell a tree let alone keep up with the daily quotas. "Give me a few minutes of your time and I'll show you what I can do," suggested the man.

When the two arrived at a grove needing to be cleared, the slender, persistent old man picked up an ax and proceeded to chop down a huge tree in record time. "That's incredible," the boss said. "Where did you learn to fell trees like that?" "Well," said the old man, "you've heard of the Sahara Forest?" Hesitantly the boss replied, "Don't you mean the Sahara Desert?" The old man produced a smile and said, "Sure, that's what it's called now."

Achievers are producers. They understand the world will not recognize them for what they could have done, should have done or would have done. Recognition is experienced by proving what you can do by doing it.

LEARN TO CELEBRATE

Sam Walton invested thirty years of his life building Wal-Mart into the nation's largest retailer. On April 5, 1992, he died of cancer. Shortly thereafter more than 15,000 stockholders of Wal-Mart Stores, Inc. bid farewell to Mr. Walton during an emotional annual meeting in Fayetteville, Arkansas, marked by tears, hugs, and singalongs dedicated to the late Arkansas billionaire.

Sam Walton created his successful empire through friendly service and reduced prices. He also learned along the way to celebrate his achievements. At age 71 he vowed to do the hula on Wall Street if his company could tally up a net pretax profit of more than 8 percent. When Wal-Mart achieved this challenging goal, Walton strapped a grass skirt over his business suit and danced along with some traditional Hawaiian dancers and musicians on the sidewalk in front of a downtown Manhattan office building.

This billionaire entrepreneur will no doubt be remembered for many of his business attributes. Among them was his youthful ability to celebrate his successes.

INSPIRED BY THE FINISH LINE

Achievers from all over the world submit themselves to the grueling demands of the Tour de France. In a *National Geographic* article titled "An Annual Madness," Gilbert Duclos-Lassalle describes the arduous experience. The bicycle race covers approximately 2,000 miles, including some of France's most difficult, mountainous terrain. Physical needs such as eating and drinking are done on the run. Temperature extremes add to the cyclists' challenges. Lassalle indicates he rides his bicycle 22,000 miles a year to train for the event. That's nearly 60 miles a day, everyday.

What kind of trophy and cash prize motivates a cycler to train so rigorously and then endure such hardship and pain? The prize is a special winner's jersey. Lassalle sums up the contestant's inspiration: "Why, to sweep through the Arc de Triomphe on the last day. To be able to say you finished the Tour de France."

Achievers are often motivated by the challenge itself. Self-discipline, preparation, and the desire to complete what they began serve as a catalyst for impressive achievement. The very thought of the finish line makes the pain worthwhile.

WHERE ARE YOU GOING?

High achievers have no desire to win a Christopher Columbus award. These awards are given to people who don't know where they are going, have no idea where they are when they arrive, and upon returning home, don't know where they've been.

How important is it to know what you want and where you're going? A study of the graduates of one Harvard class thirty years later says it all: 80 percent had no specific goals, 15 percent had ones they only thought about, and 5 percent had written goals (dreams with deadlines). The 5 percent, measured by net assets, had not only surpassed the goals they wrote down for themselves but, as a group, had more net worth than the other 95 percent combined. Impressive!

·   ·   ·

A man driving through the Black Hills near Mount Rushmore ran into a snowstorm and lost all sense of direction. Then he peered out his side window and saw a snowplow. Relieved, he kept as close to the vehicle as he could while it removed snow from the pavement. At times the heavy snowfall made it difficult to follow the machine.

After a while the plow stopped and the operator got out and walked over to the car. "Mister, where are you headed?" the driver asked.

"I'm on my way to Montana," the man responded.

"Well, you'll never get there following me. I'm plowing out this parking lot!"

If you're not getting anywhere fast, maybe it's time to decide exactly where you want to go and exactly what you want to achieve. Blindly following someone else may be a dead-end trip.

ACHIEVEMENT IN PERSPECTIVE

After completing his term as thirtieth President of the United States, he issued his famous "I do not choose to run" statement. Reporters bombarded him with questions seeking more details concerning this decision. One persistent journalist refused to leave this line of questioning. "Exactly why don't you want to be President again?" he grilled.

Calvin Coolidge, undoubtedly frustrated with the probes, looked the reporter straight in the eye and responded, "Because there's no room for advancement."

Although humorous and true, we can make a serious application. Never allow the anticipation of achievement to outweigh the realization of it. Coolidge didn't allow the grandeur of his office to shade his perspective on other valuable achievements. He realized that being President was the ultimate in politics but life existed outside of that world.

ACTION

- There are risks and costs to a program of action. But they are far less than the long range risks and costs of comfortable inaction.

  John F. Kennedy

- Some people wait so long for their ship to come in, their pier collapses.

  John Goddard

- Unless a capacity for thinking be accompanied by a capacity for action, a superior mind exists in torture.

  Benedetto Croce

- Everybody ought to do at least two things each day that he or she hates to do, just for practice.

  William James

- Human beings thrive on action. Stagnation does not wear well with us. We are said to have our origins as hunter-gatherers. We run and we chase. We are problem-solvers. We must be continuously tested and we continuously test ourselves. And it will not end until our lives end because it is life itself.

  Art Buchwald

- To become successful you must be a person of action. Merely to "know" is not sufficient. It is necessary both to know and do.

  Napoleon Hill

- To mobilize yourself, decide what you want, determine what will get you what you want, then act—do what will get you what you want most to achieve.

  Nido Qubein

- Apply yourself. Get all the education you can, but then, by God, do something. Don't just stand there, make it happen.

  Lee Iacocca

- I think there is something more important than believing: Action! The world is full of dreamers, there aren't enough who will move ahead and begin to take concrete steps to actualize their vision.

  W. Clement Stone

■ Action is indeed therapy. It erases doubts and fears, anxieties, and worries. It capitalizes on failures and mistakes and turns them into positive influences. It exercises the mind for problem solving and for creativity. It develops poise under pressure and uses wisdom and experience to consider alternatives and to provide a back-up plan. It calls forth the best in us all, and it becomes the password to success. Action is work, and work is happiness.

George Shinn

■ You will learn and grow according to the nature and consequences of your actions.

Robert Anthony

■ It doesn't matter how many people say it cannot be done or how many people have tried it before; it's important to realize that whatever you're doing, it's your first attempt at it.

Wally "Famous" Amos

■ No matter what business you're in, you can't run in place or someone will pass you by. It doesn't matter how many games you've won.

Jim Valvano

■ To do anything in the world worth doing, we must not stand back shivering and thinking of the cold and danger, but jump in, and scramble through as well as we can.

Sydney Smith

■ The critical ingredient is getting off your butt and doing something. It's as simple as that. A lot of people have ideas, but there are few who decide to do something about them now. Not tomorrow. Not next week. But today. The true entrepreneur is a doer, not a dreamer.

Nolan Bushell

■ You'll never get ahead until you start advancing.

Robert Schuller

■ The great composer does not set to work because he is inspired, but becomes inspired because he is working. Beethoven, Bach, Mozart settled down day after day to the job at hand with as much regularity as an accountant settles down each day to his figures. They didn't waste time waiting for inspiration.

Ernest Newman

■ Ingenuity, plus coverage, plus work, equals miracles.

Bob Richards

■ Both tears and sweat are salty, but they render a different result. Tears will get you sympathy, sweat will get you change.

Jesse Jackson

■ Things do not happen; things are made to happen.

John F. Kennedy

THE BREAKFAST OF A CHAMPION

There must be a reason why the Bible never mentions the intentions, dreams, or ideas of the apostles. However, an entire book is specified as the "Acts of the Apostles." It was the performance of these dedicated people that drew the attention of biblical writers. Their incredible achievements are attributed to undying dedication and ceaseless action.

I have no idea whether Lillian Katz drew her inspiration from the apostles but her drive produced impressive results. As a 24-year-old, pregnant with her first child, Lillian sought a way to increase her family's income. Using $2,000 saved from wedding gifts, she purchased a few supplies, and submitted an ad to *Seventeen* magazine promoting personalized handbags and belts. It was 1951, and the thought of putting a person's initials on products was somewhat revolutionary. "Be the first to sport that personalized look," read the ad.

The orders came, business grew, and today, her mail-order catalog company, Lillian Vernon Corporation, enjoys annual sales of $140 million. She, of course, no longer fills orders at her kitchen table, but employs 1,000 people to process 30,000 weekly orders.

Action-oriented people realize "they who want milk should not sit in the middle of a field and wait for a cow to back up to them." Lillian Katz didn't wait around for someone to offer her the opportunity to increase her family income or hope she would win the lottery. She made action the breakfast of a champion.

DECISION BACKED BY ACTION

Suppose you had five birds sitting on a wire and three of them decided to fly. How many birds would you have left on the wire?

Five birds remain. Making a decision to fly without acting on the decision is a waste of energy. The momentum to do something about our decisions is energized by action.

In 1932, during the Great Depression, a young man graduated from college with a degree in social science. He had absolutely no idea what he wanted to do with his life and besides, jobs were hard to come by. To occupy his summer and earn a little money, he went back to an old job, lifeguarding at a local swimming pool.

The father of some children he was teaching to swim took a liking to this young man and became interested in his future. He encouraged him to look inside himself and decide what he most wanted to do. Acting on the counsel, the young lifeguard spent several days searching his heart. He made a concrete, emphatic decision to become a radio announcer.

The soul-searching results were shared with his mentor who told him to begin taking the necessary action to make his dream come true. The young man packed his bags and set out to break into the radio business. His high hopes were stymied some when he hitchhiked to Chicago and failed to secure employment. Determined, he continued making contacts across Illinois and into Iowa. Finally, at WOC in Davenport, his pursuit paid off and he was offered a job as a sports announcer. This experience was the first of many that required President Ronald Reagan to combine a dream with determined action.

What ideas, dreams, or good intentions have you allowed to sit idly on a wire because your decision wasn't backed by action?

LIFE'S PREREQUISITE: ACTION

Dr. Wayne Dyer wasn't satisfied being a relatively unknown professor with a new book entitled *Your Erroneous Zones*. He set out to make his book a bestseller and not depend on the publisher to do it for him. Dyer bought several hundred copies of his book and hit the road in his car, intent on educating America about the self-help book he had written.

Six months later, Dyer had traveled twenty-eight thousand miles, covering forty-seven states. He personally delivered between fifteen and sixteen thousand copies of his book to America's book stores.

Dr. Dyer didn't stop at delivering books. He sought out feature writers and interviewers resulting in eight hundred publicity interviews.

Because of Dyer's do-it-yourself action, *Your Erroneous Zones* became a number one bestseller, and Dr. Wayne Dyer achieved acclaim as an author and professional speaker.

•   •   •

When asked about his entrepreneurial success as founder of Atari, Nolan Bushell responded, "The critical ingredient is getting off your butt and doing something. It's as simple as that. A lot of people have ideas, but there are few who decide to do something about them now. Not tomorrow. Not next week, but today. The true entrepreneur is a doer, not a dreamer."

• • •

Cavett Robert, one of this nation's outstanding public speakers, wrote, "A constructive life is built of the things we do—not of the things we don't do. Never forget that the only material which can be used in building a life is positive action."

Take it from a best-selling author, an entrepreneur, and a legendary professional speaker—life, success, achievement, and ultimately, self-satisfaction are preceded by action.

NOTHING IS ACCOMPLISHED ON THE SIDELINES

A group of animals and insects decided to organize a football game. Somehow, the teams were organized according to size. All the big animals, including the bears, lions, elephants, and giraffes, were on one team. Rabbits, squirrels, gophers, and insects formed the second team.

The game got off to a lopsided start, and at the end of the first quarter, the big animals were leading 56 to 0. By halftime, their lead had expanded to 119 to 0. The small animals and insects had produced little offensive yardage and were unable to make a single tackle.

As the second half started, the lion received the kickoff on the 25-yard line and was tackled on the 37-yard line. On first down, the bear went up the middle and was toppled at the line of scrimmage for no gain. On the next play, the cheetah attempted to run around an end but was tackled for a one-yard loss. The cheetah looked around at the bottom of the pile and saw a centipede smiling back at him. He looked at the centipede and said, "Did you tackle me? This is the first time I've been tackled all day."

"I sure did," the gutsy, multi-legged critter responded. "I also tackled the lion and bear."

One of his rabbit teammates questioned, "Where were you the first half when we failed to muster a single tackle?"

The centipede replied, "I was tying my shoes!"

The centipede is a positive role model for those people who are continually sitting on the sidelines. They intend to do something significant as soon as all of the conditions are right. They expend considerable energy and time preparing to take action. When they finally get around to making sure all their shoes are tied . . . it's too late.

DO YOUR PART

A good and faithful man fell upon financially hard times. Every time he turned around, it seemed another demand was placed upon him until finally, as the saying goes, he was "so poor he couldn't pay attention." One night in his distress, he dropped to his knees, lifted his eyes toward heaven, and prayed, "Dear God, I am destitute. Please let me win the lottery—soon!" The next week, he was optimistic his condition would change. After three months, his faith began to waver, and by the end of a year, he became angry that he had not yet won a single dime.

"Are you there, God?" he pleaded. "I believed you would help me, yet an entire year has passed without you answering my prayers."

Suddenly, a dark cloud appeared in the sky, lightning flashed, and a voice boomed from the heavens: "I hear you . . . I hear you. In fact, I've heard your every prayer, but give me a break. The least you could do is buy a lottery ticket."

Here's a profound thought: Those who decide to wait to be rescued from their undesirable circumstances will undoubtedly wait a very long time. "Keep on going and chances are you will stumble on something, perhaps when you are least expecting it," advised Charles Kettering. "I have never heard of anyone stumbling on something sitting down."

TAKE A SHOT AT IT!

A famous novelist was lecturing to a group of college students determined to pursue literary careers. In the opening statement of his talk, he asked, "How many of you really want to be writers?" A flurry of hands shot into the air. "In that case," he continued, returning his notes to his coat pocket, "the best advice I can give you is to go home and write." Then he exited the room.

The value of a book, educational program, good piece of advice, or lofty ambition is much like the value of buying a new car. You can spend a tidy sum for a new car, but until you start the engine, put it in gear, take your foot off the brake, and depress the gas, nothing will happen. Similarly, reading these inspirational anecdotes on action is of little value unless you get yourself in gear.

Wayne Gretzky, the leading scorer in hockey history, reflected on the comment of an early coach who was frustrated with his lack of scoring in an important game. "Wayne," he said privately, "you miss 100 percent of the shots you never take."

Likewise, people miss 100 percent of any goal, job task, dream, or project unless they take a shot at it. Journalist Kathy Seligman once said, "You can't hit a home-run unless you step up to the plate. You can't catch fish unless you put a line in the water. You can't reach your goals unless you actually do something."

JUST DO IT!

In the *Star Wars* sequel, *The Empire Strikes Back*, Yoda, the Jedi teacher, tries to implant into Luke Skywalker the means of engaging the "force" that is the greatest power in the universe. He says to his pupil, "Luke, there is no try, there is either do or not do."

The following story has been around longer than Luke Skywalker and magnifies the importance of *doing*: There once were four people named Everybody, Somebody, Anybody, and Nobody. An important job had to be done, and Everybody was sure that Somebody would do it. Anybody could have done it, but Nobody did it. Somebody got angry about that, because it was Everybody's job. Everybody thought Anybody could do it and that Somebody would do it. But Nobody realized that Everybody thought Somebody would do it. It ended up that Everybody blamed Somebody when Nobody did what Anybody could have done.

Be somebody who makes things happen. How? In the words of a famous shoe manufacturer: "Just do it!"

ADVERSITY

- Crises force our attention on the disorder in our thinking and can save us as we teeter on the brink of an even greater disaster.

  David McNally

- Pain nourishes courage. You can't be brave if you've only had wonderful things happen to you.

  Mary Tyler Moore

- In times like these, it helps to recall that there have always been times like these.

  Paul Harvey

- Have courage for the great sorrows of life and patience for the small ones. And when you have finished your daily task, go to sleep in peace. God is awake.

  Victor Hugo

- The way I see it, if you want the rainbow, you gotta put up with the rain.

  Dolly Parton

- Show me someone who has done something worthwhile, and I'll show you someone who has overcome adversity.

  Lou Holtz

- Good timber does not grow with ease; the stronger the wind, the stronger the trees.

  J. Willard Marriott

- Talking about your grievances merely adds to those grievances. Give recognition only to what you desire.

  Thomas Dreier

- You have to accept whatever comes and the only important thing is that you meet it with courage and with the best you have to give.

  Eleanor Roosevelt

- Watch out for emergencies. They are your big chance!

  Fritz Reiner

- Adversity is an experience, not a final act.

Michael LeBoeuf, Ph.D.

- Has any man ever obtained inner harmony by simply reading about the experiences of others? Not since the world began has it ever happened. Each man must go through the fire himself.

Norman Douglas

- Never measure the height of a mountain until you have reached the top. Then you will see how low it was.

Dag Hammarskjold

- In this life we will encounter hurts and trials that we will not be able to change; we are just going to have to allow them to change us.

Ron Lee Davis

- It will always hurt to be laughed at, snubbed, ignored or attacked by others. But I would remind you that the human personality grows through adversity, provided it is not crushed in the process.

James Dobson

- I know God will not give me anything I can't handle. I just wish that He didn't trust me so much.

Mother Teresa

- You gotta play the hand that's dealt you. There may be pain in that hand, but you play it. And I've played it.

James Brady

- We have no right to ask when a sorrow comes, "Why did this happen to me?" Unless we ask the same question for every joy that comes our way.

Philip E. Bernstein

TURN ADVERSITY INTO AN ADVANTAGE

The village blacksmith was a brilliant crafter of useful tools. As he pumped the bellows, the furnace fire was prepared. Into the intense heat the blacksmith placed a piece of iron until it reached an almost transparent state. The metal was removed from the fire and placed on the anvil, and with a heavy hammer the crafter pounded the iron made pliable by the heat.

The iron was transformed by this repeated process. After the final shape was achieved, the hot iron was placed into water. The drastic temperature change tempered the iron and gave it durability and strength. The heat, hammer, and water together developed strength that could be achieved in no other way.

The human spirit is formed, matured, and strengthened through the adversities of life. "If you will call your troubles experiences," wrote John R. Miller, "and remember that every experience develops some latent force within you, you will grow vigorous and happy, however adverse your circumstances may seem to be."

*   *   *

Representative Fred Grandy shared an anecdote that makes good sense for those struggling with day-to-day adversity. It seems there was an old farmer who had suffered through a lifetime of troubles and afflictions that would have leveled an ordinary mortal. But through it all he never lost his sense of humor.

"How have you managed to keep so happy and serene?" asked a friend.

"It ain't hard," said the old fellow with a twinkle in his eye, "I've just learned to cooperate with the inevitable."

An Asian saying advises, "When fate throws a dagger at you, there are only two ways to catch it, either by the blade or by the handle." "Cooperating with the inevitable" requires us to catch adversity by the handle and use it as the tool for which it was intended.

*   *   *

Albert Einstein suggested that "in the middle of every difficulty lies opportunity. Whenever challenged by life's difficulties, it would be advantageous to realize adversity is unavoidable and then to determine how these seemingly ill-fated events will be used to strengthen us. Keep in mind that wherever you are, whatever your circumstances may be, whatever misfortune you may have suffered, the music of your life has not gone.

Consider these examples from history where the handle of adversity was used to create opportunity:

Henry Ford failed and went broke five times before experiencing success.

Beethoven rose above his deafness to compose harmonious music.

John Bunyan wrote *Pilgrim's Progress* while confined to a prison cell for his views on religion.

The Greek orator Demosthenes overcame a lifetime of stuttering to rally people with his touching speeches.

Deaf, speechless, and blind since early childhood, Helen Keller achieved greatness experienced by few without such handicaps. "The marvelous richness of human experience would lose something of rewarding joy if there were not limitations to overcome," commented Helen Keller. "The hilltop hour would not be half so wonderful if there were no dark valleys to traverse."

In the 1952 Olympics, a young Hungarian boy split the bull's eye on the target again and again. His eye-hand coordination won him a gold medal. Then disaster struck. He lost his right shooting arm. Four years later he returned to Melbourne and split the bull's eye as he had done before—using his left hand.

As an elementary student actor James Earl Jones stuttered so badly he communicated with friends and teachers using written notes. Today, he is known for the richness and power of his voice.

Experiencing a lifetime of personal failures and setbacks, Winston Churchill persevered to become Prime Minister of England at age 62.

Charlie Steinmetz described himself as "ugly, deformed, and a dwarf." Yet he developed his scientific mind to introduce the world to new inventions.

By now you no doubt get the point. Adversity can only strip the music from life if we allow it to. Washington Irving believed "little minds attain and are subdued by misfortunes; but great minds rise above them."

Remember the movie *Private Benjamin* starring Goldie Hawn? Goldie plays a young woman who enlists in the Army on the recruiter's promise of condominium living, maid service, and other unavailable niceties. She is horrified to learn the grim realities of base and barracks living. In addition, a series of unfortunate events earns her the label of incompetent. It was unlikely she would graduate.

However, during the final stages of her training the entire base is involved in war games. She and three comrades serendipitously capture the entire "blue team" (the enemy). As a result she wins the favor of the commander and upon her graduation from basic training is assigned to his command in the Thornbirds. (This was a plum assignment and she was the only female selected.)

The day before her first parachute jump, Private Benjamin meets the commander on the road and expresses her concern about meeting his expectations and fulfilling the confidence he has expressed in her. The commander assures her of his support and replies with a statement that has formed his career as a Thornbird: "Remember, life is a series of challenges to be met and mastered."

Just as the cherished oyster, Private Benjamin endured the adversity and challenges of outside irritations, applied the resources within her, and produced a valuable pearl. Her success was born of adversity.

•   •   •

J. B. Phillips's paraphrase of James 1:2-4 puts this matter in perspective: "When all kinds of trials crowd into your lives, my brothers, don't resent them as intruders, but welcome them as friends! Realize that they have come to test your endurance.

But let the process go on until that endurance is fully developed, and you will find you have become men (and women) of mature character . . ."

Most people would no doubt enjoy a life free from flat tires, clogged toilets, broken arms, lost jobs or damaged relationships. There is a slim to nothing chance that trouble will cease to come our way. But actually, the absence of adversity might be the biggest disaster of all.

Consider the words of an anonymous poet:

> Looking back, it seems to me
> All the grief, which had to be,
> Left me when the pain was o'er
> Richer than I'd been before.

HEROES IN THE ANNALS OF ADVERSITY

David Rothenberg

I marvel at the incomprehensible difficulties, repeated setbacks and uncontrollable circumstances experienced by people who refused to quit.

The first name that comes to mind is David Rothenberg. David's father, in a fit of anger, went into his room, poured kerosene all over the room and on little David, and then lit him on fire. David miraculously lived through the ordeal although 95 percent of his body was covered with third-degree burns. Doctors estimate that David will have approximately five thousand operations in his lifetime to a body that virtually has no skin.

At age seven, David Rothenberg had the courage and audacity to respond to his life-changing experience with these words:

> I am alive!
> I am alive!
> I am alive!
> I didn't miss out on living! And that is wonderful enough for me.

Richard Bach and Richard Hooker

Remember Richard Bach? His 10,000-word story about a "soaring" seagull was rejected by eighteen publishers. Macmillan finally agreed to publish the *Jonathan Livingston Seagull* manuscript in 1970. Within five years, it had sold over seven million copies in the U.S. alone.

Another author, Richard Hooker, labored for seven years to complete his humorous war novel only to have it rejected by twenty-one publishers. Morrow took a risk and published the unique novel, *M*A*S*H*. The risk paid off and

M*A*S*H became a bestseller, prompting a blockbusting movie and long-running popular television series.

Kirk Gibson

According to a Detroit news article, Kirk Gibson is a baseball player who knows how to live with pain. In 1980, he tore the cartilage in his wrist. Two years later, he severely sprained his left wrist. In 1983, he was out for knee surgery, and in 1985 he required seventeen stitches after getting hit in the mouth with a wild pitch. In addition, he bruised a hamstring muscle, injured his right heel, and suffered a sore left ankle. His worst injury involved severe ligament damage to his ankle in 1986, a year predicted to be his best. When asked about pain, Gibson was quoted as saying "There are pluses and minuses in everything we do in life . . . But the pluses for my career, myself, and my family make it worth it. It's the path I choose."

Dave Dravecky

Dave Dravecky began his baseball career in 1982 with the San Diego Padres and played there until midway through the 1987 season when he was traded to the San Francisco Giants. He was a National League all-star and pitched in two NL championships and one World Series game.

Dave Dravecky pitched his last baseball game on August 15, 1989. His newest book, *When You Can't Come Back*, captures the agonizing, yet inspirational transition he has made after losing his left arm to cancer.

According to an interview with *USA Today*, Dravecky readily admits to the mental challenges, depression, and family strain this amputation at the height of his career caused. But there is monumental courage driving his life. Dravecky says his faith in God is everything. "I've come to understand that God is really shaping and molding my character. I've come to realize that real growth of character takes place in the valleys of life."

The cancer cost Dravecky his left arm and his career but not his zest or purpose for living.

Fanny Crosby

Fanny Crosby was six weeks old when a minor eye inflammation appeared. Careless medical treatment left her totally and permanently blind. In spite of her disability, she wrote more than eight thousand songs in her eighty-eight years of life. Fanny always believed her blindness was a gift from God that helped the words flow from her pen. Perhaps the first poem she wrote best expressed her special spirit.

> Oh, what a happy soul I am,
> Although I cannot see,
> I am resolved that in this world
> Contented I will be . . .

Wilma Rudolph

Track star Wilma Rudolph won three gold medals in the 1960 Olympics, but to get there she had to overcome enormous hurdles.

Wilma was born prematurely and complications developed that led to contracting double pneumonia twice, as well as scarlet fever. A later bout with polio left her with a crooked leg and a foot twisted inward. As a result, Wilma spent most of her childhood in braces.

Wilma's adversity created a determined spirit. She wanted out of her braces and by age eleven, she began sneaking around without them. Finally she told her doctor what she had been doing and proved to him, by slipping off her braces and walking around, that she no longer needed them. The doctor gave her permission to go without "sometimes," which in Wilma's mind meant never again.

By age thirteen, Wilma made the basketball and track teams. Two years later, she was chosen to participate with the Tennessee State University "Tigerbelles" during the summer. A teammate got her interested in pursuing the Olympic team.

At age sixteen, Wilma reached the semifinals in the 200-meter dash at the 1956 Olympic games and won a bronze metal as a member of the women's 400-meter relay. But she wanted a gold and vowed to be back in 1960 to carry out her commitment.

A demanding training program ensued along with paying her way through Tennessee State University and maintaining the B average required to stay on the track team.

When the 1960 Olympics rolled around, Wilma Rudolph was ready. In three electrifying performances she won the heart of eighty thousand fans and came home with three gold medals. She became the first American woman to win three gold medals in track and field.

It is doubtful that any Olympic champion has overcome such crippling adversity as Wilma Rudolph.

·   ·   ·

Isabel Moore wrote, "You must do the best you can with what you have and what you are and what you have become." Blindness, pain, cancer, disability, rejection, or abuse couldn't destroy our heroes of adversity. Self-pity, worry, despair and hopelessness were eliminated from their thinking. They endured, overcame, excelled, and triumphed. And you can too!

A MIXED BLESSING

Californians endured a five-year drought that gradually moved them toward a statewide crisis. People worried about the future as they watched the water tables drop drastically. Environmentalists, media, politicians, and conservation officials encouraged people daily to conserve as the picture of the future grew bleak.

Then, beginning in the first quarter of 1991, the rains came. Within a few weeks almost a foot of moisture dampened the Los Angeles area. Heavy moisture intermittently fell throughout the year and people celebrated the end to a demanding battle with nature.

Their prayers were answered. What a blessing! Right? Maybe. Maybe not. According to newspaper reports, one prominent official considered the rains a setback, even a disaster. From his perspective, the state was close to establishing a long-term water conservation policy when the rains eased the crisis and interrupted water-saving plans.

Adversity can be the springboard for change. The Chinese symbol for crisis has a dual meaning: danger and opportunity. The key is to use the energy that adversity creates to generate long-term solutions and thereby capitalize on new or expanded opportunities. Homer said it this way: "Adversity has the effect of eliciting talents which in prosperous circumstances would have lain dormant."

FROM ADVERSITY CAME HOPE

Dr. Henry Viscardi, the founder of Long Island's Human Resources Center for Disabled Children and Adults, understands the challenges facing the 240 people his organization serves. He has first-hand experience with the adversity of disability.

Dr. Viscardi was born without legs and spent his first seven years in the charity wards of several hospitals. Leather pockets were designed to fit on his stubs so he could walk. Yet the world was unkind and ignorant of the challenges facing a person living in a body 3 feet 8 inches tall.

At twenty-six, Viscardi's challenge was taken seriously by Dr. Robert Yanover. Soliciting the talents of a crafter, artificial legs were designed to fit young Henry. Imagine suddenly being able to see things never noticed before or reaching items previously reserved for those of normal height.

A miracle had occurred which transformed his life. Viscardi helped armless and legless veterans at Walter Reed Hospital during World War II adjust to their new challenges. And then came marriage, four daughters and a dream to make it possible for physically challenged people to live meaningful lives.

Henry Viscardi turned his adversity into an opportunity to teach thousands of physically challenged people to believe in themselves and their abilities. His undying and tireless commitment produced more than facilities, more than services— he provided hope.

THAT'S THE BREAKS

When asked the secret of his success, J. C. Penney replied, "Adversity. I would never have amounted to anything had I not been forced to come up the hard way."

Walt Disney could probably relate. When he submitted his first drawings for publication, the editor told him he had no artistic talent.

Robert L. Ripley was excited about entering a career in Major League Baseball. Grueling practices and training prepared him for his first pitching debut. A broken arm in the first game brought his career to a sudden halt, and doctors warned him not to engage in any work that would cause undue strain to his arm.

Ripley turned his attention to drawing. He landed a job as a newspaper sports cartoonist, and the spark for a lifetime career was created. His word pictures, penciled drawings, and creative flair were enjoyed by everyone listening to the radio, watching television, or reading a newspaper.

We remember and enjoy Robert L. Ripley exposing the world to its own peculiarities and gaining fame through Ripley's *Believe It or Not*.

Be thankful for your setbacks. They just might be an open door leading to future success. Penney, Disney, and Ripley would suggest that discouraging people, daily hassles, and even broken arms might be just the break you need to go beyond where you are. That which doesn't break us builds us.

A VOICE IN THE NIGHT

A playful story is told of a man walking home from work in the dark of night. Not noticing a large hole in the street produced by recent digging, he fell in. Every effort to escape was futile, so he leaned back in the corner and fell asleep.

A short time later another walker found himself quickly descending to the bottom of the hole. He too struggled and strained to find a way out. Exhausted, he was about to sit down and wait for the morning light when he heard a sluggish voice in the darkness say, "Forget it, fella. You can't get out."

In a split second he was out!

Isn't it amazing how all of a sudden the man was able to jump a little higher, put forth a little more effort, climb a little farther to escape his predicament. The "voice in the night" provided just the motivation he needed.

ADVICE

- If you really want to advise me, do it on Saturday afternoon between 1:00 and 4:00 o'clock, and you've got 25 seconds to do it, between plays. Not on Monday. I know the right thing to do on Monday.

Alex Agase

- A person is silly who will not take anyone's advice, but a person is ignorant who takes everyone's advice.

Anonymous

- The trouble with advice is that you can't tell if it's good or bad until you've taken it.

Frank Tyger

- When we ask for advice, we are usually looking for an accomplice.

Marquis de la Grange

- Most of us ask for advice when we know the answer but want a different one.

Ivern Bell

- Advice is what we ask for when we already know the answer but wish we didn't.

Erica Jong

- Accept good advice gracefully—as long as it doesn't interfere with what you intended to do in the first place.

Gene Brown

- Advice is like snow; the softer it falls, the longer it dwells upon, and the deeper it sinks into the mind.

Samuel Taylor Coleridge

STRICTLY ADVISORY

Lucy, in the *Peanuts* cartoon, is the ultimate advice giver. In one cartoon, Lucy, the center fielder, is exhorting Charlie Brown, the pitcher, to strike out the batter, "to win one for a change." Yet when the batter hits the ball to center field, Lucy makes no effort to catch it. Charlie Brown asks in astonishment, "If you're so interested in winning, why didn't you try to catch the ball?"

"My role is strictly advisory," replies an indifferent Lucy.

WHOOPS!

A man went to see a doctor after feeling out-of-sorts for a month. "Have you been treated by anyone else?" asked the doc.

"No, sir," the man said, "but I did go see a pharmacist."

The doctor scolded him for seeking a layperson's advice. " What kind of idiotic advice did he give you?"

The man thought for a minute. " He told me I should come and see you."

AGE

- People grow old by deserting their ideals. Years may wrinkle your skin but to give up interest wrinkles the soul. When the wires are all down and your heart is covered with the snows of pessimism and the ice of cynicism, then, and then only, are you grown old.

  General Douglas MacArthur

- The secret of staying young is to live honestly, eat slowly, and just not think about your age.

  Lucille Ball

- Aches and pains are your body's way of telling you something. And have you ever noticed that your body becomes more and more talkative as you grow older?

  Anonymous

- Midlife crisis is that moment when you realize your children and your clothes are about the same age.

  Bill Tammeus

- How do you know when you're old? When you double your current age and realize you're not going to live that long.

  Michael J. Leyden II

- You are as old as you feel right after you try to demonstrate how young you feel.

  Anonymous

- Middle age is actually the prime of life. It just takes a little longer to get primed.

  Anonymous

- There are four stages of humankind: Infancy . . . childhood . . . adolescence . . . and obsolescence.

  Art Linkletter

- Age should not have its face lifted, but it should rather teach the world to admire wrinkles as the etchings of experience and the firm lines of character.

  Ralph Barton Perry

- To me, old age is always fifteen years older than I am.

  Bernard M. Baruch

- I think we're finally at a point where we've learned to see death with a sense of humor. I have to. When you're my age, it's as if you're a car. First a tire blows, and you get that fixed. Then a headlight goes, and you get that fixed. And then one day, you drive into a shop and the man says, "Sorry, Miss, they don't have this make anymore."

  Katharine Hepburn

- The older you get, the greater you were.

  Lee Grosscup

- Time table: Age is the time when we find that we can't do all the things that we could, and it takes twice as long and costs twice as much to look even half as good.

  Anonymous

- Old age is no place for sissies.

  Bette Davis

- Old men are dangerous: it doesn't matter to them what is going to happen to the world.

  George Bernard Shaw

- Live your life and forget your age.

  Frank Bering

- Retirement at 65 is ridiculous. When I was 65, I still had pimples.

  George Burns

- A person doesn't become old until his regrets take the place of his dreams.

  John R. Noe

- Retirement is a wonderful dream. After all, you can only suck in your stomach for so long.

  Burt Reynolds

- First you forget names; then you forget faces; then you forget to zip up your fly; and then you forget to unzip your fly.

  Branch Rickey

- When you're young and you fall off a horse you may break something. When you're my age and you fall, you splatter.

  Roy Rogers

- Middle age is when your classmates are so gray and wrinkled and bald they don't recognize you.

  Bennett Cerf

- If you carry your childhood with you, you never become older.

  Abraham Sutzkever

- The really frightening thing about middle age is the knowledge that you'll grow out of it.

  Doris Day

- Everybody wants to live a long time, but nobody wants to be old.

  Adolph Abrams

- I've discovered the secret of eternal youth. I lie about my age.

  Bob Hope

- Most people say that as you get old you have to give up things. I think you get old because you do give up things.

  Senator Ted Green

- There are many stereotypes about growing old. We are not useless, toothless and sexless. In fact, old people have a special place in society. My generation has been part of more changes than any other. We have to share that knowledge. We are the whistle blowers, the social critics. We are the ones who must be advocates for disarmament and safe, renewable sources of energy.

  Maggie Kuhn

■ I don't live in the past. You know, some people tell me they've got this mental image of me frozen in time, like it was 1958 forever. Well, it's not. I like getting old. Just remember, you only live once. And if you do it right, once is enough.

Ernie Banks

■ Old age is like everything else. To make a success of it, you've got to start young.

Fred Astaire

■ . . . as we age, we actually handle our life situations with much more skill and satisfaction.

Dr. Jonas Salk

■ Just remember when you're over the hill, you begin to pick up speed.

Charles Schulz

■ In youth we learn; in age we understand.

Marie Ebner-Eschenbach

■ Once you get to be one hundred, you have made it. You almost never hear of anyone dying who is over one hundred.

George Burns

ADDING LIFE TO YEARS

"We have added years to man's life. Now we face an even greater challenge," says Louise M. Orr, "adding life to these years. In other words, we have given the American people the opportunity to enjoy nearly twice as many years as did their ancestors and now we have the obligation to help turn old age into something more than a chronological period of life."

Whose responsibility is it to add life to the years? Some might say society, while others believe each individual must take that responsibility on themselves. But almost everyone agrees with Art Linkletter, that "attitude is everything." His message to senior citizens is this: "If you're old, enjoy it."

"Senior citizens should look forward to old age. Demand your right to be independent, to have dignity, and to have your questions answered."

Linkletter believes seniors should work if they are able, exercise, eat well, and even enjoy a bit of romance. On sex, Linkletter says, "I can still talk about it for hours."

•   •   •

Age is not a time of life—it is a state of mind. On her eightieth birthday, Helen Keller declared, "One should never count the years—one should instead count one's interests. I have kept young trying never to lose my childhood sense of wonderment. I am glad I still have a vivid curiosity about the world I live in."

Never losing a sense of wonderment and curiosity must have inspired a band of fifteen Illinois widows to form their Happy Tooters band. Armed with kazoos, tambourines, and soap bottles filled with beans, they've kept their youthful spirit alive performing in retirement homes.

How about the country's possibly oldest and definitely most unique rap group—Old Guys With New Socks. Ranging from age sixty to seventy-five, this spirited music sensation performs raps with lyrics about shuffleboard, pension checks, and all matters of retirement living.

Professional golfer Chi Chi Rodriguez is a crowd-pleasing player on the senior tour. He loves life and his attitude keeps the aging process in perspective.

Whether seventeen or seventy, the heart is our source of wonder, enthusiasm, joy, and appetite for adventure. We are as young as we allow ourselves to be. As the saying goes, age is a matter of mind; if you don't mind, it doesn't matter.

Final thought: Consider this compelling question posed by Satchel Paige: "How old would you be if you didn't know how old you was?"

OLDER IS BETTER!

Statistic gatherers tell us that on an average day, 8,838 Americans turn 13, 10,951 turn 40, another 6,000 Americans turn 65, and 35 turn 100. So, who cares?

What matters is this . . . what we do with the information, wisdom, and experience gathered over the years.

At 6:13 A.M. on September 14, 1979, James "Doc" Counsilman, Indiana University's swimming coach, slid into the waters of the English Channel. Coated with grease to ward off the frigid waters, "Doc" began his 72-stroke-per-minute venture. Thirteen hours and seventeen minutes later, "Doc" Counsilman set a world record as the oldest person ever to swim the English Channel. Not a bad achievement for fifty-eight years old.

Jack LaLanne, the well-known exercise evangelist, celebrated his seventieth birthday by towing seventy boats containing seventy people for a mile across Long Beach Harbor. To add a little challenge, he did it by holding the rope in his teeth while handcuffed and wearing leg shackles. At 75, he still exercises two hours daily, works on books and videos, and travels 150,000 miles in a year conducting seminars.

Shirley Chanaca, a 66-year-old retired school nurse from Stroudsburg, Pennsylvania, takes flying lessons, works out three times a week in a fitness center, and now is a black belt in karate.

Remember Judge Joseph Wapner from "The People's Court"? At sixty-nine, the judge plays doubles tennis, walks three or four miles several times a week, does sit-ups twice daily, and makes about twenty speeches a year.

Jessica Tandy, at age seventy-four, opened jubilantly on Broadway in a challenging role as Amanda in a revival of Tennessee William's *The Glass Menagerie.*

Goethe finished *Faust* a few years before his death at age eighty-three.

William Gladstone took up a new language at age seventy.

Dr. Lillien J. Martin learned to drive an automobile when she was seventy-six years old and founded The Old Age Center in San Francisco, where she worked with older people as students until her death at 91.

Margaret Thatcher became Britain's first female prime minister at age fifty-three and Winston Churchill initiated his protest against Hitler as prime minister at sixty-five. He returned to the House of Commons as a member of Parliament at eighty. When Churchill was interviewed on his eighty-seventh birthday, a young reporter commented, "Sir Winston, I hope to wish you well on your one hundredth birthday." Churchill quickly replied, "You might do it. You look healthy."

At seventy-five, Ed Delano of California bicycled 3,100 miles in thirty-three days to attend his fiftieth college reunion in Worcester, Massachusetts.

Adolph Zukor was the chairperson at Paramount Pictures at ninety-one.

At sixty-four, Francis Chichester sailed alone around the world in a 53-foot yacht.

Alexander Graham Bell perfected the telephone at fifty-eight and solved the problem of stabilizing the balance in airplanes while in his seventies.

Mark Twain wrote "Eve's Diary" and "The $30,000 Bequest" at seventy-one.

W. K. Kellogg started his famous cereal business at forty-six.

Christopher Hewett, star of ABC's "Mr. Belvedere," started a whole new career in TV production in his sixties.

Sally Conlin began a career working with wayward girls and opening a halfway house in the slums of Minneapolis at sixty-five.

Corrie ten Boom boldly professed her Christian faith and traveled the world evangelizing into her eighties.

In the 1989 New York Marathon, more than 10,000 (approximately 42 percent) of the runners who finished were over forty. Fifty-six of the finishers were over seventy, and the oldest came in at ninety-one.

John Wesley traveled 250,000 miles on horseback, averaging 20 miles a day for 40 years, preached 4,000 sermons, produced 400 books, and knew ten languages. At eighty-three, he was annoyed that he could not write more than 15 hours a day without hurting his eyes, and at eighty-six, he was ashamed he could not preach more than twice a day. He complained in his diary that there was an increasing tendency to lie in bed until 5:30 in the morning.

•　•　•

Older is better! Researchers studying the lives of 400 famous people found that 35 percent of the group's achievements came when they were between sixty and seventy; 23 percent when they were between seventy and eighty; and 8 percent when they were over 80. It doesn't take a mathematician to conclude the world's greatest work has been achieved by people over sixty.

• • •

Aging guidelines have been offered throughout the years. Compare them to your own experiences. You know you're getting older when . . .

Everything hurts . . . and what doesn't hurt, doesn't work.

The gleam in your eyes is from the sun hitting your bifocals.

You feel like the morning after . . . and you didn't go anywhere.

Your "little black book" contains only names ending in M. D.

You get winded playing cards.

Your children begin to look middle-aged.

You know all the answers. But nobody asks you all the questions.

You look forward to a dull evening.

You walk with your back straight and your head held high . . . trying to get used to your new bifocals.

Your favorite part of the newspaper is "twenty-five years ago today."

You turn the lights out for economic rather than romantic reasons.

You sit in a rocking chair and can't get the darned thing going.

Your knees buckle and your belt won't.

Dialing long distance wears you out.

You suddenly remember that your wedding anniversary was yesterday.

You just can't understand people who are intolerant.

You burn the midnight oil until 9 P.M.

Your back goes out more often than you do.

Your pacemaker makes the garage door go up when you watch a pretty girl go by.

You sink your teeth into a steak . . . and they stay there!

Surely you were able to chuckle at least once while reading these characteristics on aging. If not, I'm sorry. Maybe this prayer from an unknown author will rejuvenate your spirit:

God keep my heart attuned to laughter
When youth is done;
When all the days are gray days, coming after
The warmth, the sun.
God keep me then from bitterness, from grieving,
When life seems cold;
God keep me always loving and believing
As I grow old.

In a poem, *Ode to Retirement,* by Len Ingebrigtsen, are these lines:

"The reason I know my youth is all spent?
My get up and go has got up and went."

One woman, when asked her age, quickly commented: "I'm too young for Medicare and too old for men to care."

AGING AND BROKE

Napoleon Hill said, "The most common cause of fear of old age is associated with the possibility of poverty."

The U. S. Department of Labor would agree. According to their statistics, only three out of every one hundred Americans reach age sixty-five with any degree of financial security. Ninety-seven out of one hundred Americans who are sixty-five and over must depend on their monthly Social Security checks to survive.

In addition, only five of every one hundred Americans who are in the higher-income professions such as law and medicine reach age sixty-five without having to depend on Social Security.

Three out of one hundred people plan, save, and invest their money to insure a comfortable retirement. One such person entrusted all her finances to her financial planning son. On her sixty-fifth birthday, he tried to convince his mother to enjoy the money she had accumulated through wise investing. "Mother," he said, "you have sufficient funds to allow you to do what you want until you're one hundred years old."

"And then what will I live on?" she replied.

Fred Astaire had good advice concerning financial planning when he said, "to make a success of old age, you have to start young."

CHRONOLOGICALLY GIFTED

William Lutz, writing in *Esquire* magazine, observes, in referring to the aged, "the term *senior citizen* has worn thin." The new phrase is *chronologically gifted*. Also, older people no longer live in the old folk's home. These days, they live in a senior congregate living community for the chronologically gifted.

One such "chronologically gifted" woman was being escorted by her daughter to visit a senior congregate living community. The daughter had high hopes of persuading her mother of the benefits of living there instead of staying on the family farm by herself.

After a brief visit, the daughter enthusiastically reflected, "People sure were having fun. When I'm their age, living there would be perfect."

"That's great," the mother replied. "I'll be sure to visit you."

A chronologically gifted couple entered a hotel lobby and requested the bridal suite. "You want what?" queried the registration clerk. "Don't get any ideas," the elderly man replied. "If I asked for the restaurant it doesn't mean I want to cook."

•   •   •

Ol' Joe wasn't too pleased with the physical results of his aging. He had a toupée custom designed, worked out at the health club, bought a little red convertible sports car, and invited a young woman out to dinner. Riding down the freeway with the top down, Joe was struck by a bolt of lightning and died.

At heaven's gate, he requested that Saint Peter escort him to God. Once in His presence, Joe asked, "God, why me?"

"Oh, Joe," replied God, "I didn't recognize you."

Why is it these chronologically gifted people possessed such a zestful approach to life?

Look up *gifted* in your nearest thesaurus and you will find such synonyms as *talented, ingenious, superior,* or *well-endowed*. Age plus gifted equals an unparalleled knowledge of what makes life meaningful. One critical element chronologically gifted people possess is experience, and through experience comes wisdom. Put it all together and the result is quality life.

AMERICA

- I am tired of hearing that democracy doesn't work—it isn't supposed to work. We are supposed to work it.

  Alexander Woolcott

- There is nothing wrong with America that the faith, love of freedom, intelligence, and energy of her citizens cannot cure.

  Dwight D. Eisenhower

- Americans have not fully realized their ideals. There are imperfections. But the ideal is right. What our country needs is the moral power to hold it.

  Calvin Coolidge

- America is only another name for opportunity.

  Ralph Waldo Emerson

- Ours is the only country deliberately founded on a good idea.

  John Gunther

- What's right about America is that although we have a mess of problems, we have great capacity—intellect and resources—to do something about them.

  Henry Ford II

- Double—no triple—our troubles and we'd still be better off than any other people on earth.

  Ronald Reagan

- America's beauty is not only in its features; its beauty is in the character underneath those features.

  Luci Swindoll

- There can be no fifty-fifty Americanism in this country. There is room here for only hundred-percent Americanism.

  Theodore Roosevelt

- America is never wholly herself unless she is engaged in high moral principle. We as a people have such a purpose today. It is to make kinder the face of the nation and gentler the face of the world.

  George Bush

- The things that will destroy America are prosperity-at-any-price, peace-at-any-price, safety-first instead of duty-first, the love of soft living and the get-rich-quick theory of life.

  Theodore Roosevelt

- What is the essence of America? Finding and maintaining that perfect, delicate balance between freedom "to" and freedom "from."

  Marilyn vos Savant

- America is like a gigantic boiler. Once the fuse is lighted under it, there is no limit to the power it can generate.

  Winston Churchill

- There can be no daily democracy without daily citizenship.

  Ralph Nader

- America did not invent human rights. In a very real sense, it is the other way around. Human rights invented America.

  Jimmy Carter

- I look forward to an America which will not be afraid of grace and beauty.

  John F. Kennedy

- We've got our problems, I know, but it's my strong conviction that there's a lot more good about America than there is wrong.

  Gerald Ford

- Democracy does not guarantee equality, only equality of opportunity.

  Irvin Kristol

- America is a construction of mind, not of race or inherited class or ancestral territory.

  Robert Hughes

ONE NATION UNDER GOD

Olympic runner Kip Mibey from Kenya chose a novel way to say thank you. He ran from Santa Monica, California, to the Statue of Liberty in New York to thank Americans for their help in feeding the African people. At the conclusion of his journey a letter was transcribed with this message: "I ask myself what makes America . . . Is it because they are still maintaining democracy, or because they are, as they say, a 'melting pot'? But I concluded that she is great because she is 'one nation under God.'"

Likewise, French writer Alexis de Tocqueville, after visiting America in 1831, said, "I sought for the greatness of the United States in her commodious harbors, her ample rivers, her fertile fields, and boundless forests—and it was not there. I sought for it in her rich mines, her vast world commerce, her public school system, and in her institutions of higher learning—and it was not there. I looked for it in her democratic Congress and her matchless Constitution—and it was not there. Not until I went into the churches of America and heard her pulpits flame with righteousness did I understand the secret of her genius and power. America is great because America is good, and if America ever ceases to be good, America will cease to be great!"

What is it that makes America special? De Tocqueville, Kip Mibey, along with countless citizens and visitors to America believe America's banner of "one nation under God" sets us apart in principle and practice. History will undoubtedly credit America's strength to a trust in God.

ONLY IN AMERICA

According to reporters, Ronald Reagan related the following joke to Mikhail Gorbachev during the 1985 U. S./Soviet summit in Geneva.

An American and a Soviet citizen were debating who had more freedom. The American said, "I can march into the Oval Office in the White House and say, 'Mr. President, I don't like the way you're running our country.'" And the Soviet citizen said, "Well, I can do that too. I can walk into General-Secretary Gorbachev's office in the Kremlin and say, 'Mr. Secretary, I don't like the way President Reagan's running his country.'"

Gorbachev did laugh, but more important, the freedom Americans enjoy was reaffirmed.

LIVING IN FREEDOM

Former president Richard Nixon, speaking at the dedication of the Ronald Reagan Presidential Library, said: "Thirty-two years ago in Moscow, Soviet Premier Nikita Khrushchev jabbed his finger into my chest and said, 'Your grandchildren will live under communism.' I replied, 'Your grandchildren will live in freedom.' At that time, I was sure he was wrong. I was not sure I was right. Now we know. Thanks in great part to the strong and idealistic leadership of President Ronald Reagan, Khrushchev's grandchildren now live in freedom."

WHAT DO YOU SEEK?

Go, seeker, if you will, throughout the land . . . Observe the whole of it, survey it as you might survey a field . . . It is your oyster—yours to open if you will . . . Just make yourself at home, refresh yourself, get the feel of things, adjust your sights, and get the scale . . . To every man his chance—to every man, regardless of his birth, his shining, golden opportunity—to every man the right to live, to work, to be himself, and to become whatever thing his manhood and his vision can combine to make him—this, seeker, is the promise of America.

Thomas Wolfe

ATTITUDE

- No one really knows enough to be a pessimist.

  Norman Cousins

- I will say this about being an optimist—even when things don't turn out well, you are certain they will get better.

  Frank Hughes

- Attitudes are caught, not taught.

  Elwood N. Chapman

- In the long run, the pessimist may be proved right, but the optimist has a better time on the trip.

  Daniel L. Reardon

- Positive thinking is the key to success in business, education, pro football, anything that you can mention . . . I go out there thinking that I'm going to complete every pass.

  Ron Jaworski
  Former NFL Quarterback

- It may not be your fault for being down, but it's got to be your fault for not getting up.

  Steve Davis

- If you want to change attitudes, start with a change in behavior.

  William Glasser

- Exhilaration of life can be found only with an upward look. This is an exciting world. It is cram-packed with opportunity. Great moments wait around every corner.

  Richard M. Devos

- Remember, whatever game you play, 90 percent of success is from the shoulders up.

  Arnold Palmer's father

■ ... positive thinkers are not the majority. In the coffee of life, they are only the cream, enriching and lightening the rest of the cup. At least, they don't get so many lumps these days.

> *Richard Gaylord Briley*
> Are You Positive?

■ The mind can convince a competent person that he is incompetent or an adequate person that he is highly talented. Unfortunately, self-doubt and negative attitudes seem to have a more powerful influence on the mind than positive attitudes. Usually a person is not aware that he is setting himself up or limiting his capabilities.

> *Bruce Bowman*

■ All is perspective. To a worm, digging in the ground is more relaxing than going fishing.

> *Clyde Abel*

■ Nothing can stop the man with the right mental attitude from achieving his goal; nothing on earth can help the man with the wrong mental attitude.

> *W. W. Ziege*

■ Attitude is the reflection of a person and our world mirrors our attitude.

> *Earl Nightingale*

■ A person's attitude toward himself has a profound influence on his attitude toward God, his family, his friends, his future, and many other significant areas of his life.

> *Bill Gothard*

■ A happy person is not a person in a certain set of circumstances, but rather a person with a certain set of attitudes.

> *Hugh Downs*

■ You can't make an overdraft on the bank of right mental attitude all your life and bring the account up to date with one deposit.

> *Zig Ziglar*

■ An optimist thinks the glass is half full; a pessimist thinks the glass is half empty. A realist knows that if he sticks around, he's eventually going to have to wash the glass.

> *Los Angeles Times Syndicate*

■   There is very little difference in people. But that little difference makes a big difference. The little difference is attitude. The big difference is whether it is positive or negative.

W. Clement Stone

■   It's not so much what happens to us, as what happens *in* us that counts, or what we think has happened to us.

Tim Hansel

■   Attitude is the speaker of our present;
    It is the prophet of our future.

John. C. Maxwell

THE MAGNITUDE OF ATTITUDE

Two young women working in a community hospital decided to quit their jobs. They were tired of dealing with ungrateful, complaining patients, back-biting between employees, and an apathetic administration. Just before quitting, though, these two women decided to try an experiment. They resolved, just for the fun of it, to bend over backwards for everyone they encountered on their last day of work.

So, no matter how someone looked at them, talked to them, or treated them, they overwhelmed people with encouragement, courtesy, and appreciation. Before long, an amazing transformation took place. Patients didn't seem so miserable, staff even smiled at each other, and the administration seemed surprisingly interested in their affairs.

The two women experienced a basic law of nature: For every action there is an equal and opposite reaction. The very situations that caused frustration were reflections of their own attitudes.

•   •   •

Harvard psychologist William James said: "The greatest discovery of my generation is that a human being can alter his life by altering his attitudes of mind."

Can it be? Can our lives actually be enhanced by altering our attitudes? Does success or failure have anything to do with mental attitude?

Art Linkletter would respond affirmatively. Linkletter says, "Things turn out the best for the people who make the best out of the way things turn out."

For those of you tempted not to read on . . . not to endure another "sermon" on positive attitude, stick with me. Consider these attitude-altering axioms capable of pole vaulting you into elevated living:

Attitude Axiom #1: Attitude affects quality of life. A positive attitude won't let you do anything, but it will help you do everything better than a negative attitude will. I've worked with winners and encountered losers. I've experienced the epitome of optimism as well as negativism. There have been people who lived life to the fullest and people who just existed. My conclusion is that what people possess inside will affect what is happening without.

Author James Allen put it this way: "A person cannot travel within and stand still without." Like it or not, we become on the outside what we are inside. "Attitude is the reflection of a person," commented Earl Nightingale, "and our world mirrors our attitude."

Simply put, our attitude is the way we see events, people, and circumstances in life. It is an internal belief system responsible for the quality of our life's experiences. Ultimately, what we produce or experience depends on attitude.

Attitude Axiom #2: Attitude is a choice. Robert Louis Stevenson was bedridden much of his life with tuberculosis. One day, his wife heard him hacking loudly and said, "I suppose you still believe it is a wonderful day." Turning toward a window ablaze with sunlight, Stevenson responded, "I do! I will never let a row of medicine bottles block my horizon."

Circumstances are uncontrollable. Life's events happen. Our responsibility is to choose our responses—our attitude. Situations may color your view of life, but you have been given the power to choose what the color will be.

Attitude Axiom #3: Attitudes alter abilities. Professor Erwin H. Schell, one of America's most respected authorities on leadership, says, "Obviously, there is something more than facilities and competence that makes for accomplishment. I have come to believe that this linkage factor, this catalyst, if you will, can be defined in a single word—attitude. When our attitude is right, our abilities reach a maximum effectiveness and good results inevitably follow."

People who believe they can't do something are usually right—and so are those who believe they can. Our attitude toward a task will trigger the body's ability to respond to it.

Football coaching great Lou Holtz speaks frequently concerning the correlation between ability and attitude. He believes, "Ability is what you are capable of doing. Motivation determines what you do. Attitude determines how well you do it." So, to cultivate abilities, sow a healthy attitude.

Attitude Axiom #4: People with a positive attitude anticipate adversity. That's right. Optimistic people do not have their heads in the clouds believing nothing will go wrong because they have a positive attitude. Actually, the opposite is true.

Positive people know challenging events, adversity, and tough situations are inevitable. J. Sidlow Baxter in his book *Awake, My Heart*, beautifully addresses this concept. "What is the difference between an obstacle and adversity? Our attitude toward it. Every opportunity has a difficulty and every difficulty has an opportunity. If the best things are not immediately possible, then immediately make the best of the things that are possible."

Remember the words of Ellen Glasgow, an American novelist who wrote many realistic novels about life in the South after the Civil War: "No life is so hard that you can't make it easier by the way you take it." A person with a healthy attitude takes difficult situations in stride, learns from each experience, and prepares for the next encounter. It's a great approach and fosters a winning lifestyle.

Attitude Axiom #5: Attitude affirms success . . . and failure. A man attending a business convention in Las Vegas decided to spend the evening "observing" the events on the casino floor. Tempted by the opportunity to make it big, he placed a two-dollar bet at the roulette table. His number won. He continued betting and winning. Within a short time, he had accumulated $50,000 in winnings.

Elated with his good fortune, he made his way to the cashier. Before reaching the window, he felt the urge to bet one more time. He went back to the roulette table and wagered his entire winnings on 14 red. The wheel spun round and round and finally stopped on 12 black. His entire winnings were lost. The fellow turned from the table and made his way back to the hotel room.

"Well," his wife asked, "did you bet any money?"

"Sure did."

"How did you do?"

"Not bad," he responded. "I lost two dollars."

Now that's a positive attitude. Positive people keep success and failure in perspective. In fact, these people tend to remove the word *failure* from their vocabulary. Words such as *experience, results, challenge, temporary setback,* and *unsuccessful attempt* are preferred.

But, you say, this is just a matter of semantics. No, it is a process of conditioning our minds to use (forgive me) failure as a stepping stone to success.

I am convinced that with the right attitude, all the setbacks in the world will not make you a failure. On the flip side, with the wrong mental attitude, all the help in the world will not make you a success.

Attitude Axiom #6: Actions alter attitudes. Making the magnitude of attitude work for you begins with acting in a manner consistent with the mental state you desire. William James said, "I don't sing because I'm happy, I'm happy because I sing." Behavior is not always subject to emotion but the way we feel is a direct result of our actions. Psychologist William Glasser advises: "If you want to change attitudes, start with a change in behavior."

You are who and what you are today because of the attitudes you choose. Will the future be a repeat of the past? The choice is yours.

"AS WITHIN, SO WITHOUT"

The Greek poet Hermessianex lived about four hundred years before Christ. Although we don't know much about him, Hermessianex left us a four-word phrase still meaningful today. He said, "as within, so without." The attitude you possess within determines external attractions. Taken a step farther, as you are within, so will be the quality of your life.

Consider the experience of Sydney J. Harris of the *Chicago Daily News* while walking one evening with a friend, a Quaker, to get a newspaper. The vendor was discourteous and cold as he made change but Harris's friend remained polite and gave him a warm greeting as he left.

"A sullen fellow, isn't he?" Harris asked.

"Oh, he's that way every night," shrugged the friend.

"Then why do you continue to be so kind to him?" Harris asked.

"Why not?" his friend responded. "Why should I let him decide how I'm going to act?"

The Quaker obviously understood the principle of "as within, so without." Only one person has the power to determine the attitude within and thereby the quality of life without. Guess who?

A MATTER OF PERSPECTIVE

An optimist and a pessimist combined their resources and went into business together. Sales were fantastic, and after the first three months the optimist was elated: "What a great beginning. Customers love our products, and we're selling more every week." "Sure," replied the pessimist, "if things keep going like this, we'll have to order more inventory."

•   •   •

Scottish minister Alexander Whyte was known for his uplifting prayers and sermons from the pulpit. He gained a reputation for always finding something to be grateful for.

One Sunday morning, the weather was damp, rainy, and gloomy. One less-than-positive member of the congregation thought to herself, "Certainly Reverend Whyte can't think of anything for which to be thankful for on a crummy day like this." Much to her surprise, however, Whyte began the service by praying, "Thank you, God, for a brand new day—and that it is not always like this."

•   •   •

When Robert Fulton's first American steamboat was finished, a trial run was scheduled on the Hudson River. A curious crowd gathered to watch the fate of the *Clermont*. One skeptical observer predicted, "They'll never get it running." But the *Clermont* did run. In fact, the steamboat picked up speed as black billows of smoke poured from its stack. The crowd erupted in celebrating applause. How about the negative skeptic? He shook his head in disbelief as he turned to walk away and then commented, "They'll never get it stopped."

•   •   •

And then there was the farmer who was known to have an attitude problem. A neighbor stopped by to visit one day and commented on his bumper crop, "You must be pleased with this year's results." "Well, it is no doubt the best I've ever had. But," he continued, "such a heavy crop is hard on the soil."

•   •   •

Some people see the positives in every situation, while others go through life seeking their induction into the negative attitude hall of fame. It's all a matter of perspective.

RISING ABOVE PARALYZING CIRCUMSTANCES

A promising athletic career was cut short for Mal Hancock. As a high school student, he experienced a fall that left him paralyzed from the waist down. Challenging and heartbreaking times followed as Mal attempted to make the necessary physical and mental adjustments.

While in the hospital, Mal developed a keen sense of humor about the sights and sounds he observed. He began to record his observations and experiences on paper in the form of cartoons. It wasn't long before the hospital staff would stop by to see what Mal had drawn, probably secretly hoping they were included in his hospital humor. His cartoons were becoming the center of attention.

Mal sold one of his cartoons to a magazine, which later launched him into a career as a cartoonist. Mal Hancock's name appears on cartoons in the *Saturday Evening Post*, *TV Guide*, and on the cover of his own book, *Hospital Humor*.

Mal Hancock learned he could not control the events in his life but he could control his reaction to those events. He took a life-changing disaster and turned it into an opportunity to express his humorous impressions of the world around him. Attitude is the powerful force determining the outcome of life's "paralyzing" circumstances.

MUD OR SUNSHINE?

Concerning attitude, John Maxwell wrote, "When we become conditioned to perceived truth and closed to new possibilities, the following happens: We see what we expect to see, not what we can see. We hear what we expect to hear, not what we can hear. We think what we expect to think, not what we can think."

Such was the case with Henry J. Kaiser's construction crew. While building a levee along a river bank, a violent rainstorm flooded the earth-moving machinery and destroyed the work that had been done. As Kaiser approached the worksite to assess the damages, he found his crew bemoaning the mud and the buried earth-moving equipment.

As his workers surrounded him, Kaiser asked, "Why are you so glum?"

"Can't you see the disaster?" they asked. "Our equipment is covered with mud."

Smiling, Kaiser asked, "What mud?"

"You must be kidding. Look around you. We are surrounded by a sea of mud. How can you say you don't see any?"

"Well," said Henry Kaiser, "what I see is clear blue sky filled with bright sunshine. I've never known mud to sustain itself against the powerful sun. Soon it will be dried up and then we will be able to move our equipment and start over. Furthermore, our attitude will not only affect how we see reality but will also affect the reality itself. Sun or mud, the choice is yours."

The difference between sun or mud is a matter of perspective. Again, what we expect to see we see. This delightful story involving Henry J. Kaiser reinforces our choice to look at any situation from more than one point of view.

BELIEF

- I never cease being dumbfounded by the unbelievable things people believe.

  Leo Rosten

- Few will have the greatness to bend history itself, but each of us can work to change a small portion of events . . . It is from numberless acts of courage and belief that human history is shaped.

  Robert F. Kennedy

- Our beliefs about what we are and what we can be precisely determine what we will be.

  Anthony Robbins

- A person does what they must—in spite of personal consequences, in spite of obstacles and dangers and pressures—and that is the basis of all human morality.

  JohnF. Kennedy

- No man can afford to express, through words or acts, that which is not in harmony with his own beliefs, and if he does so, he must pay by the loss of his ability to influence others.

  Napoleon Hill

- You never know how much you really believe anything until its truth or falsehood becomes a matter of life and death. It is easy to say you believe a rope to be strong as long as you are merely using it to cord a box. But suppose you had to hang by that rope over a precipice. Wouldn't you then first discover how much you really trusted it?

  C. S. Lewis

- The only thing that stands between a man and what he wants from life is often merely the will to try it and the faith to believe that it is possible.

  Richard M. De Vos

- Somehow I can't believe that there are any heights that can't be scaled by a man who knows the secret of making dreams come true. This special secret, it seems to me, can be summarized in four c's. They are curiosity, confidence, courage, and constancy, and the greatest of these is confidence. When you believe in a thing, believe in it all the way, implicitly and unquestionably.

Walt Disney

■ Believe that you will succeed. Believe it firmly, and you will then do what is necessary to bring success about.

Dale Carnegie

ONE STEP FURTHER THAN BELIEF

America's first commercial jet service began with a Boeing 707 flight in 1958. The next month, according to National Public Radio's "Morning Edition," a passenger on a propeller-driven DC-6 airliner struck up a conversation with another passenger, who happened to be a Boeing engineer.

The traveler asked the engineer about the new jet aircraft. The man spoke convincingly about the extensive testing Boeing had done on the jet engines. He explained how the company had long experience with aircraft engines. "Have you flown on the new 707 jet?" asked the passenger. The engineer replied, "I think I'll wait until it's been in service awhile."

This Boeing engineer believed in his company, he believed in the aerodynamic principles of flight, and he enjoyed flying. But until he stepped foot on the Boeing 707, his beliefs lacked credibility.

Susan B. Anthony believed in the rights of women. She organized a group of like-minded advocates who met frequently to discuss their convictions. A Sons of Temperance meeting in Albany, New York, where Anthony was a delegate, refused to let her take the platform. This anti-woman action prompted Anthony and her supporters to initiate the Women's State Temperance Society of New York.

Anthony spent her life promoting women's rights. Although her compaign to include women in the Fourteenth Amendment never succeeded, she had the honor of seeing the ratification of the Nineteenth Amendment before her death in 1920.

Unlike the Boeing engineer, Susan B. Anthony acted on her beliefs. John Dryden said, "They can conquer who believe they can." And, we should add, who are willing to act on the conviction of their beliefs.

GET IN THE WHEELBARROW

The story is told about the famed Zumbrati who walked a tightrope across Niagara Falls. Conditions were less than ideal. It was a windy day and the performer was thankful to have made it safely across.

One of those waiting to congratulate him was a man with a wheelbarrow.

"I believe that you could walk across pushing this wheelbarrow," the man told him.

Zumbrati shook his head and said he felt fortunate to have accomplished the feat without a wheelbarrow.

The man urged him to try. "I believe that you can do it," he said.

The aerialist graciously declined, but the man kept after him.

Finally, the performer said, "You really do believe in me, don't you?"

"Oh, I do," the man assured him.

"Okay," Zumbrati replied. "Get into the wheelbarrow."

So if you really believe . . . get in the wheelbarrow. Cast off the concerns, doubts, fears, and self-imposed limitations because once you believe something is true, whether or not it is, you will then act as if it is.

BLESSED BATS BOLSTER BELIEF

Josh O'Riley, baseball manager for the San Antonio Club of the Texas Baseball League, was experiencing a successful season. All nine of his starters were batting over .300 and it became the consensus of sportswriters and fans that this time they were destined for a league championship.

Then disaster struck. Suddenly, the entire team fell into a slump and their bats turned cold. The once inspired San Antonio team lost seventeen of their next twenty games. The players became increasingly discouraged and convinced they were jinxed. The team lost belief in themselves. Their thoughts now centered on defeat rather than that once achieveable championship.

Then Josh O'Riley heard about a traveling evangelist who was preaching in the community. Crowds were gathering to hear his sermons and it was widely broadcast that this man could perform miracles. A light came on in O'Riley's mind. He grabbed every baseball bat in the dugout, placed them in a wheelbarrow, and went off to hear the Reverend Slater.

Upon his return, O'Riley announced to his team that each bat had been blessed by the Reverend Slater. They were now assured success. A "miraculous" turnaround occurred. The team was reinspired and went on to beat Dallas for the championship. For years, baseball players paid handsome amounts of money to get their hands on a "Slater Bat."

A blessed bat? Maybe not. But the players believed their bats had been blessed, and therein lies the key. We must believe we are capable before the results will ever reflect our capabilities.

ELBERT HUBBARD'S CREDO

Elbert Hubbard was a classic salesperson. In 1894, at the age of thirty-five, he retired after a highly successful soap-selling career. He later attained success as a magazine publisher, marketer of books, furniture and other products, and direct-mail specialist. Hubbard believed in the possibility of the American Dream and loved to share his philosophy with others. He wrote the following credo to express his beliefs:

"I believe in myself. I believe in the goods I sell. I believe in the firm for whom I work. I believe in my colleagues and helpers. I believe in American business methods. I believe in producers, creators, manufacturers, distributors, and in all industrial workers of the world who have a job and hold it down. I believe that truth is an asset. I believe in good cheer and in good health, and I recognize the fact that the first requisite in success is not to achieve the dollar or to confer a benefit, but that the reward will come automatically and usually as a matter of course. I believe in sunshine, fresh air, spinach, applesauce, laughter, buttermilk, babies, and chiffon, always remembering that the greatest word in the English language is sufficiency. I believe that when I make a sale, I make a friend. And I believe that when I part with a person, I must do it in such a way that when they see me again, they will be glad and so will I. I believe in the hands that work, in the brains that think, and in the hearts that love."

CHANGE

- Change is happening faster than we can keep tabs on and threatens to shake the foundations of the most secure American business.

U. S. Congress Office of Technology

- If you thought it yesterday, if you're thinking it today, you won't think it tomorrow.

Faith Popcorn
The Popcorn Report

- If something has been done a particular way for fifteen or twenty years, it's a pretty good sign, in these changing times, that it is being done the wrong way.

Elliot M. Estes
Former GM President

- One change makes way for the next, giving us the opportunity to grow.

Vivian Buchen
Welcome Change

- In this fast-paced, modern world, it only takes a fraction of the time it used to for a luxury to become a necessity.

Doug Larson
United Feature Syndicate

- Both tears and sweat are salty, but they render a different result. Tears will get you sympathy, sweat will get you change.

Jesse Jackson

- We're dealing with a world of change, and a crucial element is discovering change.

Charles J. Hess
Using Intuition to Uncover Stock Values

- Change is the law of life, and those who look only to the past or the present are certain to miss the future.

John F. Kennedy

■ You can change anything you want, but you can't change everything you want.

John Rogers
Peter McWilliams
Do It

■ Our dilemma is that we hate change and love it at the same time; what we want is for things to remain the same but get better.

Sydney Harris

■ Fashions changed, changed again, changed faster and still faster: fashions in politics, in political styles, in causes, in music, in popular culture, in myths, in educations, in beauty, in heroes and idols, in attitudes, in responses, in work, in love and friendship, in food, in newspapers, in entertainment, in fashion.What had once lasted a generation now lasted a year, what had lasted a year lasted a month, a week, a day.

Bernard Levin
The Pendulum Years

■ Progress is a nice word. But change is its motivator and change has its enemies.

Robert F. Kennedy

■ Most bold change is the result of a hundred thousand tiny changes that culminate in a bold product or procedure or structure.

Thomas Peters

■ The change in the nineties will make the eighties look like a picnic, a walk in the park. Simply doing what worked in the eighties will be too slow.

Jack Welch
GE Chairman

■ Maturity is the ability to live in peace with that which we cannot change.

Ann Landers

■ We must change to master change.

Lyndon B. Johnson

■ The very key to our success has been our ability, foremost among nations, to preserve our lasting values by making change work for us rather than against us.

Ronald Reagan

■ We live in a time of paradox, contradiction, opportunity, and above all, change. To the fearful, change is threatening because they worry that things may get worse. To the hopeful, change is encouraging because they feel things may get better. To those who have confidence in themselves, change is a stimulus because they believe one person can make a difference and influence what goes on around them. These people are the doers and the motivators.

Buck Rogers
Getting the Best Out of Yourself & Others

■   The individuals who will succeed and flourish will also be masters of change:adept at reorienting their own and others' activities in untried directions to bring about higher levels of achievement. They will be able to acquire and use power to produce innovation.

Rosabeth Moss Kanter
Author and Harvard Business School professor

I'LL DO IT MYSELF

What do you do if you've invested sixteen years of your life with a company and your ideas for change are disregarded?Ask Liz Claiborne.

Claiborne was a clothing designer with the Jonathan Logan Company. She believed their limited variety of patterns and sizes were insufficient to meet the changing needs of their market. Efforts to convince management that body types and style preferences warranted innovation in design fell on deaf ears.

Undiscouraged, Claiborne became a vehicle for stylish and affordable women's apparel by starting her own company. Her versatile designs appealed to the growing number of women in the workforce and to store buyers. Liz Claiborne, Inc. experienced enviable growth throughout the 1960s, 1970s, and 1980s, ultimately attaining the number-one position in the woman's fashion industry.

Proactive change agents act upon the convictions of their beliefs regardless of the resistance presented by outside forces.

OLD IDEAS IN A NEW MARKET

Machiavelli wrote in *The Prince* that, "there is nothing moredifficult to take in hand, more perilous to conduct, or more uncertain in its success, than to take the lead in the introduction of a new order of things, because the innovator has for enemies all those who have done well under the old conditions and lukewarm defenders in those who may do well under the new."

The innovative Sony Corporation found itself in this Machiavellian predicament. They were one of the first makers of the Betamax Home Video Equipment. For a few years, Beta dominated the video market until a few other companies began developing VHS. Consumers seemed to prefer the VHS format, and that market took off like wildfire. Tape companies manufactured limited Beta videos, but Sony continued with their idea. Management believed they had a superior product and refused to make VHS, even though retail outlets were loading their shelves with this design.

The reality of this costly situation finally soaked in and Sony succumbed to the financial fiasco.

Leon Martel, in *Mastering Change, the Key to Business Success* (NAL, 1987) describes three common traps that keep us from recognizing and using change:

1. Believing that yesterday's solutions will solve today's problems.

2. Assuming present trends will continue.

3. Neglecting the opportunities offered by future change.

Don't get caught in the trap of believing that old ideas will succeed in a new market.

CAPITALIZING ON CATASTROPHE

Columnist Pete Hamill reported on a turbulent situation that required adapting to change. He described a region in Puerto Rico where people with limited means live in houses made of wood. Periodically a hurricane invades, creating waves that destroy the houses. As the waters recede the dismantled wooden homes are carried out to sea. The homeless people wait for the stormy waters to subside and for the wood to float back to shore. The people then begin rebuilding their community. Homes are redesigned in different styles and configurations using the same wood.

These Puerto Rican people display the enviable ability to use their talents and creativity to capitalize on a natural catastrophe.

RESPONDING TO CHANGING LIFESTYLE

In an article about the challenges facing leaders in a rapidly changing business world, the *Royal Bank Letter* from Canada stated, "Someone once described management as 'a Chinese baseball game.' In this mythical sport, both the ball and the bases are in motion. As soon as the ball is hit, the defending players can pick up the base bags and move them to anywhere in fair territory. The batters never know in advance where they must run to be safe." The author commented, "The metaphor refers to the terrific pace of change in business today."

Al Neuharth, chairperson and CEO of Gannett Company, was uneasy about the changes he observed in the newspaper industry. Afternoon papers such as *The Washington Star, The PhiladelphiaBulletin,The Cleveland Press* and *The Minneapolis Star*had met their demise. American's lifestyles were changing and instead of reading the newspaper when they came home from work, the television became their news source. Local papers were finding it increasingly difficult to deal with rising publishing costs, and advertising revenues fell short of the needed levels.

Neuharth and his team recognized that "the bases were being moved." Capitalizing on new technology and zeroing in on the public's desires, a daily national newspaper was created. *USA Today* was born.

MOVING TO THE SIDE OF THE ROAD

In 1971, Bantam published Alvin Toffler's *Future Shock,* which heightened our awareness of the impact of change on our society. Toffler predicted that "millions of ordinary, psychologically normal people will face an abrupt collision with the future...many of them will find it increasingly painful to keep up with the incessant demand for change that characterizes our time."

People tend to resist any idea, behavior, or process that threatens their existing beliefs. The message of *Future Shock* upset many because it confronted their present comfort zones. How could such absurd predictions contain any credibility? Yet, such closed-minded responses only reaffirmed the futurist's contention that people may not resist change but we do resist having to change.

A group of Amish people pulled up stakes from their religious settlement in the Midwest and moved to a remote area in Peru.

When asked their reason for doing so, one of them responded, "We got tired of having to move our wagons to the side of the road to let the cars go by."

They were, of course, voicing the frustration they felt from being pressured to change.

Many people today are fearful of "moving their wagons to the side of the road to let the cars go by."

John Steinbeck was probably right when he suggested, "It is the nature of man as he grows older to protest against change, particularly change for the better."

THE TOUGHEST THING TO CHANGE

"The world is too big for us. Too much going on, too many crimes, too much violence and excitement. Try as you will, you get behind in the race, in spite of yourself. It's an incessant strain, to keep pace... And still, you lose ground. Science empties its discoveries on you so fast that you stagger beneath them in hopeless bewilderment. The political world is news seen so rapidly you're out of breath trying to keep pace with who's in and who's out. Everything is high pressure. Human nature can't endure much more!"

This editorial represents the majority thinking today. However, it appeared on June 16, 1833, in the *Atlantic Journal.* Not much has changed, has it? Change remains—and probably always will be—a threat to the security of humankind.

•   •   •

The research of a Canadian neurosurgeon discovered some dramatic truths about the human mind's reaction to change. He conducted various experiments which proved that when a person is forced to change a fundamental belief or opinion, the brain undergoes a series of nervous sensations equivalent to distressing torture.

Change is not something to be feared. Rather it is something we should welcome—for without change, nothing in this world would ever grow or blossom, and no one in this world would ever move forward to become the person they want to be.

The toughest thing to change is our approach to change. Maybe it's time for a mind transfusion that welcomes the advent of change. Expect change; it is inevitable. Your decision is to decide whether it is to be by consent or coercion.

CHOICES

- God has given us two incredible things: absolutely awesome ability and freedom of choice. The tragedy is that, for the most part, many of us have refused them both.

  Frank Donnelly

- Our lives are a sum total of the choices we have made.

  Dr. Wayne Dyer

- You are free to choose, but the choices you make today will determine what you will have, be, and do in the tomorrow of your life.

  Zig Ziglar

- I had a life with options but frequently lived as if I had none. The sad result of my not having exercised my choices is that my memory of myself is not of the woman I believe I am.

  Liv Ullmann

CONDITIONED BY EXPERIENCE

According to an Associated Press report, a young boy panted and pawed for attention after he was rescued from a dirt-floored pen at his grandparents' home, where he was kept along with sixty dogs.

He howled. He reared back on his haunches, tilted his head and looked up, said the boy's Department of Human Services foster parent. "He acted like a little dog," she testified at a child neglect trial.

The grandparents said the boy's behavior was natural for a four-year-old and he was imitating cartoon characters he saw on television.

The foster parents said the boy continued to behave strangely after he was brought to their home, including fetching toys with his mouth. He ran wildly through the house, crashing into walls, and most of the time he ran on all fours. If he wanted attention, he would run up to them and paw at their bodies, rub his head on them, and whimper.

This unbelievable account places testifiable significance on the importance of a child's experiences. The environment in which we dwell will have a significant influence on the behaviors we exhibit.

Choose carefully who, where, and what experience you want your life exposed to. The four-year-old had no choice. You do.

CHOOSING CHOICES CAREFULLY

We are who we are today because of the choices we made yesterday. Likewise, tomorrow will become the result of today's choices. Mary Crowley, successful businessperson and author, says this about choices: "We are free up to the point of choice, then the choice controls the chooser."

I am told the Canadian Northlands experience only two seasons, winter and July. As the backroads begin to thaw, they become muddy and vehicles traveling through the backcountry leave deep ruts. The ground freezes hard during the winter months, and the highway ruts become a part of the traveling challenges. For vehicles entering this undeveloped area during the winter, there is a sign which reads, "Driver, please choose carefully which rut you drive in, because you'll be in it for the next 20 miles."

Choose carefully the path your life takes. Once you choose, your choices will control you.

COMMITMENT

- If you don't invest very much, then defeat doesn't hurt very much and winning is not very exciting.

  Dick Vermeil

- Are you a fanatic? A manager must care intensely about running a first-class operation; if his golf game is what he thinks about while shaving, the business will show it.

  Warren Buffett

- There is only one way to succeed in anything and that is to give everything. I do and I demand that my players do. Any man's finest hour is when he has worked his heart out in a good cause and lies exhausted on the field of battle . . . victorious.

  Vince Lombardi

- Commitment is the enemy of resistance for it is the serious promise to press on, to get up, no matter how many times you are knocked down.

  David McNally

- Irrevocable commitments that offer no loopholes, no bail-out provisions, and no parachute clauses will extract incredible productivity and performance.

  Robert Schuller

- No steam or gas ever drives anything until it is confined. No Niagara is ever turned into light and power until it is tunneled. No life ever grows until it is focused, dedicated, disciplined.

  Harry Emerson Fosdick

- I can't imagine a person becoming a success who doesn't give this game of life everything he's got.

  Walter Cronkite

- A total commitment is paramount to reaching the ultimate in performance.

  Tom Flores

■ There's a difference between interest and commitment. When you're interested in doing something, you do it only when it's convenient. When you're committed to something, you accept no excuses; only results.

Kenneth Blanchard

HOW COMMITTED ARE YOU?

Leaders, dreamers, inventors, aspiring professionals and all who desire achievement must understand the first step is to make a binding commitment to invest their life and talents toward all pursuits deserving their best efforts.

Vince Lombardi expected and even demanded total commitment from his Green Bay Packers. Every time a football player goes out to ply his trade, he's got to play from the ground up—from the soles of his feet right up to his head. Some guys play with their heads, and sure, you need to be smart to be number one in anything you try. But most important, you've got to play with your heart. If you're lucky enough to find a guy with a lot of head and a lot of heart, he'll never come off the field second.

General Billy Mitchell had to fight the entire bureaucracy of the U.S. Army and Navy, and get court-martialed in the process, before he finally convinced Congress to create the United States Air Force. General Mitchell played the game with a lot of head and a lot of heart. So did Margaret Sanger. As a nurse, she promoted the idea of birth control and had to leave the country for fear of arrest. Her relentless commitment eventually formed Planned Parenthood Federation of America.

Committed people desire the successful outcome of their pursuits with astounding depth and intensity. There is no room for apathy or lowered motivation. Their commitment provides a constant source of renewal and energy that rejects indifference.

•   •   •

A newspaper reporter secured an exclusive interview with the devil. The reporter was especially interested in the deceptive techniques around which the devil had built his reputation. What is the most useful tool you use on people? he asked. Is it dishonesty? Lust? Jealousy?

No, no, no, chuckled the devil. The most useful weapon I possess is apathy.

How true! An "I don't care" attitude will strip life from the loftiest dreams. Devotion, dedication, and duty add energy and possibility to the smallest ambition.

Through commitment Erma Bombeck grew her local "At Wit's End" column into a nationally syndicated feature.

Sportswriters and football fans predicted the 1988 football season would be the end for Joe Montana. Joe Montana believed differently. After back surgery in 1986, he attempted an unsuccessful comeback and found himself benched late in the 1988 season. Montana earned back his starting position and went on to lead the Forty-niners to their third Super Bowl victory of the 1980s. Talk to Montana about commitment.

Andrew Carnegie spoke of people like Joe Montana. He said people fall into three basic categories: those who did not do all their duty, those who only professed to do their duty and those who did their duty plus a little more.

A little bit more . . . what a concept. The Carnegies, Bombecks, and Montanas of this world are prime examples. So is Bill Cosby.

Dropping out of Temple University as a junior, Cosby became a starving comedian. But he made a commitment to make good. His education and training as a comedian included staying up till all hours of the night talking to seasoned comics, researching material, and working on new routines.

Quoted in the *Dallas Times Herald*, Cosby had this to say: "Anyone can dabble, but once you've made that commitment, then your blood has that particular thing in it, and it's very hard for people to stop you."

Once again, we're faced with the prerequisite to success: commitment. Is there any way around it? It's doubtful.

.   .   .

Former pro basketball star Bill Bradley shared how at the age of fifteen he attended a summer basketball camp that affected his life. The camp was run by "Easy" Ed Macauley, a former college and pro star. "Just remember that if you're not working at your game to the utmost of your ability," Macauley told his assembled campers, "there will be someone out there somewhere with equal ability who will be working to the utmost of his ability. And one day you'll play each other, and he'll have the advantage."

Bradley, who today is a U.S. Senator, saw in those words a totality of truth. He took them to heart and made them the guiding principle of his life.

Lou Holtz, Notre Dame's football coach, learned the value of commitment. He admits that in the first few years of his marriage he was looking for a "way out." Then he realized the issue wasn't the marriage but his lack of commitment to making it work. Later, he felt an urge to coach professional football. After a short stint with the New York Jets, Holtz discovered it was only a job and he lacked a real commitment to it. Today, Lou Holtz is an evangelist of this truth: All human success is the result of a persistent commitment.

.   .   .

Michelangelo's career as a sculptor and painter wasn't handed to him on a silver platter. Although he possessed great talents, his accomplishments and fame came only after he invested himself to the point of physical exhaustion. Michelangelo spent years lying flat on his back on a scaffold painting the fresco in the Sistine Chapel. By the time he completed this magnificent project, he was virtually blind from the paint that had dripped in his eyes. Now that's commitment! Because

Michelangelo was willing to invest himself, he created art that has been admired for more than four centuries.

People willing to invest themselves will improve the quality of their life as well as the world around them. Organizations, communities, and religious and educational institutions fortunate enough to have committed people will excel. The world cannot help but smile on the efforts of dedicated, hard-earned successes.

•   •   •

Dr. Anthony Campolo, professor of Sociology at Eastern College in Pennsylvania, author, and dynamic speaker, consolidates our thoughts on commitment with this statement: "What you commit yourself to be will change what you are and make you into a completely different person. Let me repeat that. Not the past but the future conditions you, because what you commit yourself to become determines what you are—more than anything that ever happened to you yesterday or the day before. Therefore I ask you a very simple question: What are your commitments? Where are you going? What are you going to be? You show me somebody who hasn't decided, and I'll show you somebody who has no identity, no personality, no direction."

Until one is committed, there is hesitancy, the chance to draw back, always ineffectiveness. Concerning all acts of initiative and creation there is one elemental truth, the ignorance of which kills countless ideas and splendid plans: The moment one definitely commits oneself, then Providence moves too. All sorts of things occur to help one that would never otherwise have occurred. A whole stream of events issues from the decision, raising in one's favor all manner of unforeseen incidents, meetings, and material assistance, which no man could have dreamed would have come his way. I have learned a deep respect for one of Goethe's couplets:

> Whatever you can do, or dream you can, begin it.
> Boldness has genius, power and magic in it.

IT TAKES HEART!

When asked the secret of his success, Charles Dickens responded, "Whatever I have tried to do in life, I have tried with my heart to do well." This statement also reflects the reason Washington Redskins wide receiver Art Monk is a leading pass receiver in pro football.

Monk's commitment to develop his talents is visible in an exhausting exercise regimen. For the past ten years, during the off season, Monk arrives at the Redskin park at 9:00 A. M. and lifts weights for 75 minutes. Then he runs six 200-meter sprints and fifteen 150-meter sprints. After dinner he runs an additional two or three miles to loosen up from the stiffness caused by his daytime regimen.

Now, contrast Monk's commitment to the new army recruit who was rudely awakened by his drill sergeant after his first night in the barracks. "Rise and shine," screamed the sergeant, "it's four-thirty!"

"Four-thirty," the rookie moaned. "Sergeant, you'd better go back to bed. We have a big day ahead of us tomorrow."

Some folks never do understand that dreaming their way through life is not a great option. It is time to wake up and realize it takes heart to prepare ourselves for the grueling real world.

"I'LL GIVE EVERYTHING I HAVE"

President Eisenhower readily admitted that public speaking was not his forte. Addressing an audience one day he told the following story:

"A neighboring farmer had a cow that he wanted to sell. We went over to visit the farmer and asked him about the cow's pedigree.

"The old farmer didn't know what *pedigree* meant, so we asked him about the cow's butterfat production. He told us he didn't have any idea what it was. Finally we asked him if he knew how many pounds of milk the cow produced each year.

"The farmer said, 'I don't know. But she's an honest cow, and she'll give you all the milk she has.'

"I said, 'I'm like the cow. I'll give you everything I have.' "

What a simple yet profound illustration of commitment.

•   •   •

Racing horse Broadway Ltd. (a son of Man o' War) never espoused and I'll-give-it-everything-I-have mentality. Back in 1928, he cost his owner $65,000 and with marvelous ability managed never to win a race. Then in 1930, competing for a $900 purse, Broadway Ltd. in a burst of inspiration made the final turn in front. Assured of victory . . . he dropped dead.

Commitment is a lifetime exercise in giving everything you have. People who are unconditioned to this way of life should refrain from periodic energy bursts . . . it could prove fatal.

UNCOMMON COMMITMENT

What happens when you get up at 4:45 A.M. six days a week, swim 6,000 meters before school every morning, and then return after classes for another rigorous workout? If your name is Janet Evans, the outcome is three gold medals in the 1988 Olympics, followed by additional success in 1992. Janet has had a passion for swimming since she was three years old. Her commitment to be the best allowed her to stand with the American flag in Seoul, Korea, to be recognized for her achievements.

What happens when you commit a lifetime to entertainment? Combine that with fifty years of freely sharing your talents for the benefit of others and you may end up in the *Guinness Book of Records* as the world's most decorated and honored man in entertainment. This celebrated status is reserved for Bob Hope.

Beginning with his first radio show for armed services personnel in 1941, Hope began a tradition of conducting benefit shows, founding and directing charitable organizations and giving of his time and wealth. At age ninety, Hope credited his staying power to a commitment that involves lifting the human spirit.

What happens when an unemployed Westinghouse worker is committed to providing a reading service? Turned down by various publishers, he and his wife put their ideas into a little magazine. Printing difficulties, subscription challenges, and limited resources couldn't crush their spirit. At the time of their death, De Witt and Lila Wallace enjoyed 100 million readers, 30 million subscribers, 18 million in the United States and the rest worldwide. Their *Reader's Digest* became a phenomenal publishing success story.

Uncommon commitment allows common people to produce uncommon results.

THEY CALLED HIM "UGY"

Eugene Orowitz was a scrawny tenth grader in New Jersey whose friends warmly called him "Ugy."

Eugene was a self-proclaimed non-athlete. He was shy, self-conscious, and lacked confidence. One day while watching his high school track team practice, the coach half jokingly asked him if he would like to try. When Ugy gripped the javelin and let it fly, everyone watching was amazed to see it soar into the grandstand. From that day on he practiced day and night to extend his distances. Before he left high school, Ugy had thrown the javelin 211 yards, achieving a national high school record. His accomplishment brought him a college track scholarship in California and later, serious consideration about Olympic competition. However, a torn shoulder muscle eventually halted his javelin-throwing career.

Denied an Olympic performance, he remained committed to pursuing a career of equal excitement. Helping a friend rehearse for a part in a play, he caught the dramatic bug and enrolled in acting school at Warner Brothers.

Eugene Orowitz (alias Michael Landon) became a television superstar, famous for his roles in *Bonanza, Little House on the Prairie,* and *Highway to Heaven.* Although few people are aware of Landon's beginnings, his commitment to be the best is permanently impressed in the minds of his fans.

COMMUNICATION

- The real art of conversation is not only to say the right thing in the right place, but to leave unsaid the wrong thing at the tempting moment.

  Dorothy Nevill

- There may be no single thing more important in our efforts to achieve meaningful work and fulfilling relationships than to learn to practice the art of communication.

  Max De Pree

- Silences regulate the flow of listening and talking. They are to conversations what zeros are to mathematics—crucial nothings without which communication can't work.

  Gerald Goodman
  The Talk Book

- A manager's personal style—how good he or she is at exchanging information—contributes more to a department's efficiency than the results of any structured or organizational brilliance.

  Mark H. McCormack

- In interpersonal communication, there must be an ongoing and perceived consistency between what you say and how you say it.

  Janet G. Elsea

- Communication is a process (either verbal or nonverbal) of sharing information with another person in such a way that he understands what you are saying. "Talking" and "listening" and "understanding" are all involved in the process of communication.

  Dr. H. Norman Wright

- Where there's simplicity words can be taken at face value. One says what one means and means what one says.

  Albert Day

- The most important thing in communication is to hear what isn't being said.

  Peter Drucker

- Communication does not begin with being understood, but with understanding others.

  W. Steven Brown

- Most conversations are just alternating monologues. The question is, is there any real listening going on?

  Leo Buscaglia

- I like people who refuse to speak until they are ready to speak.

  Lillian Hellman

- The way we communicate with others and with ourselves ultimately determines the quality of our lives.

  Anthony Robins
  Unlimited Power

- Good communication is as stimulating as black coffee, and just as hard to sleep after.

  Ann Morrow Lindbergh

- Man does not live by words alone, despite the fact that sometimes he has to eat them.

  Adlai Stevenson

- The right word may be effective, but no word was ever as effective as a rightly timed pause.

  Mark Twain

- One way to prevent conversation from being boring is to say the wrong thing.

  Frank Sheed

- Anything that begins, "I don't know how to tell you this" is never good news.

  Ruth Gordon

- An intellectual is a man who takes more words than necessary to tell more than he knows.

  Dwight D. Eisenhower

- Talk low, talk slow, and don't say too much.

  John Wayne

■   A sharp tongue and a brilliant mind are never found in the same skull.

Anonymous

■   When it comes to body language, there are some who have better vocabularies than others.

Doug Larson

■   Many people who have the gift of gab don't know how to wrap it up.

Arnold H. Glasow

THE POWER OF WORDS

Communication has the potential of being a powerful positive tool in a person's repertoire of skills. The words we use often determine the success and failure of our interactions.

According to research psychologists, the average one-year-old child has a three-word vocabulary. By fifteen months children can speak nineteen words. At two years of age, most youngsters possess a working knowledge of 272 words. Their vocabulary catapults to 896 words by age three, 1,540 by age four, and 2,072 words by age five. By age six the average child can communicate with 2,562 words.

Our word accumulation continues to grow yet effective use of them does not necessarily follow. Even though the average adult speaks at a rate of 125 to 200 words per minute and up to 18,000 words per day, this does not mean messages have been clearly relayed. "Words, like glasses," wrote Joseph Joubert, "obscure everything which they do not make clear."

•   •   •

Take, for example, the confusing yet creative communicator Casey Stengel. Addressing his baseball team one day he said, "Now all you fellows line up alphabetically by height." What was the message? Who knows?

Stengel's unique usage of the English language became known as "Stengelese." He once said, "I've always heard that it couldn't be done, but sometimes it don't always work." How profound.

Believe it or not, Stengel held a position on the board of directors for a California bank. According to the *Wall Street Journal*, Casey described his responsibilities this way: "There ain't nothing to it. You go into the fancy meeting room and you just sit there and never open your yap. As long as you don't say nuthin' they don't know whether you're smart or dumb."

We all possess our own form of Stengelese. Whether it's the way we use the English language to convey our messages or how we interpret what others say to us. Either way, the results are the same: frequent misunderstanding.

. . .

I personally like the story of the two people who met at an art show. "What do you do?" asked the young woman.

"I'm an artist," came the reply.

"I've never met a real live artist. This is so exciting. I always wanted a personal portrait done. Could you do that?"

"Oh, sure," replied the artist, "that's my specialty!"

"That's great!" she exclaimed. "I do have one special request. I want the painting done in the nude."

"I'll have to think about that and get back to you," responded the startled artist.

A few days later he called the potential customer with his decision. "I'm willing to do the painting as you requested," he said, "but with one stipulation. I want to leave my socks on. I need somewhere to put my paintbrushes."

I can almost hear you groan after reading this story. How could the artist be so naive? Yet, how many times do we misinterpret simple messages because of our own perception of the sender's meaning or intent?

It has been said, "a message sent is only as good as the receiver's perception of it." One factor contributing to the difficulty of insuring accurate perceptions is the receiver's definition of the words sent. The 500 most common used words in the English language have over 14,000 definitions. No wonder verbal interactions tend to create confusion and misunderstanding.

. . .

Mark Twain put it this way, "The difference between the right word and the almost right word is the difference between lightning and the lightning bug."

Joseph Conrad commented, "Words have set whole nations in motion and upheaved the dry hard ground on which rests our social fabric. Give me the right word and the right accent and I will move the world."

Consider also the wisdom of Sigmund Freud: "Words have a magical power. They can bring either the greatest happiness or deepest despair; they can transfer knowledge from teacher to student; words enable the orator to sway his audience and dictate its decision. Words are capable of arousing the strongest emotions and prompting all men's actions."

. . .

Words. They are powerful. Choose them carefully. Organize not only your thoughts before you speak, but determine which words best communicate the message you want to send. One final thought: Attempt to speak in the other person's language rather than your own.

Consider Lee Iacocca's comments about the leader as communicator: "It's important to talk to people in their own language. If you do it well, they'll say, 'God, he said exactly what I was thinking.' And when they begin to respect you, they'll follow you to the death."

A FEW WORDS APTLY SPOKEN

Calvin Coolidge said, "I have never been hurt by anything I didn't say."

Maybe this statement explains why Coolidge became known as the president of few words. For example, one Sunday he returned home from church services and was asked by his wife, "What did the minister speak on?"

"Sin," replied Coolidge.

Wanting to know more about the sermon she pressed her husband for details, to which Coolidge responded, "I think he was against it."

On another occasion a woman approached President Coolidge at dinner and blurted, "I have a bet with my friend, Mr. President, that I can get you to say more than two words."

Coolidge simply replied, "You lose."

Shakespeare believed, "Men of few words are the best men." I guess that would make Coolidge pretty good.

MAKE SURE THEY UNDERSTAND

Communication comes from the Latin root *commune*, which means "held in common." To make communication work, we have to make sure that the people we're talking with understand what we're saying as well as we do. Consider this scenario:

A construction worker approached the reception desk in a doctor's office. The receptionist asked him why he was there. "I have shingles," he said.

She took down his name, address, medical insurance number, and told him to have a seat.

Fifteen minutes later a nurse came out and asked him what he had. "Shingles," he replied. She took down his height, weight, and a complete medical history and told him to wait in the examining room.

A half hour later, a nurse came in and asked why he was here. "I have shingles," he replied again. She took his blood pressure, a urine specimen, and told him to take off his clothes and wait for the doctor.

An hour later, the doctor came in and asked him what he had. He said, "Shingles."

The doctor said, "Where?"

He said, "Outside in the truck. Where do you want them?"

Make sure people understand what you're trying to say.

Communication is not simply sending a message. It is creating shared meaning and understanding—swiftly, clearly, and precisely.

SILENCE IS GOLDEN

"Silence," wrote G. K. Chesterton, "is the unbearable repartee." Publius, the Greek sage, put his finger on the value of silence when he admitted, "I have often regretted my speech, never my silence."

If the great American inventor Thomas Edison was writing this anecdote, he would tell you about the time he learned a valuable lesson about silence. When the Western Union Company offered to buy his newly invented ticker, Edison had no idea how much to ask for it. He asked for and was granted a few days to think about the purchase price.

Edison and his wife talked about the offer. Although stunned by Mrs. Edison's suggestion to ask for $20,000, he hesitantly agreed and set out to meet Western Union officials.

"What price have you decided on?" the Western Union representative asked.

When Edison attempted to tell him $20,000, the figure stuck to the roof of his mouth. He stood speechless. Impatient with the pending silence, the Western Union businessperson finally blurted, "How about $100,000?"

"Speech is great, but silence is greater," said Carlyle. Thomas Edison would no doubt agree: His unintended silence reaped valuable profits.

SILLY EXAMPLES OF SILLY COMMUNICATION

Communication is serious business. Yet, we can't help but chuckle at the comical results our communication efforts sometimes produce. Relax and allow the following examples to tickle your jocular vein.

• • •

Two guys were walking down a country road when Pete said to Joe, "Look at that cow with one eye."

So Joe directly placed his hand over one eye to look at the cows.

• • •

"The events in our household this past week have left me in a state of consternation," lamented Mrs. Jones.

Her friend quickly advised, "Why don't you try prune juice?"

• • •

A traveling salesperson stopped at a fast-food restaurant for a cup of coffee. When the server delivered the coffee, the friendly salesperson attempted to make conversation.

"Looks like rain," the salesperson said.

"I don't make this stuff," the server responded, "I just serve it."

COURAGE

- Courage is not the absence of fear; rather it is the ability to take action in the face of fear.

  Nancy Anderson
  Work with Passion

- Moral courage is a more rare commodity than bravery in battle or great intelligence.

  John F. Kennedy

- You gain strength, courage and confidence by every experience in which you really stop to look fear in the face. You are able to say to yourself, "I lived through this horror. I can take the next thing that comes along." You must do the thing you think you cannot do.

  Eleanor Roosevelt

- Every human being on this earth is born with a tragedy, and it isn't original sin. He's born with the tragedy that he has to grow up. A lot of people don't have the courage to do it.

  Helen Hayes

- Few will have the greatness to bend history itself, but each of us can work to change a small portion of events . . . it is from numberless acts of courage and belief that human history is shaped.

  Robert F. Kennedy

- I am tired of hearing about men with the "courage of their convictions." Nero and Caligula and Attila and Hitler had the courage of their convictions . . . But not one of them had the courage to examine their convictions or to change them, which is the true test of character.

  Sydney Harris

- One of the most courageous things you can do is identify yourself, know who you are, what you believe in, and where you want to go.

  Sheila Murray Bethel
  Making a Difference

■   Courage comes from acting courageously on a day-to-day basis.

Brian Tracy

■   All our dreams can come true—if we have the courage to pursue them.

Walt Disney

THE HEART OF COURAGE

Mark Twain reminds us, "Courage is mastery of fear—not absence of fear." Courage, contrary to popular belief, is not the absence of fear. Courage is the heart to act in spite of fear.

During World War II, a military official summoned General George Patton in Sicily. As he praised Patton for his courage and bravery, the General interrupted: "Sir, I am not a brave man . . . The truth is, I am an utter craven coward. I have never been within the sound of gunshot or in sight of battle in my whole life that I wasn't so scared that I had sweat in the palms of my hands."

Years later, when George Patton's autobiography was published, it contained this significant statement by the general: "I learned very early in my life never to take counsel of my fears."

"Courage," said Eddie Rickenbacker, "is doing what you're afraid to do. There can be no courage unless you're scared."

THE LAUREL BURCH STORY

Laurel Burch had the courage to be different, to dream, and to create The Spirit of Womankind jewelry. Her journey to prosperity encourages the faint-hearted among us.

"I once met a man in the jungles of Bali," says Laurel. "We didn't have more than two or three words in common, but when he saw my drawings, he threw his head back and his eyes sparkled. He beamed, his face was illuminated. His delight was universal. Now he carves the mythical menageries that cluster like shrines in my house, my shops, and my displays. All ways of life increase one's sense of spirit. All offerings come back in such ways.

"When I was a girl, I used to collect little stones in bags. I delighted in their shapes and colors. When I got home, I'd put them in different arrangements and love them. When I started school I'd rarely come straight home. I'd meander around seeking secret hideouts I knew were full of treasures from other worlds. I remember always dreaming beyond what I knew, then coming up with something that made the dreams come true. When I was seven, I put on shows in my garage for the neighborhood kids. I'd collect money from them, then figure out what I was going to do.

"I ran away from home at fourteen and ended up in a Catholic boarding school. That summer, when the boarders went home, it was thirty nuns and me. I didn't have parents, I didn't have friends. I created my world out of imaginary cultures, other worlds, fantasy animals. I converted my room into the hideouts of my childhood. I'd put on a grass skirt and dance to recorded music from Bora Bora, read *The Prophet*, or pretend I was a flamenco dancer. Mother Superior didn't approve. I often wonder what she did with the grass skirt.

"For the longest time nobody validated what I was doing. In high school, I was the one with hair down to my waist, who made exotic coffees, who lit candles in my bedroom—and who wound up in the Haight in 1966. I thanked the friends who sheltered me and my two babies with gifts of necklaces and earrings made of wire hammered into twists using the flat bottom of a frying pan I'd bought at the flea market. I shaped coins, beads, and bones I found on the street into things that looked as though they came from faraway peoples. I thought of them as the spirit of life that creation gives to all people.

"I thought having two kids 'stacked the deck' against me, but by combining Egyptian beads, Chinese coins, and odds and ends from around the world, I could hold onto my inside self. I worked in a jewelry store for $1.25 an hour, of which fifty cents had to go for baby-sitting. I had no idea my own time had value and I sold my creations for $2.00 a pair.

"It might have gone on that way forever, but one day I walked into a Ghiradelli Square store owned by Lois Smith, wearing a necklace of metal and beads I'd made. She loved it and asked me to make and sell jewelry for her and other stores. I delivered my first pieces wrapped in Japanese mulberry paper and decorated my first invoices with drawings of little mythopoetic animals.

"At first my reputation grew by word of mouth. Then I went to New York and bumped into an old friend. She took one look at the jewelry on my neck (overlooking the baby strapped to my back) and said, 'Come on, we're going to *Vogue*.' The result was two pages in *Vogue* and three pages in *Harper's Bazaar*."

When all the odds were against her, Laurel Burch mustered the courage to go on. Her story is an encouragement to all who hesitate to elevate their life to the next level.

CREATIVITY

- Creativity is especially expressed in the ability to make connections, to make associations, to turn things around and express them in a new way.

Tim Hansen

- I submit that creativity will never be a science—in fact, much of it will always remain a mystery, as much of a mystery as 'what makes the heart tick?' At the same time, I submit that creativity is an art—an applied art, a workable art, a learnable art—an art in which all of us can make ourselves more and more proficient, if we will.

Alex Osborn

- Creativity involves taking what you have, where you are, and getting the most out of it.

Carl Mays

- All things are created twice: first mentally; then physically. The key to creativity is to begin with the end in mind, with a vision and a blueprint of the desired result.

Stephen R. Covey

- Ingenuity, plus courage, plus work, equals miracles.

Bob Richards

- Creativity is like a muscle—it has to be stretched and exercised regularly to keep it fit and functioning.

Gloria Hoffman and Pauline Graivier
Speak the Language of Success

- Creativity is a highfalutin' word for the work I have to do between now and Tuesday.

David Ogilvy

- Creativity is the natural extension of our enthusiasm.

Earl Nightingale

■   Creativity has been built into every one of us; it's part of our design. Each of us lives less of the life God intended for us when we choose not to live out the creative powers we possess.

Ted Engstrom

■   One of the major factors which differentiates creative people from lesser creative people is that creative people pay attention to their small ideas.

Roger von Oech

■   The greatest enemy of your creative powers is smug complacency—being satisfied with less than what you are capable of doing.

Nido Qubein

■   The creative person is the master rather than the slave of his imagination.

Michael LeBoeuf, Ph.D.

■   Be brave enough to live creatively. The creative is the place where no one else has ever been. You have to leave the city of your comfort and go into the wilderness of your intuition. You can't get there by bus, only by hard work, risking, and by not quite knowing what you're doing. What you'll discover will be wonderful: yourself.

Alan Alda

TAPPING OUR CREATIVE JUICES

R. Buckminster Fuller was a man of many talents. His entire adult life was spent as an inventor, engineer, architect, poet, and star-gazer. Most importantly, "Bucky," as his friends referred to him, was a creative thinker. He was responsible for the invention, development, and implementation of over 170 patented ideas. He authored twenty-four books and made fifty-seven trips around the world sharing his abundant supply of ideas with others.

As a young, nonconforming student, Fuller was expelled from Harvard in his freshman year. His enthusiasm and creativity remained undampened. Fuller would often spend up to 22 hours a day studying math, architecture, and physics. His self-acquired knowledge, combined with his creative ideas, made him a man ahead of his time and a leading innovator. In fact, he was often branded a kook because his ideas seemed so impossible at the time. However, the put-downs and criticism had little effect on Bucky and he continued to create, design, and invent up until his death.

R. Buckminster Fuller is considered one of the greatest innovators of this century. His creative genius stemmed from this simple yet profound thought: "People should think things out fresh and not just accept conventional terms and the conventional way of doing things."

Murray Spangler developed a mindset similar to Bucky Fuller's. As a department store janitor, Spangler suffered considerable discomfort from the dust his broom stirred up. The wheezing and coughing prompted him to find an unconventional way to clean floors.

"Why not eliminate the sweeping," he thought, "and suck up the dust instead." His friend, H. W. Hoover, financed the first awkward but functional vacuum cleaner. Spangler's futuristic, uncluttered thinking allowed him to overcome personal discomfort and go beyond conventional thinking.

•   •   •

Pablo Picasso embodied a revolutionary approach to creativity. One day, he was standing outside his house looking around the yard. A rusty old bicycle resting against the porch caught his attention. Picasso focused on the metal frame of the bike and noticed the handlebars resembled the horns of a bull. Removing the handlebars from the bike, he proceeded to his studio and created a sculpture of a charging bull. Picasso tapped his creative imagination to turn the ordinary into something dramatic. Picasso's creative success was attributed to the ability of expanding on one theme to create another.

Later in his life, Picasso shared the secret for escaping tunnel vision. "Every act of creation is first of all an act of destruction," preached Picasso. One must first break down the barriers of present limitations and restrictive thoughts and destroy old habits that strangle our creative efforts. Then and only then can our creative genius be explored.

Creativity expert Dr. Roger von Oech says "Challenging the established rules is necessary to awaken our creativity" (*A Whack on the Side of the Head: How to Unlock Your Mind for Motivation*, New York: Warner Books, 1988). von Oech tells how in the winter of 333 B.C., the Macedonian general Alexander and his army arrive in the Asian city of Gordium to spend the winter. Alexander is told about the legend surrounding the town's famous knot, the "Gordian Knot." According to local prophecy, whoever is able to untie this exceptionally complex knot will become king of Asia. Alexander is fascinated by the local legend and asks to be shown the knot so he can attempt to untie it. He studies the strangely tied rope and makes numerous fruitless attempts to locate the rope's end. Unscathed by his failure to unfasten the knot, he approaches the challenge using Picasso's advice. Alexander pulls out his sword and slices the knot in half . . . thereby inheriting control of Asia.

Creative people are constantly on the lookout for new ideas. They recreate and rearrange the present by finding novel ways to approach specific problems. They use their creativity to find new solutions, sometimes by using unrelated ideas as they fit the present situation. While this approach tends to invite criticism, creative thinkers continue to think things out fresh, knowing that novel ideas often solve complex problems.

Novel ideas may produce criticism from the masses, but Everett M. Rogers suggests that "when 5 percent of society accepts an idea, it becomes imbedded in the population. When 20 percent agrees, it's unstoppable." Even the unstoppable get criticized.

> "You can't put a crocodile on a shirt to replace the pocket. Nobody will buy them!"
>
> "You want to sell me a chicken recipe? You'll never get this idea off the ground, Colonel Sanders!"
>
> "I'm sorry, but your *Gone With the Wind* manuscript will have little public appeal."
>
> "Mr. Bell, please remove that silly toy from my office. There is no room in the market for a telephone."
>
> "Watches with no hands? You're crazy!"
>
> "How dumb do you think I am? You can't put music on a roll of tape."

The history books are full of people who realized creativity begins with destroying perceived limitations and remaining untouched by criticism.

·   ·   ·

Finally, Albert Einstein represented the best of creative thinkers when he observed, "To raise new questions, new possibilities, to regard old problems from a new angle, requires creative imagination." Creativity emerges out of personal commitment to raise new questions, explore new possibilities, focus on old problems from a new angle, and be willing to implement ideas that may not be in tune with the conventional way of doing things.

Charles Darrow was a salesperson who lived during the Great Depression. When sales positions dried up, he squeezed out a living walking dogs, washing cars, and doing other assorted odd jobs. In the evening, he worked on developing a board game that several people could play at once. Darrow had visions of every home owning one of his games.

The first company to purchase his idea sold 5,000 games in the first year. Parker Brothers later purchased the game, beefed up the marketing, and today, 20,000 of these games are sold every week.

Darrow's willingness to pursue new possibilities resulted in America's favorite board game—Monopoly™.

·   ·   ·

How about the young salesperson asked by the Hookless Fastener Company how to increase the sale of zippers. He suggested they replace the buttons on the front of men's trousers with zippers. This unconventional idea was almost scrapped. A trial run took this nontraditional idea from skepticism to a standard in the clothing industry.

Here's an old problem. How do you stop a train? George Westinghouse no doubt raised a few railroad executives' eyebrows when he suggested a train could be stopped by using wind. His imagination was unstoppable. Westinghouse Air Brakes became conventional equipment on American trains.

A discussion on new possibilities wouldn't be complete without considering George de Mestral. While brushing burrs out of his wool pants and his dog's coat, de Mestral became curious about the tenacity of the burrs. Concentrated observation of the burrs under a microscope revealed hundreds of tiny hooks snagged in mats of wool and fur. Years later, he made a connection, and the invention of Velcro™ fasteners was born. George de Mestral looked at an old problem with new eyes. He raised new questions and sought new possibilities. Einstein would have been proud.

Three challenges evolve from our discussion:

- Think things out fresh . . . be unconventional.
- Destroy the old, then create new.
- Tap your imagination. Consider new ideas, ask new questions, raise new possibilities.

• • •

Dr. Michael LeBoeuf advises, "Don't let other people define your creative potential. No one, including you, knows what you're capable of doing or thinking up."

In a three-month creativity study, psychologists researched the characteristics of creative people. Education, family backgrounds, and a variety of personal preferences were all considered as possible variables. In the end, one single common factor was found to determine an individual's creativity—attitude. Simply stated, creative people think they are creative.

Creative potential is one of the great God-given tools available to us. The extent to which we develop this gift depends on our attitude toward it. No one knows for sure what they're capable of and therein lies the excitement.

Pursue your creative possibilities at full speed. Develop the quality of imagineering.

The Aluminum Company of America defines *imagineering* as the ability to let your imagination soar and then engineering it to make it happen. Dream your dream. Organize your plan. Take action and never give up!

LIMITING FEARS

Society, tradition, and self-imposed limitations build barriers to developing a creative spirit. Although creativity is a learnable behavior, Don Koberg and Jim Bagnall maintain the following fears severely hinder the cultivation of creativity:

- fear of making mistakes
- fear of being seen as a fool
- fear of being criticized
- fear of being misused
- fear of being alone
- fear of disturbing tradition and making changes
- fear of being associated with "taboos"
- fear of losing the security of habit
- fear of losing the love of the group
- fear of truly being an individual

GOING FROM ROOM TO ROOM

Milton Erickson, a world-famous hypnotherapist, relates this story from *My Voice Will Go With You* (New York: Norton):

I asked a student, "How do you get from this room into that room?"

He answered, "First you stand up. Then you take a step . . ."

I stopped him and said, "Name all the possible ways you can get from this room into that room."

He said, "You can go by running; by walking; you can go by jumping; you can go by hopping; by somersaulting. You can go out that door, go outside the house, come in another door and into the room. Or you could climb out a window if you want to."

I said, "You said you would be inclusive but you made an omission which is a major omission. I usually illustrate, first, by saying, 'If I want to get into that room from this room, I would go out that door, take a taxi to the airport, buy a ticket to Chicago, New York, London, Rome, Athens, Hong Kong, Honolulu, San Francisco, Chicago, Dallas, Phoenix, come back by limousine, and go in the backyard and then through the back gate into the back door and into that room.' And you thought only of forward movement! You didn't think of going in backwards, did you? And you didn't think of crawling in."

The student added, "Or of sliding on my stomach either."

Humans limit themselves by thinking unimaginatively. Stretching ourselves beyond the usual and customary will yield new experiences, ideas, and unchartered territory.

EXCERPTS ON CREATIVITY

A small Kwik-Shop in Des Moines, Iowa, earns the medal for creative adjusted marketing. When their supply of Christmas candy canes didn't sell, they merely changed their advertising. All 34-cent candy canes were remarked as "Valentine's Candy," now selling for 19 cents apiece.

Nobel Laureate Jonas Salk was asked how he went about inventing the polio vaccine. He responded: "I pictured myself as a virus or a cancer cell and tried to sense what it would be like."

L.L. Bean loved hunting but despised coming home with wet feet and soggy leather boots. In 1911, he noticed a pair of rubber galoshes in a local dry goods store and a picture appeared in his mind. Why not combine leather uppers for support and rubber bottoms to create waterproof comfort? L.L. Bean's success bears evidence to the quality of his idea.

F. W. Woolworth's creative flair was displayed when a nearby merchant resented his competition and hung a large sign outside his store reading, "I have been doing business in this spot for over fifty years." The following day, Woolworth hung up his own sign. It read, "Established a week ago. All new merchandise."

During the 1904 World's Fair in St. Louis, Missouri, a hot waffle vendor applied creativity to turn disaster into a popular invention.

The vendor ran out of paper plates, so he could not serve his hot waffles. All other merchants withheld their plates, attempting to make as much money as they could.

A nearby ice cream seller suggested the waffle vendor buy ice cream from him at a reduced rate and sell it himself. And thus he did, dishing up the ice cream in small cups. But what could he do with all the waffle ingredients?

While selling another person's wares, a creative idea struck him like a bolt of lightning. At home, the next day his wife helped him produce a batch of one thousand waffles and pressed them thin with a hot iron. Each waffle was rolled into a circular pattern with a point at the bottom. The next morning this creative vendor put scoops of ice cream in his waffles and cornered the market with his "cone shaped waffle." Of course, we know it as the ice cream cone.

. . .

What do you do with rejected sandpaper materials? One man at 3M gave substantial effort to answering this question. In fact, management felt he was wasting too much time and fired him. However, he continued to come to work. Oh, how things change for persistent creative people! His dogged determination ultimately landed him the position of vice-president of 3M's roofing granules division. What about his quest for an answer to using rejected sandpaper material? You'll find the product on the roof of your house in the form of asphalt shingles.

. . .

Years ago, one of Ripley's famous *Believe It or Not* cartoons pictured a plain bar of iron worth $5.00 and pointed out that if you forged the iron into horseshoes, it would then be worth $10.50. If you used the iron for making needles, it would then be worth $3,285. And if you turned the iron into watch springs, the value would soar to $250,000. There's a big difference between $5.00 and $250,000. The difference is applied creativity.

Our excerpts on creativity feature people who were not satisfied with preserving raw material but felt compelled to transform ideas to their most valuable state.

THERE'S GOT TO BE AN EASIER WAY

Ole Evinrude was in love and engaged to be married. Ole and his fiancée took advantage of a beautiful summer day to row across the lake and enjoy a private picnic on the other side. Just as they finished setting up the picnic, his fiancée discovered they had forgotten the dessert.

Ole made his way back to the boat, rowed to the other side, picked up the dessert, and began the lengthy row back to his sweetheart. About midpoint, Ole was beat. The heat, humidity, and physical exertion left Ole low on energy, and although his ice cream was melting his creative thought mechanisms remained sharp. "There has got to be an easier way," he thought to himself.

That exasperated thought prompted the invention of the world's first portable outboard motor. Ole's experimentation began in 1906. By 1909, he had produced the first commercially successful outboard motor. In 1910, he was granted a U.S. patent for his invention. Ole Evinrude's outboard motor company went on to dominate the market for years.

Two questions continue to haunt me. First, did Ole and his fiancée ever have their picnic? Second, did they get married and live happily ever after?

CRITICISM

- The trouble with most of us is that we would rather be ruined by praise than saved by criticism.

  Dr. Norman Vincent Peale

- The longer you dwell on another's weakness, the more you infect your own mind with unhappiness.

  Hugh Prather

- I never criticize a player until they are first convinced of my unconditional confidence in their abilities!

  John Robinson

- I was never as good as all the credit I got, and never as bad as the criticism I received.

  Roger Smith

- Honest criticism is hard to take, particularly from a relative, a friend, an acquaintance, or a stranger.

  Franklin P. Jones

- When it comes to critics, remember that nobody will ever get ahead of you as long as he is kicking you in the seat of the pants.

  Tony Randall

- Sticks and stones may break our bones, but words will break our hearts.

  Robert Fulghum

AN UNDESIRABLE KNACK

Lucy, of *Peanuts* cartoon fame, is renowned for her critical spirit and caustic comments. On one occasion she told Charlie Brown, "You are a foul ball in the line drive of life."

In another strip, Linus had his security blanket in place and his thumb resting safely in his mouth, but he was troubled. Turning to Lucy, who was sitting next to him, he asked, "Why are you always so anxious to criticize me?"

The response was typical Lucy: "I just think I have a knack for seeing other people's faults."

Exasperated, Linus threw up his hands and asked, "What about your own faults?"

Without hesitation, Lucy explained, "I have a knack for overlooking them."

Lucy is not the only one who believes their knack or calling in life is to point out and correct the weaknesses of others. Unfortunately, these same people are customarily blind to their own shortcomings.

It might be wise for those who possess the gift of criticism to consider the wise words of Frank A. Clark, "Lots of faults we think we see in others are simply the ones we expect to find there because we have them."

SLAM TACTICS

While being interviewed on CNN's "Larry King Live," Donald Trump lowered the boom on King.

King's interview with the New York real estate tycoon was just under way when Trump said, "Do you mind if I sit back a little? Because your breath is very bad. It really is. Has this been told to you before?"

King responded, "No."

"Okay, then I won't bother."

A confused King continued, "That is how you get the edge. See, that little thing you threw me right then—that no one has ever told me."

"Has nobody ever told you that? You are kidding?"

"Nobody."

"Okay, Larry, your breath is great!" Trump concedes.

According to network producers, Donald Trump was just demonstrating how he gets the edge in negotiations. Sounds like a real win-win approach. I can just see the *New York Times* bestseller list with this title, *Slam Your Way to the Top*.

Before deciding to employ such a strategy, consider the words of Lord Chesterfield: "People hate those who make them feel their own inferiority."

PECKED TO DEATH

Refuse to pick at another person's weak spots. In visiting with a turkey expert I learned that when a turkey is wounded and has a spot of blood on its feathers, the other turkeys will peck at that spot until they literally peck the wounded turkey to death. Can you believe any animal would be so cruel and stupid as to keep pecking at the wound of another?

I wonder how many people go home at night pecked to death. In the midst of personal or professional difficulties, they hear such things as, "Perhaps I shouldn't say this, but . . . ," or "I don't mean to criticize, but . . . " Then the critic justifies his or her actions by saying, "I was just trying to help."

Continual or untimely pecking can immobilize and destroy the healthiest of people as well as those who are already bleeding.

THANKS FOR THE HELP

According to a story that appeared in the *St. Louis Post Dispatch*, umpire Bill Guthrie was working an afternoon baseball game. The visiting team catcher made it his business to protest Guthrie's every call.

Guthrie endured the heckling for three innings and then it got the best of him. In the fourth inning, when the catcher started to complain, Guthrie promptly stopped him. "Son," he said gently, "you've been a big help to me calling balls and strikes, and I appreciate it. But I think I've got the hang of it now. So I'm going to ask you to go to the clubhouse and show them how to take a shower."

Too many times people try to be the expert at everything and find it necessary to criticize the work others are doing. We can learn as the catcher did, there's no sense arguing with the one calling the game when your job is to play the game. Learn your job. Do it well and let others do what they have been hired to do.

CUSTOMER SERVICE

■ Don't worry about profits, worry about service.

Thomas Watson, Sr.

■ The individual (the customer) perceives service in his or her own terms.

Arch McGill

■ There is only one boss. The customer. And he can fire everybody in the company from the chairman on down, simply by spending his money somewhere else.

Sam Walton

■ Quality in a service or product is not what you put into it. It is what the client or customer gets out of it.

Peter Drucker

■ If you don't genuinely like your customers, the chances are they won't buy.

Thomas J. Watson, Jr.

■ Whether service is your primary product or only a part of it, delivery must be effective, efficient, and dependable if it is to have value to the customer. The service must be predictable and uniform; the customer has to be able to depend on what it will look like in delivery, how long it will take to deliver, and what it will cost. A Big Mac is a Big Mac is a Big Mac.

Karl Albrecht and Ron Zemke

■ Service is just a day-in, day-out, ongoing, never-ending, unremitting, persevering, compassionate type of activity.

Leon Gorman

■ Every great business is built on friendship.

J. C. Penney

■ Customer service in America stinks.

Tom Peters

■ Above all, we wish to avoid having a dissatisfied customer. We consider our customers a part of our organization, and we want them to feel free to make any criticism they see fit in regard to our merchandise or service. Sell practical, tested merchandise at reasonable profit, treat your customers like human beings—and they will always come back.

L.L. Bean

■ What we are doing is satisfying the American public. That's our job. I always say we have to give most of the people what they want most of the time. That's what they expect from us.

William Paley

■ Any business arrangement that is not profitable to the other fellow will in the end prove unprofitable to you. The bargain that yields mutual satisfaction is the only one that is apt to be repeated.

B. C. Forbes

■ A well-run restaurant is like a winning baseball team. It makes the most of every crew member's talent and takes advantage of every split-second opportunity to speed up service.

Ray Kroc

■ In former periods, business was identified as secular and service as sacred. In proportion as we have discerned that between secular and sacred no arbitrary line exists, public awareness has grown that the Golden Rule was meant for business as much as for other human relationships.

J. C. Penney

COMMITMENT FROM THE TOP

Ray Kroc, founder of McDonald's, instituted service as a primary value. His management influence remains at the heart of McDonald's day-to-day operation. I ran across a checklist at McDonald's used for training front counter people. It spelled out McDonald's ten commandments for customer treatment.

1. The Customer is the most important person in our business.
2. The Customer is not dependent on us—we are dependent on the customer.
3. The Customer is not an interruption of our work; but the purpose of it.
4. The Customer does us an honor when calling on us. We are not doing the customer a favor by serving him/her.
5. The Customer is part of our business, not an outsider. The Customer is our guest.

6. The Customer is not a cold statistic, but flesh and blood: a human with feelings and emotions like our own.

7. The Customer is not someone to argue with or match wits with.

8. The Customer is one who brings us his/her wants. Our job is to fill them.

9. The Customer is deserving of the most courteous and attentive treatment we can provide.

10. The Customer has the right to expect an employee to present a neat, clean appearance.

McDonald's is also willing to respond to their consumers. For instance, the "Styro-Wars" blasted McDonald's for using packaging manufactured by a process that emitted chlorofluorocarbons into the atmosphere. McDonald's agreed first to separate out and recycle (eventually phase out) the polystyrene "clam shells" and cups used to keep Big Macs warm and soft drinks cold.

This type of responsiveness sends a message to customers and front-line employees. Management believes in and lives their commitment to customer service.

•   •   •

In his book *The Regis Touch*, marketing expert Regis McKenna relates a story about Max Poll, CEO of Barnes Hospital in St. Louis. Poll, disguised as a patient, has someone wheel him around the hospital on a gurney to get a feel for what it's like to be a patient at Barnes. He says he doesn't see much except for the ceiling, but what he hears provides insight into the level of service the hospital provides.

Poll understands that empathy toward the patient's experience provides a valuable guide to quality service.

•   •   •

According to an October 22, 1990, article in *Business Week*, the designing of the Lexus at Toyota included extensive customer involvement. The chief engineer, Ichirou Suzuki, spent weeks interviewing U.S. customers about hobbies and values. From this, he concluded that the consumer was more conservative than he had initially believed. As a result, Suzuki designed the interior of the Lexus with a soft, comfortable feeling.

In an ongoing attempt to keep lines of communication open with its customers, each Lexus employee in the U.S. places at least one call per week to a Lexus owner. This information is used to continually improve the product.

TREATING CUSTOMERS LIKE GUESTS

Al Boyajian has been operating his famous Sears Restaurant in San Francisco approaching four decades. His long-time, loyal patrons are willing to wait up to forty-five minutes to be seated. Boyajian's obsession with quality and service produces between 800 and 900 checks a day from breakfast and lunch.

What makes the Sears Restaurant such a popular eating establishment? It is probably Boyajian's operating philosophy that states, "My customers will be treated like guests in my own home."

Sol Polk operates under a similar commitment. Sol started with nothing several years ago and now sells upwards of $60 million worth of appliances in a year. He has become known as the appliance king of Chicago.

Sol Polk credits the majority of his success to a simple attitude toward his shoppers. "Customers," says Polk, "should be treated like they are guests in my home."

For most of us, guests are treated as important people in our lives. How important do your customers feel?

ANY TIME FOR ANY REASON

Eighty years ago, Leon Leonwood Bean started his business in Freeport, Maine, based on this simple customer service premise: "Sell good merchandise at a reasonable profit; treat your customers like human beings and they'll always come back for more."

L. L. Bean sells a variety of outdoor apparel, sporting goods, and camping equipment. Every item is unconditionally guaranteed.

Their customer service philosophy has a simple application. If a customer is unsatisfied, he or she may return any item at any time for any reason.

It is evident that customer service is not a new phenomenon. The quest for quality service can be found in L. L. Bean's simple philosophy: "Any time for any reason."

AN EXPENSIVE LESSON

USA Today carried a story that headlined: "Bank gets $2M lesson." It began when John Barrier went to Old National Bank in Spokane, Washington, to cash a $100 check.

When Barrier tried to get his parking slip validated to save 60 cents, a receptionist refused, saying he hadn't conducted a transaction.

"She said you have to make a deposit," Barrier said. "I told her I'm considered a substantial depositor and she looked at me like . . . well."

He asked to see the manager, who also refused to stamp the ticket.

Barrier went to bank headquarters vowing to withdraw his $2 million-plus unless the manager apologized. No call came.

"So the next day I went over and the first amount I took out was $1 million. But if you have $100 in a bank or $1 million," he says, "I think they owe you the courtesy of stamping your parking ticket."

THIS I PLEDGE

"From this day forward, I solemnly promise and declare that every customer that comes within ten feet of me, I will smile, look them in the eye, and greet them, so help me Sam."

That pledge is executed by Wal-Mart associates in conjunction with Sam Walton's commitment to low prices every day and unquestionable customer service. If you want to be a part of the Wal-Mart family, be ready to raise your right hand, make the pledge and then live it.

"Always remember," said Walton, "a promise we make is a promise we keep."

AN UPSIDE-DOWN APPROACH

Jan Carlzon gained international recognition by transforming Sweden's national airline into a successfully profitable operation. In 1981, Carlzon became president of Scandinavian Airline Systems and in one year managed to turn a $54 million profit in an airline that had been losing $17 million.

How did such a metamorphosis take place?

Carlzon made it happen by turning the organization chart upside down. He preached, taught and lived the philosophy that the airline should be customer driven. Employees who dealt directly with the customer were put in charge of making decisions that affected the customer. Needless to say, customers responded positively to the upside-down organization chart and so did employees who dealt with customer requests and concerns.

"The only thing that counts in the new Scandinavian Airline Systems," proclaims Carlzon, "is a satisfied customer. We are going to be the best airline in the world, and that means putting the customer first in everything we do."

•   •   •

General Norman Schwarzkopf, commander of the Allied Forces in the Gulf War, came home a hero.

In an interview with David Frost, Schwarzkopf was asked, "What's the greatest lesson you've learned out of all of this?"

The articulate General replied, "I think that there is one really fundamental military truth. And that's that you can add up the correlation of forces, you can look at the number of tanks, you can look at the number of airplanes, you can look at all these factors of military might and put them together. But unless the soldier on the ground, or the airman in the air, has the will to win, has the strength of character to go into battle, believes that his cause is just, and has the support of his country . . . all the rest of that stuff is irrelevant."

STAGGERING STATISTICS

Although business owners are increasingly sensitive to providing quality customer service, many remain ignorant of the devastating effects lousy service produces. The Research Institute of America conducted a study for the White House Office of Consumer Affairs. Their findings should provide ample fuel for businesses apathetic about customer service.

> The average business will hear nothing from 96 percent of unhappy customers who receive rude or discourteous treatment.

> Ninety percent who are dissatisfied with the service they receive will not come back or buy again.

> To make matters worse, each of those unhappy customers will tell his or her story to at least nine other people, and 13 percent of those unhappy former customers relate their stories to more than twenty people.

> Additional research indicates that for every complaint received, the average company has twenty-six customers with problems, six of which are "serious" problems.

> Only 4 percent of unhappy customers bother to complain. For every complaint we hear, twenty-four others go uncommunicated to the company—but not to other potential customers.

> Of the customers who register a complaint, between 54 percent and 70 percent will do business again with the organization if their complaint is resolved. That figure goes up to 95 percent if the customer feels that the complaint was resolved quickly.

> Sixty-eight percent of customers who quit doing business with an organization do so because of company indifference. It takes twelve positive incidents to make up for one negative incident in the eyes of customers.

These staggering statistics bring to mind the story of the airline passenger who found a roach in his salad. Arriving at his hotel that evening he immediately wrote an angry letter to the airline to register his complaint. By the time he returned to his office from the business trip, a reply from the airline awaited him.

The letter said, "Dear Sir: Your letter caused great concern to us. We have never before received such a complaint and pledge we will do everything within our power to insure such an incident will never happen again. It might interest you to know that the employees serving you have been reprimanded and the entire plane is being fumigated. Your concern has not fallen on deaf ears."

Needless to say, the man was impressed. Then he noticed an interoffice memo inadvertently stuck to the back of his letter, with this message: "Send this character the 'Regular Roach Letter.'"

Customers expect a sincere and personal response to their complaints. Flippant, rehearsed, or apathetic responses only serve to aggravate an already detrimental situation. Tom Peters and Nancy Austin, writing in *A Passion for Excellence,* say, "There are two kinds of companies. The first, the most typical, views the complaint as a disease to be got over, with memory of the pain rapidly suppressed. The second ... views the complaint as a luscious golden opportunity."

What pains are you taking to insure that your customers are not receiving a 'Regular Roach Letter' but rather that each situation becomes an opportunity to develop a loyal customer?

GIVE 'EM WHAT THEY WANT

An avid canine lover invented a new dog food. He eventually sold his patent to the seventh-ranked dog food manufacturer. They immediately designed fancy packaging, found a mascot, and spent millions of dollars on marketing.

Unfortunately, the product didn't sell, sending the sales force and marketing department into a frenzy. A brainstorming session was called to evaluate the situation. One question dominated the discussion: "Why isn't our dog food selling?"

Everyone voiced their opinions and excuses, but few solutions were suggested. The agonizing question remained: "Why won't dogs eat our food?"

After much discussion, a member of the team who had remained silent suggested, "Maybe dogs don't like it!"

Moral of the story: Fancy packaging, sophisticated marketing and solicited testimonials produce nothing unless the customers like what they buy. A simple solution is to find out what people want and offer it. Find a need and fill it.

•   •   •

Management at Harley-Davidson will attest to the effectiveness of this approach. A few years ago sales were declining and executives were pondering the mystery, "Why aren't people buying our motorcycles?" Vaughn Beals, Harley-Davidson CEO, decided to get an answer, according to the January/February 1989 issue of *Success* magazine. He told his senior management team to pack their bags, straddle their seats, and hit the road. Beals wanted to find out what motorcycle enthusiasts wanted in a bike and the best way to find out was by going to their rallies and rubbing shoulders with potential and present Harley owners.

Upon his return, Willie G. Davidson, vice president of Styling, initiated a plan to incorporate the best ideas in future designs. Gas tanks were sculpted, chrome added, and the chassis chopped.

Focusing on customer satisfaction and designing a product bikers wanted worked. Harley captured 60 percent of the domestic motorcycle market.

The words of James Balkcom fit perfectly here. "The quality of any product or service is what the customer says it is."

DEATH

- I'm not afraid to die. I just don't want to be there when it happens. It is impossible to experience one's death objectively and still carry a tune.

  Woody Allen

- Death is not the greatest loss in life. The greatest loss is what dies inside us while we live.

  Norman Cousins

- Death is nature's way of saying, "Your table is ready."

  Robin Williams

- I can't die. I'm booked.

  George Burns

- Dropping dead is still the largest cause of death in our society.

  Anonymous

- I am ready to meet my Maker. Whether my Maker is prepared for the ordeal of meeting me is another matter.

  Winston Churchill

- We need to be reminded that there is nothing morbid about honestly confronting the thought of life's end and preparing for it so that we may go gracefully and peacefully. The fact is, we cannot truly face life until we have learned to face the fact that it will be taken away from us.

  Billy Graham

A FRANKLIN DISCOURSE

The following letter, dated February 12, 1756, was written to Elizabeth Hubbard. Benjamin Franklin attempts to console a sorrowing heart and at the same time share his views on death:

Dear Child,

I condole with you, we have lost a most dear and valuable relation, but it is the will of God and Nature that these mortal bodies be laid aside, when the soul is to enter into real life; 'tis rather an embryo state, a preparation for living.

A man is not completely born until he is dead. Why then should we grieve that a new child is born among the immortals? A new member added to their happy society. That bodies should be lent us is a kind and benevolent act of God.

When they become unfit for these purposes and afford us pain instead of pleasure—instead of an aid, become an incumbrance and answer none of the intentions for which they were given—it is equally kind and benevolent that a way is provided by which we may get rid of them. Death is that way.

We ourselves often prudently choose a partial death. In some cases a mangled painful limb, which cannot be restored, is willingly cut off. He who plucks out a tooth, parts with it freely, since the pain goes with it; and thus a person surrenders the whole body, and departs at once, for with it goes all pain and possibilities of pain, all diseases and suffering.

Thus, we are invited abroad on a party of pleasure that is to last forever. Perhaps a loved one has gone before us. We could not all conveniently start together, and why should we be grieved at this, since we are soon to follow, and we know where to find him or her.

Adieu.

Benjamin Franklin

THE SHADOW OF DEATH

Death seems to have a mysterious air about it. Some people fear it, others are ready to die . . . but not yet, and of course there are those who wish death would knock soon. The certainty that someday we will die and the mystery of how we will die generate fear.

Publius wrote in the first century B.C., "The fear of death is more to be dreaded than death itself." He had a point.

• • •

Evangelist Billy Graham relates an experience of Donald Grey Barnhouse in his book *Facing Death* (World Books, 1987). Barnhouse, a noted Bible teacher in the first half of the twentieth century, lost his first wife to cancer and was left with three children all under 12. As Barnhouse and his family were driving to the funeral service, a large truck passed them and cast a substantial shadow across their car. Turning to his oldest daughter, who was staring sadly out the window, Barnhouse asked, "Tell me, sweetheart, would you rather be run over by that truck or its shadow?" Pondering her father's peculiar question, she responded, "By the shadow, I guess. It can't hurt you." Barnhouse then shared this wisdom with his children: "Your mother has not been overridden by death, but by the shadow of death. That is nothing to fear."

Charles Spurgeon added this insight to the Barnhouse example: "Death in its substance has been removed, and only the shadow of it remains . . . Nobody is afraid of a shadow, for a shadow cannot block a man's pathway for even a moment. The shadow of a dog can't bite; the shadow of a sword can't kill."

DESIRE

- The difference between desire and drive is the difference between expressing yourself and proving yourself.

  Larry Wilson

- Desire alone is not enough. But to lack desire, means to lack a key ingredient to success. Many a talented individual failed because they lacked desire. Many victories have been snatched by the underdog because he wanted it more. So if you desire intensely and you act upon it, then everything stands within your reach.

  Anonymous

- Desire creates the power.

  Raymond Holliwell

- It sometimes seems that intense desire creates not only its own opportunities, but its own talents.

  Eric Hoffer

- Nothing stops the man who desires to achieve. Every obstacle is simply a course to develop his achievement muscle. It's a strengthening of his powers to accomplishment.

  Eric Butterworth

- Desire is the effort of an unexpressed possibility within you, seeking expression without, through your action.

  Wallace D. Wattles

- You do not succeed because you do not know what you want, but because you don't want it intensely enough.

  Frank Crane

- A passionate desire and an unwearied will can perform impossibilities or what may seem to be such to the cold, timid, and feeble.

  Sir John Simpson

■ Desire is the key. If you've got desire, you can be anything you want to be in America today, provided you have two things: a specific goal and a plan.

A. L. Williams
Pushing Up People

■ The will is more important than the skill when it comes to scaling a wall.

Robert Schuller

■ If you have the will to win, you have achieved half your success. If you don't, you have achieved half your failure.

David Ambrose

■ Not only must you know what you want, but you must really want what you want, if you are to get what you want.

Anonymous

■ As long as you derive inner help and comfort from anything, you should keep it. Only give up a thing when you want some other condition so much that the thing no longer has any attraction for you, or when it seems to interfere with that which is more greatly desired.

Mohandas K. Gandhi

■ Lord, grant that I may always desire more than I can accomplish.

Michelangelo

DESIRE DEMONSTRATED

Look up the word *desire* in your thesaurus and you'll find synonyms like *hunger, craving, longing,* and *yearning.*

Desire motivated inventors like Thomas Edison to dream of a lamp that could be operated by electricity. Despite ten thousand failures, he relentlessly pursued his venture.

Desire kept young W. Clement Stone on Chicago's street corners selling newspapers. Desire later made him one of the wealthiest people in America as principal owner of Combined Insurance Corporation of America.

Desire gave Florence Chadwick the courage to swim the English Channel from England to France. Enduring agonizing cramps and near-death exhaustion, Chadwick swam sixteen hours to be declared the greatest female swimmer of all time.

Desire made Jim Marshall one of the most indestructible players in professional football. Marshall started 282 consecutive games and played defensive end until he was forty-two. Teammate Fran Tarkenton once described Marshall as "the most amazing athlete to play in any sport."

Desire energized my boyhood hero, John Havlicek, to earn the nickname "Mr. Perpetual Motion." As a Boston Celtic, Havlicek gave 100 percent every game for sixteen straight seasons. Hustle, leadership, and guts made Havlicek a player by which others were measured.

People with desire work harder, are obsessed with their goals, and are driven by an intense thirst to be better.

THE ODDS WERE AGAINST HIM

A young boy growing up in west Tennessee had a burning desire. It appeared, however, his disadvantaged childhood would restrict his dreams. Told that he was from the "wrong side of the tracks," he nonetheless sustained his desire to do and be something special.

He had a battered, secondhand guitar but had no idea how to tune or play it. His cousin, country singer Lonzo Green, came for a visit and met an anxious youngster wanting to learn the guitar. Lonzo took the time to tune the instrument and teach the lad a few basic chords. The boy from the wrong side of the tracks now had something to build his dreams on.

In a few short years he turned a slim opportunity into a career that won the hearts of Americans everywhere. Elvis Presley sustained his hunger for music even though the odds were against him.

Emerson's comment, "Desire is possibility seeking expression," perfectly explains Elvis' pursuit of musical eminence.

DETERMINATION

■ I hope someday to have so much of what the world calls success, that people will ask me, "What's your secret?" and I will tell them, "I just get up again when I fall down."

Paul Harvey

■ The difference between the impossible and the possible lies in a man's determination.

Tommy Lasorda

■ When you know what you want and you want it badly enough, you will find the ways to get it.

Jim Rohn

■ You have to be single minded, drive only for one thing on which you have decided. And if it looks as if you might be getting there, all kinds of people, including some you thought were your loyal friends, will suddenly show up ... to trip you, blacken you, and break your spirit.

John R. Noe

■ Be like a postage stamp. Stick to something until you get there.

Josh Billings

■ We can learn to soar only in direct proportion to our determination to rise above the doubt and transcend the limitations.

David McNally
Even Eagles Need a Push

■ What this power is I cannot say; all I know is that it exists and it becomes available only when a man is in that state of mind in which he knows exactly what he wants and is fully determined not to quit until he finds it.

Alexander Graham Bell

DETERMINATION OF A CHAMPION

Determination best describes what it took for Sylvester Stallone to achieve his phenomenal success.

As a child, Stallone was frequently beaten by his father and told he had no brains. He grew up a loner and emotionally anguished. He was in and out of various schools. An advisor at Drexel University told him that, based on aptitude testing, he should pursue a career as an elevator repair person.

He opted to pursue an acting career, but his imbalanced life produced one failure after another. Stallone remained determined to learn the profession, using his acting failure to also try his hand at writing. His undying determination through thick and thin allowed him to see setbacks as stepping stones. "You see," said Stallone, "success is usually the culmination of controlling failure."

Stallone was inspired one night by watching Muhammed Ali fight Chuck Wepner. The excitement of the crowd watching the underdog go the distance awakened his talent and allowed Stallone to write the *Rocky* script in just three and a half days.

Stallone's writing reflected his own determined effort to find emotional, physical and mental balance in his life. In *Rocky I*, Rocky Balboa trained and prepared his body and mind to go fifteen rounds. He didn't win the fight but won the hearts of the crowd by reaching his goal. *Rocky II* developed around a fighter determined to win the world championship—and he did. Perhaps *Rocky III* best captured Stallone's desire to find himself. Rocky Balboa grows soft and loses his crown. His determination to develop his talents and remain the best were extinguished by the comfort of the good life. Rocky's one-time foe, Apollo Creed, inspired and challenged him to get back on track. Rocky returned to the sweaty gym, revitalized his winning hunger, and ultimately regained his world championship.

Through time, determination, and effort, Sylvester Stallone built a life, a career, and a future.

DRIVEN BY DETERMINATION

Civil rights leader Vernon Jordan reflected that at the beginning of his career, people constantly advised him to lower his sights. "But," Mr. Jordan says, "the more people tried to discourage me, the more determined I got!"

Determined people possess the stamina and courage to pursue their ambitions despite criticism, ridicule, or unfavorable circumstances. In fact, discouragement usually spurs them on to greater things.

•　　•　　•

Teddy Roosevelt spent endless childhood hours bedridden. Severe asthma limited his ability to play like other kids, and as he lay in bed struggling to breathe, Teddy was afraid to go to sleep for fear he would not wake up. His younger brother,

Elliott, became his protection against neighborhood bullies. Yet Teddy was determined to become strong mentally and physically. His desire to become self-sufficient fortified him through a daily exercise routine and hours of weight lifting. He became an avid reader and absorbed books on every conceivable subject. As a Harvard student, Roosevelt became known for his energy and enthusiasm.

•   •   •

Sugar Ray Leonard was an Olympic gold medalist, world professional champion and wealthy. What more could he want? Leonard made it clear he wanted to challenge Marvin Hagler for the middleweight championship.

Had Sugar Ray Leonard gone crazy? How could a boxer who hadn't fought in five years and then nearly lost his vision in one eye challenge for the world middle-weight championship? Marvin Hagler had gone undefeated in the last decade, yet a determined Leonard said he would be ready. Leonard's desire to prove he was the best middleweight boxer in the world possessed him. He initiated a demanding training program realizing Hagler was already in tip-top condition. Leonard sacrificed himself for the opportunity to win.

On the night of the fight in Las Vegas, Hagler worked the ring like a charging bull. Leonard danced, pranced, and avoided the champion's powerful blows. When all was said and done, Sugar Ray went home with $11 million and the world middleweight championship. Leonard, driven by determination, defied the odds— and the skepticism of boxing fans.

The world marveled at Sugar Ray's comeback to defeat Marvin Hagler. Leonard did not land a knockout punch but through mental toughness, physical stamina, and an obsession for winning, he regained his title as middleweight champion of the world.

•   •   •

Achievers are resolute in their goals and driven by determination. Discouragement is temporary, obstacles are overcome, and doubt is defeated, yielding to personal victory. General George Patton, Jr., said this about determination: "You need to overcome the tug of people against you as you reach for high goals."

STARTING OVER

It is unlikely that Candace Cable Brookes will ever sign lucrative contracts to endorse sports equipment. She is, however, a first-rate athlete, winning races all over the world using her arms. You see, Candace lost the use of her legs in an automobile accident. Not content with having others care for her in her wheelchair, Candace decided to make the best with what she had. She possessed ambition, determination, and two good arms. That combination helped her become a champion wheelchair racer.

Calamity often becomes the catalyst for success in a whole new area. Only those with the determination to go on will make a fresh start and encounter new horizons.

Sara Long of Cedar Rapids, Iowa, was not pleased when she found herself in a Cedar Rapids welfare line. She didn't plan to be there, nor did she plan to stay there. Sara enrolled in a small-business education program, overcame the welfare stigma, and now her new business is off to a roaring start. Nannies of Iowa, a nannie placement service, was featured in *The New York Times* and Sara appeared on the *Joan Rivers Show*.

Opportunity awaits those with the determination to change their life.

SUPERSTAR

Katharine Hepburn had only one career aspiration. She fell in love with silent movies as a child and dreamed of becoming a movie star. Throughout her education she participated in theatrical activities, and upon graduation from college Hepburn set her course to become an actress.

The road to her dream was not easy. Hepburn was fired from several stage roles, criticized for talking too fast, considered ornery and difficult to work with, and evaluated as too bony, thin, and mannish to be successful on stage.

Accompanied by unwavering determination, Hepburn sought the assistance of a voice and drama coach who nurtured her through a variety of stage roles. Eventually, one of her performances drew great reviews and led to a movie contract.

Today, Hepburn says, "I came to think that the more insulting the press was, the more it stimulated me." And stimulated she stayed. Hepburn went on to win the Academy Award for best actress four times, has published an autobiography and is in great demand for interviews.

How amazing that the woman who was told she had a voice like a rasp and a skeleton body achieved superstar status!

EXHILARATION OF VICTORY

General George S. Patton encouraged his followers to "accept the challenges, so that you may feel the exhilaration of victory."

Florence Nightingale nominated herself to accept the challenge of upgrading hospital standards, improving patient care, enhancing sanitation, and promoting nursing education. The efforts of this Englishwoman transformed hospitals from a place where people die to a place of hope and healing.

Nightingale faced a double challenge. Her own ill-defined illness restricted the activity of her adult life. But she was adamantly committed to meet the challenge of caring for injured soldiers and ailing people.

During the Crimean War, she arose by 4:30 A.M. to leave for the battlefields, where inferior medical care caused British soldiers to die unnecessarily. After incredible exploits, saving lives with her contingent of trained nurses, Nightingale returned home to England. Restricted to her sick bed, she somehow managed to establish, at age forty, the Nightingale School and Home for Nurses in London. She created a medical revolution from her bed and continued to mastermind and direct those efforts until her death at age ninety.

Florence Nightingale never enjoyed the benefits of a typical lifestyle but was determined to be victorious in her lofty challenge. Speaking of challenges, John Norley said, "All things are difficult before they are easy." The difficulties Nightingale endured eased the pain of many.

DREAMS

- I'm a big fan of dreams. Unfortunately, dreams are our first casualty in life—people seem to give them up, quicker than anything, for a "reality."

  Kevin Costner

- A dream is an ideal involving a sense of possibilities rather than probabilities, of potential rather than limits. A dream is the wellspring of passion, giving us direction and pointing us to lofty heights. It is an expression of optimism, hope, and values lofty enough to capture the imagination and engage the spirit. Dreams grab us and move us. They are capable of lifting us to new heights and overcoming self-imposed limitations.

  Robert Kriegel

- If you have a dream, give it a chance to happen.

  Richard de Vos

- Having your dreams fulfilled can be far more therapeutic than having them analyzed.

  Hyatt Resorts advertisement

- Nothing is as real as a dream. The world can change around you, but your dream will not. Responsibilities need not erase it. Duties need not obscure it. Because the dream is within you, no one can take it away.

  Tom Clancy

- Nothing much happens without a dream. For something really great to happen, it takes a really great dream.

  Robert Greenleaf

- Hold fast to dreams for if dreams die,
  Life is a broken-winged bird that cannot fly.
  Hold fast to dreams for when dreams go,
  Life is a barren field frozen with snow.

  Langston Hughes

- Dreams are powerful reflections of your actual growth potential.

  Denis Waitley and Reni L. Witt
  The Joy of Working

■ Show me somebody who doesn't dream about the future and I'll show you someone who doesn't know where he is going.

Anonymous

■ People are never more insecure than when they become obsessed with their fears at the expense of their dreams.

Norman Cousins

■ Ever since I was a little boy, I dreamed I would do something important in aviation.

Neil Armstrong

■ Dreaming illustrates your hidden capacities and your unawakened ability.

Peter Daniels

■ Since it doesn't cost a dime to dream, you'll never shortchange yourself when you stretch your imagination.

Robert Schuller

■ Realistic people with practical aims are rarely as realistic or practical in the long run of life as the dreamers who pursue their dreams.

Hans Selye

■ Your dreams can come true. I'm living proof of it. I left home at seventeen and had nothing but rejections for twenty-five years. I wrote more than twenty-five screenplays, but I never gave up.

Michael Blake
Author of Dances with Wolves

AIM HIGH

A college professor prepared a test for his soon-to-be-graduating seniors. The test questions were divided into three categories and the students were instructed to choose questions from only one of the categories. The first category of questions was the hardest and worth fifty points. The second, which was easier, was worth forty points. The third, the simplest, was worth thirty points.

Upon completion of the test, students who had chosen the hardest fifty-point questions were given As. The students who had chosen the forty-point questions received Bs. Those who settled for the easiest thirty-pointers were given Cs.

The students were frustrated with the grading of their papers and asked the professor what he was looking for. The professor leaned over the podium, smiled, and explained, "I wasn't testing your book knowledge. I was testing your aim."

An anonymous writer once commented, "Make no small plans for they have no power to stir your soul." Robert Kriegel put it this way, "The key is to have a dream that inspires us to go beyond our limits." Not only are people short on dreams but even those with dreams often set their sights low enough to protect themselves from failure.

•   •   •

Writer W. P. Kinsella was not afraid of aiming high. He envisioned an Iowa corn farmer and a dream to reunite a father and son, one of whom was dead, for a game of baseball.

Kinsella transformed that dream into the novel, *Shoeless Joe.* Film director Phil Alden Robinson read the book and set about to achieve his own dream to write and direct a film based on the book. Robinson further dreamed that Kevin Costner would agree to play the farmer.

This culmination of dreams produced the movie *Field of Dreams.* The production was a tremendous Hollywood success and even enjoyed the recognition of being an Academy Award nominee. Oh, the power of a dream.

James Allen wrote: "Dream lofty dreams, and as you dream, so shall you become. Your vision is the promise of what you shall one day be. One who cherishes a beautiful vision, a lofty ideal, will one day realize it."

Be bold with your dreams! Don't settle for the easy questions. Aim high. Create your own "field of dreams."

RESPONDING TO BROKEN DREAMS

Jimmy Carter dreamed of becoming governor of Georgia. And he did. He dreamed he could achieve the presidency of the United States. And he did. Then what? Dreams were shattered as world events and the Iran hostage crisis ended his presidency on a sour note.

Real dreamers know that failure never eliminates the dream. Failure is the opportunity to reconstruct your dreams.

Jimmy and Rosalyn Carter dedicated themselves to a new dream of helping the poor through Habitat for Humanity. By building low-cost housing, staying actively involved in global peace-making efforts, human rights, and international health issues, and establishing the Carter Center, the Carters have rebounded from political disappointment to find excitement in helping others, teaching Sunday school, and writing books.

Rosalyn wrote, "If we have not achieved our early dreams, we must either find new ones or see what we can salvage from the old. If we have accomplished what we set out to do in our youth, then we need not weep like Alexander the Great that we have no more worlds to conquer. There is clearly much left to be done, and whatever else we are going to do, we had better get on with it."

Although dreams collapse, real dreamers never do. The fulfillment of your dreams lies within you and you alone. When you understand and accept this, then nothing or no one, can deny you the pursuit of your dreams.

THE AMERICAN DREAM

In 1931, historian and Pulitzer prize winner James Truslow Adams coined the phrase "The American Dream" in a treatise called *The Epic of America*. Adams described the dream this way: "It is not a dream of motor cars and high wages merely, but a dream of social order in which each man and each woman shall be able to attain the fullest stature of which they are innately capable, and be recognized by others for what they are, regardless of the fortuitous circumstances of birth or position."

This familiar phrase has often been invoked by writers, philosophers, and politicians to explain their own convictions. It has become a prevailing justification for individual dreams and pursuits. "There are those who will reply that freedom of man and mind is nothing but a dream," said Archibald MacLeish. "They are right. It is. It is the American Dream."

•   •   •

Ray Kroc believed in the American Dream. While selling paper cups to restaurants in the 1920s, he worked his way up to becoming one of the company's top salespeople.

Confident that more could be done in the restaurant business, he left the sales position to market a machine that could mix several milkshakes at one time. His travels brought him in contact with two brothers who owned a restaurant that bought his machines. Kroc became a partner in this highly successful restaurant and continued to dream about going beyond making forty-eight milkshakes at one time on the eight multi-mixer machines.

Ultimately, Kroc bought out the two brothers, kept their name on the business, focused on building a fast-food restaurant chain, and built McDonald's into a billion-dollar industry.

The "freedom of man and mind" is not a dream. It produces dreams. Ray Kroc didn't wait for someone to bring him an idea that would work. He could have been satisfied with his impressive milkshake maker but instead constantly challenged his thinking by focusing on what more he could do to revolutionize the food industry. Therein are dreams born!

•   •   •

David McClelland, the Harvard psychologist, has extensively studied high achievers. He has concluded that successful people possess one common characteristic: they fantasize and dream incessantly about how to achieve their goals. Taking that one step further, James Allen says, "Dreams are the seedlings of reality."

The American Dream is a seedling of reality waiting to be nurtured, fertilized, and harvested by those with the courage to pursue it.

Denver entrepreneur Barbara Grogan, commenting in *Esquire* magazine, says, "The world is chock full of negative people . . . They have a thousand reasons why your dreams won't work, and they're ready to share them with you at the drop of a hat. Well, this sounds trite, but you just have to believe in yourself and in your ability to make your dreams come true."

•   •   •

Here are some people who believed in themselves and their dreams:

After his older brother was shot down and killed in World War II, Dick Clark listened to the radio to ease his painful loneliness. He began dreaming of someday becoming an announcer on his own show. "American Bandstand" was the product of this man's dream.

Ski instructor Pete Seibert was considered crazy when he disclosed his dream to start a ski resort. Standing on the summit of a mountain in the Gore Range in Colorado, Seibert finalized a dream he had since age twelve and began the challenge of convincing others that it was possible. Seibert's dream is now a reality called Vail.

Two brothers-in-law had a simple dream of making $75 a week. They started their own business that advertised a single product served thirty-one different ways. Baskin-Robbins Ice Cream was a dream come true for its founders—as well as ice-cream lovers everywhere.

Bank of America exists today because A. G. Giannini dreamed of starting a financial institution that served "the little guy." Although a high school dropout, Giannini believed his concept could become a national bank. By making unheard-of automobile and appliance loans, his dream became a reality by the time of his death in 1949.

After Sybil Ferguson lost 56 pounds, her neighbors wanted to learn her secrets. A support group began to meet each morning to discuss their weight-loss experiences and to encourage one another. Sybil latched onto this successful support-group idea and franchised it throughout the United

States and Canada. The Diet Center, with over $45 million in annual reve-
nues, made a personal dream to lose weight an international weight-loss
program.

Living in a government-funded housing project in Pennsylvania, Mike
Ditka dreamed of escaping the mines of his home state. Capitalizing on his
dream and athletic ability, he achieved notoriety as a pro football player
and head coach of the Chicago Bears.

These notable people testify to the exciting phenomenon that if you have a dream
and nurture it, be passionate about it, and act upon it, you can experience the
realization of it.

EDUCATION

- A graduation ceremony is an event where the commencement speaker tells thousands of students dressed in identical caps and gowns that *individuality* is the key to success.

  Bob Orben

- The primary purpose of a liberal education is to make one's mind a pleasant place in which to spend one's time.

  Sidney J. Harris

- Next in importance to freedom and justice is popular education, without which neither freedom nor justice can be permanently maintained.

  James A. Garfield

- The classroom—not the trench—is the frontier of freedom now and forever-more.

  Lyndon B. Johnson

- Education's purpose is to replace an empty mind with an open one.

  Malcolm S. Forbes

- It is the purpose of education to help us become autonomous, creative, inquiring people who have the will and intelligence to create our own destiny.

  Dr. Neal Postma and Dr. Charles Weingardner
  The School Book

- You see, real ongoing, lifelong education doesn't answer questions; it provokes them.

  Luci Swindoll

- People will pay more to be entertained than educated.

  Johnny Carson

- The most important function of education at any level is to develop the personality of the individual and the significance of his life to himself and to others. This is the basic architecture of a life; the rest is ornamentation and decoration of the structure.

  Grayson Kirk

■   The essence of our effort to see that every child has a chance must be to assure each an equal opportunity, not to become equal, but to become different—to realize whatever unique potential of body, mind, and spirit he or she possesses.

John Fischer

■   A great teacher never strives to explain his vision—he simply invites you to stand beside him and see for yourself.

Reverend E. Inman

■   If you can read and don't, you are an illiterate by choice.

Danny Cox

HUMOR IN EDUCATION

Imagine how many times a day in this country students say or do something that raises the laughter quotient of adults. School is now in session. Try putting yourself in the following situations and enjoy.

•   •   •

From *Good Living* comes this story:

One morning, a new substitute teacher entered her assigned class and asked a little boy his name.

"Jule," he replied.

"No, not Jule," she said. "You should not use contractions. Your name is Julius." Turning to the next boy, she asked, "And what is your name?"

"Bilious," he replied.

•   •   •

Anthony Robbins tells the story about a teacher who knew how to handle rowdy situations. All the kids in her class arranged to drop their books at exactly 9:00 A.M. as a prank to throw the teacher off. Without missing a beat, she put down her chalk, picked up a book, and dropped it too. "Sorry I'm late," she said. After that, she had the kids eating out of her hand.

Now that is a teacher who thinks on her feet.

•   •   •

Speaking of teachers, I ran across this definition of a teacher: "One who can drink three cups of coffee before 8:00 A.M. and hold it until 3:30."

•   •   •

"Mommy, Mommy," shouted the excited second grader, "I made 100 at school today!"

"I'm so proud of you sweetheart! Tell Mommy about it."
"Well, I made 50 in spelling, 30 in math, and 20 in English."

•   •   •

A mother was upset over her little girl's report card and called her teacher at school. "Isn't she trying?" she asked the teacher. "She certainly is," came the reply.

•   •   •

"Son, I'm worried about you being at the bottom of the class."
"Don't worry, Dad, they teach you the same stuff at both ends."

•   •   •

From my son's science teacher comes this memorable anecdote:
A knowledgeable teacher shared his final session on astronomy. "So you see, students, the universe is an incredible creation. As an example, the heavens contain 117,971,423,641 stars."
The class rowdy immediately raised his hand and quipped, "How do you know?"
Accustomed to this student's constant challenges, the teacher immediately responded, "If you don't believe me, count them for yourself."

•   •   •

Two parents of eighth-graders were discussing their children's educational experiences. Said one mother: "My son is not doing the greatest. Just the other day, the teacher asked, 'Who is Betsy Ross?' and he answered, 'lead singer for the Supremes.' "

•   •   •

I love the story about the student who was describing his new teacher to his parents: "She's mean but she's fair," he explained.
"How's that?" his mother asked.
"Well, she's mean to everyone."

•   •   •

Exhausted from a day of continual harassment, the substitute teacher shook her finger at the unruly class. "All right, kids," she shouted, "do anything you please! Now let's see you disobey that!"

•   •   •

"Son, why do you hate school so much?"
"I don't. I just hate the principle of the thing!"

•   •   •

The "People in the News" segment of the Des Moines Register reported this interesting tidbit: It seems Mark Twain got two high school students in Beaver Falls, Pennsylvania, into trouble. When they read a line by Twain for the daily quotation over the school's public address system, administrators weren't amused. "First, God created idiots," the quote goes. "That was just practice. Then he created school boards." Jessica McCartney, 17, and Heidi Schanck, 18, were banished to a conference room after reading the quote.

•   •   •

A ninth-grader was complaining about the amount of material she had to learn for her history exam.

Finally, her mother could take it no longer. "It is important for you to understand the events of history and how they affect us today. I got straight A's in history."

"That was easy for you, Mom," the daughter responded. "You lived through most of it."

•   •   •

Finally, a high school senior reluctantly showed his dad the grades on his first semester report card.

"Son, how do you explain four F's and one D?" his father demanded.

"Well, Dad, I guess I spent too much time on that one subject."

•   •   •

Education is a serious endeavor, but thank goodness it has its lighter moments.

CLASSROOM INSIGHTS

A Champaign, Illinois, second-grade teacher was concerned by her students' lack of awareness of early American proverbs. She decided to introduce them to these pithy pearls of wisdom by giving them the opening words of a proverb and having the children write their own finish. Here are some of the results:

A penny saved . . . isn't much.

The bigger they are . . . the better I like them.

You can lead a horse to water . . . but they always want something else.

Two heads . . . are worse than two feet.

A bird in the hand . . . is liable to go to the bathroom.

Don't count your chickens . . . before you wash your hands.

You can't teach an old dog . . . because he can't see very well.

Early to bed . . . stinks!

If at first you don't succeed . . . eat fruit.

THINK ABOUT IT

A study conducted by the U.S. Department of Health, Education, and Welfare reported the following:

Learners retain:

10 percent of what they read;

20 percent of what they hear;

30 percent of what they see;

50 percent of what they see and hear;

70 percent of what they say;

90 percent of what they say and do.

DAMAGING RESEARCH

A study by the National Parent-Teachers Organization revealed that in the average American school, eighteen negatives are identified for every positive that is pointed out. The Wisconsin study revealed that when children enter the first grade, 80 percent of them feel pretty good about themselves, but by the time they get to the sixth grade, only 10 percent of them have good self-images.

MURPHY'S LAWS OF LEARNING

Murphy is known for his law that states: "If anything can go wrong, it will." But until now, his Laws of Learning have officially gone unnoticed. These laws, conveniently divided into "Student Laws" and "Teacher Laws," are nonetheless familiar to everyone in a school setting. And thanks to Tom Royer, writing in the Rural Electric Nebraskan, now you know who to blame them on.

No doubt you've witnessed the First Student Law, which states, "If you didn't do your homework, there will be a surprise quiz worth 40 percent of your grade."

Other student laws include the following:

- You will get the hardest grading teacher in your poorest subject.
- Each year, you will have one teacher with bad breath, one teacher who talks down to you, and one teacher who takes an instant dislike to you. Likely they'll be the same teacher.
- The slower the teacher is in passing out the tests and giving instructions, the longer the test.

- The night with the most homework is also the night with the best TV programs.
- Study hall is noisiest when you have to cram for a test the next period.
- If you are a good athlete, at least one of your teachers will dislike athletes and announce that all sports are a waste of time.
- If you are a poor athlete, at least two of your teachers will be coaches teaching courses required for graduation.
- The day of the open-book test, you'll leave your book at home.
- If there's been a "surprise" quiz every Friday for the last four weeks, and you spend all of Thursday night studying, this particular Friday the teacher will be absent.

As if Murphy's Student Laws weren't enough to wreak havoc in the classroom, there are a number of Teacher Laws written by his former teachers (including his mother, who gave up teaching after she had him in class). They are as follows:

- Your favorite student will move away before the term is half over.
- Your worst behaved class will meet the last period of the day.
- In a classroom of twenty students, ten will pay no attention to you, five will disrupt the class at least once a day, three will be hyperactive, and of the two remaining good students, at least one will be absent.
- The students with the worst behavior problems from all of your classes will be in your study hall, homeroom, or both.
- No matter what subject you teach, at least 25 percent of each class will proclaim the subject is a waste of time. If you teach art, music, physical education, or a foreign language, the percentage rises to 80 percent.
- If you feel that sports are emphasized too much, at least 75 percent of your class will be athletes.
- Give an open-book test and at least three students will complain about not knowing there was going to be a test (they forgot their books, too).
- Decide not to give your usual Friday quiz as a gift to the class and at least half of them will complain.

These are but a few of the Laws of Learning that generations of students and teachers have added to Murphy's best known original law—which was written after he took the S.A.T. test.

STARTLING DISCOVERY

Jaime O'Neill has taught for about twenty years in community colleges. Over the years, he has become increasingly concerned about the lack of knowledge among his students. It's not that he was concerned about their lack of technical knowledge or complex facts, but that so many of the general "facts" they thought they knew were downright inaccurate.

So he decided to do something about it. Hoping to show to his students just how lacking they were in the basics, he devised an eighty-six question quiz on general knowledge. He gave it to his college English class.

Twenty-six people in the classroom, ranging in age from eighteen to fifty-four, all of whom had completed at least one quarter of college work, participated in O'Neill's experiment. The eighty-six questions covered simple facts about the world around them—facts about people, facts about geography, facts about life in general. Professor O'Neill was so startled by what he discovered that he recorded his findings and later wrote them in a Newsweek article entitled "No Allusions in the Classroom" (September 1985). Here's a sampling of his results:

Ralph Nader is a baseball player. Charles Darwin invented gravity. Christ was born in the sixteenth century. J. Edgar Hoover was a nineteenth-century president. "The Great Gatsby" was a magician in the 1930s. Sid Caesar was an early Roman emperor. Mark Twain invented the cotton gin. Jefferson Davis played guitar for the Jefferson Airplane. Dwight D. Eisenhower served as president during the seventeenth century. Socrates was an American Indian chieftain.

O'Neill continued: "My students were equally creative in their understanding of geography. They knew, for instance, that Managua is the capital of Vietnam, that Cape Town is in the United States, and that Beirut is in Germany. Bogota, of course, is in Borneo (unless it is in China). Camp David is in Israel, and Stratford-on-Avon is in Grenada (or Gernada). Gdansk is in Ireland. Cologne is in the Virgin Islands. Mazatlan is in Switzerland. Belfast was variously located in Egypt, Germany, Belgium, and Italy. Leningrad was transported to Jamaica; Montreal to Spain."

And on and on it went. Most students answered incorrectly far more often than they answered correctly. Several of them meticulously wrote, "I don't know" eighty-six times, or eighty times, or sixty-two times . . .

ENCOURAGEMENT

- No matter how busy you are, you must take time to make the other person feel important.

  Mary Kay Ash

- We live by encouragement, and we die without it—slowly, sadly, angrily.

  Celeste Holm

- You never know when a moment and a few sincere words can have an impact on a life.

  Zig Ziglar

- A person may not be as good as you tell her she is, but she'll try harder thereafter.

  Anonymous

- Three billion people on the face of the earth go to bed hungry every night, but four billion people go to bed every night hungry for a simple word of encouragement and recognition.

  Cavett Robert

- There is no more noble occupation in the world than to assist another human being—to help someone succeed.

  Alan Loy McGinnis

- Few things in the world are more powerful than a positive push. A smile. A word of optimism and hope. A "you can do it" when things are tough.

  Richard M. De Vos

- Outstanding leaders go out of the way to boost the self-esteem of their personnel. If people believe in themselves, it's amazing what they can accomplish.

  Sam Walton

- I have yet to find the man, however exalted his station, who did not do better work and put forth greater effort under a spirit of approval than under a spirit of criticism.

  Charles Schwab

■ I've compared offensive linemen to the story of Paul Revere. After Paul Revere rode through town everybody said what a great job he did. But no one ever talked about the horse. I know how Paul Revere's horse felt.

Gene Upshaw

■ When someone does something good, applaud! You will make two people happy.

Samuel Goldwyn

■ People love others not for who they are but for how they make us feel!

Irwin Federman

■ Silent gratitude isn't very much use to anyone.

G. B. Stern

■ If you think that praise is due him
Now's the time to slip it to him,
For he cannot read his tombstone
When he's dead.

Berton Braley

■ There are two things people want more than sex and money . . . recognition and praise.

Mary Kay Ash

■ A compliment is verbal sunshine.

Robert Orben

■ Every man needs a blind eye and a deaf ear, so when people applaud, you'll only hear half of it, and when people salute, you'll only see part of it. Believe only half the praise and half the criticism.

Charles Spurgeon

■ The deepest craving of human nature is the need to feel appreciated.

William James

■ Ninety percent of the things we do are prompted by a desire to feel important. People have a way of becoming what you encourage them to be—not what you nag them to be.

Scudder N. Parker

OPERATION APPRECIATION

"There are high spots in all of our lives," wrote George Matthew Adams, "and most of them come about through encouragement from someone else. Encouragement is oxygen to the soul."

A few years ago a television newscaster happened upon a man dressed up in a stupid-looking red Spiderman suit. He had placed suction cups on his hands and feet to climb the side of one of the tallest buildings in the world. He climbed 125 stories. When he came over the top, there was thunderous applause, as well as police and reporters waiting for him. They asked, "Why in the world would you risk your life climbing this tall building?" He thought for a moment and then responded, "I love to hear the applause."

It seems hard to believe that this man felt he had to climb 125 stories in a silly comic strip suit to get the applause of people. Yet how many times do people we live and work with feel the same way? They struggle to accomplish great, unusual things just to be noticed.

•   •   •

Just as children learn to get attention any way they can—even by misbehaving— some adults learn that the only way to get attention is by doing something wrong.

When Mary arrives at work late, we take note and say, "Mary, you're late."

Mary thinks to herself, "Wow, this is the first time you've spoken to me in weeks." So Mary starts showing up late all of the time and tells a co-worker, "Now that I'm coming in late, people notice me—in fact, they're holding special meetings just to talk about me."

Sound farfetched? Maybe. Maybe not.

The reality is, we live in a nit-picking, fault-finding world where people find it easier to criticize the bad than recognize the good.

•   •   •

I am learning every day that our success as leaders, parents, teachers, and friends is dependent on our ability to create an environment that brings out the best in people. In other words, help people believe in themselves and in their abilities.

How? I have an idea. Implement Operation Appreciation in your organization, home, school, and community. Begin each day by asking yourself these questions:

- What will I do today to express faith in people?
- How will I give people courage to do their best?
- What specific actions will I take to recognize people for who they are and what they can achieve?

When we eliminate unrealistic expectations, allow for failure without punishment, and appreciate people's efforts, the foundation is laid for people to excel.

A lot of people have gone further in their life than they thought they could because someone else thought they could.

Whoever you are, wherever you might be, there are talents to be uncovered in people around you. Give encouragement to the talents you see in others. Compliment them, assure them, stimulate them to make the best possible use of their potential abilities.

Some of you might be saying to yourself, "I've heard all of this before. It's old hat."

Consider this. In a leadership workshop for middle- and upper-level managers, I asked each person to write down ten good things about one of their employees. Soon, one person stood up with the finished list. However, the majority of the group had not yet made a mark on their paper. They had heard it all before but how many had made it a part of their lifestyle?

•　　•　　•

Socrates said: "I can't teach you anything, I can only make you think." Here are some thoughts that might prompt you to action:

> People love us not for who we are but for how we make them feel. As Emerson said: "Our chief want in life is somebody who shall make us do what we can."

> Goethe believed, "The way you see people is the way you treat them and the way you treat them is what they become." Gandhi refused to see the bad in anyone. Many people in India exceeded their self-imposed limitations because of Gandhi's expressed faith in them.

> Humorist Robert Henry said, "People do not live by bread alone. They need buttering up once in awhile." Failure to provide recognition leads to psychological malnutrition. Approach people knowing they wear a sign on their forehead that reads: MMFI-AM—Make Me Feel Important-About Me.

> Sincere praise makes it possible for people to pay you one of life's sweetest compliments: "I like myself better with you." It has also been found that humans strive to live up to the compliments paid them.

> Don't try to change what people are. Rather, develop what they have. According to Kahlil Gibran, "Our worst fault is our preoccupation with the faults of others." If you want to get the best out of someone, you must look for the best that is in them. People can only use their strengths to excel, not their limitations.

> Become a talent scout among people and put your discoveries into words of appreciation. Remember, it's O.K. to send flowers, but they have a limited vocabulary.

Perhaps all these thoughts about showing appreciation and encouraging people boils down to a simple personal commitment. We need to acquire the attitude of believing in others.

Operation Appreciation is something anyone can do and everyone needs. A compliment or encouraging word can help dreams and ambitions become reality.

CELEBRATING OTHERS' SUCCESS

Roger Ailes asks this penetrating question, "Do you bring other people up or down?" He continues, "This may be the most important question facing you in your career and life."

A natural follow-up would be, "How are you bringing other people up?" "What specific things do you do every day to show others their importance to you?"

One of the most difficult, yet meaningful actions we can take to encourage others is celebrate their success. Forty thousand fans were in attendance in the Oakland stadium when Rickey Henderson tied Lou Brock's career stolen base record. According to USA Today, Lou left baseball in 1979 but faithfully followed Henderson's prestigious career and was excited about his success. Realizing that Rickey would set a new record, Brock was quoted in USA Today as saying, "I'll be there. Do you think I'm going to miss it now? Rickey did in 12 years what took me 19. He's amazing."

Imagine how Rickey Henderson felt knowing the person whose stolen base record he was about to break was excited about his achievements. Envy or jealousy might have been more natural feelings for Lou Brock but encouragers set self-interest aside and rejoice in the happiness of others.

MARRED FOR LIFE

The name Star Daily is prominent throughout England. His reputation as a notorious vicious killer, ruthless armed robber, and hardened man was rooted in his childhood.

Daily's teacher routinely called on him to stand and read a passage in front of his class. He would step to the front of the room, hesitantly take the book from his teacher and attempt to do what he was instructed. The words seemed to run together and the harder he tried, the more inept he became. He repeatedly stumbled through the passages as the snickers from the classroom reverberated in his mind.

On one occasion Daily was having an unusually difficult time with the reading assignment. Open laughter ensued in the classroom and even his sister buried her head in laughter and embarrassment. As he turned to the teacher for support, she too was hiding her laughter.

Crushed, this timid little boy exploded in anger. He threw the book against the wall and ran out the door. As he exited he screamed, "You will fear me! You will hate me! But this will be the last time you laugh at me!" As he ran, he killed, looted and demeaned all those he came in contact with for the remainder of his life.

The word encouragement means "to put courage into." Encouragement provides the support people need to pursue their dreams and aspirations. It also fuels inspiration needed to face day-to-day challenges.

Life could have been different for Star Daily. He wasn't born a criminal, and I wonder what might have happened had he experienced the courage to face his fears.

POWER OF POSITIVE PRAISE

Compliments are like potato chips. Once you've had one you look for more.

Offering compliments based on a person's character or actions inspires them to perform in such a manner that invites additional praise. People tend to live up to the compliments they receive.

William James said, "All of us, in the glow of feeling we have pleased, want to do more to please."

Combine this truth with the psycholinguistic research that indicates a person's mind takes 48 percent longer to understand a negative statement than a positive one and compliments become a dynamic force in motivating others.

The story is told of a newspaper cartoonist who amused himself one summer day by sending telegrams to twenty acquaintances selected at random. Each message contained only one word, "Congratulations." As far as he knew, not one of them had done anything in particular to be congratulated on. However, each took the message as a matter of fact and wrote him a letter of thanks. Everyone who received the message had done something that they regarded as clever and worthy of congratulations.

The power of praise is limited only by its lack of use. How many people do you know who could benefit from a sincere "congratulations" or "great job" or possibly even "you're the best"? Silent appreciation doesn't mean much. Let others know your positive regards toward them. They'll live up to your compliment.

ENTHUSIASM

- If you don't have enthusiasm, you don't have anything.

Kemmons Wilson, Sr.

- The important thing to remember is that if you don't have that inspired enthusiasm that is contagious, whatever you do have is also contagious.

Danny Cox

- Nothing good or great can be done in the absence of enthusiasm.

Tom Peters

- Enthusiasm is the electric current that keeps the engine of life going at top speed. Enthusiasm is the very propeller of progress.

B. C. Forbes

- Enthusiasm is the yeast that makes your hopes rise to the stars.

Mike Wickett

- I prefer the folly of enthusiasm to the indifference of wisdom.

Anatole France

- Godly enthusiasm is not a fire of our own kindling . . . If a man, however, has caught fire, let me not quench the Spirit by dampening the ardor of his pure devotion. Enthusiasm is not contrary to reason; it is reason—on fire.

Peter Marshall

- First make sure that what you aspire to accomplish is worth accomplishing, and then throw your whole vitality into it. What's worth doing is worth doing well. And to do anything well, whether it be typing a letter or drawing up an agreement involving millions, we must give not only our hands to the doing of it, but our brains, our enthusiasm, the best—all that is in us. The task to which you dedicate yourself can never become a drudgery.

B. C. Forbes

- Our spirits grow gray before our hairs.

Charles Lamb

- The real secret of success is enthusiasm.

  Walter P. Chrysler

- Passion is in all great searches and is necessary to all creative endeavors.

  W. Eugene Smith

- Enthusiasm and joy are Siamese twins—it's hard to find one without the other.

  Peter McWilliams and John Rogers
  Do It

- Every man is enthusiastic at times. One man has enthusiasm for 30 minutes — another man has it for 30 days, but it is the man who has it for 30 years who makes a success in life.

  Edward B. Butler

- We act as though comfort and luxury were the chief requirements of life, when all that we need to make us happy is something to be enthusiastic about.

  Charles Kingsley

- For as long as I can remember whatever I was doing at the time was the most important thing in the world for me . . . I have found enthusiasm for work to be the most priceless ingredient in any recipe for successful living.

  Samuel Goldwyn

- Enthusiasm is a vital element toward the individual success of every man or woman.

  Conrad Hilton

- Enthusiasm is self-confidence in action!

  Franklin Field

- I feel sorry for the person who can't get genuinely excited about his work. Not only will he never be satisfied, but he will never achieve anything worthwhile.

  Walter P. Chrysler

- Apathy can be overcome by enthusiasm and enthusiasm can be aroused by two things: first, an idea which takes the imagination by storm; and second, a definite, intelligible plan for carrying that idea into action.

  Arnold Toynbee

■ Like the chicken and the egg, enthusiasm and success seem to go together. We suspect, however, that enthusiasm comes first. If you hope to succeed at anything in this world, polish up your enthusiasm and hang on to it.

John Luther

■ When enthusiasm is inspired by reason, is practical in application, reflects confidence, and spreads good cheer, raises morale, inspires associates, arouses loyalty, and laughs at adversity, it is beyond price.

Coleman Cox

■ Fires can't be made with dead embers, nor can enthusiasm be stirred by spiritless men. Enthusiasm in our daily work lightens efforts and turns even labor into pleasant tasks.

James Mark Baldwin

■ No matter how trifling the matter at hand, do it with a feeling that it demands the best that is in you.

Sir William Osler

A DAILY PASSION

The word enthusiasm comes from the Greek roots en and theos and means "God within." It is a fire, a passion within. Real enthusiasm is not something you "put on" and "take off" to fit the occasion. It is a way of life.

Apparently Theodore Roosevelt possessed that kind of passionate lifestyle. In 1883, according to Bernard Levin, writing in Enthusiasms (Crown Publishers), Roosevelt went buffalo hunting in the Badlands of South Dakota with a single companion, Joe Ferris. They nearly died of thirst, and they slept on the ground, saddles their only pillows. One night wolves caused their horses to bolt, and it took some time for the fleeing beasts to be recaptured. The men went back to sleep; it began to rain heavily and they awoke, finding themselves lying in four inches of water. Shivering between sodden blankets, Ferris heard Teddy Roosevelt exclaim, "By Godfrey, but this is fun!"

Now that's enthusiasm!

FUN TO BE AROUND

Who would you rather be around? Someone who exudes vitality, enthusiasm, and a zest for life or a pessimistic, downtrodden bore? When given the choice, the majority of people from all walks of life would rather befriend the optimistic, enthusiastic, upbeat person.

Here's a case in point. General William Westmoreland was once visiting a platoon of paratroopers in Vietnam. During the conversation, the general asked this question: "How do you like jumping out of planes?" The first paratrooper responded, "I love it, sir." "How do you like jumping?" he asked the next. "It's a fantastic experience, sir!" exclaimed the soldier. "I couldn't imagine not doing it." "How do you like it?" he asked the third. "I'm scared to death, sir, and don't much like it," he honestly replied. "Then why do you do it?" the general queried. "Because I love being around guys who enjoy it."

Most of us would agree with John G. Shedd who said, "I like the person who bubbles over with enthusiasm. Better to be a geyser than a mud puddle."

Do people enjoy being around you? Are you the type of person who attracts others because of your enthusiasm for even the undesirable tasks? If you want to be liked, show that you like life by your enthusiasm.

NEW RULE

When Vince Lombardi took over as coach of the Green Bay Packers, he was not handed a winning team on a silver platter. The Packers were at the bottom. In 1958, they lost ten out of twelve games, tied one, and won one. When he addressed the players at spring training camp in June 1959, Lombardi was faced with a dispirited football team.

According to an article in Guideposts magazine, Lombardi said, "Gentlemen, we are going to have a great football team. We are going to win games. Get that!"

"Now how are we going to accomplish that?"

He continued, "You are going to learn to block, run, and tackle. You are going to outplay all the teams that come up against you. Get that!"

Then he threw in a new twist: "You are to have confidence in me and enthusiasm for my system. Hereafter, I want you to think of only three things: your home, your religion, and the Green Bay Packers, in that order! Let enthusiasm take hold of you—beginning now!"

He later expounded on his enthusiasm expectation. "If you aren't fired with enthusiasm," he exclaimed, "you will be fired, with enthusiasm."

Virtually the same players as the year before went on to win seven games that year, a division title the next year, and a world championship in the third year. Their renewed passion for the game produced astounding results.

How would a renewed enthusiasm for what you do enhance the outcome? How would your mood, actions, and performance be altered if you knew that being unenthusiastic would get you fired?

EXAMPLE

- A Chinese general put it this way: If the world is to be brought to order, my nation must first be changed. If my nation is to be changed, my hometown must be made over. If my hometown is to be reordered, my family must first be set right. If my family is to be regenerated, I myself must first be.

  A. Purnell Bailey

- We expect our leaders to be better than we are . . . and they should be—or why are we following them?

  Paul Harvey

- As a leader or a manager in your organization, you must start to behave in a manner that is congruent with the behavior you expect from your employees. The top managers in any organization must model the behavior they desire for the rest of the company.

  Karl Albrecht
  Service America

- When you walk what you talk . . . people listen.

  Anonymous

- Your job gives you authority. Your behavior earns you respect.

  Irwin Federman
  A Personal View of Leadership

- Leaders of the high-performing companies communicate their vision in their daily actions. The best testament is the living testament.

  James A. Belasco

- I won't accept anything less than the best a player's capable of doing . . . and he has the right to expect the best that I can do for him and the team!

  Lou Holtz

- People look at you and me to see what they are supposed to be. And, if we don't disappoint them, maybe, just maybe, they won't disappoint us.

  Walt Disney

EXAMPLE 133

- I've always found that the speed of the boss is the speed of the team.

  Lee Iacocca

- Never do anything you wouldn't be willing to explain on television.

  Arjay Miller

- We tend to idealize role models when we are scared or uncertain. Alas, we can be models of what we are, and no more than that.

  Judith Bardwick

- One man practicing sportsmanship is far better than fifty preaching it.

  Knute K. Rockne

- The foundations of character are built not by lecture, but by bricks of good example, laid day by day.

  Leo B. Blessing

- We must be the change we wish to see in the world.

  Mohandas K. Gandhi

- Be such a man, and live such a life, that if every man were such as you, and every life a life like yours, this earth would be God's Paradise.

  Phillips Brooks

- People may doubt what you say but they will believe what you do.

  Anonymous

HOW BRIGHT IS YOUR LANTERN?

Dwight L. Moody tells the story of a blind man in a large city sitting at a street corner with a lantern beside him. A passerby noticed the man and inquired why he had a lantern, since he was blind and the light of it was the same as the darkness. The blind man simply replied, "So that no one may stumble over me."

That's an interesting thought, holding up a lantern so others won't stumble. As I read that a couple of situations crossed my mind.

As reported in Our Daily Bread (September 6, 1987), the Department of Transportation in a large city was recently embarrassed. They discovered that four of the top ten parking violators in the city were their employees who were responsible for ticketing illegally parked vehicles. A double check on the computer showed that four employees owed between $5,000 and $8,000 each in unpaid parking tickets.

It's mighty difficult to expect the public to respect the law when those administering it are prime violators. I believe that would be an excellent example of causing someone to stumble.

On the flip side, there are those people who take their example seriously. Kirby Puckett, the Minnesota Twins centerfielder, had this to say in an interview: "Kids take a liking to me because they're about my size. It's nice to have somebody kids can look up to. I didn't give this role to myself, but I accept the responsibility. Everybody should have somebody to look up to. If all these other guys thought about that, maybe they wouldn't be having so many problems."

Puckett realizes that base hits, homeruns, and spectacular catches are going to put him in the limelight. His responsibility is to make sure the light reveals a character kids can look up to—and adults for that matter.

The noted eighteenth-century philosopher and skeptic David Hume was kidded by some of his friends for going to church on Sunday to hear the Scottish minister, John Brown, preach. Hume silenced his friends with this reply, "Well, I don't believe everything he says, but he lives everything he believes. And once a week I like to hear a man who believes what he says."

David Hume's response is the desire all people have of their role models. "Please," we ask, "let your life be a living example of what you speak." Whether religious leaders, company executives, spouses, little league baseball coaches, big league players, political leaders, teachers, friends, the message is the same. Let your lantern burn brightly so others won't stumble.

A SAD IRONY

There's irony in Mark Twain's comment that "few things are harder to put up with than the annoyance of a good example."

As a young boy Twain knew church leaders who owned and abused slaves. He heard people professing to be Christians use foul language and practice dishonesty during the week while speaking piously in church on Sunday. Bible teachers used the scripture to justify slave ownership. Although he saw genuine Christianity in family members, the lousy example of church leaders turned him off toward things religious.

Although Twain said a good example was an annoyance, I must believe he felt a poor example was a travesty.

ROLE MODEL

According to Jim Naughton, writing in The Washington Post, Chicago Bulls star, Michael Jordan, is one of America's most admired men, particularly among young people. Jordan's popularity has something to do with his acrobatic elegance and something to do with how serious he is about this role-model image.

EXAMPLE 135

He recently organized a foundation to raise money for child-oriented charities. Jordan also works face to face. David Rothenberg, the young California boy whose father set him on fire, was invited to sit on the Bulls bench with his hero. Jordan receives roughly thirty requests each week from dying children whose last wish is to meet him, and he fulfills as many requests as he can. Each child who sits on the bench receives the sneakers that Jordan wore in the game.

The opportunity for disappointment, however, rests heavily. "The good part about being famous is being able to help people," Jordan says. "The hard part is every day you have to be in a good mood, because that is what people expect. You learn to get good at it."

I'D RATHER SEE A SERMON

According to The Life of Francis d'Assisi, Francis once invited a young monk to join him on a trip to the local village to preach. Honored to be asked and excited to learn from the master, the monk readily accepted.

All day long he and Francis walked through the streets, byways, and alleys caring for the needs of the poor and helpless along the way. They rubbed shoulders with hundreds of people. At day's end, the two headed back home. Not even once had Francis addressed the gathered crowds, nor had he talked to anyone about the gospel. Greatly disappointed, his young companion, said, "I thought we were going into town to preach." Francis responded, "My son, we did preach. We were preaching while we were walking. We were watched by many and our behavior was closely observed. It is of no use to walk anywhere to preach unless we preach everywhere as we walk!"

Like it or not, we're preachers everyday. People will believe what we do long before the messages we preach.

THE BOORS OF SUMMER

Dale Murphy, star Philadelphia Phillies right fielder and father of seven boys, is so unfailingly good and polite that teammates call him "Father Murphy," reported the Philadelphia Inquirer (July 7, 1991). When he was asked which athletes his sons like most, he named two basketball players and one hockey player. "Those are all great role models," he added.

"But what about baseball players?" someone asked.

"Ummm, I'd have to think about that."

Never mind artificial turf and the designated hitter rule. The most troubling change in baseball in recent years has been the demeanor of those who play it.

In 1990, for instance, Cincinnati Reds relief pitcher Rob Dibble, angry with himself even though his team won, loosed a post-game fastball into the seats, plunking a young teacher on the arm. Philadelphia Phillies centerfielder Lenny

Dykstra spent much of his time answering questions about how he lost some $78,000 in illegal poker games. He also managed to bounce his car off a couple of trees after a teammate's bachelor party. His blood-alcohol level would have staggered an ox. In 1989, then Oakland Athletics outfielder Jose Canseco tried to squeeze money from fans by describing his wife's body on a 900 telephone number.

Maybe it wouldn't mean so much if these were marginal players. But they are among the best in the game, and these cases reflect a pattern. In 1990, a marketing firm surveyed 1800 American adults and ranked more than 300 athletes in terms of "likability." Just two active baseball players—Bo Jackson of the Chicago White Sox and Texas Rangers pitcher Nolan Ryan—made the top 75.

In 1990, baseball's reigning Most Valuable Players, Barry Bonds of the National League and Rickey Henderson of the American League, started sniveling over their salaries. Henderson showed up late for spring training, sulked openly and suggested that $3 million a year was not enough to buy his best performance. Bonds, who was awarded only $2.3 million in an arbitration case he lost, merely threatened to punch out the world.

Should we expect players to be any different? You take a boy with athletic talent and begin coddling him in Little League. You teach him early that he will be forgiven for poor behavior because he is special. You ignore his indiscretions, cheer his heroics. By the time he is a young man, he is earning a CEO's salary. Someone is there to carry his bags, book his hotel rooms, bring his food. He never waits in line, and everything is free, from the fifteen unopened boxes of shoes that clutter his locker to the nicest meals in the finest restaurants.

So why should we be shocked when Mike Marshall stages a one-day strike because the Red Sox won't pay a traffic ticket that his wife got at the stadium?

Spectators are getting fed up. "Players have complained and moaned for years," says baseball's deputy commissioner, Steve Greenberg. "But when my dad (Hall of Famer Hank Greenberg) was earning $7,000 a season, it elicited some sympathy. Who feels sorry for someone earning $3 million? The knee-jerk reaction is to tell him to get a real job."

Maybe the media are to blame. Perhaps the problems began when journalists stopped portraying players as gods and began exploring more than just how they played. If Babe Ruth were a Yankee today, would the tabloids ignore his drinking and sexual escapades?

"The players today don't trust the media, and maybe they shouldn't," says Philadelphia broadcaster Bill Campbell. "But today's players are also more self important. If it's convenient for them, they'll help you. If not, their attitude is 'The hell with you.'"

One of these multimillion-dollar players might defend himself by saying, "I signed up to play baseball. I didn't sign up to be anyone's role model."

Perhaps not. But a certain obligation should go with all that money and celebrity. Someone who has been handed the keys to the American dream should at least follow the road map. Players owe something to the game of baseball and its fans.

EXAMPLE 137

"The sports world," wrote Bill James, author of the Baseball Abstract books that bear his name, "is a refuge in a world of laziness and sloth, indecision and lack of commitment, hedged values and shortcuts. In society at large, we use sports to express and defend our values as well as to teach them."

Whether they like it or not, athletes are heroes. That is their job.

EXCELLENCE

- Excellence demands that you be better than yourself.

  Ted Engstrom

- Quality doesn't mean we have to be 100 percent better in any one thing; it means we strive to be 1 percent better in 100 things.

  Jan Carlzon

- Quality is never an accident; it is always the result of high intention, sincere effort, intelligent direction and skillful execution; it represents the wise choice of many alternatives.

  Willa A. Foster

- Desire is the key to motivation, but it's the determination and commitment to an unrelenting pursuit of your goal—a commitment to excellence—that will enable you to attain the success you seek.

  Mario Andretti

- If you don't do it excellently, don't do it at all. Because if it's not excellent, it won't be profitable. If it is not excellent, it won't be fun and if you're not in business for fun or profit, what the hell are you doing here?

  Robert Townsend

- Real excellence does not come cheaply. A certain price must be paid in terms of practice, patience, and persistence—natural ability notwithstanding.

  Stephen Covey

- It's the little things that make the big things possible. Only close attention to the fine details of any operation makes the operation first class.

  J. Willard Marriott

- Quality involves living the message of the possibility of perfection and infinite improvement, living it day in and day out, decade by decade.

  Tom Peters

- If you believe in unlimited quality and act in all your business dealings with total integrity, the rest will take care of itself.

  Frank Perdue

■ Good, better, best; never rest till "good" be "better" and "better" best.

Mother Goose

■ Some people may have greatness thrust upon them. Very few have excellence thrust upon them. They achieve it. They do not achieve it unwittingly, by doin' what comes naturally, and they don't stumble into it in the course of amusing themselves. All excellence involves discipline and tenacity of purpose.

John Gardner
Excellence

■ I want you to start a crusade in your life—to dare be your best.

William Danforth

■ The compulsion to excellence assures excitement!

Robert Schuller

■ I would rather perform at 90 percent of an excellence standard than 110 percent of an adequacy standard.

Don Beveridge

EXCELLENCE . . .

We talk about it, think about it, write of it, and some of us might even contemplate trying to achieve it. But, what is it?

Maybe you would agree with Satchel Paige: "Ain't no man that can avoid being born average, but ain't nobody got to be common."

The great author Charles Dickens said, "Whatever I have tried to do in my life, I have tried with all my heart to do well. What I have devoted myself to, I have devoted myself to completely."

A. W. Tozer provides a possible definition and a shot of inspiration in his comment to "let your heart soar as high as it will. Refuse to be average."

However you define excellence, it is important to keep in mind that it is not a project, act, or job description; excellence is a way of life. It includes going beyond the normal call of duty, stretching our perceived limits, and holding ourselves responsible for being our best.

Excellence comes from striving, maintaining the highest standards, paying attention to little details, and being willing to go the extra mile.

John Wooden, the legendary basketball coach at U.C.L.A., subscribed to basic life-enhancing, winning principles. He consistently emphasized the need for constant improvement and steady performance. John Wooden believed that "the mark of a true champion is to always perform near your own level of competency."

Excellence can simply be doing your very best. In everything. In every way. In every situation.

In other words, only those who settle for mediocrity are always at their best. Unfortunately, the mediocre seldom realize what they have settled for.

•   •   •

The great industrialist and philanthropist Andrew Carnegie addressed a graduating class one day saying, "There are several classes of young people. There are those who do not do all their duty, there are those who profess to do their duty, and there is a third class far better than the other two, that do their duty and a little more . . . Do your duty and a little more and the future will take care of itself."

How true! People who get by with as little effort as possible, settle for less than they are capable of, or wait for someone to come along and inspire them often believe life is shortchanging them. Yet life only gives back to them what they put into life. And their future will take care of itself as well.

Entertain these enduring excellence entities to enter the ecstasy of excellence:

1. Consider your commitment.

   "The quality of a person's life," said Vince Lombardi, "is in direct proportion to their commitment to excellence, regardless of their chosen field of endeavor." Isaac D'Israel put it this way: "It is a wretched taste to be gratified with mediocrity when the excellent lies before us."

   When you feel a compelling, constant, daily desire to do everything in your life as well as it can constantly be done, you will touch the borders of excellence.

2. Pay the price.

   Excellence in any endeavor is not automatic. As Dr. Stephen Covey says, "Real excellence does not come cheaply. A certain price must be paid in terms of practice, patience, and persistence—natural ability notwithstanding." Review those three Ps again—each is necessary for paying the price.

3. Exceed expectations.

   Challenge yourself to exceed self-imposed and other limitations. Go a step beyond the customary or ordinary. Give just a little more than normal. Bishop Gore said, "God does not want us to do extraordinary things; he wants us to do ordinary things extraordinarily well." When people perform the common things in life in an uncommon way, the world will sit up and take notice.

   I understand that Smuckers, the jelly and jam maker, has a policy of filling its containers with more product than the official weight indicates. It doesn't matter whether the consumer weighs their jar of jam or not. What is important is that Smuckers is committed to do more than they are required to do.

4. Never settle for good enough.

Winston Churchill exemplified this quality. He said, "I am easily satisfied with the very best."

Former Secretary of State Henry Kissinger asked an aide to prepare a report. The aide worked day and night to analyze the information and complete his report. Shortly after receiving the finished product, Mr. Kissinger returned it to his aide with a note: "Redo it." The aide diligently went about his task, turned it in and again was told to redo it. After the third time the aide asked to see Kissinger. "I have completed this report three times," he said, "and this is the best job I can do." Kissinger replied, "In that case, I'll read it now."

Hallmark cares enough to send the very best. How do you know? They said so. How about you? Are you the best? Do you believe it?

•   •   •

One final thought.

When you think you've arrived at excellence and can now relax . . . BEWARE.

Contemplate the lesson learned from a master window washer. Upon doing a superb job with the windows on the 116th floor of the Empire State Building, she made the mistake of stepping back to admire her work.

ONE PERCENT BETTER

It has been said that excellence results from doing 100 things 1 percent better rather than one thing 100 percent better.

Peters and Waterman, in their bestseller In Search of Excellence (Harper & Row, 1982), put it this way: "The essence of excellence is the thousand concrete, minute-to-minute actions performed by everyone in an organization to keep a company on its course."

WalMart founder Sam Walton was a believer in tending to the details. One day while visiting a competitor's store, which was in total disarray, Sam Walton pointed out to one of his executives a procedure he liked. "Why aren't we doing this?" he asked. Rather than criticize or put down his rival's chaos, Walton was looking for one thing that would give his company an edge and make them 1 percent better.

How about taking a walk through your organization? What one, three, or seventeen areas can you identify where 1 percent better is possible?

Adopt the concept that "finished never is." The Japanese have a word for it—kaizen, meaning "continuous improvement." In other words, the status quo is never acceptable. Make it 1 percent better.

PAY ATTENTION TO THE LITTLE THINGS

Vince Lombardi, the immortal coach of the Green Bay Packers, taught that, "excellence is achieved by the mastery of fundamentals."

Leo Rosten tells the story of a widower who had for years and years been eating at the same restaurant. On this Friday night, he sat down at his usual table and his waiter, as usual, put before him the usual salad. Mr. Smith ate the salad. The waiter removed it, as usual, and, as usual, replaced it with a bowl of chicken soup.

As he started off, Mr. Smith called out, "Waiter!"

"What?" said the waiter.

"Please taste this soup," said Mr. Smith.

The waiter frowned. "It's the chicken soup you always have."

"Taste it," said Mr. Smith.

"Listen, Mr. Smith, in all the years you have eaten here, did you ever once have a bad bowl of chicken soup?"

"Waiter—taste—the—soup!" said Mr. Smith.

"All right, all right, Mr. Smith, I'll taste it. So, where's the spoon?"

"Aha!" replied Smith.

Fancy products, gimmicks, and catchy slogans are not facilitators of excellence. Tasty chicken soup without a spoon rarely impresses anyone. If you want excellence, pay attention to the little things. If it's mediocrity you want, forget the fundamentals.

•   •   •

A religious cartoon depicted a worker looking up at a billboard. He had just painted the words "Beleive and you shall be saved." From a cloud overhead a hand protruded, the forefinger pointing at the misspelled word beleive. God's voice thundered from the heavens, "I before E except after C." It's one of the fundamentals of spelling.

What fundamentals might be overlooked in your organization? Are there small things that tend to be taken for granted?

Identify your business fundamentals. Evaluate the possibilities. Take action.

IT'S ALL AROUND US

H. L. Mencken, the long-time editor of the famous American Mercury magazine, shouted to his employees, "It's coming in the doors!" Everyone stopped what they were doing and looked at their boss.

"It's up to the bottom of the desk! It's up to the seats of our chairs."

"What are you talking about?" asked one of his confused colleagues.

"It's all around us. Now, it's to the top of our desks," shouted Mencken as he jumped to the top of his desk.

"What do you mean?" inquired the newsroom staff.

"Mediocrity. We're drowning in mediocrity!" Mencken shouted as he jumped from his desk and exited, never to return.

Eccentric? Maybe. Overly critical? Possibly. Is there a message? Definitely! As the saying goes, the value of one's life is in direct proportion to one's commitment to excellence.

Mencken refused to be associated with any cause, organization, or project bogged down in mediocrity. He also made it his responsibility to make sure others knew of his distaste for substandard performance.

Ask yourself: How strong is my commitment to excellence? What am I doing to ensure excellence and inspire those around me to do the same?

NO WORSE THAN ANYONE ELSE

Pulling no punches and telling it like it is, Tom Peters exhorted a group of corporate executives toward excellence. He spoke to these leaders for several hours concerning product excellence, employee training, values, mission, and customer service.

Unable to restrain himself any longer, an irritated executive interrupted Peters to voice his dissatisfaction with the message. "I'm sick and tired of hearing all this stuff on excellence," he blurted. "Our company is no worse than anyone else's."

Wouldn't that be a great motto to hang over an organization's entrance or print on their stationery: "We're no worse than anyone else."

Imagine receiving medical treatment, buying a car seat for a child, flying with an airline, or building a home with companies who claim to be no worse than anyone else.

Neil Armstrong, the first man to walk on the moon, was asked if he was nervous contemplating his trip into space. "Who wouldn't be," he responded. "There I was sitting on top of 9,999 parts and bits—each of which had been made by the lowest bidder!"

The Ministerial Association in a small community met to discuss the declining attendance in their churches. As the leaders discussed the predicament of their individual denominations, one pastor finally interjected, "It's good to hear the rest of you are experiencing difficulty as well. At least we're no worse than anyone else."

The "we're no worse than anyone else" attitude debilitates personal and corporate excellence. Those with the courage to rise above the current level of mediocrity will enjoy a distinct competitive advantage.

It is much like the story of the two backpackers who spotted a grizzly bear stalking them. One person calmly sat down, took off her hiking boots, and put on a pair of running shoes. "What good will that do?" asked her companion. "You can't outrun the grizzly." Lacing up her shoes, the friend responded, "I just have to stay ahead of you."

A commitment to be our best and taking corresponding action are the running shoes that keep us one step ahead of the "we're no worse than anyone else" crowd.

"Once you say you're going to settle for second," said John F. Kennedy, "that's what happens to you in life, I find."

THE BEST GET BETTER

"Once you're labeled 'the best'," says Larry Bird, "you want to stay up there, and you can't do it by loafing around." In his off-season, Larry Bird lifts weights, runs, and works on new moves and shots. "If I don't keep changing," Bird told Esquire magazine, "I'm history."

Although Larry Bird is now retired from professional basketball, I'm convinced he will maintain his commitment and drive to be his best at whatever he does. Why?

The best keep getting better.

Jessica Tandy, Oscar winner for her role in Driving Miss Daisy, was asked in Vis a Vis (March 1990) if any of her performances have left her unsatisfied. "All of them," she instantly replied. "I've never come off the stage at the end of a performance and said, 'tonight, everything was perfect.' There'll always be some little thing that I'll have to get right tomorrow." Such is the reason why her performance in her following movie Fried Green Tomatoes once again won her outstanding reviews.

The best keep getting better.

No one knows for sure who invented the cupcake, but there's no question who improved it. D. R. "Doc" Rice, now in his eighties, is credited with injecting the creme filling and putting the squiggly white line atop the cupcake's chocolate icing at Continental Baking Company's Detroit plant. Rice's changes in the original formula for devil's food cake hand covered with vanilla or chocolate icing led to widespread popularity of the snack. For example, in 1989, Hostess sold 400 million cupcakes. Not bad.

The best make things better.

STATUS QUO OR STANDING OVATION

Ronald Reagan often talked about altering the status quo. "Status quo," he said, "you know, that's Latin for the mess we're in!"

One man never satisfied with the status quo is Peter Ueberroth. The son of an itinerant aluminum-siding salesperson, he went on to become Time's man of the year in 1985. Ueberroth also built one of the finest travel companies in the United States.

His commitment to a personal lifestyle of excellence is reflected in his business practices as well. For example, Ueberroth's employees wear coats and ties at all times and when an employee looks a little shabby, they are admonished to purchase new threads. Oh yes, Ueberroth customarily provides a check to cover the cost. That's putting your money where your mouth is.

Ueberroth also spearheaded a tremendously successful twenty-third Olympic games in Los Angeles. Unlike the twenty-two that preceded it, this event blasted the status quo and generated a $215 million profit. To top off this effectively orchestrated event, eighty-four thousand people attending the closing ceremonies gave Peter Ueberroth a standing ovation.

The difference between status quo and a standing ovation is found in a comment by Abraham Lincoln. "I do the very best I know how—the very best I can; and I mean to keep doing so until the end." I can only assume Peter Ueberroth would agree.

FIND YOUR SWEET SPOT

After decades of work as a consultant with major companies and prolific writing, Peter Drucker made this observation: "The great mystery isn't that people do things badly but that they occasionally do a few things well. The only thing that is universal is incompetence. However, nobody ever commented, for example, that the great violinist, Jascha Heifetz, probably couldn't play the trumpet very well."

Finding that niche, talent, or interest where excellence can be achieved is a great way to maximize your efforts. When we find that "sweet spot," as in tennis or golf, increased power and control are at our disposal.

Here's a practical example of what I mean. A young woman loaded with reference letters from prominent people and Ivy League credentials presented herself to the vice-president for Personnel at a multi-product manufacturing plant.

"What can you do? What is your specialty?" asked the personnel specialist.

"My background and training are diverse," she began. "I think I could do most anything you ask."

"Well," remarked the interviewer, "we're not interested in hiring someone who can do many things fairly well. Our company is looking for people who have developed a few talents extremely well."

•   •   •

"If a man can write a better book, preach a better sermon, or make a better mousetrap than his neighbor," said Emerson, "though he build his house in the woods, the world will make a path to his door."

Find your sweet spot and become the best you can be. Think about it—that's the way people and organizations attain the competitive edge.

Larry Bird perfects his jump shot; Katarina Witt is known for her double jumps on ice; Steffi Graf has refined her tennis serve; Wayne Gretzky excels in putting the puck where he wants it, and Joe Montana's passing accuracy is superb.

Federal Express defines dependability; Zig Ziglar exemplifies refined speaking skills; Nordstrom has capitalized on premier customer service; and Ray Kroc built a hamburger empire on quality, service, cleanliness, and value.

Take a common thing and do it uncommonly well. As Alfred North Whitehead put it, "Doing little things well is the way toward doing big things better."

LIFESTYLE OF EXCELLENCE

According to a 1986 issue of Boardroom Reports, a splendid philosophy of excellence is described in Toyota's Basic Management Handbook. Toyota believes and preaches the only acceptable quality percentage is 100 percent. Every car must be manufactured exactly according to specifications and no Toyota should ever leave the factory without passing quality tests perfectly.

Excellence is not a "sometimes" affair; it is a way of life. Every person in the organization must be committed to go beyond the "good enough" syndrome and think 100 percent quality in every facet of the organization. Then and only then can consistent excellence be achieved.

Business isn't the only area of life where good enough really isn't.

In Communicate Like a Pro (1983), Nido Qubein tells the experience of a young musician who approached an old master who had just completed the most beautiful rendition of a complex collection of great compositions he'd ever heard. "Sir," the young man said admiringly, "it must be great to have all the practicing behind you and be able to simply sit down and play like that."

"Oh!" the master replied, "I still practice eight hours every day."

"But, why? I mean, you are so good!" exclaimed the young musician.

"I wish to become superb!" answered the old master.

The old master understood the chasm that exists between good enough and superb. He was also distinctly aware that natural talent or a musical flair was not enough. Professional musical excellence demanded a daily commitment to practice and refine his skills.

Only when we are committed to doing what it takes to be superb can we begin to measure up to all that we were created to be.

TRIFLES MAKE PERFECTION

Buzzwords have a way of coming and going. Some believe that will be the case with "excellence." That may be, but the message of excellence is neither new nor will it be lost in the annals of time. Those who preceded us had their own vocabulary but the process, performance, and definition of excellence were evident.

Michelangelo received a visit from a friend as he worked diligently on a sculpture. After a brief chat, the friend left but returned later to find Michelangelo working on the same statue. Thinking the statue was nearly completed on his last visit and seeing no visible change, he exclaimed, "You haven't been working all this time on that same statue, have you?" "Indeed I have," the sculptor replied. "I've been retouching the facial features, refining the leg muscles, polishing the torso; I've softened the presentation of some areas and enhanced the eye's expression." "But all those things are insignificant," responded the visitor. "They are mere trifles." "That may be," replied Michelangelo, "but trifles make perfection, and perfection is no trifle."

"Trifles make perfection, and perfection is no trifle" is a simple message passed down in a variety of forms. Although simply spoken, the consequences have monumental impact. People and organizations who pay attention to the "little things," the seemingly insignificant, produce excellence in larger matters.

Take inventory. What details in your life or organization have you overlooked? Are there functions that appear insignificant? Renew your commitment and give attention to these finishing touches.

A VIOLIN LESSON IN EXCELLENCE

In the late seventeenth century, three rural families dominated the musical instrument industry. Working in shops located side by side in the Italian village of Cremona, these families produced the finest violins. The Amatic family hung a sign outside their shop that read, "The best violins in all of Italy." Not wanting their creations to go unnoticed, the Guarneri family posted a sign that read, "The best violins in all the world!" The famous Anton Stradivari, known to produce the finest, most expensive stringed instruments, boasted his worldwide renown by hanging a sign on his front door that simply read, "The best violins on the block!"

Zig Ziglar says, "The greatest enemy of excellence is good." These three Italian families were proud of and prominently advertised their product. They also understood the aggressive competition among them would never allow "good" to be their best. Whether our products and services are the best in the country or in the world, remember, there might be someone on the block who surpasses us.

EXCUSES

ARE YOU AN EXCUSIOLOGIST?

The exercise of making excuses is not new to our generation. We can trace this popular diversionary technique back to the Old Testament. Yes, I know Adam and Eve each made some worthless excuses but in the Book of Leviticus we find a sacred custom called the "escaped goat."

When the problems and trials of the people became overwhelming, a healthy male goat was brought to the temple. In a formal ceremony, the high priest of the tribe placed his hands on the head of the goat and read the list of problems. This process transferred the agonies and anxieties onto the goat and the goat was set free, taking the troubles with him out to pasture.

Things haven't changed much in 4,000 years. Now people use a less formal process of placing blame for their problems on something or someone else. Although the term *scapegoat* is still popular, I prefer a phrase that seems more appropriate. Avid scapegoaters become professional excusiologists. That's right, *excusiologists!*

I am reminded of the farmer who asked his neighbor if he could borrow a rope. "Sorry," the neighbor responded, "I'm using it to tie up my milk."

"You can't use a rope to tie up milk," responded the stunned farmer.

"I know," said the neighbor, "but when you don't want to do something, one excuse is as good as another."

Therein lies the motto for excusiologists: "One excuse is as good as another."

• • •

A portion of my professional career involved working in both adult and juvenile corrections. Not one person was ever guilty of the acts, behavior, or crimes for which they had been accused. Every prisoner had an excuse. "I was in the wrong place at the wrong time." "I was framed!" "I only wanted to rob the guy but when he resisted, I was forced to shoot him. It's his fault." And the list goes on and on.

Professional excusiology is not limited to criminals. How about the student who came home with four *F*'s and one *D*- on his report card? Before his father could get angry, the little boy blurted out, "I know, Dad. I've been spending far too much time on that one subject."

That's excusiology.

A little girl was being disciplined for misbehavior. In between her tears she admitted, "I didn't do it, and I promise I'll never do it again."

Oh well, not every excuse is foolproof.

• • •

The Oklahoma Department of Human Services prints a monthly list of the "worst" excuses received for nonpayment of child support. Here are two classics:

"I can't afford to pay child support. I'm too far behind on my cable bill."

"I will not allow my ex-wife to get rich on my money." (The man was required to pay $25 a week.)

Another prime case of excusiology:

A man placed on a strict weight-loss program gave in to temptation one morning and bought doughnuts at the bakery. When asked why he cheated on his diet, he said it was God's fault for opening up a parking place right in front of the bakery as he drove by.

When all else fails, blame God.

• • •

Creative employees have always been able to come up with memorable excuses for coming in late or not at all. For instance, "I thought Halloween was a holiday." Here's another one: "My astrologer warned me not to come to work before noon on Wednesday." Here's a dandy, "My parrot spoke for the first time, so I waited for him to do it again so I could tape record it." I'm not kidding. These are actual excuses. One more work-related excuse: "I lost my American Express card, and I can't leave home without it."

Exercisers produce their own set of excuses. Take the man who said he couldn't use his exercise bike because it had a flat tire.

I guess we must respect the ingenuity of these excusiologists.

• • •

Although we may chuckle at the feeble attempts people make to cover their tracks and explain away their shortcomings, one thing remains true: people continue to make excuses a ceremonious ritual. And excusiologists are especially adept.

There is a pattern that tends to develop when analyzing excuses. The first type of excuse is outright denial—refusing to admit any association, involvement or wrongdoing. Children learn this technique early on and tend to carry it with them into adulthood.

The second form of refusing responsibility is a simple, "It's not my fault" or "It's because of" excuse. This is a true form of scapegoating. Find someone else to blame. It's because of my supervisor, spouse, great uncle, mother-in-law, or some other innocent bystander.

Finally, we have the "I did it, but . . . " approach. "But" is the important word here. Excusiologists resorting to this popular antic admit to wrongdoing but then every circumstance in life becomes fair game to be blamed for the error.

O. J. Simpson once said, "The day you stop making excuses, is the day you start to the top."

The simple truth is, people who make excuses a way of life experience little to take credit for and life will continue to seem unfair.

• • •

Tennis great Virginia Wade played but failed to win the British championship at Wimbledon fifteen years straight. Previous wins at the U.S. Open, Italian Open, and the Australian Open didn't fill the gap of a winless Wimbledon.

Wade got caught up in excusiology. Bad luck, weather, poor calls, bad bounces, and a cadre of other targets were used to justify her failure to end up in the winner's circle.

In 1977, Virginia Wade took a proactive approach to her tennis game. She gave up making excuses and committed herself to winning at Wimbledon, no matter what the circumstances.

By taking personal responsibility for her own mistakes, the quality of her game, and her competitive spirit, Virginia Wade was ready to win her first Wimbledon. And she did.

• • •

The things we continue to excuse will return to haunt us over and over again. Excusiology is a dead-end way of life.

John Wooden was one of the greatest basketball coaches of all time. Wooden led his UCLA Bruins to a record-breaking number of NCAA basketball championships and gained the respect of players and spectators alike. He provided inspiration and leadership that propelled his teams to victory. One of Wooden's memorable motivating statements admonished players to take responsibility for their actions. Wooden believed, "Nobody is a real loser—until they start blaming somebody else."

Have you fallen into the habit of making excuses? Who and what will you stop blaming for failures? In what areas of your life and career can you take more control? How will you begin taking responsibility for developing a winning lifestyle?

LOST CAUSE

The coach of a high school baseball team became frustrated with the performance of his first base player. Error after error made it difficult for the other players to have faith in him and winning games depended on improved performance.

On the next day of practice, the coach grabbed a glove and headed for first base to show the player how it should be done. The first ball hit toward him took a bad hop and clobbered the coach in the chest. Next came a popper just outside the first baseline. Lost in the bright sun, the ball glanced off his glove and hit him in the forehead. Later a wild throw came from shortstop causing the coach to stretch, tearing the seat of his pants. Exasperated, the coach turned to his first base player, handed him the glove, and shouted, "You've got this position so messed up, even I can't do a thing with it."

FAILURE

- Failure is good. It's fertilizer. Everything I've learned about coaching, I've learned from making mistakes.

  Rick Pitino

- Most successes have been built on failures, not on one failure alone but several. A majority of the great historic accomplishments of the past have been the final result of a persistent struggle against discouragement and failure. A man is never beaten until he thinks he is.

  Charles Gow

- A well-adjusted person is one who makes the same mistake twice without getting nervous.

  Jane Heard

- Remember there are two benefits of failure. First, if you do fail, you learn what doesn't work; and second, the failure gives you an opportunity to try a new approach.

  Roger von Oech

- I have always felt that although someone may defeat me, and I strike out in a ball game, the pitcher on that particular day was the best player. But I know when I see him again, I'm going to be ready for his curve ball. Failure is a part of success. There is no such thing as a bed of roses all your life. But failure will never stand in the way of success if you learn from it.

  Hank Aaron

- The way to accelerate your success is to double your failure rate.

  Tom Watson, Sr.

- Now what should happen when you make a mistake is this: You take your knocks, you learn your lessons and then you move on. That's the healthiest way to deal with a problem.

  Ronald Reagan

- The freedom to fail is vital if you're going to succeed.

  Michael Korda

- The people who are really failures are the people who set their standards so low, keep the bar at such a safe level, that they never run the risk of failure.

Robert Schuller

- A man's errors are his portals of discovery.

James Joyce

- People who refuse to move ahead because they are afraid of failure do not protect their self-respect; they lose it.

Dale E. Galloway

- People are known as much by the quality of their failure as by the quality of their successes.

Mark McCormack

- You only have to do a very few things right in your life so long as you don't do too many things wrong.

Warren Buffett

- If at first you don't succeed, you're about average!

Dr. Robert Anthony

- Admire those who attempt great things, even though they fail.

Seneca

- Our business in this world is not to succeed, but to continue to fail, in good spirits.

Robert Louis Stevenson

- Don't be discouraged by failure. Failure, in a sense, is the highway to success because every discovery of what is false leads us to seek after what is true. And every fresh experience points out an error which we shall, afterwards, carefully avoid.

John Keats

- Failure is the opportunity to begin again more intelligently.

Henry Ford

■   Many of life's failures are people who did not realize how close they were to
    success when they gave up.

Thomas Edison

FAILING INTO SUCCESS

The late Senator Hubert Humphrey barely lost the 1968 presidential election after
trailing in the polls some months earlier by a large margin. It was one of his toughest
battles and no doubt, a heartbreaking loss.

Some years later Humphrey wrote, "To come as close as we finally did to winning
the highest office in this land and then to lose was hard. But in writing my
concession speech, I told myself, 'This has to be done right because it is the opening
speech of your next campaign!'"

Hubert Humphrey understood that successful people are not afraid to fail.
Although it is not an event they look forward to, achievers have the ability to accept
failure and continue on, planning for their next success.

"Acceptance of what has happened," advised William James, "is the first step to
overcoming the consequences of any misfortune."

•   •   •

Failure is a natural consequence of trying. Those who never fail have never tried
anything worth failing at. Only the risk takers see failure as one of the most powerful
of all the success laws because you only really fail when you quit trying.

"Failure is a part of success," teaches Ty Boyd. "You must expect to fail again
and again and again before you can accomplish anything worthwhile."

A real-life example of this principle occurred when a chemist, Paul Ehrlich,
discovered a drug to treat those afflicted with syphilis. It was named "Formula 606,"
because the first 605 tests were a failure.

So often world-recognized achievements seem to just happen. What the public
rarely sees are the failures that preceded achievement.

•   •   •

In an interview with the *San Francisco Examiner* (June 22, 1986), Lee Iacocca said,
"Most people are looking for security, a nice, safe, prosperous future. And there's
nothing wrong with that. It's called the American Dream."

On the other hand, the American Nightmare is the FOF (Fear of Failure) Complex.

Iacocca continued, "Fear of failure brings fear of taking risks . . . and you're never
going to get what you want out of life without taking some risks. Remember,
everything worthwhile carries the risk of failure."

The dreaded fear of failure: We hide it. We deny it. We fear it. We ignore it. We
hate it.

Face it, many people believe that if at first you don't succeed, destroy all the evidence that show you tried.

John Barrymore wisely noted, "You can only be as good as you dare to be bad." There absolutely, positively is no shortcut to success without risk. You are not a failure because you didn't reach your dream, but a success because you tried.

Never, never allow your energies to be wasted muddling around in the fear of failure.

The freedom to fail prepares people for the opportunity to succeed. A few basic principles are critical for making the failures of today stepping stones to a brighter future.

Keep failure in perspective. The young aspiring pitcher knew he was in trouble when the Little League coach approached the mound and said, "Son, I think I better have someone relieve you."

"But," the pitcher argued, "I struck this guy out last time."

"I know," said the coach empathetically, "but this is the same inning."

It has been said that dentists' mistakes are pulled. Carpenters turn theirs into sawdust. Doctors' failures are buried and lawyers' mistakes get shut up in prison. However, like the young pitcher, most of our failures end up out in the open for the whole world to see.

It is embarrassing to have mistakes, blunders, and failures exposed to everyone around you. But before the self-pity party begins, remind yourself that it could always be worse.

For instance, how would you like to have listed on your résumé, "Designed the Leaning Tower of Pisa"? The tower is twenty feet out of perpendicular. The person who planned the foundation to be only ten feet deep for a 179-foot-tall building was one sandwich short of a picnic that day.

We will never know what we can achieve until we try. If we make a mistake, fall short, or totally mess up . . . so what? That's why erasers were invented. Keep your goof-ups in perspective. They are temporary and only as big or disastrous as you allow them to become.

Failure offers a new beginning. A sportswriter once asked this question of actor, sportscaster, and former mediocre major leaguer Bob Uecker: "How did you handle pressure as a player?"

Uecker responded, "It was easy. I'd strike out and put the pressure on the guy behind me."

I'm not recommending we put the pressure on the people around us but Uecker's comment suggests a healthy approach. Once the failure is over, forget it let it die. It's time for a new beginning.

Warren Bennis and Bert Nanus, who interviewed and studied ninety successful people for their book, *Leaders: The Strategies of Taking Charge* (Harper & Row, 1986), wrote, "Failure is a beginning, the springboard to renewed efforts."

In his autobiography, *The Tumult and the Shouting,* the great sports columnist Grantland Rice gives this advice on how to use failure for future benefit: "Because golf exposes the flaws of the human swing—a basically simple maneuver—it causes more self torture than any game short of Russian roulette. The quicker the average golfer can forget the shot he had dubbed or knocked off line—and concentrate on the next shot—the sooner he begins to improve and enjoy golf. Like life, golf can be humbling. However, little good comes from brooding about mistakes we've made. The next shot in golf or life, is the big one."

Press on. B. C. Forbes, founder of *Forbes* magazine, said, "History has demonstrated that the most notable winners usually encountered heartbreaking obstacles before they triumphed. They finally won because they refused to become discouraged by their defeats. Disappointments acted as a challenge. Don't let difficulties discourage you."

Baseball manager Connie Mack who led the Philadelphia Athletics from 1900 to 1950, once said, "I've seen boys on my baseball team go into a slump and never come out of it, and I've seen others snap right out and come back better than ever. I guess more players lick themselves than are ever licked by an opposing team."

Whether your failures produce more failure or success is highly dependent on your willingness and desire to persist beyond your slump.

Build on experiences. In 1983, the Australians challenged the United States for the America's Cup. Despite America hanging on to it for 134 years, the Aussies directing their boat, *Australia III*, beat Dennis Conner's American entry in four straight races. It was a devastating and humiliating defeat.

In 1988, Dennis Conner received about $5 million in return for product endorsements. Why? After losing the competition in 1983, Dennis Conner went back to the drawing board, built on his experiences and won back the America's Cup in 1987. Conner and his sailing team learned a difficult lesson from failure and rebounded to 'sail' to success.

Failure is the foundation for success when you learn from and build on your experiences. What failures have you experienced lately? How well are you dealing with them? Are you caught up in a self-pity party? What new beginnings are possible as a result of this failure? Have you tightened your determination and persistence belt? How do you plan to build on what you've learned?

The next time failure knocks at your door, remember the encouragement of Confucius that, "Our greatest glory is not in never falling but in rising every time we fall."

REBOUNDING FROM FAILURE

Ron Guidry didn't like the taste of failure. Pitching in the major leagues for the New York Yankees was a dream come true. Management suggested he wasn't ready for the big leagues and sent him back down to the minors. With his balloon deflated, Guidry went home and told his wife, "That's it. I'm going to quit baseball rather than go back to the minors. I worked like crazy to get here and I'm not going back."

The Guidrys packed up their belongings and headed for their home in the south. At a restaurant just before the border, Guidry's wife's persistent encouragement paid. Ron decided to go to his new minor league team and give it one more shot.

The next year Ron Guidry won the Cy Young trophy, an award presented annually to the best pitcher in the major leagues.

. . .

Stacy Allison wasn't pleased with failing at her first attempt to climb Mount Everest. She admits to initially experiencing acute disappointment and discouragement. But failure ultimately became her inspiration. "I had to fail to realize that self-worth isn't built upon one accomplishment," she told the *Christian Science Monitor*. "It's built through years of setting goals and reaching them."

A year later Allison successfully reached the summit and stood on top of the world.

. . .

Richard Bach completed only one year of college, then trained to become an Air Force jet-fighter pilot. Twenty months after achieving his wings, he resigned. Then he became the editor of an aviation magazine that went bankrupt. Life became one failure after another.

Even when he wrote *Jonathan Livingstone Seagull*, Bach couldn't think of an ending. The manuscript lay dormant for eight years before he decided how to finish it—only to have several publishers reject it. Once published, the book became a top seller and Bach achieved national recognition.

. . .

When Churchhill was defeated as prime minister after leading Great Britain to victory in World War II, his wife tried to comfort him by telling him it was a "blessing in disguise." "If it is," said Churchill, "then it is very effectively disguised."

The devastation from his failure to be reelected was real. Yet, Churchill later realized it was far from the end of an illustrious career.

. . .

A young woman aspiring to land a permanent position in broadcasting found more failure than success. No United States radio station would give her an opportunity, because "a woman wouldn't be able to attract an audience." She made her way to Puerto Rico and then, paying her own way, flew to the Dominican Republic to cover and sell her stories on the uprising there.

Back in the States she valiantly pursued her passion, but after eighteen firings she wondered if a career in broadcasting was ever meant to be. Finally, she persuaded an executive to hire her, but he wanted her to host a political talk show.

She was familiar with the microphone but not politics. Using her comfortable conversational style, she talked about what the fourth of July meant to her and invited callers to do the same. The program was a hit. Listeners loved it and the network realized it.

Today, Sally Jessy Raphael is a two-time Emmy-award-winning host of her own television talk show reaching eight million viewers daily throughout the United States, Canada and the United Kingdom. Raphael used every setback, failure and firing to spur her on to something better.

* * *

Football coach Mike Ditka said, "You never really lose until you quit trying." Our examples are proof that failure is not the issue. What we do with it is.

Dr. Joyce Brothers believes "the person interested in success has to learn to view failure as a healthy, inevitable part of the process of getting to the top."

"Failure should challenge us to new heights of accomplishment," said William Arthur Ward, "not pull us to new depths of despair. Failure is delay, but not defeat. It is a temporary detour, not a dead-end street."

The value of failure comes from the rebound. Never quit trying, view your failure as natural, and remember, failure is only temporary. Bounce back!

PUTTING FAILURE BEHIND YOU

On your next opportunity to rent a video, check out *The Best of Times*. Robin Williams stars as a man unable to put in the past an incident that occurred twenty years before. His high school football team lost a critical football game because he failed to catch a pass. If only he had hung on, Taft High would have beaten Bakersfield and everything would be different.

Williams decides to recreate the game and thereby give himself a second chance. The story revolves around the difficulties he has persuading the members of both teams to reunite for a rematch, but he is committed to erase his past and the nightmare of living with his failure.

Keep in mind this is a movie. The game-deciding play happens just as it did twenty years ago, but this time Williams makes the catch and puts the past behind him.

People experience dropped passes throughout their lives. Human nature responds by wanting to do it over—to have a second chance. In real life, the plot and result remain the same.

* * *

The former governor of Texas, John Connally, whose business assets once approached $500 million, watched his business disintegrate as oil prices fell. In a television interview he said, "Oil prices fell. There was nothing we could do about it. We had leveraged our assets. We watched the assets rapidly lose value until they failed to match our liabilities. We went to Hong Kong and to the markets of the world to refinance our operations, quite confident that with the passing of time values would rise again and we would once more be solvent. But we failed. We were left with no recourse but to seek the legal protection of the courts through bankruptcy."

Mr. Connally sold his silver, horses, personal property, and other valuable assets to pay off creditors.

Oh, to be able to replay the past.

Benjamin Franklin, toward the end of his life, reflected on his past and penned the following: "When I reflect, as I frequently do, upon the felicity I have enjoyed, I sometimes say to myself, that were the offer made me, I would engage to run again, from beginning to end, the same career of life. All I would ask, should be the privilege of an author to correct in a second edition, certain errors of the first."

The second edition of our lives begins when failure is recognized, dealt with and plans set to proceed from there. Don't wait around for an instant replay to fix your dropped passes. Put the failure behind you and press on.

EVER HAD A NO-HIT EXPERIENCE?

In 1962, four young women wanted to start a professional singing career. They began performing in their church and doing small local concerts. Then came their time to cut a record. It was a flop. Another was recorded. The sales were a fiasco. The third, fourth, fifth, and on through their ninth recordings were all failures.

Early in 1964, they were booked for the Dick Clark show. He paid barely enough to meet expenses and no great contracts resulted from their national exposure.

In the summer of 1964, they recorded "Where Did Our Love Go?" This song raced to the top of the charts and the Supremes gained national recognition and prominence for their musical sensations.

Prior to their hit singles, the Supremes were known as the "No-Hit Supremes." Their musical future was bleak, but they continued to believe in their abilities and passion for their profession.

How about you? Have you ever had a no-hit experience? What did you do about it? What action are you taking to ensure your next effort is a hit?

FROM POVERTY TO PROSPERITY

George Washington Carver suggested that "ninety-nine percent of the failures come from people who have the habit of making excuses."

In 1915, Carver and other residents of Coffee City, Alabama, had reason to complain and make excuses. They were nearly starving because of the boll weevil's destruction of the cotton crop. Rather than make excuses for their predicament, Carver suggested growing peanuts instead of cotton. He developed innovative uses for peanuts and made soaps, plastics, inks, chemicals and cosmetics from peanut-derived substances. The community prospered from his innovative, no-nonsense, no-excuse handling of disaster.

Had the people of Coffee City, Alabama, decided to wallow in their impoverishment, the experience of prosperity would have remained outside their grasp.

William Marston, in his book *Take Your Profits from Defeat*, wrote, "Every success I know has been reached because the person was able to analyze defeat and actually profit by it in the next undertaking."

Well-managed failure is one of opportunity's favorite disguises.

FAILING INTELLIGENTLY

The renowned inventor Charles Kettering suggested that we must learn to fail intelligently. He said, "We need to teach the highly educated person that it is not a disgrace to fail and that he must analyze every failure to find its cause. He must learn how to fail intelligently, for failing is one of the greatest arts in the world."

Kettering gave these suggestions for turning failure into success:

- Honestly face defeat; never fake success.
- Exploit the failure; don't waste it. Learn all you can from it.
- Never use failure as an excuse for not trying again.

Kettering's practical advice reminds us that failure is a natural part of progressive living. Face it. Learn from it, and don't make excuses for failure. It doesn't get much simpler than that.

FORGIVENESS

- Love lets the past die. It moves people to a new beginning without settling the past. Love prefers to tuck the loose ends of past rights and wrongs in the bosom of forgiveness—and pushes us into a new start.

    Lewis B. Smedes

- Nothing cures like time and love.

    Laura Nyro

- Forgiveness is not an elective in the curriculum of life. It is a required course, and the exams are always tough to pass.

    Charles Swindoll

- "Eating Crow" is never pleasant—no matter how much mustard and ketchup you put on it. But usually the sooner you eat it the less unpleasant it is to the taste!

    Nido Qubein

- Forgiveness is the oil of relationships.

    Josh McDowell

- Since nothing we intend is ever faultless, and nothing we attempt ever without error, and nothing we achieve without some measure of finitude and fallibility we call humanness, we are saved by forgiveness.

    David Augsburger

- Forgiving heals your memory as you change your memory's vision.

    Lewis B. Smedes

- Forgiveness is the fragrance the violet sheds on the heel that has crushed it.

    Mark Twain

- The heart's memory eliminates the bad and magnifies the good; and thanks to this artifice, we manage to endure the burdens of the past.

    Gabriel Garcia Marquez

HEALING THE WOUNDS

D. A. Battista suggested, "One of the most lasting pleasures you can experience is the feeling that comes over you when you genuinely forgive an enemy—whether he knows it or not."

What is this pleasure-producing action called forgiveness?

Forgiveness means to erase, to forego what is due; to give up resentment; to wipe the slate clean, to release from a debt, to cancel punishment; to personally accept the price of reconciliation; to give up all claims on one who has hurt you and let go the emotional consequences of that hurt.

Dr. Paul Faulkner, writing *In Making Things Right*, says forgiveness is similar to looking at an old cut on your body that has become a tough, permanent scar. When the cut was fresh, it festered and was painful. Now that the cut has become a scar, you've forgotten the pain. In fact, you seldom think of it at all. But you can still see the scar. Similarly, it is possible to forget the hurt of past resentments. How? By cutting the line with an attitude of love and goodwill toward the people who have abused you.

Resentment forces us to "re-feel" our wounds, while forgiveness heals the wounds. Healing the wounds brings lasting pleasure.

"I DON'T REMEMBER"

Ron Lee shares the following story in *Gold in the Making*:

The story is told of a priest who lived in the Philippines. A woman in his parish deeply loved God. In fact, this woman claimed that at night she often had visions in which she talked with Christ and he talked with her. The priest, however, was skeptical of her claim; so to test her visions he said to her, "You say that you actually speak directly with Christ in your visions? Then let me ask you a favor. The next time you have one of these visions, I want you to ask Him what terrible sin your priest committed when he was in the seminary."

The sin the priest spoke of was something he had done in secret, and no one knew except him and Christ. This sin, this years-old sin, however, was such a great burden of guilt to him that he was unable to freely experience joy or peace and was unable to free himself to live in the present. He wanted forgiveness, but felt he never could be forgiven.

The woman agreed to ask the priest's question in her next time of prayer and went home. When she returned to the church a few days later, the priest said, "Well, did Christ visit you in your dreams?"

"Yes, He did," replied the woman.

"And did you ask Him what sin I committed in the seminary?" he asked rather cynically.

"Yes, I asked Him."

"Well, what did He say?"

Then she quietly responded, "He said, 'I don't remember.' "

The priest's realization that God had forgotten all he had done serves as a reminder to heed the words of the apostle Paul: "Forgive as freely as the Lord has forgiven you" (Colossians 3:13). "Be as ready to forgive others as God for Christ's sake has forgiven you" (Ephesians 4:32).

BEFORE THE SUN GOES DOWN

The Bible admonishes us, "Do not let the sun go down on your wrath."

A college sophomore got into a heated disagreement with her senior roommate one morning over a trivial issue. The underclass student took quite a beating, destroying her pride and arousing her anger. Bitterness and hurt dominated her feelings throughout the day. She ran into her roommate throughout the day and refused to talk to her.

Toward evening, a friend suggested she break the silence and heal the hurt. "Don't you think you should make-up and forgive her before you go to bed?" her friend asked. "Remember, the Bible says not to let the sun go down on your wrath."

Her friend's admonition struck a humorous chord and a smile appeared on the sophomore's face as she quipped, "I don't suppose it is possible to keep the sun from going down."

The collegian's comment was a recognition that the feelings she was holding were not benefiting the relationship and only she was responsible for altering her own attitudes through forgiveness.

Although we are unable to change universal physical laws, we can alter our unforgiving attitudes and make things right before the sun goes down.

BURY THE HATCHET

A mother brought her two arguing children together and demanded they make immediate amends. The siblings hesitantly apologized to each other, and then the younger commented, "I'm apologizing on the outside, Mommy, but I'm still angry inside."

How childish, we might say. Yet, adults tend to go through the motions of forgiveness by covering their real emotions with flippant statements. True forgiveness doesn't bury the hatchet while allowing the handle to remain exposed.

FRIENDSHIP

- Friendship is the inexpressible comfort of feeling safe with a person, having neither to weigh thoughts nor measure words.

  George Eliot

- There is no reason to make the search for friendship sound like an animal instinct. Friendship does not always come as a result of a search; it can come when we least look for it, just as it denies itself when we pursue it too earnestly and with pathetic eagerness.

  Martin E. Marty

- Friendship doesn't make you wealthy, but true friendship will reveal the wealth within you.

  Anonymous

- Be careful the environment you choose for it will shape you; be careful the friends you choose for you will become like them.

  W. Clement Stone

- Friendship is like vitamins; we supplement each other's minimum daily requirements.

  Kathy Mohnke

- By listening, by caring, by playing you back to yourself, friends ratify your better instincts and endorse your unique worth. Friends validate you.

  Gail Sheehy

- No distance of place or lapse of time can lessen the friendship of those who are thoroughly persuaded of each other's worth.

  Robert Southey

- Friends in your life are like pillars on your porch. Sometimes they hold you up, and sometimes they lean on you. Sometimes it's just enough to know they're standing by.

  Anonymous

■ The most beautiful discovery true friends make is that they can grow separately without growing apart.

Elisabeth Foley
Friendship doubles our job and divides our grief.

Anonymous

■ It is important for our friends to believe that we are unreservedly frank with them, and important to friendship that we are not.

Mignon McLaughlin

■ We gain nothing by being with such as ourselves: we encourage each other in mediocrity. I am always longing to be with men more excellent than myself.

Charles Lamb

■ A friendship founded on business is better than a business founded on friendship.

John D. Rockefeller

■ The happiest miser on earth is the man who saves up every friend he can make.

Robert E. Sherwood

■ The making of friends, who are real friends, is the best token we have of a man's success in life.

Edward Everett Hale

■ I always felt that the great high privilege, relief, and comfort of friendship was that one had to explain nothing.

Katherine Mansfield

FUTURE

- Business more than any other occupation is a continual dealing with the future; it is a continual calculation, an instinctive exercise in foresight.

  Henry R. Luce

- Your past is important, but as important as it is, it is not nearly as important to your present as the way you see your future.

  Dr. Tony Campolo

- Tomorrow is the most important thing in life. It comes to us at midnight very clean. It's perfect when it arrives, and it puts itself in our hands and hopes we've learned something from yesterday.

  John Wayne

- Our faith in the present dies out long before our faith in the future.

  Ruth Benedict

- The only way to move into the future is to let go of the past ... and the present.

  Robert Kriegel

- The trouble with our times is that the future is not what it used to be.

  Paul Valery

- Everyone's future is, in reality, an urn full of unknown treasures from which all may draw unguessed prizes.

  Lord Dunsany

- To pierce the curtain of the future, to give shape and visage to mysteries still in the womb of time, is the gift of the imagination. It requires poetic sensibilities with which judges are rarely endowed and which their education does not normally develop.

  Felix Frankfurter

- He who lives in the future lives in a featureless blank; he lives in impersonality; he lives in Nirvana. The past is democratic, because it is a people. The future is despotic, because it is a caprice. Every man is alone in his prediction, just as each man is alone in a dream.

  G. K. Chesterton

■ Hope for the moment. There are times when it is hard to believe in the future, when we are temporarily just not brave enough. When this happens, concentrate on the present. Cultivate *le petit bonheur* [the little happiness] until courage returns. Look forward to the beauty of the next moment, the next hour, the promise of a good meal, sleep, a book, a movie, the likelihood that tonight the stars will shine and tomorrow the sun will shine. Sink roots into the present until the strength grows to think about tomorrow.

Ardis Whitman

■ To understand what is happening today or what will happen in the future, I look back.

Oliver Wendell Holmes

■ The future belongs to people who see possibilities before they become obvious.

Ted Levitt

■ The future belongs to those who believe in the beauty of their dreams.

Eleanor Roosevelt

■ I'm not worried about the quarter, I'm worried about the future.

Laurence A. Tisch

■ The future is a great land; a man cannot go around it in a day; he cannot measure it with a bound; he cannot bind its harvests into a single sheaf. It is wider than vision, and has no end.

Donald G. Mitchell

■ The future is like heaven—everyone exalts it but no one wants to go there now.

James Baldwin

■ The future has several names. For the weak, it is the impossible. For the fainthearted, it is the unknown. For the thoughtful and valiant, it is ideal.

Victor Hugo

■ If you do not think about the future, you cannot have one.

John Galsworthy

■ The future is not a gift—it is an achievement.

Harry Lauder

■   Life is a series of collisions with the future; it is not a sum of what we have been, but what we yearn to be.

Dean Acheson

■   If there is hope in the future, there is power in the present.

John Maxwell

PRESSING FORWARD

Janus, the Roman god of doorways, reminds us of the importance to see the past and look toward the future.

The statues and pictures of Janus portray him as having eyes, nose, and mouth on both the front and back of his head. The rationale for this unique portrayal is to show that a doorway is simultaneously both an entrance and exit. As Janus stands in the doorway—the present—he can look forward and backward at the same time.

The month of January is named for Janus, as it indicates the end of the old year and the beginning of a fresh new year. As with Janus, we too can learn from where we've been while keeping our eyes focused on where we are going.

•   •   •

Paul Dickson encourages us to build on the positive past as we anticipate the future: "May you look back on the past with as much pleasure as you look forward to the future."

What are your memories of the past? If regrets, guilt, and other disabling memories linger, be encouraged that each day is a new day, removed from the past. Although we cannot erase the past, we need not be bound by it.

If, on the other hand, your recollections are fruitful, pleasant and endearing, build on them. The past can be an inspiration for the future. Be thankful for the opportunity to create more memories that will become a part of your memorable past.

At age seventy-five, Jacques Cousteau offered this inspiring perspective: "To yackety-yak about the past is for me time lost. Every morning I wake up saying, 'I'm still alive—a miracle.' And so I keep pushing."

NOT MUCH HOPE

A woman attending a state fair stopped by the tent of a fortune teller. Looking into her crystal ball a frown spread across the fortune teller's face as she predicted, "The next fifteen years of your life will be filled with disappointment, unhappiness, and poverty."

"Then what?" asked the anxious woman.

"You'll grow accustomed to it."

GIVING

- Success in life has nothing to do with what you gain in life or accomplish for yourself. It's what you do for others.

  Danny Thomas

- We all have something to give. So if you know how to read, find someone who can't. If you've got a hammer, find a nail. If you're not hungry, not lonely, not in trouble—seek out someone who is.

  George Bush

- If you haven't any charity in your heart, you have the worst kind of heart trouble.

  Bob Hope

- The measure of life is not its duration, but its donation.

  Peter Marshall

- You have not lived a perfect day, even though you have earned your money, unless you have done something for someone who will never be able to repay you.

  Ruth Smeltzer

- The miracle is this—the more we share, the more we have.

  Leonard Nimoy

- Man discovers his own wealth when God comes to ask gifts of him.

  Rabindranath Tagore

- The greatest pleasure I know is to do a good action by stealth and to have it found out by accident.

  Charles Lamb

- We must not only give what we have; we must also give what we are.

  Cardinal Mercier

- That which you cannot give away, you do not possess. It possesses you.

  Ivern Ball

- A committed giver is an incurably happy person, a secure person, a satisfied person, and a prosperous person.

Eric Butterworth

- Those who have not sown anything during their responsible life will have nothing to reap in the future.

George Gurdjieff

MORE THAN WATER

According to the legend, a desert wanderer happened upon a spring of cool, crystal-clear water. The water was so delightful, he decided to bring the king a sample of it. Barely quenching his own thirst, he filled his leather canteen and began his lengthy journey in the hot desert sun to the palace.

When he finally reached his destination, the water had become stale because of the old leather container in which it had been stored. The king graciously accepted the gift of his faithful subject. He tasted it with an expression of gratitude and delight, and the wanderer went his way with a joyful heart.

After he had gone, others in the king's court tasted the putrid water and asked why the king had pretended to enjoy it. "Ah," responded the king, "it was not the water I tasted, but the spirit in which it was given."

PERSONAL TOUCH

Dr. Charles Dickson tells of a man who stopped at a flower shop to have flowers wired to his mother 200 miles away. As he left, he noticed a little girl sobbing on the curb in front of the shop. When he inquired what was wrong, she explained that she wanted to buy a rose for her mother, but it cost $2.00 and she only had 75¢. He bought the rose for the girl and offered her a ride home. She agreed if he would also take her to her mother. She directed him to a cemetery where she placed the rose on a freshly dug grave. The man returned to the flower shop and cancelled the order. Instead, he got in his car and drove 200 miles to his mother's home to personally deliver a bouquet of local flowers.

As I write this chapter, Mother's Day is one day away. Is it possible that I have often taken the short cut to show my mother and the significant others in my life how much they mean to me? Dr. Dickson's story is a marvelous reminder of Emerson's advice that the most valuable gift we can give is a portion of ourselves.

PURE MOTIVES

Years ago, *The Chaplain* magazine told how the noted preacher Charles Spurgeon and his wife were tabbed as being stingy because they sold all the eggs their chickens laid and wouldn't give any away. Because they always made a profit on their butter, milk, and eggs, rumors circulated that they were greedy.

The Spurgeons, however, endured the criticism graciously, and only after the death of Mrs. Spurgeon was the truth revealed. The records showed that their entire profits had been used to support two needy, elderly widows whose husbands had spent their lives in Christian ministry.

Our giving may not always be understood, but like the Spurgeons, our responsibility is to give as our heart dictates. What appears on the surface has little significance when our motives are pure.

A UNIQUE TWIST

A missionary was sitting in a small corner restaurant reading a letter delivered from home. As she opened the letter, a crisp, new twenty-dollar bill caught her attention. Needless to say, she was pleasantly surprised, but as she read the letter, her eyes were distracted by the movement of a raggedly dressed man on the sidewalk leaning against a light post in front of the building. She couldn't get his peculiar condition and stature off her mind. Thinking that he might have greater financial need than her, she slipped the bill into an envelope on which she quickly penned "persevere." Leaving the restaurant, she nonchalantly dropped the envelope at the stranger's feet.

Turning slowly, he picked it up, read it, watched the woman walk away, and smiled as he tipped his hat and went his way.

The next day walking down the street, she felt a tap on her shoulder. She found the same shabbily dressed man smiling as he handed her a roll of bills. When she asked what they were for, he replied: "That's the money you won, lady."

"Persevere paid five to one."

There is a serious moral to this story: It is impossible to unselfishly give of ourselves without being blessed in return. As Edwin Markham put it, "All that we send into the lives of others comes back into our own."

A SURE-FIRE INVESTMENT

I recently read about a father who, one evening after supper, settled into his easy chair with a stimulating book on investing. Barely into the first chapter, his vivacious and charming three-year-old entered the den. "Daddy," she said with that hard-to-resist tone of voice, "will you read to me?"

He looked at the title of his book which guaranteed lifelong wealth and then at his daughter's *Miss Piggle Wiggle.* "Hop up here, sweetheart. Let's find out what Miss Piggle Wiggle is up to."

Giving means sacrificing our desires to meet the needs of others. This father realized that giving of himself would reap greater dividends than any investment strategy.

GIVING MAKES LIVING WORTHWHILE

Rod Serling's "Twilight Zone" series once featured a story about a gambler who dies and is transported to a room where there is a gambling table and a dealer. Every time he rolls the dice, he scores. Every hand he holds is a winner. The living quarters are plush and supplied with everything he wants. At first, the man believes he is in paradise. He should be happy, but he is completely and totally alone. The fun of sharing his winnings with someone else is missing. He finally concludes that he is not in heaven, as he had first thought. He is in hell.

Albert Einstein believed that "only a life lived for others is worth living." It might also be said that, "only a life lived giving to and sharing with others is worth living."

MAKING DREAMS COME TRUE

It was June 1981. A 67-year-old man stood eyeball to eyeball in front of a graduating class of 61 sixth-grade students in a poverty-stricken Harlem neighborhood. He struggled to maintain the interest and attention of the predominantly African-American and Latino audience. Historically, statistics showed the majority of these students would exit the education system long before they graduated from high school.

"You must dream," he began. "Dream about how things could be . . . what you want your life to be. Don't allow the ghetto to engulf your education and your thinking. Stay in school. Get your high school education, and I will . . ."

I will what? A sense of urgency struck this man who had attended this very school many years earlier. He recalled how graduating from high school at age fourteen, he went to work in a restaurant. One night a man at one of his tables asked, "Why aren't you in college?" The customer was a trustee at Swarthmore College. A meeting was arranged with the Dean of Students and the young man began his college education with a full scholarship. Now a multi-millionaire, what could he say to these children that would make a difference in their lives?

"Get your high school education, and I will . . . I will give you each a college scholarship!" Eugene Lang implanted hope in their lives, and nearly 90 percent of that class went on to graduate from high school. His "I Have a Dream" program has made it possible for kids to make their dreams come true.

LOST CAUSE

Malcolm Kushner relates the story of a man who chaired the charity committee of his local hospital (*The Light Touch: How to Use Humor for Business Success*, Simon & Schuster, 1990). He reviewed all the fundraising records, and he discovered that the richest person in town had never made a donation. So he went to visit him. He said, "Our records show that you're the richest person in town, but you've never contributed to the hospital." And the rich man said, "Do your records also show that my widowed mother was left absolutely destitute? Do they show that my brother is totally disabled? Do they show that my sister was abandoned with four young children?" By now the chairperson felt really ashamed. He said, "Well, no, our records didn't show that." And the rich man said, "Well, I don't do anything for them, so why would I do anything for you?"

Maybe this selfish man could learn from Charles Dickens' *Christmas Carol*. In it, Ebenezer Scrooge was portrayed as a mean, selfish, unhappy old man who was only interested in making money and serving his own needs. As the story progresses, Scrooge begins to realize his shortcomings and a transformation ensues. He begins to laugh and play, share, and help. His skinflint personality gives way to happiness and generosity, and he is liberated from a life of self-centeredness.

GOALS

- The primary purpose of goal-setting is to pull change in the direction you have chosen—one which fits your expertise and overall plan.

  Jim Tunney

- While we are here we should set goals and achieve them, make the best of things, make others feel good about themselves, and be happy with what we are and what we are doing.

  Janet Evans

- Happiness, wealth, and success are by-products of goal-setting; they cannot be the goal themselves.

  John Condry

- Goals give you the specific direction to take to make your dreams come true.

  Bob Conklin

- Goal setting is a logical fulfilling approach to dynamic living.

  Peter Daniels

- One reason we don't attain our goals is that we often focus on how far away we are from feeling satisfaction rather than how far we've come.

  Fred Pryor

- The future does not get better by hope, it gets better by plan. And to plan for the future we need goals.

  Jim Rohn

- Don't concern yourself with how you're going to achieve your goals. Leave that to a power greater than yourself. All you need to know is where you are going and the answers will come to you.

  Dorothea Brandt

- At this very moment you are WHO you are and WHERE you are because of what you've allowed to inhabit your goal-box.

  Richard Gaylord Briley

- Goals can give you power in your life. A person or an organization without a goal is powerless.

  Lewis Timberlake
  Timberlake Monthly

- Winners make goals; losers make excuses!

  Anonymous

- Losers always concentrate on activities, but high achievers concentrate on planning and making every moment count in their efforts to reach progressively higher intermediate goals.

  John R. Noe

- It must be born in mind that the tragedy of life doesn't lie in not reaching your goal. The tragedy lies in having no goal to reach. It isn't a calamity to die with dreams unfulfilled, but it is a calamity to not dream. It is not a disgrace not to reach the stars, but it is a disgrace to have no stars to reach for. Not failure, but low aim is sin.

  Helmut Schmidt

SPECTATOR OR PARTICIPANT?

In *Do Right With Lou Holtz*, coach Holtz proclaims, "I'm a firm believer in goals. Take a good look at me. You'll notice I stand five feet ten, weigh 152 pounds, wear glasses, speak with a lisp, have a physique that appears like I've been afflicted with beriberi or scurvy most of my life. The only reasons why I can stand up as head football coach at the University of Notre Dame are: I have a great wife and I am very goal oriented."

Being chosen to coach the Notre Dame football team was one of the 107 lifetime ambitions Holtz listed on a piece of paper in 1966. Unemployed at the time, Holtz dreamed of dinner at the White House, an appearance on the "Tonight Show," jumping out of a plane, and other aspirations befitting this over-achiever.

"Don't be a spectator," Holtz exhorts, "don't let life pass you by."

Chuck Givens would agree. As a kid, he wrote down 181 goals he wanted to achieve in his life. First on his list was writing a song that would hit the top of the Nashville charts. At age twenty-two, his hit song "Hang on Sloopy" earned him enough to start a recording studio. A few weeks later it burned to the ground, yet Givens believed if he could do it once, he could do it again. To date Givens has achieved 160 of his 181 goals, and I doubt he is finished.

How many goals have you set? How powerful are your plans and desires to achieve them? What price are you willing to pay to make them come true?

Your answers will determine whether you want to be a spectator or an active participant in the game of life.

THE SECRET TO SCORING

An unknown author said, "The purpose of goals is to focus our attention. The mind will not reach toward achievement until it has clear objectives. The magic begins when we set goals. It is then that the switch is turned on, the current begins to flow, and the power to accomplish becomes reality."

Wayne Gretzky experienced the power and magic of goals. At age 17, he was an outstanding athlete intent on pursuing a career in either soccer or hockey. His first love was hockey, but when he tried out for the pros, he was told, "You don't weigh enough. At 172 pounds, you are over fifty pounds lighter than the average player. You won't be able to survive on the rink."

An old Greek proverb says, "Before you can score, you must have a goal." And Wayne knew how to score. "I go where the hockey puck is going," he said. He made liars of those who doubted his abilities by becoming hockey's all-time leading scorer. Gretzky had a goal undaunted by the naysayers.

Today, Wayne Gretzky enjoys a multimillion-dollar hockey contract and endorsements producing equal wealth. He is living proof that it is not as important to know where the puck is as it is to know where it is going.

SET YOUR COURSE

Imagine a pilot coming over the intercom and announcing: "I have some good news and some bad news. The bad news is we have lost one engine and our direction finder. The good news is we have a tail wind and wherever we are going we are getting there at a rate of 600 miles an hour."

I don't know about you, but I would be a little disconcerted by the news. Yet, people often fly along like this plane—directionless, lacking energy, but being pushed swiftly along by the winds of circumstances.

David Mahoney advises, "The important thing is not where you were or where you are, but where you want to get."

Where do you want to get? What do you most want to accomplish? What do you want your professional life to be like in three years? How about your personal life? Set your course and apply all power available to you.

WHERE AM I GOING?

The life and words of Justice Oliver Wendell Holmes have provided us with unlimited wisdom and encouragement. One amusing account is especially applicable to our discussion of goals.

While traveling on a train, Holmes had misplaced his ticket. Watching him fumble through his belongings and pockets in growing frustration, the conductor tried to ease his mind. "Don't worry about it, Mr. Holmes. I'm sure you have your ticket somewhere. If you don't find it during the trip, just mail it in to the railroad when you reach your destination."

Appreciative of the conductor's empathy, yet dismayed by his predicament, he looked the conductor in the eye and responded: "Young man, my problem is not finding my ticket. It's to find out where in the world I'm going."

STRAIGHT AHEAD AND STEADY

When I was a teenager, a local farmer hired me to help him complete fall plowing. My first day on the tractor was disastrous. As I watched the plow turn the soil behind me little did I realize that by the time I reached the end of the field, the row was noticeably crooked. Toward the end of the day the farmer arrived to survey my work. The crooked rows prompted him to give this advice: "You can't plow a straight row if you continuously look back. You must keep your eyes focused straight ahead."

So it is with life. Plowing our way into the future is powered by meaningful and specific goals. Focusing on the past, what lies behind, will prevent us from effectively pursuing our future. Goals provide the direction for us to focus our energies on what lies ahead.

THERE'S POWER IN GOALS

I know of a young man who, despite his weight problem, became a successful model and actor. You may remember him as one of the first men to wear the grapes in the Fruit of the Loom commercials.

But, even though he was successful, he didn't feel good about himself. Finding the following note on his car one day inspired him to do something about his problem: "Fat people die young. Please don't die.—An Admirer."

This young man went on a crash diet and lost nearly 110 pounds within three months. The dramatic weight loss wrecked his body and resulted in his hospitalization.

After this devastating experience, he decided to start all over and learn how to lose weight safely through good nutrition and proper exercise. After he learned this, he wanted to share his knowledge with others like himself who were troubled by obesity.

He was so enthusiastic about his newfound knowledge and about helping others that people became immediately attracted to him. He eventually made weight-loss education his business—and enthusiasm his partner!

Today, Richard Simmons is recognized all over America for his weight-loss crusade and has become a wealthy and famous man. But he couldn't have done it without his enthusiasm and the ability to set goals.

GROWTH

- We cannot become what we need to be by remaining what we are.

  Max De Pree

- You are the same today that you are going to be five years from now except for two things: the people with whom you associate and the books you read.

  Charles "Tremendous" Jones

- What you become is far more important that what you get. What you get will be influenced by what you become.

  Jim Rohn

- The business of expanding your consciousness is not an option. Either you are expandable or you are expendable.

  Robert Schuller

- Unless you try to do something beyond what you have already mastered, you will never grow.

  Ronald E. Osborn

- If you don't have the power to change yourself, then nothing will change around you.

  Anwar Sadat

- All growth is a leap in the dark, a spontaneous unpremeditated act without benefit of experience.

  Henry Miller

- If we don't change, we don't grow. If we don't grow, we are not really living. Growth demands a temporary surrender of security.

  Gail Sheehy

- I worry that our lives are like soap operas. We can go for months and not tune in to them, then six months later we look in and the same stuff is still going on.

  Jane Wagner

EXPAND YOUR WORLD

A favorite fish of many hobbyists is the Japanese carp, commonly known as the koi. The fascinating thing about the koi is that if you keep it in a small fish bowl, it will only grow to be two or three inches long. Place the koi in a larger tank or small pond and it will reach six to ten inches. Put it in a large pond and it may get as long as a foot and a half. However, when placed in a huge lake where it can really stretch out, it has the potential to reach sizes up to three feet.

You've probably already figured out the simple point to this illustration. The size of the fish is in direct relation to the size of the pond.

A comparable analogy can be made concerning people. Our growth is determined by the size of our world. Of course, it is not the world's measurable dimensions that are important, but the mental, emotional, spiritual, and physical opportunities we expose ourselves to.

Realizing that growth comes from the inside and not the outside, we come to the realization that unless we expand who we are, we'll always have what we've got.

•   •   •

Many people get in the habit of saying no to new experiences, preferring to be locked into a comfort zone that restricts their growth. Life becomes habitual rather than experiential.

John Stuart Mill said, "The perpetual obstacle to human advancement is custom." To the degree we're living our lives based on "that's the way I've always done it," our comfort zone has more control of us than we have of ourselves.

Existing in a world governed by habit leads to mediocrity and dullness. If we refrain from pushing out the walls of our comfortableness, they will contract to restrict any fresh ideas, exciting opportunities, or possibilities from entering.

Life is a smorgasbord, a variety of tasty, delicious choices. People locked into a comfort-zone approach pass over any entries that may be foreign to them. Their selection is based on familiarity. As a result, many delicious choices are passed over.

•   •   •

What you become is far more important than what you are. Why? Because the only way life gets better is when you do. Develop an appetite for the unique and unusual. When you choose ideas, thoughts, information, activities, suggestions, and insights not in your usual repertoire, life becomes more than repeating one day after another.

I am reminded of the woman who heard about an opening in her organization that would mean a promotion for her. She made application, but someone who had been with the organization far less time than she was hired instead. She went to the director of personnel and asked why. The director responded, "I'm sorry, but you haven't had twenty-two years of experience as your application states; you've had only one year's experience twenty-two times."

This unfortunate situation occurs far too often. The woman has never improved, grown, or extended beyond her initial value to the organization. "The business of expanding your consciousness is not an option," writes Robert Schuller. "Either you are expandable or you are expendable."

Do you desire a promotion in life? How many times in the last month have you felt trapped? Are there opportunities you have passed over because you felt inadequate? Have you found yourself admiring or even envying others' good fortune?

• • •

Harry Truman said, "Life is iffy." We enjoy life more *if* we expose ourselves to the unfamiliar. We become more valuable *if* we are growing and stretching. Work will be more fulfilling and satisfying *if* we decide to be our best. The *ifs* are endless.

Are you looking for an above-average job, salary, or life? These honorable desires are not things you pursue; they are part of what you develop and become. Become an above-average person.

One of the best ways to become an above-average person is by following Mark Twain's advice: "Do something every day that you don't want to do." Ouch! That sharp arrow definitely pierces our comfort zone. Keep in mind that winners are people who are willing to do the things losers refuse to do—even when they don't want to.

Zig Ziglar recommends: "Go as far as you can see and when you get there, you will always be able to see farther." You see, growth is exciting! As we expand our comfort zone, additional opportunities appear. These new things expand us more and the growth process continues.

Although you may be tempted to stop or coast, don't do it. The comfort zone will contract once again. Work through discomforts, adversity, and temptations. You will become stronger. The key is undying commitment to exceed yourself.

• • •

The Swiss philosopher Henri Frederic Amiel reminds us, "He who is silent is forgotten; he who does not advance falls back; he who stops is overwhelmed, out distanced, crushed; he who ceases to grow becomes smaller; he who leaves off, gives up; the condition of standing still is the beginning of the end."

So what can we do? Listen to Charles Garfield, author of *Peak Performers* (Avon Books, 1986): "Searching for the peak performer within yourself has one basic meaning: You recognize yourself as a person who was born not as a peak performer but as a learner. With the capacity to grow, change, and reach for the highest possibilities of human nature, you regard yourself as a person in process. Not perfect, but a person who keeps asking: What more can I be? What else can I achieve that will benefit me and my company? That will contribute to my family and my community?"

Why doesn't everyone want to grow? I don't have an answer to that, but here are a few suggestions for those ready to see, give, share, grow, experience, and enjoy new heights.

1. Eliminate all self-imposed limitations. Growth inhibitors such as procrastination, excuses, apathy, blame, and closed-mindedness need to be addressed and overcome. If you are excited about where you are going, you won't want anything to derail your efforts.

2. Evaluate life patterns and habits that restrict your desire to break through mediocrity. Habits are a primary determinant of what we become.

3. Answer the question: What can I begin doing today that would make a difference in my life? Start with all the small things you can do to expand yourself and the quality of your life. Build on them.

Remember the words of J. C. Penney: "No one need live a minute longer as he is, because the creator endowed us with the ability to change ourselves." Healthy, growing, fulfilled people continually strive to expand their social, mental, spiritual, and physical capacities.

ONE EGG AT A TIME

Aesop possessed the uncanny ability to communicate powerful life messages through his fables. The simplicity, elegance, and neatness of his literary genius are matched only by the instructive and challenging points.

Take, for example, the fable about the goose and the golden egg. It is the story of a poor farmer who one day visits the nest of the goose and finds at her side a glittering yellow egg. Convinced this must be a trick, he is about to throw it away but on second thought, takes it home—where he discovers to his delight that the egg is pure gold. The farmer becomes fabulously rich by daily gathering one golden egg from the nest of his special goose. As he grows rich, he becomes greedy and impatient. Hoping to secure all the gold at once, he kills the goose and opens her, only to find nothing.

Nice story but irrelevant to us, right? Wrong. Growth is a daily grind composed of successes, failures, lost opportunities, progress, and change. Thinking it can be attained in one fell swoop is deceptive and results in losing a fortune of daily activities that comprise the process of growth.

BREAKING BARRIERS

Scientists said it couldn't be done. Chuck Yeager had different plans. On October 14, 1947, he took a flight that broke the sound barrier and its "invisible brick wall." The doom and gloom experts, who predicted that both the pilot and aircraft could not endure such speeds without damage, were mystified. Yeager attained an air speed of 700 miles per hour in his Bell Aviation X-1 plane, and three weeks later, accelerated to an incredible 1,612 miles per hour. So much for the impenetrable barrier.

In his autobiography, Yeager reflects, "After all the anxiety, after all the anticipation, breaking the sound barrier was really a let-down. The sonic barrier, the unknown, was just a poke through jello, a perfectly paved speedway."

The historical, myth-destroying event turned out to be a walk in the park. All the hoopla surrounding breaking down flight barriers existed only in people's minds. Yeager continued, "Later, I realized that this mission had to end in a let-down because the real barrier wasn't in the sky but in our knowledge and experience of supersonic flight."

What so-called "invisible brick walls" are stunting your ability to grow? Beware: The "human barriers" contrived in your mind produce impenetrable personal limitations.

REVIVING YOUR LUSTER

Stanley Marcus emulated innovative leadership as he built the retail giant Neiman-Marcus Department Store. It became known as an international symbol of taste and excellence. Not only was he a retailing genius, he also possessed the ability to inspire growth in others and was committed to the same for himself. The flavor of his inspiration is evident in a favorite story he shared with his employees. Marcus says:

> One of the most popular of my 'sermons' dealt with my comparison of human beings to brass. I cited a visit to the bridge of a naval vessel where the brass gleamed like gold. I asked the captain how often they had to shine the brass.
>
> He replied, "Every day. The minute you stop polishing it, it starts to tarnish."
>
> I correlated this incident to human beings, saying, 'None of us is made of gold, we're made of brass, but we can look like gold if we work hard at polishing ourselves as the sailor polishing the brass on the ship. We humans can be better than we really are if we will make the effort.'
>
> That sounds trite, but it must have made an impression on many hundreds of people, for almost every week some member of our staff came up to me and said, "I'm sure polishing my brass today."

Apathy, routine, repetition, lack of challenge and on and on are life tarnishers. The luster can be returned by putting forth the shining effort that gives your talents, qualities, and dreams their intended gleam and sparkle. Keep in mind the advice of the ship's captain: "Keep polishing, for the minute you stop, the brass starts to tarnish."

A PRIMER ON GROWTH

The poet Robert Browning said, "My business is not to remake myself, but to make the absolute best of what God made."

How? First, consider the advice of Mark Twain, who said, "Take your mind out every now and then and dance on it. It is getting all caked up." Twain knew people had a tendency to get in a rut by settling into a set way of thinking and performing.

Consider the frog hopping about one day when he happened to slip into a large pothole along a country road. All his attempts at jumping out fell short. Soon a dog came upon the frog trapped in the hole and offered to pull him out. He, too, failed. After various country animals made gallant attempts to help the poor frog, they finally gave up. "We'll go back and get you some food," they said. "It looks like you're going to be there a while." However, not long after they took off to get food, the frog hopped past them. They couldn't believe it! "We thought you couldn't get out!" they hollered out. "Oh, I couldn't," replied the frog, "but you see, there was a big tractor coming right at me, and I had to."

It is when we have to get out of the potholes and ruts of life that we make changes. As long as we are settled and comfortable, growth is doubtful. Dance on your brain!

•   •   •

Next, expand your mind. Successful, growing people know the value of reading books. A recent Gallup Poll showed that high-income people read an average of nineteen books a year.

An old epigram says, "The person who can read and doesn't has no advantage over the person who can't read." Reading is not a leisure luxury but a life-enhancing necessity.

Henry David Thoreau encouraged expanding our world through reading when he said, "How many a person has dated a new era in their life from the reading of a book? The book exists for us, perchance, which will explain our miracles and reveal new ones. The at-present unutterable things we may find somewhere uttered. These same questions that disturb and puzzle and confound us have in their turn occurred to all the wise men; not one has been omitted; and each has answered them according to his ability, by his word, and his life."

Before getting too excited about just reading books, consider the admonition of F. W. Robertson. "It is not the number of books you read, nor the variety of sermons you hear, but it is the frequency and earnestness with which you meditate on these things till the truth in them becomes your own and part of your being, that insures your growth."

•   •   •

The third principle in our panacea is stretch, improve, transform. Nothing was so feared by seafarers in the days when ocean vessels were driven by wind and sail as the doldrums. The doldrums existed in the part of the ocean near the equator, where calms, squalls, and light breezes stifled the sailor. The old sailing vessels caught in the doldrums would be helpless for days and weeks, waiting for the wind to blow.

Human doldrums produce the same immovable results. However, an internal prevailing wind gives people an edge. We can move forward, thereby allowing us to stretch and improve. Breaking through the stagnating doldrums requires a commitment to become better tomorrow by beginning today. Stretch yourself each day to accomplish more than the day before.

·   ·   ·

It has been said, the largest room in the world is the room for improvement. Improvement is possible when self-imposed limitations are destroyed. Fleas can be trained by placing them in a shoe box with a lid on it. Fleas jump, so they hit the lid over and over again until Excedrin Headache 347 occurs. The fleas will continue to jump, but they no longer jump high enough to hit the lid. Now, it has been shown that you can take the lid off and the fleas won't jump out of the box. They can't. The fleas have conditioned themselves to jump a little lower.

Fleas, and of course humans, are capable of jumping higher by transforming their old limitations. A few years ago, Transformer™ toys made their debut in time for holiday shopping. These fascinating toys could be changed from a truck to a robot and back to a truck again. A few strategic moves transformed the toys from one object into another. Toymakers smiled all the way to the bank as consumers were intrigued with purchasing two toys for the price of one.

Another form of transformation is possible with a simple bar of iron. In its rough form, the bar is worth approximately $5.00. Create horseshoes from that bar of iron and it is now valued around $50.00, or if you made it into needles, the value would be $5,000. But take that bar of iron and transform it into springs for a Swiss watch, the ultimate value could reach half a million dollars.

The raw material remains the same. However, what is important is how that material is formed and developed.

Whether transforming toys, a bar of iron, or human beings, the message is the same. Value increases as stretching, growing, and transformation take place.

Caution: Refrain from becoming like the head hunter who bought himself a new boomerang and then spent the rest of his life trying to throw the old one away. Transformation and growth is a "metamorphosis" to a new way of doing things. Growth is not so much a matter of throwing away the old as it is capitalizing on a more effective lifestyle.

FROM WEAKLING TO WINNER

At 97 pounds dripping wet, he was a sickly and skinny high schooler. He was picked on, laughed at, and ostracized. Thick glasses, arch supports, and a shoulder brace further complicated his self-concept and acceptance by others. The constant rejection and his own self-deprecating lifestyle prompted him to drop out of high school.

His life became directionless and empty. Then one day, his life took a right turn. He attended a health lecture and made a decision that his future would not be a repeat of the past. He junked his junk food diet, began exercising two hours a day, and gradually changed his physical appearance, self-image, and attitude about life. This one-time frail, self-conscious teenager opened his own health club in California. His passion for improving one's status led him door to door, promoting and selling his new exercise business. He was committed to changing the lifestyles of people in Oakland, California, and beyond.

Jack LaLanne has been an exercise evangelist and practitioner for five decades. National and international recognition followed his devotion to personal growth. To much of the world, Jack LaLanne is known as "Mr. Exercise." He would be the first to tell you that personal success is directly attributable to one's conscious decision not to let the future be a repeat of the past.

IMPRISONED OR FREE?

Papillon was condemned to life imprisonment on Devil's Island. His meaningless existence was further frustrated by a recurring nightmare. Repeatedly, he would see himself standing before a harsh tribunal.

"You are charged," the leader would shout, "with a wasted life. How do you plead?"

"Guilty," was the only right answer. "I must plead guilty."

The prisoner Papillon knew the meaning of wasted life. Yet, many people have created their own self-imposed prisons. Failure to capitalize on our freedoms leaves us wasted and unfulfilled. So, prisoner or free, the decision to grow is ours.

CHOOSE A DOOR

Bob Conklin, co-founder of Personal Dynamics and chair of the board for the Conklin Company, is a prolific writer and motivational speaker. He tells a silly yet profound story about a fellow in New York whose life was bungling along rather miserably and so decided to consult a psychiatrist to help him change. He selected an address on Park Avenue and entered the doctor's reception room, tastefully appointed but without a receptionist. There were two doors, one marked "Men" and the other, "Women."

He went through the door for "Men" and came upon two other doors, one marked "Extrovert" and the other marked "Introvert." Knowing he was an introvert, he opened that door and found himself in a room with two more doors. One read "Those Making at Least $20,000" and the other, "Those Making Less than $20,000."

He knew he made less than that sum so he entered that door—and found himself back on Park Avenue!

The man learned a valuable lesson about the habitual barriers to change and growth that, for most people, are more painful to learn. Habitual actions, limiting self-talk, and thinking others are responsible for us lead to a dead end or worse yet, the realization we will be what we've always been.

This story is a valuable reminder that we are accountable for our own lives. We are responsible for what we are, where we are going, and what we become. Happiness, success, peace, well-being, and growth result from our own choices and decisions, not others'. So, choose your door wisely.

•   •   •

In an even sadder scenario, there are people who can make choices that affect their destiny, but limit their own growth. You never learn how to grow. You can only learn how to learn how to grow. Think about that.

You will never learn all there is to know about personal growth. So you acquire a curious lifestyle that keeps you sharp and aware of all that is available to you. Move ahead and maintain an open mind that draws in nourishment from the world around you and the experiences you encounter.

Unfortunately, people who remain isolated and do not expose themselves to nurturing opportunities, don't realize what they are missing. Nineteenth-century inventor John Ericson came to that realization. Although he had a childhood buddy who became a world-renowned violinist, Ericson never went to a concert, believing music was a waste of time. His friend, Ole Bull, entered Ericson's shop one day with violin in hand. He began playing even when Ericson initially objected. Soon Ericson noticed his workers dropping their tools to listen and he too became enthralled. When Ole quit playing, his lifelong friend quickly encouraged, "Don't stop now! Go on! I never knew until now what I've been missing in my life!"

What have you been missing? Try different techniques. Avoid self-limiting attitudes. Expose yourself to new learning situations. Get to know the people around you a little better. Risk failure. Encourage your growth potential and soak up nature's nourishment.

HAPPINESS

- Most people ask for happiness on condition. Happiness can be felt only if you don't set any conditions.

Arthur Rubinstein

- Happiness is a conscious choice, not an automatic response.

Mildred Barthel

- Happiness cannot be traveled to, owned, earned, worn, or consumed. Happiness is the spiritual experience of living every minute with love, grace, and gratitude.

Denis Waitley

- A happy person is not a person in a certain set of circumstances, but rather a person with a certain set of attitudes.

Hugh Downs

- Happiness is an inside job.

Wally "Famous" Amos

- Those only are happy who have their minds on some object other than their own happiness . . . on the happiness of others . . . on the improvement of mankind . . . even on some art or pursuit, followed not as a means, but as itself an "ideal end."

Greta Palmer

- Monday is a day designed to add depression to an otherwise happy week.

Jim Davis's Garfield the Cat

- There are eight requisites for contented living: health enough to make work a pleasure; wealth enough to support your needs; strength to battle with difficulties and overcome them; grace enough to confess your sins and forsake them; patience enough to toil until some good is accomplished; charity enough to see some good in your neighbor; faith enough to make real the things of God; hope enough to remove all anxious fear concerning the future.

Johann Wolfgang von Goethe

188

■ Happiness is looking at all the good and bad in any given moment—both within us and around us—and then choosing to focus upon the good.

> *John Rogers and Peter McWilliams*
> Wealth Is Happiness

■ The best advice on the art of being happy is about as easy to follow as advice to be well when one is sick.

> *Madame Swetchine*

■ We look for happiness in possession of the external—in money, a good time, somebody to lean on, and so on. We are impatient, hurried, and fretful because we do not find happiness where we look for it.

> *John Dewey*

■ Happiness depends upon ourselves.

> *Aristotle*

■ The man who makes everything that leads to happiness depend on himself, and not upon other men, has adopted the very best plan for living happily.

> *Plato*

■ Happiness is in the taste, and not in the things.

> *La Rochefoucauld*

■ The happiness of your life depends on the quality of your thoughts.

> *Marcus Aurelius Antoninus*

■ The Constitution of America only guarantees pursuit of happiness—you have to catch up with it yourself. Fortunately, happiness is something that depends not on position but on disposition, and life is what you make it.

> *Gill Robb Wilson*

■ Happiness lies in good health and a bad memory.

> *Ingrid Bergman*

■ Unhappiness is in not knowing what we want and killing ourselves to get it.

> *Don Herold*

■ The secret of happiness is not discovered in the absence of trials, but in the midst of them.

Ted Nace

■ To experience happiness, we must train ourselves to live in this moment, to savor it for what it is, not running ahead in anticipation of some future date nor lagging behind in the paralysis of the past.

Luci Swindoll

■ Happiness is not created by what happens to us, but by our attitudes toward each happening.

Walter Heily

■ May we never let the things we can't have, or don't have, or shouldn't have, spoil our enjoyment of the things we do have and can have. As we value our happiness, let us not forget it, for one of the greatest lessons in life is learning to be happy without the things we cannot or should not have.

Richard L. Evans

■ Success is getting what you want; happiness is wanting what you get.

Charles F. Kettering

■ Nothing gives such complete and profound happiness as the perpetually fresh wonder and mystery of exciting life.

Norman Vincent Peale

PURSUIT OF HAPPINESS

Benjamin Franklin was concluding a moving speech on the guarantees of the Constitution when a heckler shouted out, "Aw, those words don't mean anything. Where's all the happiness you say it guarantees us?" Franklin smiled and calmly silenced his critic. "My friend, the Constitution only guarantees the American people the right to pursue happiness; you have to catch it yourself."

SEARCHING FOR HAPPINESS

"A man travels the world over in search of what he needs and returns home to find it," observed George Moore.

Count Maurice Maeterlinck's *The Bluebird* illustrates this point. A woodcutter's boy and girl, Tyltyl and Mytyl, keep a blackbird in a cage in their home. What they want, however, is the bluebird of happiness. The two siblings set out from their modest hut in search of the desired bluebird. The twosome wander through many lands but return home disappointed and discouraged. Then, to their dismay, the blackbird they had lent to an ill child next door had turned into a bluebird. The fabulous bluebird of happiness was theirs all the time.

Happiness is not a possession we search for. Rather, it is a blessing present in everything we experience. The moral is to quit searching for happiness but start realizing and enjoying happiness where you are.

WEALTH IN HAPPINESS

Hetty Green never made the headlines to applaud her achievements. During her lifetime, however, she was the richest woman in the world. Green reportedly maintained a balance of $31 million in one bank and upon her death left an estate of $95 million. The desire for wealth consumed her, yet her lifestyle earned her a listing in the *Guinness Book of World Records* as "the greatest miser"—and one of the meanest.

Her miserly lifestyle included living on cold oatmeal so she wouldn't have to pay for the heat. Her son was forced to have his leg amputated because she refused to pay for an operation to save it. The cause of her death in 1916 was a convulsion prompted by an argument about the virtues of skim milk.

Hetty Green was rich but lived an impoverished life. Although she lived, there was no life in her living.

One day a newspaper reporter found himself in the presence of the fabulously wealthy J. Paul Getty. In his best interviewer's voice he asked, "Mr. Getty, what is it that money cannot buy?"

Getty pondered the reporter's question then responded, "I don't think it can buy health, and I don't think it can buy a good time. Some of the best times I have ever had didn't cost any money."

Jay Gould, the American millionaire, had plenty of money. As he was dying, Gould lamented, "I suppose I am the most miserable man on earth."

There is no happiness in wealth, but there is countless wealth in the experience of happiness.

CHANGE OF HEART

An Indian fable acquaints us with a mouse who, like all mice, was afraid of cats. A local wizard empathized with him and offered to help the mouse dispel his fear. So with the mouse's blessing, the wizard turned him into a cat. The cat, however, was afraid of dogs. So the wizard did his thing and turned the cat into a dog. Afraid of tigers, the dog was soon turned into a tiger. The wizard discovered the tiger was afraid of big game hunters and exclaimed in disgust, "You're hopeless! What you need is a change of heart. And that I cannot give you."

What marvelous insight for humankind. If we want to be happy, a change of heart is required.

Football announcer Don Meredith says, "If 'ifs' and 'buts' were candy and nuts, we'd all have a Merry Christmas." We can contrive a myriad of "ifs" and "buts" for not being happy. But if we wait around for our fears to vanish and our dreams to come true before we can be happy, then our fate will be comparable to the mouse's.

THE SECRET OF THE TOUCHSTONE

Raimundo de Ovies tells a story that, when the great library of Alexandria was burned, one book was saved. But it was not a valuable book, and so a poor man, who could read a little, bought it for a few coppers. It was not very interesting; yet there was a most interesting thing in it! It was a thin strip of vellum on which was written the secret of the "touchstone."

As J. Martin Kohe tells it in *Your Greatest Power*, the touchstone was a small pebble that could turn any common metal into pure gold. The writing explained that it was on the shores of the Black Sea, lying among thousands and thousands of other pebbles which looked exactly like it. But the secret was this: The real touchstone would feel warm, while ordinary pebbles are cold. So the man sold his few belongings, bought some simple supplies, camped on the seashore, and began testing pebbles. This was his plan.

He knew that if he picked up ordinary pebbles and threw them down again because they were cold he might pick up the same pebble hundreds of times. So, when he felt one that was cold, he threw it into the sea. He spent a whole day doing this and there were none of them the touchstone. Then he spent a week, a month, a year, three years; but he did not find the touchstone. Yet he went on and on and on this way.

One morning he picked up a pebble and it was warm . . . and he threw it into the sea. He had formed the habit of throwing pebbles into the sea. He had gotten so into the habit of throwing them into the sea, that when the one he wanted came along, he still threw it away.

Such is the pursuit of happiness. Searching for that one magic pebble, people expend countless energy and effort. The search is desperate and habitual and even when the supposed happiness-producing experience is realized, it too is cast aside.

Happiness is enjoying each pebble-like life experience because we've decided to focus on the good in all of life's moments.

HONESTY

- Truth has no special time of its own. Its hour is now—always.

  Albert Schweitzer

- They say honesty pays, but it doesn't seem to pay enough to suit most people.

  Anonymous

- Honesty means integrity in everything. Honesty means wholeness, completeness; it means truth in everything—in deed and in word.

  Orison Swett Marden

- The truth is incontrovertible, malice may attack it, ignorance may deride it, but in the end; there it is.

  Winston Churchill

- When regard for truth has been broken down or even slightly weakened, all things will remain doubtful.

  Saint Augustine

- Truth is tough. It will not break, like a bubble, at a touch. Nay, you may kick it about all day, and it will be round and full at evening.

  Oliver Wendell Holmes

- Some of the finest cheating in the world has been done under the guise of honesty.

  Henry H. Crane

- Those who exaggerate in their statements belittle themselves.

  C. Simmons

- Real integrity stays in place whether the test is adversity or prosperity.

  Charles Swindoll

- Integrity is the glue that holds our way of life together.

  Billy Graham

HONESTY IS FOR WINNERS

Before humankind lie two paths—honesty or dishonesty. The ignorant embark on the dishonest path; the wise on honest. Thomas Jefferson believed, "Honesty is the first chapter in the book of wisdom." Yet, we are in danger of disregarding the "honesty is the best policy" philosophy.

A recent *USA Today* poll found that only 56 percent of Americans teach honesty to their children. In addition, a Louis Harris poll turned up the regrettable fact that 65 percent of high school students would cheat on an important exam.

Could it be we are becoming a nation content with taking the ignorant path? There is substantial reason for us to revitalize the importance of honesty.

For instance, in 1982, the Forum Corporation of Boston, Massachusetts studied 341 salespeople from eleven different companies in five different industries. The purpose of their study was to determine what accounted for the difference between the top producers and average producers.

Guess what? When the study was finished, it was not skill, knowledge, or charisma that separated the best from the average. Forum Corporation found the difference was attributable to honesty. When customers can trust their salesperson, they will buy from them.

Before we throw the value of honesty out the window, maybe it is time to reevaluate why it has been so important to those before us.

"Old Blood and Guts" General George Patton was misunderstood, criticized— and beloved. No one can deny the fact he knew how to build a winning army. Soldiers who fought alongside Patton knew this legendary warrior was a man of truth and therefore they trusted him. Porter B. Williamson, an officer on Patton's staff, said Patton, "spoke the truth with such a forceful attitude whether it was pleasant information or not. His constant command to the staff was, 'Get the facts, get the truth and get it to the troops.'"

Patton's team was a winner. Honesty still produces winners and sets them apart from all of the rest—and it always will.

MARK TWAIN SPINOFF

"I am different from Washington," declared Mark Twain. "I have a higher, grander standard of principle. Washington could not lie. I can lie, but I won't."

Twain's comment makes me think of a few people confronted with the temptation to lie. After fishing for crappie all day and not getting so much as a nibble, the fisher went back to shore, loaded up his boat and began the drive home. Before reaching home, he stopped at a grocery store advertising fresh fish.

"Throw me a dozen of the biggest fish you have," he said to the woman at the counter.

"Throw them? Why?"

"Because I'm going to catch them. I may be a lousy fisher, but I'm not a liar."

I'll bet that guy can tell some creative fish stories.

·   ·   ·

Here's another classic story told to me by an attorney friend who represented a man arrested for robbery.

"You are sure," queried the lawyer of his client, "that you have told me all the truth? If I am to successfully defend you, I need to know the whole truth."

"Yah, you know it all," the man responded.

"Good. I am confident we can get your case dismissed on lack of evidence. Now, one more time, have you given me all of the facts?"

"Hey man, I've told you everything . . . except where the money is hidden."

Whoops!

·   ·   ·

And then there is the lady who mailed a check to the Internal Revenue Service for $300. Enclosed with the check was this note: "I cheated on my income tax last year and have not been able to sleep since. This check covers half of what I owe. If I continue to have trouble sleeping, I will send you the other half."

Would you call this a half-truth?

Mark Twain was right. We all can lie but it is those committed to the truth who maintain their integrity.

NO RECALL NEEDED

A newspaper reporter once asked Sam Rayburn, "Mr. Speaker, you see probably a hundred people a day. You tell each one 'Yes' or 'No' or 'Maybe.' You are never seen taking notes on what you told them, but I have never heard of you forgetting anything you have promised them. What is your secret?"

Rayburn carefully eyed his questioner and replied, "If you tell the truth the first time," he replied, "you don't have to remember."

GOLFERS' DILEMMA

"Mary, why don't you play golf with Jane anymore?" asked a friend.

"Would you play golf with someone who kicked the ball with her foot when you weren't watching?" Mary asked.

"I guess not," admitted the friend.

"Would you want to play with someone who lied about their score?" Mary continued.

"No, I sure wouldn't," the friend agreed.

"Neither did Jane," replied Mary.

HUMILITY

- Those who travel the high road of humility are not troubled by heavy traffic.

  Senator Alan K. Simpson

- Awareness of both your limitations and your potential enhances humility.

  Sheila Murray Bethel

- What the world needs is more geniuses with humility. There are so few of us left.

  Oscar Levant

- Get someone else to blow your horn and the sound will carry twice as far.

  Will Rogers

- Humility must always be the portion of any man who receives acclaim earned in the blood of his followers and the sacrifices of his friends.

  Dwight D. Eisenhower

- Success and humility make good partners in your life. Allow them to compliment each other.

  Thomas A. Bruno

- It is no great thing to be humble when you are brought low; but to be humble when you are praised is a great and rare attainment.

  Saint Bernard

- Don't be so humble; you're not that great.

  Golda Meier

- Humility is not renunciation of pride but the substitution of one pride for another.

  Eric Hoffer

- The proud man counts his newspaper clippings—the humble man, his blessings.

  Bishop Fulton J. Sheen

HOW SMALL IS SMALL ENOUGH?

Theodore Roosevelt was known by those closest to him as a nature lover. It is said that after an evening of talk with his friend, William Beebe, the two would take a walk together. As they explored the vastness of the darkened universe, each marveled at the Milky Way, the big and little dippers and the enormity of the number of visible stars, realizing the minuteness of their stature compared to the universe. Finally, Teddy Roosevelt would break the silence and say, "Now, I think we are small enough. Let's call it a night."

• • •

Sir Winston Churchill, always the comic, once targeted a political colleague with this remark: "He is a modest man, and he has much to be modest about." Although intended as a slam, Churchill had a point. Is it not true that all of us have much to be modest about?

When you put yourself on a mighty pedestal and elevate yourself above the rest of the world, just keep in mind that the size of your funeral is going to depend a lot on the weather. Now that will help you keep things in perspective.

PUT IN MY PLACE

It took me three years to work up the nerve to take my wife along with me on a speaking engagement. My wife's approval would be the ultimate compliment and encouragement as I endeavored to become a respected public speaker. I feverishly memorized the key points, practiced my illustrations, and worked on voice fluctuation.

When I stepped on the podium that night I was confident of my ability to deliver a flawless and inspiring speech. Forty-five minutes flew by and the crowd applauded my efforts. The pride swelled up inside of me as individual audience members shook hands and thanked me for a memorable address.

In the car on the way home, I turned to my wife and asked, "Sweetheart, how many great speakers do you think there are in the world today?"

She smiled, placed her hand on mine and softly said, "One fewer than you think, dear." Ouch!

A thin line exists between having confidence in our abilities and being proud or conceited. Sometimes others have a better view of our position than we do. If you can handle their honesty, an objective outsider might be able to help you keep yourself from crossing that thin line.

NO SWOLLEN HEAD HERE

One of my boyhood baseball idols was Carl Yastrzemski, first baseman for the Boston Red Sox. As he approached his three-thousandth career hit, fans and reporters took special interest. As the historic number drew closer, "Yaz" was bombarded by reporters' questions.

One reporter, seeking a comment from the Yaz, asked, "Aren't you afraid of all this attention going to your head?"

Yastrzemski flashed a smile and said, "I look at it this way. I've been at bat over 10,000 times. That means I've failed 7,000 times at plate. That fact alone will prevent me from getting a swollen head."

HUMOR

- Nothing is better than the unintended humor of reality.

  Steve Allen

- We sing "Make a Joyful Noise Unto the Lord" while our faces reflect the sadness of one who has just buried a rich aunt who left everything to her pregnant hamster.

  Erma Bombeck

- Why humor? Why not humor? I'd rather it be my ally than my enemy.

  Robert Orben

- Though a humorist may bomb occasionally, it is still better to exchange humorists than bombs. And . . . you can't fight when you're laughing.

  Jim Boren

- Humor is a proof of faith.

  Charles M. Schulz

- I deeply believe in humor; not in jokes. Humor is spectacular!

  Tom Peters

- The kind of humor I like is the thing that makes me laugh for five seconds and think for ten minutes.

  William Davis

- Humor used at the proper time can help break the "panic cycle" that so often accelerates the patient's illness or state of mind. Laughter can broaden the focus and diffuse the intensity of negative thoughts, thereby aiding the patient's ability to gain control.

  Norman Cousins

- Humor and depression are incompatible. Except in severe cases, humor relieves the grip of depression. At times of tragedy, many people seek to laugh, rather than cry.

  Joel Goodman

■ A sense of humor has been linked with longevity. It is a possibility that the mental attitude reflected in a lively sense of humor is an important factor predisposing some people toward long life.

Raymond Moody, M.D.

■ Humor happens when two worlds collide. Something unexpected has to happen that jolts you up and out of the normal pattern and then you start laughing. Humor is the synapse between the regular and the surprising. Every time we laugh, we are making a leap between two worlds.

Margie Brown

■ What is a sense of humor? Surely not the ability to understand a joke. It comes rather from a residing feeling of one's own absurdity. It is the ability to understand a joke—and that the joke is oneself.

Clifton Fadiman

■ Humor has always been an expression of the freedom of the human spirit. It is an ability to stand outside of life's flow and view the whole scene—the incongruities, the tragedies outside our control, the unexpected.

Dr. Terry L. Paulson

■ A sense of humor is what makes you laugh at something that would make you mad if it happened to you.

Herm Albright

■ Although humor is an "intangible" it has a direct impact on communication flow, work environment, and productivity.

Malcolm L. Kushner

■ Imagination was given to man to compensate for what he is not. A sense of humor was provided to console him for what he is.

Horace Walpole

■ Humor is laughing at what you haven't got when you ought to have it.

Langston Hughes

■ After God created the world, He made man and woman. Then, to keep the whole thing from collapsing, He invented humor.

G. Mordillo

- Humor is just another defense against the universe.

Mel Brooks

- Comedy is acting out optimism.

Robin Williams

- You don't have to teach people to be funny. You only have to give them permission.

Dr. Harvey Mindess

- If you could choose one characteristic that would get you through life, choose a sense of humor.

Jennifer James

- The essence of humor is an expectation that comes to nothing.

James C. Humes

- Everything is funny as long as it's happening to somebody else.

Will Rogers

- Good humor is a tonic for mind and body. It is the best antidote for anxiety and depression. It is a business asset.

Glenville Kleiser

- No one would have been invited to dinner as often as Jesus was unless he was interesting and had a sense of humor.

Charles Shultz

- There are three rules for creating humor, but unfortunately no one knows what they are.

Laurence Peter

- Analyzing what's funny is like dissecting a frog in a laboratory. After you've finished, nothing remains.

William James

- Humor is something that thrives between man's aspirations and his limitations. There is more logic in humor than in anything else. Because, you see, humor is truth.

Victor Borge

- If I had no sense of humor, I should long ago have committed suicide.

Mohandas K. Gandhi

- A good sense of humor helps to overlook the unbecoming, understand the unconventional, tolerate the unpleasant, overcome the unexpected, and outlast the unbearable.

Anonymous

AN UNEXPECTED RESPONSE

A December 12, 1983, article in *Fortune* Magazine addressed the topic "Executives Ought to Be Funnier." One example involved auto executive Eugene Cafiero. When he was president of Chrysler, Cafiero traveled to England to meet with employees at a troubled plant there. Conflict between management and the union employees was intense. As Cafiero entered the plant he was confronted by a man who loudly exclaimed, "I'm Eddie McClusky and I'm a communist." The composed Chrysler executive extended his hand and replied, "How do you do. I'm Eugene Cafiero and I'm a Presbyterian." The subsequent laughter squelched this potentially explosive confrontation.

Conflict is undoubtedly a serious issue. Its impact, however, can be minimized and subdued by a sense of humor.

Consider this story told by Malcolm Kushner in *The Light Touch: How to Use Humor for Business Success*, Simon & Schuster, 1990: Police Officer Adelle Roberts was investigating a routine domestic disturbance call—a husband-and-wife fight. As she parked her patrol car in front of the offenders' house, a television flew out of a second-story window. Loud voices argued as she walked to the front door and knocked. An angry man screamed, "Who is it?" Roberts knew that if she said "Police," it would make things worse. Instead, she replied "TV repairman." The man started laughing and opened the door. A favorable atmosphere had been established for resolving the dispute.

IDEAS

- Nothing is more dangerous than an idea when it is the only one you have.

  Emile Chartier

- You'll find boredom where there is the absence of a good idea.

  Earl Nightingale

- The best way to get a good idea is to get a lot of ideas.

  Linus Pauling

- Once a new idea springs into existence, it cannot be unthought. There is a sense of immortality in a new idea.

  Edward De Bono

- Good ideas are not adopted automatically. They must be driven into practice with courageous patience.

  Admiral Hyman Rickover

- Ideas lose themselves as quickly as quail, and one must wing them the minute they raise out of the grass—or they are gone.

  Thomas Kennedy

- Ideas are like rabbits. You get a couple and learn how to handle them, and pretty soon you have a dozen.

  Anonymous

- There's an element of truth in every idea that lasts long enough to be called corny.

  Irving Berlin

- I'm not impressed with the power of a corporate president. I am impressed with the power of ideas.

  Ken Mason
  President of Quaker Oats

- A new idea is delicate. It can be killed by a sneer or a yawn; it can be stabbed to death by a quip and worried to death by a frown on the right man's brow.

  Charles Brower

■ I would swap a whole cartload of precedents anytime for one brand-new idea.

Luther Burbank

■ All great ideas are controversial or have been at one time.

George Seldes

■ Good ideas, like good pickles, are crisp, enduring, and devilishly hard to make.

Rushworth M. Kidder
The Christian Science Monitor

MOVERS AND SHAKERS

It has been said that once a new idea springs into existence, it cannot be unthought. There is a sense of immortality in a new idea. Maybe that's why Ira Hayes is an avid believer that ideas precede success. Hayes, former vice president of advertising at National Cash Register and respected platform speaker suggests that everybody should possess an "idea-of-the-week book."

On the platform, Hayes reveals his personal idea book which is filled with his ideas from thirty disciplined and creative years. He has programmed his life to come up with one good idea a week.

"The movers and shakers of tomorrow," says Hayes, "will be those who have the resolve to write down an idea, despite its source, and to keep trying it, despite any resistance they encounter."

Movers and shakers. History is laced with people who had an idea and then applied their resources to make the idea a reality. For instance, traveling through the south several years ago, Kemmons Wilson realized families found it difficult to find affordable hotels. So he opened one, then two, and eventually the Holiday Inn chain was born. Today, "The World's Innkeeper" is the world's largest hotel chain.

Betty Nesmith, working as an executive secretary in 1951, noticed that the speed of new electric typewriters was resulting in increased typing errors. She developed a mixture of water-based paint and a coloring agent that blended with the paper being used. Five years later, Nesmith was working full-time to fill the onslaught of orders for her concoction. In 1979, she sold her Liquid Paper Corporation to Gillette for $47.5 million. A single idea, practically applied, increased typists' effectiveness and Nesmith's pocketbook.

Then there was George Thomas. Looking for an efficient way to apply deodorant, his mind focused on the ballpoint pen and (puff!) came up with roll-on deodorant.

Product engineer and frequent traveler John Todd was tired of forgetting his shampoo and having to wash his hair with soap. Serious brainstorming led Todd to ultimately create free amenities for hotel guests with the brand name printed on one side and the hotel's name on the other. His simple idea resulted in annual revenues of $11.7 million.

It has been said that ideas are more than information; they consist of information with legs attached. Our examples of successful, history-making ideas were only as fruitful as the energetic people behind them. They were movers and shakers. Ira Hayes never intended his "idea a week" binder to be an empty exercise. Doing something with your ideas is critical. An idea without legs is an exercise in futility.

Ask yourself: How many ideas have I generated this year? This month? This week? What action have I taken to make them a reality?

DO YOU HAVE A BETTER IDEA?

The El Cortez Hotel in San Diego is the birthplace of an architectural first.

Management at this elegant hotel determined their single elevator was not sufficient for getting their guests to and from their rooms and the lobby. Deciding an additional elevator was needed, engineers and architecture experts were contracted to solve the problem.

They proposed cutting a hole in each floor from the basement to the top of the hotel. As the experts stood in the lobby discussing their plans, a hotel janitor overheard their conversation.

"What are you up to?" he asked.

One of the planners explained the situation and their proposed solution. The janitor responded, "That's going to make quite a mess. Plaster, dust, and debris will be everywhere."

One of the engineers assured him it would work fine because they were planning to close the hotel while the work was being completed.

"That's going to cost the hotel a healthy amount of money," the janitor exclaimed, "and there will be a lot of people out of jobs until the project is completed."

"Do you have a better idea?" one architect asked.

Leaning on his mop, the janitor pondered the architect's challenge and then suggested, "Well, why don't you build the elevator on the outside of the hotel."

Looking at each other in amazement, the architects and engineers responded, "That's never been done before . . . let's do it."

Hence the El Cortez became the originator of a popular architectural feature.

Moral of the story: It doesn't necessarily take a trained expert to come up with the best idea.

PROFITABLE FOOD FOR THOUGHT

Mike Brennan did more than rise from a grocery stocker to supermarket owner. He also carefully observed the shopping habits of his customers. Brennan noticed how many shoppers used calculators when they shopped and an idea sprouted. A durable, water-resistant calculator that attaches permanently to the handle of a shopping cart went from an idea to test marketing.

Will grocery customers actually buy his calculators? Only time will tell. So, to encourage use of the calculators, Brennan is offering advertising space on each calculator for a monthly fee. As the customer interacts with the calculator, advertisers promote their product all the way to the check-out stand.

Mike Brennan plans to smile all the way to the bank with his projected revenues in the millions.

Maybe it's the nature of supermarket people to come up with good ideas. In 1937, Sylvan Goldman, the owner of two supermarket chains, noticed that customers rarely bought more items than they could carry in their two arms. An idea arose. Why not come up with a four-wheel device for shoppers to cart their items in. The shopping cart was born and thus, an ingenious method for "helping" shoppers spend more money by carrying more items to the check-out counter. Goldman is credited with inventing a four-wheeled vehicle outnumbered only by the automobile.

GREAT IDEAS WITH UNIQUE BEGINNINGS

Karl Vesper reported in *New Venture Strategies* (Prentice Hall, 1990) that most ideas come from unlikely, often overlooked sources. Vesper cites the following examples:

- Leo Gerstenzang thought of Q-tips when he saw his wife trying to clean their baby's ears with toothpicks and cotton.
- Ott Diffenbach came up with cellophane soda straws when he twisted the wrapper from a cigarette pack and saw he had created a tube.
- King C. Gillette had been looking for a throwaway product ever since having a conversation with the inventor of pop-bottle caps. When he found his razor dull, he thought of the safety razor with disposable blades.
- Ole Evinrude got angry when the ice cream in his rowboat melted before he got to his island picnic spot—so he invented the outboard motor.
- Ralph Schneider decided to form Diners Club one night after he lost his wallet.
- Charles Strite was fuming at the burnt toast in the factory lunchroom where he worked—and thought up the automatic toaster.

HOW NOT TO SELL AN IDEA

Ideas can be put to death as quickly as they are born. General Foods, not wanting to squelch employees' new ideas, made their supervisors aware of "killer phrases" to avoid, such as:

"Now here's a sketchy idea of what I have in mind, for you to kick holes in . . ."

"Here's an idea for what it's worth . . . I'm not sure I like it myself . . ."

"This probably won't work, but . . ."

"This may sound screwy to you, but maybe there's some way we can use it . . ."

"This isn't too practical, perhaps, but . . ."

"This may not work here, but let me tell you about it anyway. . ."

"I'd like to go over this for a minute or two, even at the risk of boring you . . ."

Do any of these sound familiar?

IDEA GENERATORS PRODUCE LIFE ALTERATIONS

Roy Speer and Lowell Paxson had a profitable idea. Their careful observation of people's lifestyles led these two men to three conclusions: (1) People like to shop; (2) people like to watch TV; and (3) people like to shop or watch TV anytime they please.

Their idea? The Home Shopping Network, Inc., a 24-hour-a-day TV shopping channel. The idea appealed to TV watchers and shoppers everywhere, generating hundreds of millions of dollars in revenues annually.

•　　•　　•

Thousands of other ideas are dramatically altering our lifestyles. From Mary Phelps Jacob's use of two lace handkerchiefs and a pink ribbon in 1914 to invent the first bra to Jacqueline Clark's "Nanny Franchises" established in thirty locations. Fast food, Jiffy Lube, One-Hour Martinizing, and super discount stores are the brainchildren of idea generators.

•　　•　　•

Norman Vincent Peale was approached by a young man who wanted to start his own business but lamented that he had no money.

Peale reportedly responded to him, "Empty pockets never held anyone back. Only empty heads and empty hearts can do that."

Ideas that influence our lives spring from people who are not concerned with what they lack, but people who focus their attention and persistence on making their idea a success.

A NOVEL IDEA

Of all the ideas addressed in this section, Will Parish's receives my vote for being the most novel. Parish, a former lawyer and conservation specialist, was well aware of rising energy costs and diminishing fossil fuel resources, as well as the enormous problems associated with waste disposal.

While in India, he ate a meal heated by flaming cow dung. That's right, cow dung. Lights flashed, whistles blew, lightning struck, fireworks went off (maybe not, but a novel idea was created). Parish formed National Energy Associates, which now burns 900 tons of "cow chips" a day, producing enough megawatts to light 20,000 American homes. Parish says he now combines doing well with doing good, and *Fortune* magazine labeled him the world's true "entre-manure."

My second place vote goes to Leisure Time Development, Inc. They've developed a unique way to keep dieters honest (or at least aware of what they eat). Through miniature technology, they manufacture a tiny tape-player that is placed inside a refrigerator. Every time the door is opened, a voice shouts, "Are you eating again? No wonder you look the way you do. Do yourself a favor and shut the door." Dieters beware!

•   •   •

There's more to reputable ideas than the idea itself. Motivational author, William Davis, in an article entitled, "Let Me Through, I Have an Idea," says: "It is a popular myth that the essence of innovation is having ideas. If only it were that simple. An idea is merely the starting point; innovation is about making things happen, which is a great deal more difficult. Intrinsically, ideas have little value. It is only when they are implemented by determined people that they become influential."

Having an idea is a great beginning but it could become wishful thinking. For additional ways to make your ideas valuable, go on to the chapter on Innovation. You will find inspiration and guidance to make your ideas innovative reality.

IMAGINATION

- Measure a person by the stretch of his imagination.

  Robert Schuller

- The imagination is far more powerful than the will.

  Peter Daniels

- To develop imaginative powers, we must specialize in our own fields but be alert to new ideas from any source and continually seize and set down our inspirational flashes when they come to us.

  Carl Holmes

- Imagination is the preview of life's coming attractions.

  Larry Eisenberg

- It's exciting to imagine how many things may exist which we cannot possibly imagine.

  Ashleigh Brilliant

- The most interesting people are the people with the most interesting pictures in their minds.

  Earl Nightingale

- Imagination in business is the ability to perceive opportunity.

  Abraham Zaleznik

- Man is so constituted as to see what is wrong with a new thing, not what is right. To verify this, you have but to submit a new idea to a committee. They will obliterate 90 percent of rightness for the sake of 10 percent of wrongness. The possibilities a new idea opens up are not visualized, because not one person in a thousand has imagination.

  Charles F. Kettering

- To raise new questions, new possibilities, to regard old problems from a new angle, requires creative imagination.

  Albert Einstein

- Imagineering: The ability to let your imagination soar and then engineering it to make it happen.

  Aluminum Company of America

- The man who has no imagination has no wings.

  Muhammad Ali

- Imagination, not invention, is the supreme master of art as of life.

  Joseph Conrad

- Imagination will often carry us to worlds that never were. But without it, we go nowhere.

  Carl Sagan

IMAGING YOUR WAY TO SUCCESS

"The great successful men of the world have used their imagination" says Robert Collier. "They think ahead and create their mental picture in all its details, filling in here, adding a little there, altering this a bit and that a bit, but steadily building—steadily building."

Successful people envision desired outcomes. They are not surprised by their achievements as they were already faultlessly executed in their mind. Jack Nicklaus explained his imaging technique in his book, *Golf My Way* (Simon & Schuster, 1976). "First I 'see' the ball where I want it to finish, nice and white and sitting up high on the bright green grass. Then the scene quickly changes, and I 'see' the ball going there: its path, trajectory, and shape, even its behavior on landing. Then there's a sort of fade-out, and the next scene shows me making the kind of swing that will turn the previous images into reality."

Curtis Carlson, Founder of the Carlson Companies and best known as the inventor of Gold Bond Stamps as well as being one of the wealthiest people in Minnesota, has spent his life building and expanding. When asked what personal qualities contributed to the building of his successful empire, Carlson responded, "I think my success is the result of my ability to see, to imagine how things can be. I'm not distracted by how things are."

Maxwell Maltz would concur with that philosophy of business building. "For imagination sets the goal 'picture' which our automatic mechanism works on," explains Maltz. "We act, or fail to act, not because of 'will' as is so commonly believed, but because of imagination."

Walt Disney was the giant in the world of imagination. On Saturdays Disney took his daughters to a local park to ride the merry-go-round and play. While sitting on a bench eating snacks and watching his children enjoy their rides on the carousel,

Disney imagined an elaborate family park filled with happy families. He put every detail into place. From the pirates of the Caribbean to Main Street USA, Disneyland is the result of Disney's ability to create the future in his mind. This pioneer of family amusement had no similar facilities to draw ideas from. He relied on his imagination to design the original blueprint.

From Napoleon Hill's *Law of Success* (Success Unlimited, 1977), comes this summarizing thought:

"Just as the oak tree develops from the germ that lies in the acorn, and the bird develops from the germ that lies asleep in the egg, so will your material achievements grow out of the organized plans that you create in your imagination. First comes the thought; then organization of that thought into ideas and plans; then transformation of those plans into reality. The beginning, as you will observe, is in your imagination."

INNOVATION

- The innovator is someone who has the capacity not just of envisioning the future in an abstract, day-dreaming, fantasizing kind of way, but has the interest and the capability and the drive to actually do something about that vision.

  William Thompson

- Innovation is not a random process. When it works, it works because someone has identified a real need, and found a way to bring new ideas or new technologies to bear on that need.

  Lewis W. Lehr

- Innovation is resisted by individuals who are unwilling to risk the status they have achieved and jealously guard their own job against any change.

  William T. Brady

- Make a technical contribution; innovate, don't emulate.

  David Packard

- Any business that does not learn how to innovate within the next few years will not be around by the year 2000.

  Peter F. Drucker

- The entrepreneur finds a need and fills it. The innovator anticipates or creates a need and fills it.

  Denis E. Waitley and Robert B. Tucker
  Winning the Innovation Game

- Pardon the grammar, but even if it "ain't broke" today, it will be tomorrow. Today's innovations are tomorrow's antiques.

  Robert Kriegel
  If It Ain't Broke . . . Break It

- Innovation has to be linked to a market-driven mentality, tied in with customer needs. It can't be done in a vacuum, or as innovation for its own sake.

  Jim Beard

212

A NOVEL PROFESSION

Before an illustrious career in films, W. C. Fields pursued a novel way to make a living. He worked as a professional drowner in Atlantic City. Fields would swim into the ocean, pretend to drown, and wait to be rescued by a lifeguard. While rescue efforts were administered, beach vendors sold their hot dogs and soft drinks to the curious crowds. W. C. Fields later collected a percentage of the profits.

No wonder Fields enjoyed a successful career in acting.

SNEAKY ... SNEAKY

The story is told of a man who attempted to cross the Canadian border on his motorcycle. He carried two saddlebags strapped across his seat. The border guards questioned, "What's in your saddle bags?"

"Rocks," the man replied.

The guards emptied the bags to inspect them. Finding nothing but rocks, they sent the man on his way with bags full of rocks.

A few weeks later, the same scenario occured and so on every two or three weeks for several months. The guards endured the cycle rider's entry over the border with saddle bags full of rocks.

Finally, one week, the guards could no longer stand it. "We know you are smuggling something across the border but every time we check your saddle bags, there's nothing in them but rocks. It's driving us crazy. Tell us what you're up to and we promise not to turn you in."

"It's quite simple," the man smiled, "I'm smuggling in stolen motorcycles."

MAKING A MINT WITH A HOLE

The well-known candy with the hole in the middle was not always so popular. In 1913, Edward John Noble, a young, vivacious advertising salesperson, purchased his first roll of Life Savers. Impressed with the taste, round shape, and name of the mints, he approached the company with an advertising proposal. "Not interested," they said, "but we'll sell you the rights to Life Savers."

Noble's decision to take the company up on their offer was initially a catastrophe. The little mints had a short shelflife due to inferior packaging. Stores handling the mints were hesitant to purchase more inventory even though Life Savers were now being wrapped in foil to seal in the flavor.

Noble was not willing to abandon his product. Being an ingenious salesperson, he used a new marketing approach to pursue new customers. Life Savers mints were prominently placed next to cash registers in saloons, restaurants, and cigar stores with a lofty five-cent price tag.

Edward John Noble's innovative approach later became known as counter merchandising and Life Savers continue to enjoy center stage on candy displays. Noble turned a struggling round mint with a hole in it into a "mint."

INNOVATIVE MARKETING

"Business has only two functions," writes Peter Drucker, "marketing and innovation."

Consider these phrases posted on separate roadside signs: A peach looks good . . . with lots of fuzz . . . but man's no peach . . . and never was . . . Burma Shave! In 1925, Burma Shave knew they had a great product but were ineffective in marketing it. So, their roadside advertising was implemented. Today, the Burma Shave commercials are highly recognized as memorable trivia.

Here's another exemplary approach combining innovation and unique marketing. A small garage-based company took a single product, biodegradable soap, broke the customary marketing trends and amassed a fortune.

Using multi-level marketing, Amway left its competitors green with envy. First, they produced a quality product, developed unique packaging, attached distinctive labeling, and then used direct salespeople to sell their product. It is working to the tune of an estimated $1 billion in annual revenues.

Domino's Pizza shocked the industry with their original idea: "Guaranteed delivery in 30 minutes or $3.00 off." Quick service is now a minimum standard in the food industry.

Innovative marketing—could it be the third function of business?

PURSUIT OF POSSIBILITIES

Innovators oppose "to do" lists. Their lives are governed by "to create" lists. Rather than getting caught up in activity, they are incessantly pursuing new possibilities and refining existing ones. Here's a few examples to show you what I mean.

A few years ago, Coca-Cola sold two basic cola drinks: Coke and Tab. Today, the Coca-Cola Company markets Coca-Cola Classic, New Coke, Caffeine-Free Coke, Diet Coke, Caffeine-Free Diet Coke, Cherry Coke, and Diet Cherry Coke. Consumers can purchase these products in cans, glass bottles, and plastic bottles. A total of at least 42 combinations are now available.

The Campbell Soup Company recognized the need for a product appealing to two-income households who have less time to spend in the kitchen. The innovators went to work designing a line of frozen dinners more nutritious than customary TV dinners realizing it would cost the consumer a little more. As a result, the Campbell

Soup Company introduced its Le Menu line of frozen dinners. As Denis Waitley says, "Innovators anticipate or create a need and fill it." So it is with the Campbell Company.

The name Levi Strauss is immediately recognized by millions of jeans wearers. Levis determined a need for a comfortable, looser fitting yet stylish casual pant that would appeal to their lifelong baby boomer jeans buyers. Designers and marketers went to work on their innovative plan to produce and market Dockers.

Bold, bright, eye-catching store displays replaced drab and uninviting areas in men's departments. Shoppers were attracted to the colorful displays and ultimately the casual appeal of the Dockers slack.

Innovation rejuvenated the Levi Menswear Division taking Dockers sales from $1 million in 1986 to $500 million in 1990.

UCLA's legendary basketball coach John Wooden changed the pace of college basketball by introducing the fast break. His team struggled with excessive turnovers while perfecting the fast-break offense. Today, nearly every team in the country uses Wooden's innovation. But, only Wooden won ten national collegiate championships in 12 years. This remarkable achievement in sports history is credited to a coach who believed failure and mistakes were opportunities to succeed. Although Tom Peters said it, John Wooden would no doubt agree that, "The essence of innovation is the pursuit of failure . . . to be able to try things and make mistakes . . . without getting shot."

Prior to World War I, Clarence Birdseye was scratching out a living as a fur trader in Labrador. He observed that when catching a fish in subzero temperatures, the fish would freeze hard and fast when brought up through the ice. He further noted that when thawed, the fish were tender and moist, just like fresh fish.

This casual observation, recalled a decade later, made Clarence Birdseye a pioneer of frozen foods. Northern aboriginal people had practiced quick freezing for centuries but Birdseye introduced it to the general public. His refinement of nature's process created a multi-billion dollar industry.

An unknown philosopher once declared, "If you keep doing what you've always done, you'll keep getting what you've always got." Pepsi Cola decided to break tradition by investing heavily in the blow-and-fill plastic bottle. These containers could be produced more cost effectively, thereby reducing the cost to customers as well as allowing consumers to see what they were buying. Instead of "getting what they always got," Pepsi-Cola increased their market share in food market chains.

The mind of an innovator is never at rest. Creating and refining are a way of life. Innovators applaud failures, knowing failures produce great ideas, destroy barriers to creative thinking, and recognize that there is no innovation without risk.

SECOND GUESSING AN INVENTION

The man who designed the instant replay 30 years ago isn't sure it was a smart invention.

According to an Associated Press Release, Tony Verna, producer-director-instant replay creator, says, "You can't exaggerate anymore. You can't say a guy jumped six feet in the air because the replay will show you're a liar."

Instant replay made its debut on December 7, 1963, during CBS's telecast of the Army-Navy game in Philadephia.

"The idea came to me out of frustration," Verna said. "Before replays, football telecasts were filled with dead spots. You spent a lot of time watching receivers walk back to the huddle after incomplete passes. It really destroyed the momentum of the telecast. Replays gave you something to show during the pauses. It seemed to make the game go faster."

What started out as an experiment quickly became a regular television feature. Today, instant replays are as much a part of sports telecasts as the announcers and athletes.

Until recently, replays were even used to review controversial calls—a situation that creates long delays and contradicts the purpose of instant replay's creation.

"It's ironic," Verna laments, "the reason I started instant replays was to keep the momentum going. Now the replays are slowing the whole thing down."

KINDNESS

- It is not genius, nor glory, nor love that reflects the greatness of the human soul; it is kindness.

  Henri-Dominique Lacordaire

- Have you had a kindness shown? Pass it on.

  Henry Burton

- Kindness consists in loving people more than they deserve.

  Joseph Joubert

- People who overlook little slights and keep reaching out to help one another with acts of kindness will have very little problem maintaining harmonious relationships.

  Richard Strauss

- Kind words are the music of the world. They have a power that seems to be beyond natural causes, as though they were some angel's song which had lost its way and come back to earth.

  Anonymous

- Two important things are to have a genuine interest in people and to be kind to them. Kindness, I've discovered, is everything in life.

  Isaac Bashevis Singer

- Constant kindness can accomplish much. As the sun makes ice melt, kindness causes misunderstanding, mistrust, and hostility to evaporate.

  Albert Schweitzer

- Lead the life that will make you kindly and friendly to everyone about you, and you will be surprised what a happy life you will lead.

  Charles M. Schwab

- Kind words can be short and easy to speak, but their echoes are truly endless.

  Mother Teresa

- Kindness can become its own motive. We are made kind by being kind.

  Eric Hoffer

LAUGHTER

- I have always felt that laughter in the face of reality is probably the finest sound there is and will last until the day when the game is called on account of darkness. In this world, a good time to laugh is any time you can.

  Linda Ellerbee
  Prime Time Live, ABC News

- Laughter and good humor are the canaries in the mine of commerce—when the laughter dies, it's an early warning that life is ebbing from the enterprise.

  Paul Hawken

- There are three things that are real—God, human folly and laughter. The first two are beyond comprehension. So, we must do what we can with the third.

  John F. Kennedy

- A good hearty laugh is worth ten thousand "groans" and a million "sighs" in any market on earth.

  Napoleon Hill

- If you wish to glimpse inside a human soul and get to know a man, don't bother analyzing his ways of being silent, of talking, of weeping, or seeing how much he is moved by noble ideas; you'll get better results if you just watch him laugh. If he laughs well, he's a good man.

  Fyodor Dostoyevsky

- If I were given the opportunity to present a gift to the next generation, it would be the ability for each individual to learn to laugh at himself.

  Charles Schultz

- Laughter has a scientifically demonstrable exercise impact on several body systems. Muscles are activated; heart rate is increased; respiration is amplified with increase in oxygen exchange. Mirthful laughter is followed by a state of compensatory physical tension.

  William F. Fry, M.D.

- What I want to do is to make people laugh so that they'll see things seriously.

  William K. Zinsser

218

■ Love makes the world go round, but it's laughter that keeps us from getting dizzy.

Anonymous

■ An onion can make people cry, but there has never been a vegetable invented to make them laugh.

Will Rogers

■ Of all the things God created, I am often most grateful he created laughter.

Charles Swindoll

■ Laughter is much more important than applause. Applause is almost a duty. Laughter is a reward.

Carol Channing

■ Why we laugh is generally because we have seen or heard something that is at variance with custom.

Art Young

■ I am persuaded that every time a person smiles—but much more so when laughing, it adds something to this fragment of life.

Laurence Sterne

■ Laughter is, after speech, the chief thing that holds society together.

Max Eastman

■ Laugh and the world laughs with you. Cry and you may not cry alone, but you'll get a group discount.

Etruscan Philosopher

■ We are all here for a spell; get all the goods laughs you can.

Will Rogers

■ You can turn painful situations around through laughter. If you can find humor in anything, you can survive it.

Bill Cosby.

■ May you always have a smile on your face and laughter in your heart.

Anonymous

LAUGHTER: THE CHEAP MEDICINE

Admit it . . . many of us have become far too serious. Smiles, chuckles, and belly laughs have been replaced with flat expressions, stomach pains, and ulcers. As Erma Bombeck says, "We sing 'make a joyful noise unto the Lord' while our faces reflect the sadness of one who has just buried a rich aunt who left everything to her pregnant hamster."

Perfection paralysis and pessimistic platitudes perpetually permeate perfectly plausible possibilities.

Humor me! Don't evaluate the quality of the sentence structure. This slightly altered alliteration accurately alludes to a few reasons for today's seriously stuffy, sanctimonious, sophistication.

In other words . . . LET'S LEARN TO LOOSEN UP!

Laughter is a cheap medicine. It distracts your attention, changes attitude and outlook of life, causes relaxation and reduction of tension, while increasing the body's natural painkillers.

In short, laughter relaxes our tensions and promotes a feeling of well-being.

I like the way Josh Billings put it: "There ain't much fun in medicine, but there's a heck of a lot of medicine in fun."

Dr. Norman Cousins, in his bestselling book *Anatomy of an Illness as Perceived by the Patient* (Bantam, 1983), takes an interesting look at the use of humor to overcome a painful and debilitating illness. Cousins found that ten minutes of good belly laughter gave him two hours of pain-free sleep. Prior to that, even his heavy medications were unable to relieve the pain caused by the severe inflammation of his spine and joints enough for him to sleep.

Cousins stumbled upon this phenomenon by chance. Doctors applied every medical technology they knew of. No relief. One day he came upon a letter from a consulting doctor who had written Cousins' personal physician. One line in that letter caught his attention. It read, "I'm afraid we're going to lose Norman." Cousins said, "At that point, I began to take more of an interest in the case."

In cooperation with his physician, Cousins began a consistent treatment of Vitamin C along with prescribed humor therapy. He would watch his favorite humorous movies and read funny books. Ten minutes of this unique prescription allowed him two hours of pain-free living. Cousins eventually recovered and in response to his experience, numerous studies have confirmed the value of laughter in healing.

Cousins also commented on another benefit of laughter. "I've never known a person," he said, "who possessed the gift of hearty laughter to be burdened by constipation." Sounds like a beneficial outcome to me.

So how do we improve our *Laughter Quotients*?

LIGHT-HEARTED LAUGHTER LIFTERS

1. Be willing to laugh at yourself.

For you straight-faced, sourpuss, solemn folk, who firmly believe you have nothing to laugh at, read this next sentence carefully. Take off all of your clothes— that's right—strip naked. Now stand in front of a mirror and sing to yourself. If that doesn't draw so much as a chuckle, get out your high school yearbook. Maybe you'll be able to manage a smile or two by reminiscing and seeing how silly you really looked.

How about the short man who quit wearing cowboy boots? He kidded others that the boots gave him a rash . . . under his armpits.

Think of all the failures, stumbling blocks, embarrassing moments, and down-right stupid things you've experienced. Now recall how six months later, you laughed about them (or should have).

2. Think funny.

Even our stressful experiences produce laughter material. It is important to remember that what we think about during those events will determine our reaction.

Take the guy who entered the doctor's examining room and exclaimed: "Sorry I didn't come sooner, Doc, but I got held up in your waiting room."

James Russell Lowell possessed a light-hearted attitude about growing old. While passing a building on the outskirts of Boston, he noticed a sign reading, "Home for Incurable Children." Turning to a friend, he remarked, "They'll get me in there some day."

How about the lady experiencing a particularly frustrating round of golf. Back in the clubhouse she laments: "I finally figured out my problem. I was standing too close to the ball . . . after I hit it."

LIGHTEN UP . . . THINK FUNNY!

As Seneca declared, "It better benefits man to laugh at life than to lament over it."

3. Listen for life's laughable moments.

Making the most of this free, lawful, healthy gift requires keen listening. Here's an example. Imagine you are the wife of a gynecologist shopping for groceries in a busy supermarket. Suddenly an excited stranger approaches you and proclaims, "I just have to tell you I adore your husband. He got me pregnant when no one else could."

Believe me, you must "hear" this conversation in your mind to experience the humor.

You are working in a school cafeteria and today is peanut butter and jelly sandwich day. A third grader picking up his lunch declares, "It is about time we got a home cooked meal."

Listen for the subtle, soft, and simple laughter moments.

4. Renew the child in you.

Preschoolers laugh up to 450 times a day (not always appropriately, I'm sure). Adults laugh an average of 15 times a day. Who do you think is healthier?

A Sunday School teacher was quizzing her class about their Old Testament knowledge.

"What do you think Noah did all that time he was on the ark?" she asked. There was silence. "Do you think he did a lot of fishing?"

"What?" sneered one boy. "With only two worms?"

Children may not find everything funny, but they have the uncanny ability to make anything funny.

As you observe and experience life, ask yourself: "How would a nine-year-old respond?" Even if you don't laugh, the exercise will brighten what you see.

A NATURAL HIGH

Consider the following description of a physical reaction: The neural circuits in your brain begin to reverberate. Chemical and electrical impulses start flowing rapidly through your body. The pituitary gland is stimulated; hormones and endorphins race through your blood. Your body temperature rises half a degree, your pulse rate and blood pressure increase, your arteries and thoracic muscles contract, your vocal chords quiver, and your face contorts. Pressure builds in your lungs. Your lower jaw suddenly becomes uncontrollable, and breath bursts from your mouth at nearly 70 miles an hour.

Although the description might resemble the electric charge needed to jump-start a car, it is actually the clinical description of laughter. The results are impressive. Laughter distracts your attention, changes attitude and outlook on life, causes relaxation and reduction of tension, increases the body's natural pain killers. Every time we laugh our stress level is lowered.

At Northwestern University, a study conducted under strict, scientific test conditions demonstrated this: The act of laughing massages the heart, stimulates blood circulation, and helps the lungs breathe easier. Another test at Fordham University reinforced the conclusion that laughter benefits the heart, lungs, stomach and other organs. It relaxes our tensions and promotes a feeling of well-being.

Need we say more?

LEADERSHIP

- The ultimate responsibility of a leader is to facilitate other people's development as well as his own.

Fred Pryor

- The leader's task, then, is to create an environment that is conducive to self-motivation.

Nido Qubein

- If people are coming to work excited . . . if they're making mistakes freely and fearlessly . . . if they're having fun . . . if they're concentrating on doing things, rather than preparing reports and going to meetings—then somewhere you have a leader.

Robert Townsend

- As a manager, the important thing is not what happens when you are there but what happens when you are not there.

Kenneth Blanchard and Robert Lorber
Putting the One Minute Manager to Work

- To be a leader means willingness to risk—and a willingness to love. Has the leader given you something from the heart?

Hubert H. Humphrey

- A business is a reflection of the leader. A fish doesn't stink just from the tail, and a company doesn't succeed or fail from the bottom.

Gary Feldmar

- Perhaps more than anything else, leadership is about the "creation of a new way of life."

James M. Kouzes and Barry Z. Posner
The Leadership Challenge

- The world of the '90s and beyond will not belong to managers or those who make the numbers dance, as we used to say, or those who are conversant with all the business and jargon we use to sound smart. The world will belong to passionate, driven leaders—people who not only have an enormous amount of energy but who can energize those whom they lead.

Jack Welch
Chairman and CEO of General Electric

- There are countless ways of attaining greatness, but any road to reaching one's maximum potential must be built on a bedrock of respect for the individual, a commitment to excellence, and a rejection of mediocrity.

  Buck Rogers

- The first and last task of a leader is to keep hope alive—the hope that we can finally find our way through to a better world—despite the day's action, despite our own inertness and shallowness and wavering resolve.

  John W. Gardner

- Leadership is a sacrifice—it is self denial—it is love, it is fearlessness, and it is humility, and it is in the perfectly disciplined will. This is also the distinction between great and little people. The harder you work, the harder it is to surrender.

  The role of the leader is to enhance, transform, coach, care, trust, and cheerlead. The activities of the leader are to educate, sponsor, coach, and counsel using appropriate timing, tone, consequences, and skills.

  Tom Peters and Nancy Austin
  Passion for Excellence

- Leaders know that the "higher up you go—the more gently down you reach."

  Sheila Murray Bethel
  Making a Difference

- I'll tell you what makes a great manager: a great manager has a knack for making ballplayers think they are better than they think they are. He forces you to have a good opinion of yourself. He lets you know he believes in you. He makes you get more out of yourself. And once you learn how good you really are, you never settle for playing anything less than your very best.

  Reggie Jackson

- The first responsibility of a leader is to define reality. The last is to say thank you. In between the leader is a servant.

  Max Dupree
  Leadership Is an Art

WHAT MAKES A LEADER?

Practically every human endeavor requires leadership. Zig Ziglar says, "Even a two-car parade gets fouled up if you don't decide ahead of time who's going to lead."

Once we know who is leading, it is critical for the leader to know how to lead. What qualities do effective leaders possess? How do they go about managing the affairs of the company while maintaining the loyalty of employees? What sets apart the mediocre from the excellent leader?

Harold Green, who built ITT from a little company into a massive conglomerate, provides a suitable introduction to this issue of leadership. In his book, *Managing* (Avon, 1985), he says this about the art of leadership: "Leadership is the very heart and soul of business management. No one really manages a business by shuffling the numbers or rearranging organizational charts or tallying the latest business school formulas. What you manage in business is people ... To my mind, the quality of leadership is the single most important ingredient in the recipe of business success."

Leaders lead people. A leader is one whom others consistently follow. People follow because they have a belief in the direction, integrity and competence of the one leading.

Irwin Federman, president and CEO of Monolithic Memories, one of the most successful of the high-tech companies in Silicon Valley, illustrates this brilliantly in the following quote: "If you think about it, people love others not for who they are, but for how they make us feel. We willingly follow others for much the same reason. It makes us feel good to do so. Now, we also follow platoon sergeants, self-centered geniuses, demanding spouses, bosses of various persuasions and others, for a variety of reasons as well. But none of those reasons involves that person's leadership qualities. In order to willingly accept the direction of another individual, it must feel good to do so. This business of making another person feel good in the unspectacular course of his daily comings and goings is, in my view, the very essence of leadership."

Management consultant and author, Joe Batten, wrote: "The tough-minded leader always gives high touch primacy over high tech. In short, people first—technology second."

J. Willard Marriott, chairman of the board of the enormously successful hotel chain, was asked: "How do you manage to be fair and nice with people and yet demand excellence from them?"

"Well, it's tough-minded management, which basically says that you treat people right and fair and decent, and in return they give their all for you."

Leaders love people. They expect the best from them. Sensitivity to employee needs, wants and concerns is at the top of their priorities. The courage to make decisions based on "what's right for people" governs their day-to-day responsibilities. People respond to such leadership.

John W. Gardner, former Secretary of the U.S. Department of Health, Education and Welfare pinpointed four moral goals of a leader:

1. releasing human potential,

2. balancing the needs of the individual and the community,

3. defending the fundamental values of the community, and

4. instilling in individuals a sense of initiative and responsibility.

These values prompt people to respond positively. When lived, and not just preached, people realize their best interest is being considered. Leaders who sincerely activate Gardner's goals will experience an upsurge in employee productivity.

Lieutenant General Zais provided this challenge: "I leave you with the one piece of advice which I believe will contribute more to making you a better leader, will provide you with greater happiness and self-esteem, and at the same time advance your career more than any other advice that I can provide you. And it doesn't call for special personality or for any certain chemistry. Any one of you can do it. And that advice is: You must care."

Zais continued, "You cannot expect the soldier to be a proud soldier if you humiliate him. You cannot expect him to be brave if you abuse him and cower him. You cannot expect him to be strong if you break him. You cannot ask for respect and obedience and willingness to assault hot landing zones, hump back-breaking ridges, destroy dug-in implacement, if a soldier has not been treated with respect and dignity which fosters unit spirit and personal pride. The line between firmness and harshness, between strong leadership and bullying . . . is a fine line. It is difficult to define. But those of us who have accepted a career as leaders must find that line. It is because judgment and concern for people are involved in leadership that only people can lead, not computers. I enjoin you to be ever alert to the pitfalls in too much authority. Beware that you do not fall into the category of the little man with a little job and with a big head. In essence, be considerate, treat your subordinates right, and they will literally die for you."

"Treat people as adults," says Tom Peters of *In Search of Excellence* (Warner Books, 1988) fame. "Treat them as partners, treat them with dignity, treat them with respect. Treat people—not capital spending and automation—as the primary source of productivity gains. These are fundamental lessons from the excellent companies research."

Zais and Peters provide an apt reminder that leaders have the responsibility to treat people with the utmost respect and dignity. Every leader works with things, ideas and people. Without ideas, things are not created and without people there are no ideas. To achieve their goals, smart leaders recognize that the morale of their people is of paramount importance. In *What Works for Me: Sixteen CEO's Talk About Their Careers and Commitments*, Thomas R. Horton quotes Richard A. Zimmerman, chairman and CEO of Hershey Foods:

Among the CEOs I know, the most successful ones have a very positive outlook. Every CEO has to be a cheerleader. At times you may feel that you can list a series of disaster scenarios for your company, and certainly you are in the best position to do that; still, you have to be a cheerleader at least part of the time . . . OK, we know it is going to be tough, but let's get at it! You need always to be encouraging and perhaps that is one of the most admired attributes that I see in most CEOs.

To ensure high morale, the Tandem computer company adopted this simple five-point creed:

1. All people are good.
2. People, workers, management and the company are all the same thing.
3. Every single person in the company must understand the essence of the business.
4. Every employee must benefit from the company's success.
5. You must create an environment where all of the above can happen.

Jim Treybig, President and CEO of Tandem Computers, substantiates this credo by declaring, "Everything starts with the manager. Does he care about people?" And, from the ancient philosophy of Lao Tzu comes this modern advice:

> The group will not prosper if the leader grabs the lion's share of the credit for the good work that has been done.
> The group will rebel and resist if the leader relies on strict controls in an effort to make things come out a certain way.
> The group members will become deadened and unresponsive if the leader is critical and harsh.
> The wise leader is not greedy, selfish, defensive, or demanding. That is why the leader can be trusted to allow any event to unfold naturally.

People leave or love their jobs for a number of reasons. Considerable research has been conducted to determine how companies can increase their retention rates. Aside from massive data, a simple question will address both loving and leaving a job. How important do people feel in their work?

What have you as a leader done to show your employees how important they are?

When was the last time you made it possible for people to be proud of their achievements?

How often do you celebrate successes? Pass on authority? Provide recognition for a job well done?

What are you as a leader doing to make work satisfying, challenging, and interesting?

Robert Townsend, former CEO of Avis Rent-A-Car, summarizes and encapsulates our thinking on what makes a leader with this comment:

> The real essence of leadership is to care about your people, to help them get as much as they can out of the business environment, and to have as much fun as they can. Anybody who can do that—and really mean it—is a leader.

WHAT DERAILS FAST-TRACK EXECUTIVES?

Why do some executives perish while others flourish? The American Management Association conducted in-depth interviews with 41 executives and found that these traits often lead to failure:

1. Insensitivity to co-workers.

2. Aloofness and arrogance.

3. Tendency to misuse information conveyed in confidence.

4. Inability to control ambition.

5. Inability to delegate assignments or promote teamwork.

6. Inability to staff effectively.

7. Inability to think strategically.

8. Overdependence on mentors.

A LEADER

I went on a search to become a leader.

I searched high and low. I spoke with authority. People listened. But alas, there was one who was wiser than I, and they followed that individual.

I sought to inspire confidence, but the crowd responded, "Why should I trust you?"

I postured, and I assumed the look of leadership with a countenance that flowed with confidence and pride. But many passed me by and never noticed my air of elegance.

I ran ahead of the others, pointed the way to new heights. I demonstrated that I knew the route to greatness. And then I looked back, and I was alone.

"What shall I do?" I queried. "I've tried hard and used all that I know." And I sat down and pondered long.

And then, I listened to the voices around me. And I heard what the group was trying to accomplish. I rolled up my sleeves and joined in the work.

As we worked, I asked, "Are we all together in what we want to do and how to get the job done?"

And we thought together, and we fought together, and we struggled towards our goal.

I found myself encouraging the fainthearted. I sought the ideas of those too shy to speak out. I taught those who had little skill. I praised those who worked hard. When our task was completed, one of the group turned to me and said, "This would not have been done but for your leadership."

At first, I said, "I didn't lead. I just worked with the rest." And then I understood, leadership is not a goal. It's a way to reaching a goal.

I lead best when I help others to go where we've decided to go. I lead best when I help others to use themselves creatively. I lead best when I forget about myself as leader and focus on my group . . . their needs and their goals.

To lead is to serve . . . to give . . . to achieve together.

Anonymous

LEARNING

- We are losing our ability to manage ideas; to contemplate, to think. We are becoming a nation of electronic voyeurs, whose capacity for dialogue is a fading memory, occasionally jolted into reflective life by a one liner: "Where's the beef?" "Today is the first day of the rest of your life." "Born again." "Gag me with a spoon." "Can we talk?"

Yes, we can talk; but only at the level of the lowest common denominator. We are imposing on our minds the same burdens that we have inflicted on our stomachs—precooked ideas—designed to appeal to the largest number of people at the lowest possible price: McThought.

Ted Koppel

- . . . that is what learning is. You suddenly understand something you've understood all your life, but in a new way.

Doris Lessing

- We never stop investigating. We are never satisfied that we know enough to get by. Every question we answer leads on to another question. This has become the greatest survival trick of our species.

Desmond Morris

- The illiterate of the future will not be the person who cannot read. It will be the person who does not know how to learn.

Alvin Toffler

- We know next to nothing about virtually everything. It is not necessary to know the origin of the universe; it is necessary to want to know. Civilization depends not on any particular knowledge, but on the disposition to crave knowledge.

George F. Will

- I don't divide the world into the weak and the strong, or the successes and the failures, those who make it or those who don't. I divide the world into learners and nonlearners.

There are people who learn, who are open to what happens around them, who listen, who hear the lessons. When they do something stupid, they don't do it again. And when they do something that works a little bit, they do it even better

230

and harder the next time. The question to ask is not whether you are a success or a failure, but whether you are a learner or a nonlearner.

Benjamin Barber

■ Learning is the essential fuel for the leader, the source of high-octane energy that keeps up the momentum by continually sparking new understanding, new ideas, and new challenges. It is absolutely indispensable under today's conditions of rapid change and complexity. Very simply, those who do not learn do not long survive as leaders.

Warren Bennis and Burt Nanus
Leaders: Strategies for Taking Charge

■ It's what you learn after you know it all that counts.

John Wooden

■ There is no substitute for knowledge.

W. Edwards Deming

■ What's an expert? I read somewhere that the more a man knows, the more he knows he doesn't know. So I suppose one definition of an expert would be someone who doesn't admit out loud that he knows enough about a subject to know he doesn't really know much.

Malcolm S. Forbes

■ We are drowning in information but starved for knowledge.

John Naisbitt

■ Compared to what we need to know or should know and someday will know, we are like children playing blind man's bluff.

Earl Nightingale

■ Isn't the knowledge that comes from experience more valuable than the knowledge that doesn't? It seems fairly obvious that a lot of scholars need to go outside and sniff around, walk through the grass and talk to the animals.

Benjamin Hoff

■ Knowledge has never been known to enter the head via an open mouth.

Doug Larson

- Never regard study as a duty, but as the enviable opportunity to learn to know the liberating influence of beauty in the realm of the spirit for your own personal joy and to the profit of the community to which your later work belongs.

Albert Einstein

- Learning new things won't help the person who isn't using what he already knows.

Anonymous

- There is more treasure in books than in all the pirates' loot on Treasure Island ... and best of all, you can enjoy these riches every day of your life.

Walt Disney

- A little learning is a dangerous thing, but a lot of ignorance is just as bad.

Bob Edward

- Learning is the noble challenge of broadening our scope.

Luci Swindoll

- In time of drastic change, it is the learners who inherit the future. The learned usually find themselves equipped to live in a world that no longer exists.

Eric Hoffer

- Only the curious will learn and only the resolute overcome the obstacles to learning. The quest quotient has always excited me more than the intelligence quotient.

Eugene S. Wilson

- People learn something every day, and a lot of the time it's that what they learned the day before was wrong.

Bill Vaughn

- Not all learning comes from books. You have to live a lot.

Loretta Lynn

- The best of all things is to learn. Money can be lost or stolen, health and strength may fail, but what you have committed to your mind is yours forever.

Anonymous

- Wisdom is the reward you get for a lifetime of listening when you'd have preferred to talk.

Doug Larson

- Wisdom is the ability to anticipate the probable effects of your decisions in other people's lives, as well as in your own life.

Denis Waitley

- Wisdom is the gift of spotting a positive idea and underscoring it by letting it become incarnated into action.

Robert Schuller

- Never mistake knowledge for wisdom. One helps you make a living; the other helps you make a life.

Sandra Carey

"BEING INFORMED" OR "GETTING INFORMED"

Perhaps you read about the work of Professor Herb Dordick of the University of Southern California Annenberg School of Communications. Professor Dordick divides people into two categories: first are those who are "being informed" and the other group are those who are "getting informed." The 10 percent of the population who are "getting informed" actively pursue new information. According to Professor Dordick, "those 'being informed' are the ones inundated with information who have no strategy to separate the noise and clutter from that which is useful, valuable, and which fuels their innovation machine."

"Getting informed" and keeping informed produces knowledge that, when applied, generates substantial payoffs. Besides, we don't want to end up like the business person who lamented, "I feel like I know more and more about less and less."

ARE YOU AHEAD OR BEHIND?

Louis L'Amour, the prolific author of novels about the American West, wrote a short story describing a man who loved books.

The man was noticed acting suspiciously as he perused the shelves in a library. He took down a leather-bound copy of Shakespeare's *King Lear* and ran his fingers gently over the cover. He opened the book and felt the pages. Suddenly he tucked it under his coat and bolted out the door.

Someone who had been watching him ran after the thief and stopped him. The man willingly surrendered the book. Then he explained. All his life he had loved books, but he had never learned to read. So he would come to the library just to hold books. He loved the way they felt in his hands. That's why he had stolen Shakespeare.

Think of the number of people who can read but have no passion for learning. Their crime equals or is greater than L'Amour's character. Mark Twain said: "The man who does not read good books has no advantage over the man who can't read them." Victor Hugo put it this way: "It is those books which a man possesses but does not read which constitute the most significant evidence against him."

Motivational speaker Jim Rohn advocates that to be a high achiever we must read. He suggests disciplining ourselves to read two books per week. That's about 100 books a year. He quips, "If you've done that for the last 10 years, you're 1,000 books ahead. If you haven't, you're 1,000 books behind."

Can you agree with Kathleen Norris that, "Just the knowledge that a good book is awaiting one at the end of a long day makes that day happier"? If so, you're probably ahead. If not, you're getting more behind every day.

IMPROVING THE MIND

Hal Stebbins said, "Perpetual hunger is the key to a full mind. When you stop learning, you stop."

At ninety-two years of age, Justice Oliver Wendell Holmes was hospitalized. His friend, President Roosevelt, stopped in to visit him and was surprised to see Justice Holmes reading a Greek Primer. "What are you doing, Oliver?" asked the president. "Reading," answered Holmes. "That much I can see," said the president, "but why a Greek Primer?" The lifelong learner Holmes answered, "Why, Mr. President, to improve my mind."

This concept of life-long learning was expressed by Mark Twain in *Life on the Mississippi*: "Two things seemed pretty apparent to me. One was, that in order to be a [Mississippi River] pilot a man has got to learn more than any one man ought to be allowed to know; and the other was, that he must learn it all over again in a different way every 24 hours."

ASKING THE RIGHT QUESTIONS

Isador Isaac Rabi, one of America's renowned physicists, relates this memory of his childhood. When he came home from school every day, his mother would ask, "Did you ask any good questions today, Isador?" Notice she did not ask "What did you learn today?"

William A. Ward remarked, "Curiosity is the wick in the candle of learning." Could it be concluded that learning is the result of asking the right questions, not necessarily striving to have all the right answers? Rabi attributed a great deal of his success to his ability to ask the right questions. As the age-old proverb says, "If you know all the answers, you haven't asked all the questions."

KNOWING WHERE TO FIND THE ANSWERS

Theodore Roosevelt told the delightful story of a business person who had consulted an attorney for legal advice. The business person was having coffee with a friend one day and he recounted the experience. "Why did you spend your hard-earned money for a lawyer?" asked his friend. "The law books in his office contain every answer you could ever want. Why didn't you just read the right book and find out the answer for yourself? It would have saved you a lot of money."

"That's true," replied the business person, "but the difference is the lawyer knew what book and what page the answer was on."

Disraeli would have appreciated that response. He said, "To be conscious that you are ignorant of the facts is a great step to knowledge."

LIFE

- I like living. I have sometimes been wildly, despairingly, acutely miserable, racked with sorrow, but through it all I still know quite certainly that just to be alive is a grand thing.

  Agatha Christie

- When in the world are we going to begin to live as if we understood that this is life? This is our time, our day . . . and it is passing. What are we waiting for?

  Richard L. Evans

- Life is really fun, if we only give it a chance.

  Tim Hansel

- Life is a blend of laughter and tears, a combination of rain and sunshine.

  Norman Vincent Peale

- Death is not the greatest loss in life. The greatest loss is what dies inside us while we live.

  Dr. Norman Cousins

- I have found that if you love life, life will love you back. I accept life unconditionally. Life holds so much—so much to be happy about always. Most people ask for happiness on condition. Happiness can be felt only if you don't set conditions.

  Arthur Rubinstein

- Don't forget until too late that the business of life is not business, but living.

  B.C. Forbes

- Life is meant to be a never-ending education, and when this is fully appreciated, we are no longer survivors but adventurers.

  David McNally
  Even Eagles Need a Push

- There is no shortcut to life. To the end of our days, life is a lesson imperfectly learned.

  Harrison E. Salisbury

■ To fully enjoy life, to derive its greatest meaning and beauty, one needs to enter into it with not only the look of involvement and happiness, but the spirit of involvement, as well.

Luci Swindoll

■ When the days are too short chances are you are living at your best.

Earl Nightingale

■ Live each day as you would climb a mountain. An occasional glance toward the summit keeps the goal in mind, but many beautiful scenes are to be observed from each new vantage point. So climb slowly, enjoying each passing moment; and then the view from the summit will serve a more rewarding climax for your journey.

Bishop Fulton J. Sheen

■ Socrates said, "The unexamined life is not worth living." I'd go a step further: "The unexamined life is impossible to live successfully."

Warren Bennis

■ The purpose of life is not to be happy. The purpose of life is to matter, to be productive, to have it make a difference that you lived at all. Happiness means self-fulfillment and is given to those who use to the fullest whatever talents God or luck or fate bestows upon them.

Leo Rosten

■ Life is a great big canvas, and you should throw all the paint on it you can.

Danny Kaye

■ Life is not a destination; it's a journey. It's not a series of goals; it's a series of steps, of events unfolding as you make your way. Life is not all about accomplishment; it's all about doing, participating, progressing, growing, learning.

Mike Hernacki

■ If I had my whole life to live over again, I don't think I'd have the strength.

Flip Wilson

■ I never lose sight of the fact that just *being* is fun.

Katharine Hepburn

■   I think of life as a good book. The further you get into it, the more it begins to
    make sense.

Harold S. Kushner

■   Life is often ambiguous and untidy. There are always loose ends. It is sticky,
    hot, cold, lukewarm at times—and frequently messy and unmanageable. Most
    of life is somewhere in between, in the middle—amidst small frustrations and
    a lot of "I don't know what to do next."

Tim Hansel

■   I've developed a new philosophy. I only dread life one day at a time.

Charlie Brown
Charles Schulz's "Peanuts"

■   The purpose of life, after all, is to live it, to taste experience to the utmost, to
    reach out eagerly and without fear for newer and richer experience.

Eleanor Roosevelt

GRAB HOLD OF LIFE

The famous author "Anonymous" was once quoted as saying, "The problem
with life is that it is so daily."

That's true. But if you are uncomfortable with that profound reality, consider the
alternative.

Thanks to medical science, people are living longer and longer. Unfortunately,
many people have not learned to take advantage of the extra years. Quantity of life
has not necessarily resulted in enhanced quality of life. Could it be that life has
become, for many, a process of daily existence and not much more?

This daily responsibility called life beckons us to make the most of the possibilities and challenges as well as the failures and setbacks. That silent admonition
has the potential to catapult us beyond a daily existence into a fulfilled life.

Two young guys joined a construction crew commissioned to build a multi-story
office building. At lunch they placed themselves on an iron girder high above the
ground and opened their lunch box. "I can't believe it," blurted Joe, "peanut butter
and jelly sandwiches. I don't like peanut butter and jelly."

With that he crumpled his sandwiches and hurled them to the ground.

Lunch on the second day produced the same scenario as Joe became visibly upset
with the sandwiches in his lunch. Once again, the sandwiches were hurled seventeen stories below.

Joe's buddy dreaded lunch on the following day. Rather than enjoying a well
earned rest, he was stuck listening to his new co-worker complain day after day.

He silently watched Joe sort through his lunch selection. And then . . . And then it happened. "I've had it with peanut butter and jelly," screamed Joe. He angrily smashed the sandwiches in his hand and thrust them to the ground below.

Unable to restrain himself any longer, Joe's buddy exclaimed: "If you don't like peanut butter and jelly sandwiches, then tell your wife not to make them anymore."

"Wait a minute," Joe quickly exclaimed, "don't bring my wife into this. I make my own sandwiches."

We may chuckle at the absurdity of this situation but it has a definite relevance to most of our lives. We all make our own sandwiches. Quality of life is determined by the ingredients we choose in filling the time between the two slices of bread . . . the beginning and end of our lives.

It probably goes without saying that to enjoy the richness of life we need to make wise choices about what we fill it with.

Remember the old television show "Let's Make a Deal" and the master deal-maker Monty Hall? People showed up for that program in the most outlandish costumes imaginable with the hope of being chosen to negotiate a deal. Monty teased them with options and tempting possibilities. In fact, before the participants had a chance to make a decision on his first offer, he would often provide them another choice to complicate their decision-making. The heart of this popular game show revolved around options and choices. Everybody went away with something (although some participants would have been better off not winning anything). It was a game of guesswork and the people who went home the happiest were the ones who guessed the right choices.

Life may at times seem to mirror the "Let's Make a Deal" process. There are certain choices in life that will be positively rewarded and others that bring disappointment. Although we do not always make the best choices, we can make the best of the choices we make.

I ran across a verse in the *Southern Statesman* newsletter that communicates perfectly what we can do to insure a quality life.

> You can't control the length of your life, but
> you can control its width and depth. You can't
> control the contour of your countenance, but you
> can control its expression. You can't control
> the other person's opportunities, but you can
> seize upon your own and make the best of them.
>
> You can't control the weather, but you can
> control the atmosphere which surrounds you. You
> can't control the distance that your head will be above the
> ground, but you can control the level
> of the contents of that head.

You can't control the other person's annoying faults,
but you can see to it that you yourself
do not develop or harbor similar propensities.

As Dr. Denis Waitley puts it, "I am behind the wheel in my life. Losers let it happen—winners make it happen." So if your life takes a turn for the worse, remember that you are the one who is driving. Of course, even when we are in control, there may be days when we feel like the bug and other days the windshield. Even so, I would suggest we stop worrying about the potholes, detours and road-closed signs and start enjoying the journey.

Two key words keep ringing in my ears. Control and Choices. Winners, those are the people living quality lives, control the choices they make and their responses to the consequences of their choices. Let me add another significant word: responsibility. Winners take responsibility for the quality of their lives by making wise choices that help them create the kind of life they desire.

When human beings come to the realization that they are in charge of their lives, they can begin taking charge to make things happen. That's when quality life takes on a pragmatic meaning. Until then, this all sounds like pie-in-the-sky philosophy.

There's an old German saying that goes, "You have to take life as it happens, but you should try to make it happen the way you want to take it." Sounds like great advice to me.

Just as practical is the advice of an unknown poet who said:

Life itself can't give you joy,
    Unless you really will it;
Life just gives you time and space,
    It's up to you to fill it.

No one ever finds life worthy of living—he or she has to make it worth living. Life is neutral. It is neither good nor bad. Just neutral. What we do with life will determine whether we view it as an adventure or a drudgery. Life doesn't do anything to you, it only reveals your spirit.

"There are only two ways to approach life," suggests Merle Shain, "as a victim or as a gallant fighter and you must decide if you want to act or react. . . . A lot of people forget that."

WHAT DO YOU WANT?

Summers were busy for Reverend John conducting evangelistic tent meetings throughout the Midwest. His most challenging moments came recruiting and inspiring local residents to attend his evening services. Driving along a country road one morning he spotted a farmer cultivating his cornfield. Reverend John made his way into the field and greeted the elderly man. Following an introduction and some small talk he proceeded to question the potential recruit.

"Are you a member of the Christian family?" he began.

"Why no," the farmer replied, "they live two miles north and one mile east."

Trying a little different approach, Reverend John continued, "Are you lost?"

"No, can't say as I am. In fact, I've been farming this land for some forty years."

Slightly flustered, Reverend John decided to be more direct. "My good friend, are you ready for 'Judgment Day'?"

The farmer perked up, "When is it?"

"I don't know," responded Reverend John, surprised by the farmer's sudden interest.

"You find out," the farmer quickly interjected, "because my wife and I probably will want to attend both days."

The evangelist's experience illustrates the dilemma experienced by many. They are seemingly unable to get what they want in life because they aren't specific about what they want. Spell it out, commit to it and keep your eyes on the desired outcome.

QUIET DESPERATION

Naturalist Henry David Thoreau is noted for his comment that most people "live lives of quiet desperation." In an effort to avoid that existence, Thoreau lived alone from 1845 to 1847 in the now-famous woods of Walden Pond, Massachusetts. In 1854, he published his experiences in the book entitled *Walden*. Thoreau wrote, "I went to the woods because I wished to live deliberately, to front only the essential facts of life, and see if I could not learn what it had to teach, and not, when I came to die, discover that I had not lived. I did not wish to live what was not life, living is so dear . . ."

The thought-provoking truths contained in Thoreau's writing have remarkable application many years later. Rather than living in quiet desperation we would do well to recognize, as did Thoreau, that "living is so dear."

LACKING ONE THING

A young artist worked painstakingly on the picture of an eagle. When the instructor came to view the painting, the artist hid nearby and waited to hear his mentor's comments. The master artist looked intently at the painting. At last he said, "It lacks only one thing." Hearing this, the young artist was heartbroken. For days he reevaluated his efforts from the initial stroke to the finishing touches. What did his masterpiece lack? Exasperated, he approached his instructor to ask what his painting lacked. "It lacks only life," the master artist responded. "With life, it would be perfect."

Is it possible the masterpiece we work so hard to create throughout our lifetime lacks the essential element of life itself?

Norman Vincent Peale addressed this beautifully when he commented: "By the good life, I mean one that is intensely interesting, even exciting. It is a life that is full of meaning and rich in satisfaction. Such a life is not free of difficulties or problems; of course not. But it does possess the power to overcome them and to attain victorious levels of experience. The good life is based on a definitive value system in which joy and enthusiasm serve as both cause and effect."

LIFE IS LIKE . . .

Have you ever noticed how easy it is to philosophize about life? Take the two ladies who met every morning for coffee at a local fast-food restaurant. They would habitually find their way to the same window booth everyday and watch the traffic go by. Their two-hour ritual was filled with silence except for periodic moments of short conversation.

While watching the traffic one lady said to her partner, "Life is like a highway."

Several minutes and cars passed before her partner answered, "I don't get it. How is life like a highway?"

An hour went by before the first lady responded, "You know, maybe life isn't like a highway after all."

Here's a profound reality: It is a lot easier to create analogies about life than it is to explain life. Add value to life; take up one of Benjamin Franklin's habits. Every day of his adult life, he set aside time to examine two questions. In the morning he asked himself, "What good shall I do today?" As the day drew to a close, his question was: "What good have I done today?" This process is sure to produce more than philosophizing about what life is like.

LIFE'S UNCERTAINTIES

One thing is certain, life is filled with uncertainty. It is impossible to know what the next twenty-four hours, or for that matter, the next hour will bring. Blessings and sorrows, success and failure, sunshine and rain are all present in life's agenda. The fear of uncertainty can have a crippling effect on our pursuit of the good life.

In the Middle Ages, European sailors refused to sail very far south. They were convinced that the middle of the earth was ringed with fire, because the farther south they traveled the hotter the temperature became. The fear of the unknown kept the Atlantic Ocean free from explorers. Sometime in the Middle Ages, a chart was drawn showing a painting of a ship turning back into the Mediterranean Sea from the Straits of Gibraltar. Above the painting appears the Latin phrase *Ne Plus Ultra*, which means, "Nothing more beyond." Had it not been for Ponce de Leon and Christopher Columbus, the Atlantic Ocean would have remained an undiscovered horizon. They challenged the myths of what might lie beyond to discover new worlds and unexplored possibilities.

How many of life's horizons go unexplored because we fear the uncertainties or are satisfied to tiptoe through life to make it safely to death without seeing what was available to us. Countless discoveries await the adventurous spirit willing to test the unknown.

ALL THE ANSWERS

The points contained in this section are encapsulated in the incident involving a 67-year-old man who called the doctor's office to schedule a physical.

Once the examination was completed, the doctor began quizzing his patient. "I have been your physician for many years; you are in great shape. Why the sudden desire for this physical?"

"I am getting married Saturday," responded the man, "and I want to make sure I am in great physical condition."

"At your age, choosing to get married is truly honorable," the doctor said. "You are in excellent health and God willing you and your bride will have many happy years together. Tell me, did your father die at an old age?"

"Did I say my father died? My father is 86 years old and in super condition."

"That's great! What about your grandfather, did he die at an old age?"

"Did I say my grandfather died? He is now 105 years old and is going to get married the same day I am. We're having a double ring ceremony. In fact, his son, my father, is going to be the best man for both of us."

"That is absolutely amazing," responded the doctor, "105 years old and he chose to get married!"

A smile appeared on the face of the groom-to-be as he replied, "Did I say he CHOSE to get married?"

Some things in life we can choose and others are thrust upon us. The privilege of choosing what we make of our life is one of the great privileges endowed by our Creator.

LOVE

■ Mental toughness is humility, simplicity, spartanism, and one other . . . love. I don't necessarily have to like my associates but as a man, I must love them. Love is loyalty; love is teamwork. Love respects the dignity of the individual. Heart and power is the strength of your cooperation.

Vince Lombardi

■ Love that lasts involves a real and genuine concern for others as persons, for their values as they feel them, for their development and growth.

Evelyn Duvall

■ Mature love involves growing from a state of receiving much and giving little toward a state of cheerfully giving everything and demanding nothing in return.

Dr. Richard Strauss

■ Love is to the heart what the summer is to the farmer's year. It brings to harvest all the loveliest flowers of the soul.

Billy Graham

■ Man must evolve for all human conflict a method which rejects revenge, aggression and retaliation. The foundation of such a method is love.

Martin Luther King, Jr.

■ Love never reasons, but profusely gives—gives like a thoughtless prodigal, its all—and trembles then lest it has done too little.

Hannah Moore

■ Love is the highest, purest, most precious of all spiritual things. It will draw out from men their magnificent potential.

Zig Ziglar

■ Love that is not expressed in loving action does not really exist, just as talent that does not express itself in creative works does not exist; neither of these is a state of mind, or feeling, but an activity, or it is a myth.

Sydney J. Harris

■ The amazing thing about love is that it is the best way to get to know ourselves.

Rollo May

■ Love is something like the clouds that were in the sky before the sun came out. You cannot touch the clouds, you know; but you feel the rain and know how glad the flowers and the thirsty earth are to have it after a hot day. You cannot touch love either; but you feel the sweetness that it pours into everything. Without love you would not be happy or want to play.

Annie Sullivan

■ Love is a moment and a lifetime. It is looking at him across a room and feeling that if I don't spend the rest of my life with him, I'll have missed the boat. Love is working together, laughing together, growing together. It is respect for each other and the people each cares about, however difficult it is sometimes to like his kinfolk or his friends. Love is wanting to shout from the rooftops the successes, little and big, of one another. Love is wanting to wipe away the tears when failure comes. Love is liking the feel of each other. It is wanting to have children together because they are the exclamation point of love. Love is laughter, especially in the middle of a quarrel.

Liz Carpenter
Getting Better All the Time

■ The more a person perceives that he/she is loved, the less they will interfere with the lives of others.

Dr. William Glasser

■ Love doesn't make the world go 'round. Love is what makes the ride worthwhile.

Franklin P. Jones

■ What the world really needs is more love and less paperwork.

Pearl Bailey

■ The cure for all the ills and wrongs, the cares, the sorrows, and the crimes of humanity all lie in the one word *love*. It is the divine vitality that everywhere produces and restores life.

Lydia Maria Child

■ Love is the immortal flow of energy that nourishes, extends, and preserves. Its eternal goal is life.

Smiley Blanton

THE SEARCH FOR LOVE

Love is an essential ingredient for success. Without it, your life suffers in emptiness. With it, life vibrates warmth and satisfaction. Search for and generate love—because if you don't, you're not living—just breathing.

Ida Fay Oglesby, writing in the *P.E.O. Record* (January 1983), tells the story of a little eight-year-old girl in a Pennsylvania orphanage who was shy, unattractive, and regarded as a problem. Two other asylums had her transferred, and now this director was seeking some pretext for getting rid of her. One day someone noticed the little girl was writing a letter. An ironclad rule of the institution was that any communication from a child had to be approved before it was mailed. The next day, the director and her assistant watched the child steal out of the dormitory and slip down to the main gate. Just inside the gate was an old tree with roots showing above the ground. They followed and watched as the child hid the letter in one of the crevices of the root. Carefully looking around, the little girl scurried back to the dormitory.

The director pounced on the note and tore it open. Then, without speaking, she passed the note to her assistant. It read, "To anybody who finds this: I love you."

Only when we experience love can we experience life to the fullest.

A LESSON FROM THE UPAS

The Upas tree grows in Indonesia, secretes poison and grows so thick it kills all forms of vegetation around it. The upas's very existence results in sheltering, shading, poisoning, and destroying its surroundings.

Unfortunately, there are people who possess the same qualities and lifestyle. They dominate, criticize, and overwhelm others while wanting attention, credit, and homage paid to them. These people have no interest in sharing themselves. They have simply not learned to love or be loved.

Several years ago a story appeared in *The Gospel Banner* that provided a clear example of an "upas person."

A fashionably dressed young woman, sightseeing in a New York City slum, shuddered over a dirty, unkempt ragamuffin playing in the filth of the gutter. "Just look at that child!" she cried. "Why doesn't someone clean him up? Where is his mother?"

"Well, it's this way, Miss," explained her guide. "The child's mother loves her child, but she doesn't hate the dirt. You hate the dirt but you don't love the child. Until love for the child and hate for the dirt get into the same heart, the poor child remains just about as he is."

It's important to consider carefully the words of the French orientalist Caussin de Perceval, "Never to judge rashly; never to interpret the actions of others in ill sense, but to compassionate their infirmities, bear their burdens, excuse their weaknesses, and make up for their defects—to hate their imperfections, but love themselves, this is the true spirit of charity."

SACRIFICIAL LOVE

Out of Alan Paton's novel, *Ah, But Your Land Is Beautiful* (MacMillan, 1983), comes this story: A girl with a terrible facial disfigurement and a blind man fell in love and married. He was the only person she cared about who wouldn't flinch from her.

One day a prominent surgeon examined the man. "I believe I can restore your sight," he said. Joy filled the man's heart, but fear gripped his wife's. Sensing her hesitation, the husband asked, "Why do you not share my joy?" "I do," she insisted. Then he said, "You have never before lied to me. Why do you lie to me now?" When she told him of her blemish, he said, "I love you so much that I will stay blind. Your happiness means more to me than my sight." He calmed her fears by closing the door to a possible miracle that might cause him to stop loving her.

The Bible says, "Greater love hath no man than to lay up his life for a friend." I would say the blind man possessed great love.

MARRIAGE

- Love at first sight is easy to understand; it's when two people have been looking at each other for a lifetime that it becomes a miracle!

  Sam Levenson

- What you are as a single person, you will be as a married person, only to a greater degree. Any negative character trait will be intensified in a marriage relationship, because you will feel free to let your guard down—that person has committed himself to you, and you no longer have to worry about scaring him off.

  Josh McDowell
  Secret of Loving

- For two people in a marriage to live together day after day is unquestionably the one miracle the Vatican has overlooked.

  Bill Cosby

- The kind of marriage you make depends upon the kind of person you are. If you are a happy, well-adjusted person, the chances are your marriage will be a happy one. If you have made adjustments so far with more satisfaction than distress, you are likely to make your marriage and family adjustments satisfactorily. If you are discontented and bitter about your lot in life, you will have to change before you can expect to live happily ever after.

  Evelyn Duvall and Reuben Hill
  When You Marry

- Success in marriage is more than finding the right person. Being the right person is even more important.

  Elof G. Nelson

- Marriage—as its veterans know well—is the continuous process of getting used to things you hadn't expected.

  Tom Mullen

- The middle years of marriage are the most crucial. In the early years, spouses want each other and in late years, they need each other.

  Rebecca Tilly

■ If you marry for money only, you will suffer . . . in comfort.

Dr. Murray Banks

■ If you want to sacrifice the admiration of many men for the criticism of one, go ahead, get married.

Katharine Hepburn

■ The trouble with some women is that they get all excited about nothing—and then marry him.

Cher

■ An archeologist is the best husband any woman can have. The older she gets, the more he is interested in her!

Agatha Christie

■ Happy marriages begin when we marry the ones we love, and they blossom when we love the ones we marry.

Tom Mullen

KEEP THE FIRES KINDLED

George Bernard Shaw described marriage as that time "when two people are under the influence of the most violent, most insane, most delusive, and most transient of passions. They are required to swear that they will remain in that excited, abnormal, and exhausting condition continuously until death do them part."

Recall the aura, the ecstasy, the perfectness of your wedding day. The vows are meticulously and faultlessly repeated. A stimulating honeymoon reinforces the idealistic glow. Nothing could ever alter the thrill of this hallowed occasion.

Then comes reality. The couple soon realizes marriage is not an ongoing celebration of celestial dimensions. It's a lifelong process of down-to-earth hard work—worth every drop of sweat it produces.

•   •   •

Building a marriage that withstands the test of time requires an understanding of the foundation on which healthy relationships are constructed.

It often appears the mortar that holds it all together is acceptance. Charles L. Allen put it this way: "One of the important things about marriage is to be accepted. Love is the basis of marriage, but there are many married people who have never felt accepted. Marriage is not a reformatory, and spouses need to reach out to each other without criticism or reservations. To live with a wife or a husband who does not accept you is a dark valley to walk through."

Marriage involves two imperfect human beings joining together. Accept your spouse for who they are, not what they would be, could be, or should be "if only they listened to you." Mature love is an unconditional acceptance and commitment to an imperfect person, for what they are, not what you would like them to be tomorrow.

I love the story of two women having lunch together, who began discussing their husbands. One said, "If all women were like me, they would all want to be married to my husband." The other woman quickly retorted, "If all women were like me, none of them would want to be married to him." The ideal mate is just a matter of perspective.

· · ·

"You can't make someone over," advised Judy Davis and Dr. Herman Weiss in *How to Get Married* (Ballantine Books, 1983). "You won't be able to make him more romantic, wittier, more outgoing, less of a gambler/drinker/smoker, or even cure his allergy to your cat. You cannot afford to become his mother, his teacher, or his therapist. Look before you leap into a relationship."

George F. Gilder, writing in *Sexual Suicide,* concurs. "A marriage is a commitment of two people," he says, "not to exchange products or services but to escape the psychology of exchange altogether. Each partner receives the other as a whole person, for what he is rather than for what he agrees to do."

· · ·

Understand. What an interesting word. If you could "stand under" me and experience what I experience, see what I see, feel how I feel, then you would know what makes me tick.

Any couple who perfects the art of understanding is on their way to a relationship made in heaven. The fact is, most of us are selfish enough to want others to see our point of view with little regard for the other person's perspective.

As the old story goes, there was a time when he talked and she listened. On their honeymoon she talked and he listened. And now that they are settled down in their own home, they both talk and the neighbors listen. And if they don't yell loud enough for the neighbors to hear, maybe nobody's listening.

First comes the desire to understand. Then, mutual openness, honesty, listening, and respect are mixed together to create empathy. It is amazing what happens when two people individually commit themselves to understand the other.

A more common scenario involves Ole and Lena. They were experiencing a little marital discord and decided to see a counselor. When the counselor asked what the difficulty was, Lena took off with a long-winded dissertation of her complaints, which lasted almost an hour. Then, after taking a deep breath, Lena added, "Well, that is my side of the story. Now I will tell you his."

We may think we know our spouse's side of the story though we have never taken the time to listen to it.

Dr. Robert C. Kolodney of the Masters and Johnson Institute in St. Louis says that less than ten percent of a couple's therapy is focused on the physical part of the relationship, even though this is why the couple thought they came for help. The focus of 90 percent of the therapy is on the areas of self-esteem and interpersonal communication.

Dr. Howard Markman offers this formula: "Communicating frequently and intimately is the best prescription for a successful marriage."

· · ·

So, understanding is our second prerequisite for a healthy relationship. The third principle is to be committed to meeting the other person's needs.

The Apostle Paul emphasized this point when he wrote, "Let each of you esteem and look upon and be concerned for not (merely) his own interests, but also each for the interest of others." (Philippians 2:4, Amplified).

I'm not so naive to believe that it is possible for any two people to completely fulfill one another's needs. If a couple could mutually satisfy even 75 percent of the other's needs, it would be a minor miracle.

So what's the point? There seems to be a discrepancy between the quality suggested and its improbable achievement.

Enter and sustain your marriage with a sincere desire to meet your spouse's needs, not to have your needs met. Although we can never fully meet someone's needs, fulfillment comes to those who see how close they can come. Being sensitive to what's important to your spouse is a lifelong endeavor.

Inspirational author and pastor Bruce Larson tells about the change that can occur in relationships between husband and wife after they have been married for a few years. He illustrates this by relating the seven stages of the common cold in the life of a young married couple.

> *The first year:* "Sugar, I'm worried about my little sweetie pie. You've got a bad sniffle and I want you to go to the hospital for a complete checkup."
>
> *The second year:* "Listen, honey, I don't like the sound of that cough. I've called the doctor and he's going to rush right over."
>
> *The third year:* "Maybe you'd better lie down, honey. Nothing like a little rest if you're feeling bad. I'll even bring you something to eat."
>
> *The fourth year:* "Look, dear, be sensible; after you've fed the kids and washed the dishes, you'd better hit the sack."
>
> *The fifth year:* "Why don't you take a couple of aspirin?"
>
> *The sixth year:* "If you'd just gargle or something instead of sitting around barking like a seal, it might help."

The seventh year: "For heaven's sake, stop sneezing! What are you trying to do, give me pneumonia?"

Does that sound at all familiar?

•　　•　　•

How about this amusing story from *The Happiness Digest*—

At breakfast one morning, a woman said to her husband, "I bet you don't know what day this is." "Of course I do," he answered as he went out the door on his way to the office. At 10:00 A.M. the doorbell rang. The woman opened the door and was handed a box containing a dozen long-stemmed, red roses. At 1:00 P.M., a foil-wrapped, two-pound box of her favorite chocolates arrived. Later, a boutique delivered a dress.

The woman couldn't wait for her husband to come home. "First the flowers, then the candy, and then the dress!" she exclaimed. "I've never spent a more wonderful Groundhog's Day in my whole life!"

And how about the man and woman married 50 years who were asked the secret of their marital bliss. "Well," drawled the old man, "the wife and I had an agreement when we first got married. The agreement was that when she was bothered about something, she would just tell me off, get it out of her system. And if I was mad at her about something, I was to take a walk. I suppose you can attribute our marital success to the fact that I have predominantly lived an outdoor life."

What I like about this couple is their commitment to each other. Their response to marriage's normal difficulties was to react in a way that would enrich the relationship.

Whether you're dealing with an illness, forgetting a special day, or involved in conflict, responding in a way that uplifts your partner will reap marvelous dividends.

•　　•　　•

Norman Wright has wisely observed that "marriage resembles a pair of shears, so joined that they cannot be separated; often moving in opposite directions, yet always punishing anyone who comes between them."

Acceptance, understanding and sensitivity to the other person's needs form the rivet that holds the shears together and allows them to work interdependently.

Walter Trobisch, in his sensitive book, *I Loved a Girl*, says you are in love "if you cannot imagine living your life without her; if you feel pain when you are away from her; if she occupies your thoughts, and inspires your dreams at all times; if her happiness means more to you than your own."

For some, those feelings were a long time ago. The fire has dwindled and the coals are cold. Yet we argue that was just the experience of falling in love. Once there, Trobisch's thoughts aren't important anymore. Right? Wrong!

Marriage and family counselor Dr. Henry Brandt writes that love is mature when a couple "enjoys being together more than being with anyone else, although others are not excluded from their lives. They discover that each can even have a good time doing something together which neither would enjoy doing alone. When they are absent from each other, each is in the background of the other's thoughts."

It has been said that in marriage, being the right person is as important as finding the right person.

Sally Wendkos Olds reported that researchers Ammons and Stinnett believe a key characteristic of happy married partners is that they "are sensitive to other people . . . they recognize the needs of others, respect their differences, consider their feelings, put themselves in the other person's shoes."

Be the right person! Keep the fires kindled!

MISSION

- For a merit environment to work, our managers must be able to teach what our mission is all about—our purpose, our vision, our values—and apply this to local (work unit) needs.

  William J. O'Brien
  President, Hanover Trust

- We are not just managing for the sake of being great managers. We are managing for the mission.

  Frances Hesselbein

- Mission starts with determining what you really care about and want to accomplish and committing yourself to it. You can always develop expertise. First, discover your preference.

  Charles Garfield

- Purpose is not simply a target that an organization chooses to aim for; it is the organization's reason for being.

  Perry Pascarella and Mark A. Frohman
  The Purpose-Driven Organization

- Only a clear definition of the mission and purpose of the business makes possible clear and realistic business objectives. It is the foundation for priorities, strategies, plans, and work assignments. It is the starting point for the design of managerial jobs and, above all, for the design of managerial structures.

  Peter Drucker

- The first thing you must do to become a great organization is spell out in writing your beliefs and purpose. Write a credo that will be a behavioral guide to every person in your company, from entry-level positions to CEO. This creed, once thought out and formalized, should become as much a part of a company's operation as its product, service, or policies.

  Buck Rogers

- American business needs a lifting purpose greater than the struggle of materialism.

  Herbert Hoover

MISSION-DRIVEN

Organizational culture is an outgrowth of a company's determined mission. When an organization decides what it is all about, every action and decision will revolve around the pursuit of this ideal.

"Mission," says Charles Garfield, "is an image of a desired state of affairs that inspires action, determines behavior, and fuels motivation."

> The largest nonprofit organization in the free world continues a proud tradition through the pursuit of its mission. The Girl Scouts of America dedicate themselves "to the purpose of inspiring girls with the highest ideals of character, conduct, patriotism, and service that they may become happy and resourceful citizens."

> For the employees of Levi Strauss & Company, this mission provides daily inspiration: "Above all we want satisfaction from accomplishments and friendships, balanced personal and professional lives, and to have fun in our endeavors."

> Delta Airline's motto simply states, "We're ready when you are."

> At W. L. Gore and Associates, the mission is "to make money and have fun."

> Ryder System Inc. seeks through their missions "to be the growing leader in providing high-quality transportation support services to business customers." As a result of this pursuit, Ryder made over ninety friendly acquisitions in the 1980s.

> At Federal Express, "People, service and profits" are at the forefront of every business- and employee-related decision: "We will produce outstanding financial returns by providing totally reliable, competitively superior global air-ground transportation of high priority goods and documents that require rapid, time-certain delivery. Equally important, positive control of each package will be maintained utilizing real-time electronic tracking and tracing systems. A complete record of each shipment and delivery will be presented with our request for payment. We will be helpful, courteous, and professional to each other and the public. We will strive to have a satisfied customer at the end of each transaction."

> The spirit of the Walt Disney Company is grounded in this mission: "We seek not to imitate the masters; rather, we seek what they sought."

> Westinghouse Furniture Systems advertises its mission as "expanding the limits of human performance."

> At Quality Inns, the vision is "to pursue excellence and become the most recognized, respected, and admired lodging chain in the world."

One section of the Hewlett-Packard corporate statement reads, "Objective: To honor our obligations to society by being an economic, intellectual, and social asset to each nation and each community in which we operate." Elsewhere, in its advertising, Hewlett-Packard announces emphatically, "Performance. Not promises."

Colgate-Palmolive Company is a leader in providing consumer products and services that meet or exceed the needs and expectations of consumers worldwide. "Our mission," they proclaim, "is to improve continuously our products and services so that our Company, our people, our business partners, and our shareholders will grow and prosper, enabling us to become the best global consumer products company."

The Minneapolis-based department store chain, Dayton Hudson, has a company mission: "Purchasing agent for its customers." This statement boldly reminds all eighty thousand plus employees that the company exists to serve the customer.

To quote Charles Garfield again, "The mission statement provides the why that inspires every how." These are but a sampling of well-known companies who know *what* they believe, thereby making the *how* and *why* simpler to define.

A SOUND PHILOSOPHY

The ServiceMaster Corporation serves as a beautiful example of a company that thoroughly integrates its corporate philosophy and mission into day-to-day affairs.

Founded by Marion E. Wade, the story of its conception, genesis and growth is told in Wade's book, *God Is My Counsel*. Kenneth T. Wessner, Chairman of the Board of ServiceMaster, states:

> The philosophy of a company determines the character and nature of business it conducts. The climate of a company is created by the concepts of managing and life that govern its policies and practices. The philosophy of ServiceMaster and the words we used to express that philosophy have been carefully conceived, nurtured, and refined through years of thought, work, and commitment. Our company philosophy is expressed in four objectives. These four statements are the foundation upon which everything we do is built.
>
> To honor God in all we do.
> To help people develop.
> To pursue excellence.
> To grow profitably.

For the people of ServiceMaster, their work is not merely the making of a living; it is a way of life.

That solid philosophy has helped ServiceMaster become one of the largest cleaning service conglomerates in the world.

MISTAKES

- Crisis can often have value because it generates transformation . . . I have found that I always learn more from my mistakes than from my successes. If you aren't making some mistakes, you aren't taking enough chances.

  John Sculley

- The trouble in America is not that we are making too many mistakes, but that we are making too few.

  Philip Knight
  Footwear News Magazine, *February 1989*

- We teach people that mistakes are like skinned knees for little children. They're painful, but they heal quickly, and they're learning experiences. My people are covered with the scars of their mistakes. They've lived out in the field; they've been shot at; they've been hit in every part of their bodies; and they're real. By the time they get to the top, their noses are pretty well broken. The chances of their getting there with a clean nose are zero.

  H. Ross Perot

- Mistakes are part of the dues one pays for a full life.

  Sophia Loren

- You know, by the time you reach my age, you've made plenty of mistakes, and if you've lived your life properly, so you learn. You put things in perspective. You pull your energies together. You change. You go forward.

  Ronald Reagan

- While one person hesitates because he feels inferior, the other is busy making mistakes and becoming superior.

  Henry C. Link

- A mistake only proves that someone stopped talking long enough to do something.

  Michael LeBoeuf

- If you're going to do something wrong, at least enjoy it.

  Leo Rosten

■ Whenever I make a bum decision, I go out and make another one.

Harry Truman

■ Give me a fruitful error anytime, full of seeds, bursting with its own corrections.

Vilfredo Pareto

■ The difference between greatness and mediocrity is often how an individual views a mistake.

Nelson Boswell

■ Have patience with all things but first with yourself. Never confuse your mistakes with your value as a human being. You're a perfectly valuable, creative, worthwhile person simply because you exist. And no amount of triumphs or tribulations can ever change that. Unconditional self-acceptance is the core of a peaceful mind.

Saint Francis de Sales

■ You cannot become a power in your community nor achieve enduring success in any worthy undertaking until you become big enough to blame yourself for your own mistakes and reverses.

Anonymous

■ I have my faults. But being wrong ain't one of them.

Jimmy Hoffa

"I GUESS I FLEW THE WRONG WAY"

More than fifty years ago, Douglas "Wrong Way" Corrigan made a forbidden New York-to-Dublin, Ireland, flight in a used Curtiss-Robin monoplane. "My compass froze. I guess I flew the wrong way," Corrigan claimed on July 18, 1938. He has maintained he thought he was returning to his home base of Long Beach, California, after federal aviation authorities denied him permission to fly to Ireland. In a 1988 article in *The Des Moines Register*, Corrigan hinted that his wrong-way explanation might change after a flight to Dublin as an honored guest for three days of ceremonies commemorating his flight. Corrigan's explanation sounded like pure blarney at the time—he was made a lifetime member of the Liars Club—but America and Ireland loved it. As punishment for his journey, the Bureau of Air Commerce suspended Corrigan from flying for five days, the five days while he was aboard a ship on the way home. Whatever the true story, Corrigan had joined the ranks of Charles Lindbergh and Wiley Post by making a solo, non-stop, single-engine crossing of the Atlantic.

A TEN-MILLION-DOLLAR EDUCATION

"The better a man is, the more mistakes he will make, for the more new things he will try," says management consultant Peter Drucker. "I would never promote into a top-level job a man who was not making mistakes . . . otherwise he is sure to be mediocre."

A now famous story at IBM involved founder Thomas Watson and one of his vice presidents who took the initiative on the development of a new product. As reported in *Fortune* (August 31, 1987), the product was a risky venture that ended up a colossal failure and cost the company $10 million. Watson called the executive into his office saying there was something he wanted to discuss with him.

Sure he was about to lose his job, the young man blurted out, "I guess you want my resignation?"

Watson replied, "You must be kidding. We've just spent $10 million educating you."

Anyone making a multi-million-dollar mistake had to learn something that would help him do a better job the next time. Drucker's comment that people who are not making mistakes are sure to be mediocre is comforting to those of us who make mistakes as a part of our daily regimen.

NOT AGAIN

I'm not sure I can agree with Jane Heard's comment that, "a well-adjusted person is one who makes the same mistake twice without getting nervous." There are some mistakes that are unhealthy to repeat and we might wonder how in the world someone could be so dense as to let that happen.

A husband and wife were enjoying an evening home together in front of the television. An action-packed adventure movie was playing and the bad guy was being chased by a police officer down a spiral mountain highway. As the speeds increased to an uncontrollable level, the wife said, "I bet you dinner at a fancy restaurant the criminal goes over the cliff." "It's a bet," said the husband. Just then the bad guy lost control on a curve and drove over the cliff.

Realizing he had just lost the bet, the husband asked, "Where do you want me to make dinner reservations?"

His wife looked over at him and said, "I feel guilty collecting on our bet. I've seen this movie before."

"So have I," the husband sheepishly responded, "but I didn't think he'd be stupid enough to drive off the same cliff twice."

WISDOM FROM EMERSON

Ralph Waldo Emerson's daughter was attending school away from her home community. In a letter to her father, she indicated that she was concerned about a past mistake that continued to haunt her. Emerson wrote the following to his daughter:

> "Finish every day and be done with it. You have done what you could. Some blunders and absurdities no doubt crept in; but get rid of them and forget them as soon as you can. Tomorrow is a new day, and you should never encumber its potentialities and invitations with the dread of the past. You should not waste a moment of today on the rottenness of yesterday."

Sounds like great advice for dealing with the small as well as big mistakes that will inevitably enter our lives.

COLOSSAL MISTAKES

When your mistakes seem big, purchase and peruse M. Hirsh Goldberg's *The Blunder Book* and your bloopers will appear trifling. According to Goldberg, the company that won the bid to construct the 100 miles of track for the Washington, D.C., subway system estimated the cost to be $793 million. When it was finished, however, it cost $6.6 billion. Goldberg said the same company that built the subway system was awarded a contract to build the Saudi Arabian city of Jubail. The initial cost projection was $9 billion. But when the project was finished, the bill came to $45 billion . . . just a mere $36 billion cost overrun.

A CLASSIC CASE OF STUPIDITY

Many years ago, in a land far away, three vagrants roamed the countryside in search of adventure. Their quest brought them to an orderly village where they created their own sense of excitement considered unacceptable by the town's people. For their serious unlawful behavior, the three were sentenced to death by the guillotine.

When the fateful day arrived, the executioner double-checked the equipment and indicated he was ready to begin. But when the first victim was placed on the guillotine, it didn't work.

"Unbelievable!" shouted the executioner. "The laws of our land dictate we must set you free."

The second drifter was positioned beneath the murderous blade and again, the guillotine stuck. He too was freed.

The third man had watched the previous equipment failure and his two friends set free. As he lay on the platform, eyes glaring up at the weapon that would end his life, he suddenly blurted, "Wait a minute, I see your problem. If you would just oil that hinge . . ."

MOTIVATION

- The only way to get people to like working hard is to motivate them. Today, people must understand why they're working hard. Every individual in an organization is motivated by something different.

  Rick Pitino

- Motivation without mobilization means only frustration.

  Nido Qubein

- The key to all motivation is desire, and the master key to creating desire is responsiveness to the needs, desires, and interests of the people you would lead.

  John R. Noe

- The world is moved by highly motivated people, by enthusiasts, by men and women who want something very much or believe very much.

  John Gardner

- Motivation describes your attitude when you would rather do one thing more than another at a particular time.

  Robert Anthony

- Nobody motivates today's workers. If it doesn't come from within, it doesn't come. Fun helps remove the barriers that allow people to motivate themselves.

  Herman Cain
  Godfather Pizza CEO

- Motivation is a fire from within. If someone else tries to light that fire under you, chances are it will burn very briefly.

  Stephen Covey

- Getting down to the nitty-gritty, most people are motivated by unconscious motives most of the time.

  Richard J. Mayer

- The motivator who can motivate everybody but himself may win the world, but he'll never enjoy it.

  Charlie "Tremendous" Jones

- If your people are headed in the wrong direction, don't motivate them.

George Odiorne

- Motivation is what gets you started. Habit is what keeps you going.

Jim Ryun

- Unlock your natural drives by doing what you enjoy.

Hans Selye

- Average people look forward to "getting off." Successful people look forward to "getting on."

Jim Rohn

- The more that people understand the value of what they are doing, the more motivated they are to do it well. Similarly, the better they understand what their individual rewards will be, that is, "what's in it for them," the more motivated they will be.

Dr. David Campbell

A WHALE OF A CHALLENGE

When was the last time you tried to make a 40-foot, 45-ton, untrained, satisfied whale do what you want it to do? Probably not lately, unless you were one of the people in San Francisco bay a few years ago. A humpback whale, affectionately named Humphrey, was migrating along the California coast when a wrong turn got him stranded. Humphrey became a national celebrity when he turned into San Francisco bay, swam under the Golden Gate Bridge, and managed to navigate 70 miles upriver. Even though it was for his own good, Humphrey resisted all attempts to get him back to salt water. Three weeks into his predicament, marine biologists lured him with the recorded sounds of feeding humpbacks. Humphrey excited the crowds as he responded to a familiar sound and followed his friends into the Pacific.

People—and whales for that matter—do things because they want to, not because someone else thinks it is a good thing to do. Motivation results from actions that satisfy inner needs. As Frank Bettger put it, "Show people what they want and how to get it, and they will move Heaven and Earth to get it."

MOTIVATED BEYOND MEDIOCRITY

Twin boys grew up in a small midwestern community where they found many people very interested in their daily activities. Tom and Terry were always small for their age and were never known to be anything but aggressive and physical. They were often the "show" for others as they would wrestle each other frequently.

As they grew up, they started to gain recognition for their individual abilities as legitimate wrestlers. They wrestled through their high school days in the lightest weights since they did not weigh the 96 pounds necessary to be identified as a legitimate lightweight. Their determination was never doubted, and by their final two years in high school, both were state champions and caught the eye of Dan Gable, head wrestling coach of the University of Iowa.

From a split home and a mother who never stopped caring, they started their college career with the assurances from the medical professionals they would grow at least a few more inches and gain some weight. During their high school days I had had an opportunity to observe the boys closely, since their mother was my personal secretary, and I listened to many difficult stories of coping with the challenge of raising two teenagers as a single parent.

The story here, however, is the relationship of these boys to their college coach, Dan Gable. Tom has shared with me on a number of occasions that Coach Gable was "the finest." I never doubted he meant that, but I did wonder at times why that would be true since I was aware of the expectations Coach Gable had for all of his athletes.

March, 1990: This morning I figured it out.

Two weeks ago, Tom, who was the Number 1 wrestler in the nation in his weight class and had won the Nationals last year, was defeated by an opponent he had beaten twice before and lost the championship match of the Big Ten Athletic Conference. In visiting with his mother, I learned two things. First, Tom was personally very depressed, and secondly, Coach Gable was very rough on him and had him working extremely hard.

As he prepared for the Nationals this past weekend, many wondered what would happen. As had been anticipated on Saturday night, he again faced the same wrestler who defeated him at the Big Ten Finals and had been identified as the most improved wrestler in the meet. Tom came from behind to win in the final period and regained his top ranking in the nation.

In Sunday's paper, Tom was quoted: "Coach Gable has had a great influence on me. He is a very important person in my life." Did he say that because the coach pushed him to excel and win big, or was there something else?

This morning I stopped to visit with the mother of Tom and Terry to share the exciting experience of having two sons become the number-one wrestlers in the nation. I noticed a large, lovely, fresh-cut flower arrangement behind her desk, and she shared with me the personal message attached. It stated, "Thank you for sharing your two sons with our family. We do love them.—The Dan Gable Family.

I think I found the answer to that relationship.

Both sons have now graduated from the University of Iowa, enrolled in graduate school, and plan to continue their career of wrestling with hopes of competing in the 1996 Olympics.

This story was shared by Bob Hoogeveen of Sheldon, Iowa. He is a personal friend of the Brands' family and says he marvels at Tom's and Terry's continual motivation to transcend mediocrity. This heartwarming account reaffirms the importance of having people believe in us, our motivation, and our potential.

GENERATE YOUR OWN MOTIVATION

Life isn't boring. Work isn't meaningless. Relationships aren't valueless. Whatever people are investing in these opportunities will be returned to them. Bored, unenthusiastic, unmotivated people wear their depressing qualities on their shirtsleeves for the whole world to see. They are constantly looking for new jobs, more exciting relationships, or an environment that appreciates them. It rarely works that way, and these people usually infect everything and everyone around them with their sluggishness.

A motivated lifestyle is enjoyed by those who create it for themselves. Zig Ziglar said he is often challenged by people wanting to know what motivation is and what it isn't. Zig says, "There are those who say that when someone goes to a motivational session they get all charged up, but a week later they're back where they were before they attended the session. In short, motivation isn't permanent . . . right?"

I remember Zig addressing that question during a "motivational" session I attended. He put it this way, "Of course motivation isn't permanent. But then, neither is bathing; but it is something you should do on a regular basis."

It is absurd to think that one seminar or speaker or book could have an immediate and permanent affect on the rest of your life. You will be required to generate that motivation on a daily basis with or without the assistance of others.

MOTIVATED BY FLAKES

At forty-six years of age, Will Kellogg found it difficult to remain motivated working for his older brother, a prominent doctor. Will was a shy person, somewhat nonsocial and without distinctive talents.

Working together, the two brothers were experimenting with producing a cereal for a patient. In the process they discovered the wheat flake, which Will tried to get his brother to mass market. Dr. Kellogg was not interested, so Will bought out his brother's portion of the cereal business and set out on his own.

There was a renewed motivation that eventually revealed Will's keen business ability, marketing genius, and customer sensitivity. Out of a less than exhilarating situation, Will Kellogg generated his own motivation to create not only Corn Flakes, but a lifetime of fulfillment.

"We don't need more strength or more ability or greater opportunity," says Basil S. Walsh. "What we need is to use what we have." That's exactly what Will Kellogg learned. He didn't possess any Olympic-level abilities, but he was motivated to make the most of what he had. In so doing, he became one of the richest people in America.

A MATTER OF PERSPECTIVE

Buck Rogers, former vice president of marketing at IBM, says in *Getting the Best Out of Yourself and Others* (Harper & Row, 1988): "Businesses aren't boring—not the publishing business, not the shoe business, not the computer business. People are boring. Drab, unexcited, unmotivated people carry their boredom with them. They take it from job to job hoping that they'll be brought out of their doldrums by a new job, new people, and a new environment. It rarely works that way; unfortunately, they usually bring down the new people around them instead of being elevated by them."

If you feel bored, penned in, unstimulated, and unmotivated, it's your responsibility to do something about it even if the company you work for seems apathetic about the conditions you perceive to be the cause.

"Well-motivated people have a sense of achievement, of being a fundamental part of the picture," writes Rogers. "If people feel proud and pleased with their performance, they will then be ready, willing, and able to achieve even more."

An amusing example of this is the man who was hired by the circus to clean up after elephants. A friend observed him in his new position and couldn't help but share his perspective. "You have the worst job of anyone I know," the friend began. "The elephant poops and you scoop. Poop and scoop. Poop and scoop. What a demeaning job. Why don't you just quit?"

"What," responded the pooper-scooper, "and give up show business?"

It is not the job we do but how we perceive it that affects our inspiration in it. This person felt important in his role. There was a sense of achievement and a feeling of belonging. Being part of the big top was motivation enough to continue scooping.

CREATIVE MOTIVATION

I read a modern fable that involved a clever retired man who bought a modest home near the junior high school. The first few weeks were marvelous and all his expectations of a relaxing retirement were being met. Then a group of teenagers began hanging around the neighborhood and entertained themselves by kicking garbage cans.

Unable to stand the constant noise, he approached the young people and softly said, "It is great to see you having a good time. I remember when I was a kid doing the same thing. It was fun." Then he continued with a strange request, "I would like to pay you each $1.00 a week for coming around and banging these garbage cans."

The youths were ecstatic and agreed to his proposal. However, in a few weeks the man informed the children that inflation made it necessary for him to cut down his payment to 50 cents a piece. Although a little disgruntled, the children agreed to continue at a reduced fee.

One morning the elderly man approached the garbage-banging children with this news, "My social security check no longer makes it possible for me to continue paying you at the going rate. I can only give you 25 cents each for your playful efforts. I hope that will be acceptable."

"What," exclaimed one kid. "You expect us to continue kicking those cans around for a lousy quarter. No way! You just lost your can bangers."

The man lived quietly ever after.

SIMPLY PUT

When Red Auerbach coached the dynasty-producing Boston Celtics, he carefully outlined each pre-game talk. Auerbach took great pride in making each pep talk an original. However, during the NBA championships one year, he found himself at a loss for words. Turning to his star player, Auerbach asked Frank Ramsay if he had any words of wisdom for the team.

Ramsay gave the invitation a little thought, then approached the blackboard and wrote, "You win . . . $10,000! You lose . . . $5,000!" That was all the pre-game pep talk the Celtics needed.

OBSTACLES

- Some people make victims of their disadvantage, while others are victimized by their disadvantages.

Robert Schuller

- If the winds of fortune are temporarily blowing against you, remember that you can harness them and make them carry you toward your definite purpose, through the use of your imagination.

Napoleon Hill

- If you want to move your greatest obstacle, realize that the obstacle is yourself—and that the time to act is now!

Nido Qubein

- History has demonstrated that the most notable winners usually encountered heartbreaking obstacles before they triumphed. They finally won because they refused to become discouraged by their defeats. Disappointments acted as a challenge. Don't let difficulties discourage you.

B. C. Forbes

- One who gains strength by overcoming obstacles possesses the only strength which can overcome adversity.

Albert Schweitzer

- An adventure is only an inconvenience rightly considered. An inconvenience is only an adventure wrongly considered.

G. K. Chesterton

- If you find a path with no obstacles, it probably doesn't lead anywhere.

Frank A. Clark

- You learn that, whatever you are doing in life, obstacles don't matter very much. Pain or other circumstances can be there, but if you want to do a job bad enough, you'll find a way to get it done.

Jack Youngblood

DREAMS THAT OBSTACLES COULDN'T DESTROY

Obstacles stimulate us to uncover dormant abilities. Out of our difficulties comes new strength. Isn't it interesting how something we despise and avoid at all costs can provide the catalyst for something wonderful.

Sheila Holzworth, who climbed to Mount Rainier's icy summit in 1981, surmounted the obstacle of blindness. Holzworth lost her sight when she was 10 years old. Her orthodontic headgear, attached to her braces, snapped and gouged her eyes. Despite her disability, she has gone on to become an international figure in athletics for the disabled. The Des Moines, Iowa, woman has joined the likes of John F. Kennedy, Gayle Sayers, Ralph Nader, and Elvis Presley in being named an Outstanding Young American by the United States Jaycees.

Dolly Conner was born with small optic nerves resulting in 20/300 vision in one eye and 20/400 vision in the other. She can't drive a car, read a magazine, or see a blackboard but she can put a basketball through a hoop. Dolly plays backup center for the Monmouth College basketball team, averaging 2.1 points and rebounds per game. Oh, by the way, she shoots at 61.9 percent accuracy. In high school she averaged 19 points and 15 rebounds, scoring 1,604 career points.

According to an Associated Press release, Chris Samele's dream of basketball greatness died just days after his high school career began. Chris's left leg was torn off above the knee in an auto accident. However, Chris always believed he would play again. He recovered and became the first person off the bench when the Red Raider Coach wanted instant offense. Samele was the team's best 3-point shooter. Samele, a shooting guard, figured his game returned to about 60 percent of what it once was, but in some ways he improved.

"My shot is even better," Samele said. "I still play real competitive. The game still means as much to me. I just can't expect to do what I used to expect of myself. Before I would rely on my natural ability. Now I have to think a lot more. There's just a lot of little tricks you have to learn—a lot of shortcuts," Samele said.

These capable people could have given up and few would have blamed them. Yet, each found new abilities, different techniques and a revitalized desire to pursue their dreams.

ENCOUNTERING LIFE'S TOLL BOOTHS

In the Mel Brooks movie *Blazing Saddles* there is a scene that perfectly captures the nature of obstacles. The good guys are being chased across the desert by the bad guys. And, of course, the bad guys are rapidly gaining on them. The situation is desperate, but the good guys come up with a plan for slowing the bad guys down.

Right in the middle of the desert the good guys set up a toll booth. The toll is a nickel. As the bad guys gallop up to the toll booth they realize they don't have enough nickels to pay their toll. So they send one of their gang back to town to get change. In the meantime, the good guys get away.

Movie watchers immediately make two conclusions. First, how ridiculous to set up a toll booth in the middle of the desert. Second, anyone with minimal insight realizes how easy it would be for the bad guys to ride around this silly toll booth. They could slip through without paying the toll. Who is going to stop them?

How in the world can we compare this scenario to life's obstacles? Thinking about obstacles in the form of toll booths, how many people encounter toll booths every day without questioning the validity? Does this toll booth have a right to be here? Are there ways around it? Should I just ignore it? Why not carry a few nickels in the event I come upon a toll booth today? Others spend so much time thinking, worrying and planning for potential toll booths, they never get around to living.

ROUGH SPOTS

A display of golf balls that spanned many years revealed how they were transformed by the addition of one significant element. The first golf balls manufactured had smooth covers. A young avid golfer experiencing financial difficulties played with a beat up golf ball. His playing partners noticed their smooth covered balls did not fly as accurately or as far.

Today, golf balls may have as many as 432 dimples. These "rough spots" enhance the ball's accuracy and distance. So it is with life. Rough spots have a tendency to sharpen our performance.

James Whitaker, the first American to reach the summit of Mt. Everest, knew what it was like to deal with rough spots. Avalanches, dehydration, hypothermia, and the physical and mental fatigue caused by the lack of oxygen at 29,000 feet all stood between him and the top of the world's highest mountain. Most of those who dared to climb it before Whitaker had failed. He succeeded.

"You don't really conquer such a mountain," he said. "You conquer yourself. You overcome the sickness and everything else—your pain, aches, fears—to reach the summit."

Ignoring, denying, or complaining about the rough spots leads to self-destruction. Achievers use the rough spots to move to the next level.

OPPORTUNITY

- We are all faced with a series of great opportunities brilliantly disguised as impossible situations.

  Chuck Swindoll

- Sometimes opportunity knocks, but most of the time it sneaks up and then quietly steals away.

  Doug Larson

- Opportunity is a moving target, and the bigger the opportunity, the faster it moves.

  Richard Gaylor Briley
  Are You Positive?

- Opportunity beckons more surely when misfortune comes upon a person than it ever does when that person is riding the crest of a wave of success.

  Earl Nightingale

- What is the difference between an obstacle and an opportunity? Our attitude toward it. Every opportunity has a difficulty and every difficulty has an opportunity.

  J. Sidlow Baxter
  Awake, My Heart

- Our problem in the immediate future will be not the lack of opportunities for the really motivated, but the lack of motivated people ready and able to take advantage of the opportunities.

  Buck Rogers

- We are the dwelling place of incredible opportunities. They live in us. With consciousness about who we are and what we are, with the awareness of the problems we're faced with, with a commitment not only to ourselves but to each other, we can make it work. We will make it work.

  John Denver

- I think luck is the sense to recognize an opportunity and the ability to take advantage of it. Everyone has had breaks, but everyone also has opportunities. The man who can smile at his breaks and grab his chances gets on.

  Samuel Goldwyn

■   If opportunity doesn't knock, build a door.

Milton Berle
One Door Closes, Another Door Opens

■   Many do with opportunities as children do at the seashore. They fill their little
    hands with sand, and then let the grains fall through, one by one, till all are
    gone.

Thomas Jones

■   Sometimes we stare so long at a door that is closing that we see too late the one
    that is open.

Alexander Graham Bell

■   The reason so many people never get anywhere in life is because when oppor-
    tunity knocks, they are out in the backyard looking for four-leaf clovers.

Walter P. Chrysler

■   Too often, the opportunity knocks, but by the time you push back the chain,
    push back the bolt, unhook the two locks, and shut off the burglar alarms, it's
    too late.

Rita Coolidge

■   Too many people are thinking of security instead of opportunity.

James F. Byrnes

■   It is often hard to distinguish between the hard knocks in life and those of
    opportunity.

Frederick Phillips

■   *You* create opportunity. *You* develop the capacities for moving toward oppor-
    tunity. *You* turn crises into creative opportunities and defeats into successes and
    frustration into fulfillment. With what? With your great invisible weapons:
    your good feelings about yourself, your determination to live the best life you
    can, and your feeling—that only you can give yourself—that you are a
    worthwhile, deserving person. You must fight for your right to fulfill the
    opportunity that God gave you to use your life well.

Dr. Maxwell Maltz
The Search for Self-Respect

■ Well, some people create their own opportunities; others go where opportunities are the greatest; others fail to recognize opportunity when they are face
to face with it.

Walter P. Chrysler

■ People who cling to illusions seldom embrace opportunities.

Gerhard Gschwandtner

■ If opportunity came disguised as temptation, one knock would be enough.

Lane Olinghouse

■ The lure of the distant and the difficult is deceptive. The great opportunity is
where you are.

John Burroughs

■ The golden opportunity you are seeking is in yourself. It is not in your environment; it is not in luck or chance, or the help of others; it is in yourself alone.

Orison Swett Marden

LOOKING FOR OPPORTUNITY

Opportunity is defined as a set of circumstances providing a chance or possibility, a stroke of good fortune which presents itself and can either be grasped or
lost.

"Opportunities? They are all around us," said Orison Swett Marden. "There is
power lying latent everywhere, waiting for the observant eye to discover it."

Circumstances, positive and negative, are constantly around us waiting to be
capitalized. When seized, opportunities surface.

Take the experience of Edward Lowe back in the 1940s. As reported in *Success*
(September 1988), he was in the business of producing a clay-based material that
would soak up oil and grease spills. One day a neighbor asked to use the compound
for her cat. It didn't track all over the house and besides that, it looked good.
Favorable circumstances presented themselves and Lowe realized he was on to
something. He began selling the compound to pet shops and went on to supply 40
percent of a $400 million cat-box filler market.

According to *Bits & Pieces* (January 1987), television repairperson Joe Resnick
became frustrated every time he installed a television antenna. The antennas came
in separate pieces and it seemed every time he was assembling one on a roof, there
were pieces missing, he would drop a necessary part from the roof, or his hands
were freezing in the frigid weather.

Resnick, determined to create a pre-assembled antenna, locked himself in a chicken shed and went to work on his obsession. Within a week he designed an antenna with aluminum arms and stabilizing tubes. He tested it; it worked marvelously. A patent was secured and Resnick called his new company Channel Master. Within three years the company was doing a million dollars' worth of business. Resnick grasped the opportunity and turned frustrating circumstances into a successful business venture.

In 1948, Gene Autry was on the lookout for a Christmas song to match the success of his popular 1947 hit, "Here Comes Santa Claus." He was ready to cut two records and had decided on three of the songs but a fourth was needed.

About that time an aspiring New York songwriter mailed Autry a recording of his number called, "Rudolph, the Red-Nosed Reindeer." Autry wasn't impressed but his wife was, and she believed children would enjoy it as well.

In the final minutes of the recording session, Autry decided to record Johnny Mark's Rudolph song as his fourth number. Autry may have thought it was silly, but it sold two and a half million copies the first year. Since then, "Rudolph, the Red-Nosed Reindeer" has been recorded by over 400 artists in virtually every language and has sold in excess of a hundred million copies.

There are no limits to our opportunities. Most of us see only a minute portion of what is possible. We create opportunities by seeing the possibilities and having the determination to act upon them. Remember, opportunities are always out there waiting to be discovered.

Cat litter, antennas, hit records, and countless other achievements fulfill Helen Schucman's belief that, "every situation, properly perceived, becomes an opportunity."

HAPPIEST, YET SADDEST

Three men were riding in the Colorado Rockies on horseback one starry, moonlit night. As they made their way along the base of the mountain, a voice thundered from the sky, commanding them to stop and dismount. They immediately followed the instruction. Then the voice continued, "Go to the riverbed and pick up some pebbles. Put them in your backpack and do not look at them til morning."

Completing their tasks, the men begin to mount up when they heard the voice again, "This will be both the happiest and saddest day of your life." With that final thought, the men went on their way.

As the sun began to brighten up the eastern sky, the riders reached into their saddle bags. To their amazement, the pebbles had turned to gold. As they celebrated their new wealth, one of the men stopped and exclaimed, "Wait! Now I know what the voice meant when he said this would be both the happiest and saddest day of our lives. Yes, we have gold, but think how rich we would be had we picked up more pebbles."

So often people go through life and at some point realize, "there could have been more." They failed to take advantage of all the opportunities around them, thereby stripping themselves of unfound treasure.

Are you filling your saddle bag with every possibility, every opportunity that comes your way? If not, why not? Don't wake up one morning to lament, "This is both the happiest and saddest day of my life."

PERSEVERANCE

- Most people give up just when they're about to achieve success, they give up at the last minute of the game, one foot from a winning touchdown.

H. Ross Perot

- To succeed, we must have the will to succeed, we must have stamina, determination, backbone, perseverance, self-reliance and faith.

B. C. Forbes

- Never despair, but if you do, WORK ON IN DESPAIR.

Edmund Burke

- The rewards for those who persevere far exceed the pain that must precede the victory.

Ted Engstrom

- I do not think there is any other quality so essential to success of any kind as the quality of perseverance. It overcomes almost everything, even nature.

John D. Rockefeller

- When the truly great people discover that they have been deceived by the signposts along the road of life, they just shift gears and keep on going.

Nido Qubein

- Perseverance does not always mean sticking to the same thing forever. It means giving full concentration and effort to whatever you are doing right now.

Denis Waitley and Reni L. Witt
The Joy of Working

- True perseverance is not forced. People who are fired up don't have to push themselves to persevere. When you are excited about what you are doing, you don't have to convince yourself to "stick to it." You have to convince yourself not to. It's not something you have to do, it's something you want to do. With passion as a base, perseverance comes naturally.

O. J. Simpson

- Many men fail because they quit too soon. They lose faith when the signs are against them. They do not have the courage to hold on, to keep fighting in spite of that which seems insurmountable. If more of us would strike out and attempt the "impossible," we very soon would find the truth of that old saying that nothing is impossible . . . abolish fear and you can accomplish anything you wish.

Dr. C. E. Welch
Founder, Welch's Grape Juice

- You can do it gradually—day by day and play by play—if you want to do it, if you will to do it, if you work to do it over a sufficiently long period of time.

William E. Holl

- Big shots are only little shots who keep shooting.

Christopher Morley

- Even the woodpecker owes his success to the fact that he uses his head and keeps pecking away until he finishes the job he starts.

Coleman Cox

- Keep going and the chances are you will stumble on something, perhaps when you are least expecting it. I never heard of anyone stumbling on something sitting down.

Charles Kettering

- How can we preserve our aspirations and at the same time develop the toughness of mind and spirit to face the fact that there are no easy victories? One is a tough-minded recognition that the fight for a better world is a long one.

John Garner
No Easy Victories

- Persistence is self-discipline in action.

Brian Tracy

A PANTHEON OF PERSEVERANCE

The desires of our heart often require unquenchable spirit, sweat, energy beyond what we think is possible, and an undying commitment. These prerequisites to success culminate in one overriding quality—perseverance.

"If an unusual necessity forces us onward, a surprising thing occurs," observed William James. "The fatigue gets worse up to a certain point, when, gradually or suddenly, it passes away and we are fresher than before!"

"We have evidently tapped a new level of energy," James continues. "There may be layer after layer of this experience, a third and fourth 'wind.' We find amounts of ease and power that we never dreamed ourselves to own, sources of strength habitually not taxed, because habitually we never push through the obstruction of fatigue."

So, how do we know when we have persevered enough? Easy. When we achieve what we set out to do, it is enough.

Dr. Seuss's first children's book was rejected by twenty-three publishers. The twenty-fourth publisher sold six million copies and Dr. Seuss died having known his perseverance resulted in entertaining, challenging, and educating millions of children.

After having been rejected by both Hewlett-Packard and Atari, Apple microcomputers had first-year sales of $2.5 million.

Marathoner Joan Benoit underwent knee surgery only seventeen days before the U.S. Olympic trials, but her determination enabled her not only to make the team, but also to win the first ever Olympic gold medal in her event.

Vince Lombardi didn't become a head coach in the NFL until he was forty-seven.

The novel *Ironweed* has been a phenomenal bestseller and Pulitzer Award winner. The author, William Kennedy, had written several manuscripts, all of them rejected by publishers, before his sudden success. *Ironweed* was rejected by thirteen publishers before finally being accepted for publication.

During their first year of business, the Coca-Cola company sold only 400 Cokes.

In his first three years in the automobile business, Henry Ford went bankrupt twice.

Michelangelo endured seven years lying on his back on a scaffold to paint the Sistine Chapel.

Inventor Chester Carlson pounded the streets for years before he could find backers for his Xerox photocopying process.

Charles Goodyear was obsessed with the idea of making rubber unaffected by temperature extremes. Years of unsuccessful experimentation caused bitter disappointment, imprisonment for debt, family difficulties, and ridicule from friends. He persevered and in February of 1839, Goodyear discovered that adding sulfur to rubber achieved his purpose.

In 1902, the poetry editor of the *Atlantic Monthly* returned the poems of a twenty-eight-year-old poet with the following note: "Our magazine has no room for your vigorous verse." Robert Frost persevered.

Michael Jordan was cut from his high school basketball team.

A junior naval officer dreamed of becoming an admiral but was discharged from the service because he had cancer. He endured four bouts with the disease and at one time, was informed he only had two weeks to live. He beat the cancer but Navy regulations forbade him from being reinstated. Then he learned it would take "an act of Congress" to get him back in the Navy, so he went after it. President Truman responded to his dogged determination and reinstated him. This man, Irwin W. Rosenberg, became Rear Admiral of the United States' Seventh Fleet.

In 1905, the University of Bern rejected a Ph.D. dissertation, saying that it was irrelevant and fanciful. Albert Einstein was disappointed but not defeated. He persevered.

Dennis Walters was a promising young golfer when a freak golf cart accident paralyzed both of his legs. He had no intent of watching golf from the sidelines. Dennis learned how to hit golf balls from a sitting position, designed a swivel seat for his golf cart and eventually drove the ball 250 yards from a sitting position. Walters went on to become a golf instructor and popular golf exhibitionist.

Frank Woolworth labored to save his first $50, and then saw three of his first five chain stores fail.

Cyrus H.K. Curtis lost over $800,000 on the *Saturday Evening Post* before it realized a dollar profit.

Bryant rewrote "Thanatopsis" a hundred times.

Pennsylvanian David W. Hartman went blind at age eight. His dream to become a medical doctor was thwarted by Temple University Medical School, when he was told that no one without eyesight had ever completed medical school. He courageously faced the challenge of "reading" medical books by having twenty-five complete textbooks audio recorded for him. At twenty-seven, David W. Hartman became the first blind student to complete medical school.

Johnny loved football and played for St. Justin High School in Pittsburgh and then attempted to make the Notre Dame team. Judged too small, he settled for playing at a smaller college. Upon graduation his bid to play for the Pittsburgh Steelers ended when he was cut. Johnny worked construction and played some amateur football while staying in contact with every NFL team. All he wanted was a chance. The Baltimore Colts responded, and he soon became one of the top quarterbacks in the league, leading the Colts to a world championship. Ultimately, Johnny Unitas was inducted into the Football Hall of Fame.

Another football player was told he was too small to be a quarterback, too slow on his feet and too weak to take the punishment. However, this young man from Georgia decided to persevere. His efforts resulted in becoming the longest lasting quarterback in the NFL. Fran Tarkenton then also passed for more yards than any quarterback in the history of the game.

One of the most successful writers of the 1970s developed his writing interest while in the Navy. For eight years he wrote a myriad of routine reports. After he returned to public life he wrote an array of stories and articles that never got published. Several years later he wrote a book that touched the world. Alex Haley and *Roots* made history.

We may never make history, become a famous athlete, invent a new product, or start a multimillion-dollar company—but whatever our dreams are, the willingness to "keep on keeping on" will determine our measure of success.

NEVER HEARD OF HIM

I love the story of the high school basketball coach who was attempting to motivate his players to persevere through a difficult season. Halfway through the season he stood before his team and said, "Did Michael Jordan ever quit?" The team responded, "No!" He yelled, "What about the Wright brothers? Did they ever give up?" "No!" the team resounded. "Did O. J. Simpson ever quit?" Again the team yelled, "No!" "Did Elmer McAllister ever quit?"

There was a long silence. Finally one player was bold enough to ask, "Who's Elmer McAllister? We never heard of him." The coach snapped back, "Of course you never heard of him—he quit!"

ONE MORE TIME

I have no idea whether this story is true, but the message is powerful. It's entitled "The Pebble of Success" and reportedly took place in 1942. According to the account, Rafael Solano was physically exhausted and defeated. As he sat on a boulder in the dry river bed he announced to his companions, "I'm through. There's no use going on any longer. See this pebble. It makes 999,999 I've picked up without finding one diamond. One more pebble makes a million, but what's the use? I quit!"

The exploration crew had spent months prospecting for diamonds in a Venezuelan watercourse. Their efforts focused on finding signs of valuable diamonds. Mentally, physically, and emotionally they were exhausted. Their clothes were tattered and their spirits weak.

"Pick up one more and make it a million," one man said. Solano consented and pulled forth a stone the size of a hen's egg. It was different than the others, and the crew soon realized they had discovered a diamond. It is reported Harry Winston, a New York jewel dealer, paid Rafael Solano $200,000 for that millionth pebble. The stone was named the Liberator and to date is the largest and purest diamond ever found.

Harriet Beecher Stowe said, "Never give up, for that is just the place and time that the tide will turn." Rafael Solano would surely agree. Just one more time!

PERSONALITY

■ He has the personality of a dial tone.

Phyllis Diller

■ The superior man is firm in the right way and not merely firm.

Confucius

■ Every bigot was once a child free of prejudice.

Sister Mary de Lourdes

■ I couldn't be two-faced. If I had two faces, I wouldn't wear this one.

Abraham Lincoln

■ Stubbornness is the energy of fools.

German Proverb

■ I have always felt sorry for people afraid of feeling, of sentimentality, who are unable to weep with their whole heart. Because those who do not know how to weep do not know how to laugh either.

Golda Meir

■ Some people are so nervous they keep the coffee awake at night.

Anonymous

■ The quintessence of all our mental and nervous disorders is over-occupation with personal ego; namely, self-centeredness. When the personality becomes centripetal, that is, ego-centered, it disintegrates. Out of extreme self-centeredness arises defensiveness, hostility, and aggressive antisocial behavior . . . to make one's self his center is self-destruction.

Paul E. Billheimer

■ If you have anything valuable to contribute to the world it will come through the expression of your own personality—that single spark of divinity that sets you off and makes you different from every other living creature.

Bruce Barton

■ Three elements enter into the building of a personality: heredity, environment, and personal response. We are not responsible for our heredity; much of our environment we cannot control; but the power to face life with our individual rejoinder—that we are responsible for.

Harry Emerson Fosdick

■ Whenever two people meet there are really six people present. There is each man as he sees himself, each man as the other person sees him, and each man as he really is.

William James

■ Every man has three characters—that which he exhibits, that which he has, and that which he thinks he has.

Alphonse Karr

■ If I keep my good character, I shall be rich enough.

Platonicus

■ Almost every man wastes part of his life in attempts to display qualities which he does not possess.

Samuel Johnson

■ A man never discloses his own character so clearly as when he describes another's.

Jean Paul Richter

■ The measure of a man's real character is what he would do if he knew he never would be found out.

Thomas Babington Macaulay

■ Rationalizing is the tactful, modern way of describing the act of fooling yourself.

Robert Quillen

■ The calm man, having learned how to govern himself, knows how to adapt himself to others and they in turn revere his strength and feel that they can learn from him and rely upon him.

James Allen

■ People are like stained glass windows. They sparkle and shine when the sun is out; but when the darkness sets in their true beauty is revealed only if there is a light within.

Elizabeth Kübler-Ross

■ Women's liberation is just a lot of foolishness. It's the men who are discriminated against. They can't bear children. And no one's likely to do anything about that.

Golda Meir

■ Stature comes not with height but with depth.

Benjamin Lichtenberg

■ People seldom notice old clothes if you wear a big smile.

Lee Mildon

■ There is no fire like passion, there is no shark like hatred, there is no snare like folly, there is no torrent like greed.

Buddha

■ Conscience takes up more room than all the rest of a person's insides.

Mark Twain

■ Character is the foundation stone upon which one must build to win respect. Just as no worthy building can be erected on a weak foundation, so no lasting reputation worthy of respect can be built on a weak character. Without character, all effort to attain dignity is superficial and the results are sure to be disappointing.

R. C. Samsel

■ Character is what we do when no one is looking. It is not the same as reputation . . . success . . . achievement. Character is not what we have done, but who we are.

Bill Hybels
Who You Are When No One Is Looking

■ Character may be manifested in the great moments, but it is made in the small ones.

Phillip Brooks

■ Be more concerned with your character than with your reputation. Your character is what you really are while your reputation is merely what others think you are.

John Wooden

IF YOU FIND ME . . .

To whom it may concern:

I am chronically human. If the following signs are observed, I am not emotionally disturbed or dying:

1. If you find me stumbling and falling, I may just be trying something new—I am learning.
2. If you find me sad it may be that I've just realized that I have been fooling myself and making the same stupid mistakes over and over again—I am exploring.
3. If you find me terribly frightened, I may just be in a new situation—I am reaching out.
4. If you find me crying, it may be because I failed—I am trying.
5. If you find me very quiet, it may be that I am planning—I will try again.
6. If you find me angry, I may have just discovered that I was not really trying—I am erring.
7. If you find me with a strange self-satisfied smile, I may have just discovered that I have everything I need for growing—I am knowing.
8. If you find me ecstatically happy, I may have finally succeeded—I am growing.

These are life signs of beings of my nature. If prolonged absence of the above indicators is observed, do not perform an autopsy without first providing a fertile opportunity for life to emerge.

Taken from: *Personal Achievement Skills Training*, Arkansas Rehabilitation Research and Training Center, University of Arkansas.

PRACTICING WHAT HE PREACHES

The Reverend Billy Graham is admired throughout the world, standing out as the epitomy of character. I remember as a young boy our family revered Graham as a person who practiced what he preached. Even in the midst of recent national evangelist scandals, Billy Graham came out unscathed. A representative from the National Council of Churches observed, "Even with his high visibility, he's a man of integrity who is concerned with people."

Harvey Mackay in his book *Beware the Naked Man Who Offers You His Shirt* (Morrow, 1990), says, "Other ministers tell funnier jokes than Billy Graham, do a better job of illustrating Bible passages, and organizing their sermons, but no one is more effective than Billy Graham in making an altar call, getting people to step forward in front of the congregation, and make a commitment."

Graham's personal qualities and lifestyle are consistent with his spiritual commitment. He draws only a reasonable salary and housing allowance as head of the 80-plus million-dollar Billy Graham Evangelist Association. Graham accepts no fees for speaking and places book royalties in a charitable trust.

Billy Graham remains on the list of the ten most respected Americans. His sincerity, moral integrity, and actions consistent with his teachings have made him the person many presidents have chosen to consult. Although I'm sure he would be the first to confess his flaws, Graham's reputation is built on solid character.

Napoleon Hill wrote, "Reputation is that which people are believed to be; character is that which people are." People who desire long-term success strive to make their reputation consistent with character.

CHURNING WITHIN

What people see on the outside and what is being felt on the inside can be separated by a turbulent river.

In 1835, a man entered the doctor's office in Florence, Italy, and requested a check-up. When the doctor inquired about his symptoms, the man replied, "I am filled with anxiety and exhausted from lack of sleep. I have been unable to eat and find myself isolated from even my closest friends."

Upon examination, the doctor determined the man was in excellent physical condition. However, he decided the man needed to get out of his rut and have a good time. The doctor suggested he attend the circus that was in town and enjoy the hilarious antics of the star performer, a clown named Grimaldi. "You could cure your sadness by enjoying the fun and laughter Grimaldi produces."

"No, no," replied the patient, "he can't help me. You see, I am Grimaldi!"

People are not always what they appear to be. Some even spend their lifetime existing in two worlds: one is what they feel inside and the other is what they allow others to see.

What masks are you wearing? Do others know you . . . really know you? Is what people see consistent with how you feel? Emotional health is balancing the internal and the external.

PERSUASION

- Most people prefer to shelve unpleasant conflict . . . It would be a good thing for them to show more endurance and courage during the negative than suffer the dissatisfaction of a poor agreement later.

  Chester Karrass
  Give and Take

- Keep in mind the better you understand what you want and why you want it, the better your chances will be of acquiring it.

  Fred Jandt
  Win-Win Negotiating

- Persuasion is converting people—no, not to our way of thinking but to our way of feeling and believing.

  Cavett Robert

- To get others to do what you want them to do, you must see things through their eyes.

  David J. Schwartz

- To get to the Promised Land, you have to negotiate your way through the wilderness.

  Herb Cohen

- Never fight too often with one enemy or you will teach him your art of war.

  Napoleon Bonaparte

- To be persuasive we must be believable; to be believable, we must be credible; to be credible, we must be truthful.

  Edward R. Morrow

- If you have an important point to make, don't try to be subtle or clever. Use a pile driver. Hit the point once. Then come back and hit it again. Then a third time—a tremendous whack.

  Winston Churchill

- We are generally the better persuaded by the reasons we discover ourselves than by those given to us by others.

  Blaise Pascal

■ Faced with the choice between changing one's mind and proving that there is no need to do so, almost everyone gets busy on the proof.

John Kenneth Galbraith

■ Tact is the art of convincing people that they know more than you do.

Raymond Mortimer

■ What convinces is conviction.

Lyndon Baines Johnson

■ Never make your appeal to a man's better nature; he may not have one. Always make your appeal to his self-interest.

Lazarus Long

AN ACCOMPLISHED DIPLOMAT

In his autobiography, Benjamin Franklin relates how he overcame the habit of autocratic persuasion (arguing) and developed himself into a noted diplomat. One day a friend was bold enough to be honest with Ben. "Your opinions have a slap in them for everyone who differs with you," the friend began. "Your friends find they enjoy themselves more when you are not around. You know so much that no man can tell you anything. Indeed no man is going to try, for the effort would lead only to discomfort. So you are not likely ever to know more than you do now, which is very little."

The advice was heeded, and the next time Franklin wanted to persuade people that his idea was good, he took a different approach. Ben believed the people of Philadelphia would benefit from street lighting. Rather than trying to persuade them to his way of thinking, he merely hung a beautiful lantern on the end of a long bracket attached to the front of his house. He kept the glass sparkling clean and lit the wick each evening as dusk settled in. Anyone walking by on the dark street could see the light from quite a distance, and it offered comfort to their stroll.

It wasn't long before Franklin's neighbors began placing lanterns outside their homes. Franklin had learned that providing a silent example was a great form of persuasion.

In his pursuit to refine his diplomacy, Franklin mastered another persuasive technique. "The best way to convince another," Franklin said, "is to state your case moderately and accurately. Then say, of course, you may be mistaken about it; which causes your listener to receive what you have to say, and like as not, turn about and convince you of it, since you are in doubt."

DON'T OVERDO IT

Sometimes people become so obsessed with achieving what they believe to be right, they fail to consider all of the options. Take, for instance, the man charged with murder who bribed his juror friend to advocate for a verdict of manslaughter.

The attorneys presented their evidence and the witnesses shared their insights. After the closing remarks, the jury deliberated for a long time, but at last brought in their verdict of manslaughter.

Upon visiting his imprisoned friend the following week, the jury member was thanked for his efforts. "You must have had a difficult time convincing them to vote for a charge of manslaughter."

"You got that right," replied the friend. "The other eleven wanted to acquit you."

The next time you are convinced that your way is the only way, remember it could come back to haunt you.

A CHANGE OF HEART

Franklin Delano Roosevelt employed his finest talents to convert a senator to his way of thinking. When a disagreeing senator blocked some vital legislation, FDR discovered that the senator was an avid stamp collector. One night, while working on his own stamp collection, Roosevelt phoned the senator to ask his assistance. Flattered by the request, the senator came over that evening to offer his expertise. The next day a vote was due on the bill, and when roll-call was taken, the senator voted for it.

The great persuader Thomas Aquinas offered this bit of advice: "When you want to convert someone to your view, you go over to where he is standing, take him by the hand (mentally speaking), and guide him. You don't stand across the room and shout at him; you don't call him a dummy; you don't order him to come over to where you are. You start where he is, and work from that position. That's the only way to get him to budge."

By getting into the senator's world, FDR was able to take him by the hand and, without any mention of the issue, lead him into his court. It probably was the only way that senator would budge from his balky position.

CONFUSED

Harry Truman said, "If you can't convince them, confuse them." There is another alternative. Give people enough time and they will confuse themselves.

The story is told of a guy who owned an elephant. It was becoming a nuisance and too expensive to maintain. So, one day he approached a friend with this proposition: "I am putting my elephant up for sale. It is only five hundred dollars. You want to buy it?"

"Not a chance," responded his friend. "What am I going to do with an elephant? My wife is allergic to the smell. I have two kids to support. We live in a small apartment. We can barely pay our bills the way it is. Besides, five hundred dollars is too much . . . I'll give you one hundred."

HALF CONVINCED

Have you ever had a situation where you felt you convinced the wrong people of the right thing? Maybe you feel like the traveling evangelist who returned home from a week of tent meetings. As his wife greeted him she asked what he preached on all week.

"I talked about forgiveness on Monday, love on Tuesday, salvation on Wednesday, holiness on Thursday, and charity on Friday."

"Were you persuasive?" the wife continued.

"Monday through Thursday I was primed, passionate, and persuasive, but Friday wasn't too successful."

"What did you tell them on Friday?"

"I told my audience it was the privilege and responsibility of the rich to give to the poor."

"How did they respond?" asked the anxious wife.

"So, so," replied the evangelist. "I convinced the poor."

POTENTIAL

- The greatest burden in life is to have a great potential.

  Charlie Brown
  Charles Schulz's "Peanuts"

- One can never consent to creep when one fells an impulse to soar.

  Helen Keller

- Unless a man undertakes more than he possibly can do, he will never do all he can do.

  Henry Drummond

- Many intelligent adults are restrained in thoughts, actions, and results. They never move further than the boundaries of their self-imposed limitation.

  John C. Maxwell

- There is no meaning to life except the meaning man gives his life by the unfolding of his powers. To "maximize our potential," we must take advantage of the resources available designed to increase our understanding of ourselves, the people around us, and the life we are now involved in. We become what we indulge ourselves in. The opportunities life offers help us tap our potential and can be explored when we are equipped with the right tools.

  Erich Fromm

- Experience by itself simply means you are growing older. Experience that is looked at and evaluated provides clues that can be the wellspring of growth into your potential.

  Bart Lloyd

- If you deliberately plan to be less than you are capable of being, then I warn you that you'll be unhappy for the rest of your lives. You'll be evading your own capacities, your own possibilities.

  Abraham Maslow

- Every man's foremost task is the actualization of his unique, unprecedented, and never-recurring potentialities, and not the repetition of something that another, and be it even the greatest, has already achieved.

  Martin Buber
  The Way of Man

■ Our past is not our potential.

Marilyn Ferguson

■ Few men during their lifetime come anywhere near exhausting the resources within them. There are deep wells of strength that are seldom used.

Richard E. Boyd

■ Have the daring to accept yourself as a bundle of possibilities and undertake the game of making the most of your best.

Henry Emerson Fosdick

■ Winning individuals do not leave the development of their potential to chance. They pursue it systematically and look forward to an endless dialogue between their potentialities and the claims of life—not only claims they encounter but the claims they invent.

John Gardner

■ I have no doubt whatever that most people live, whether physically, intellectually, or morally, in a very restricted circle of their potential being . . . we all have reservoirs of life to draw upon of which we do not dream.

William James

■ One of the most common problems in our society is unsuccessful people with great potential.

Hubie Brown

■ The undeveloped piece of property with the greatest potential is still between the ears.

Anonymous

MAXIMIZE YOUR POTENTIAL

Robert Louis Stevenson believed that, "to be what we are and to become what we are capable of becoming is the only end of life."

William James, America's renowned psychologist observed that, "compared to what we ought to be, we are only half awake. We are making use of only a small part of our physical and mental resources." That which each of us use but have not yet developed is our potential. It is my deep-down belief that each of us possesses the ability to grow far beyond our present self-imposed limitations.

Far too many people exist in a world of "what is" rather than giving thought or applying their energies to "what can be."

The great story teller Mark Twain told about a man who died and met Saint Peter at the pearly gates. Realizing Saint Peter was a wise and knowledgeable person, he said, "Saint Peter, I have been interested in military history for many years. Tell me, who was the greatest general of all times?"

Saint Peter quickly responded, "Oh, that is a simple question. It's that man right over there," as he pointed nearby.

The man said, "You must be mistaken, Saint Peter. I knew that man on earth and he was just a common laborer."

"That's right, my friend," replied Saint Peter. "But he would have been the greatest general of all time . . . if he had been a general."

Beware not to shortchange your potential. All people are created with the equal ability to become unequal. Those who stand out from the crowd have learned that all development is self-development. Growth is an individual project and the crowd will stand back to let a winner shine through.

•   •   •

The primary tool each of us must carry is desire. Emerson said, "Desire is possibility seeking expression." Desire alone is not enough. But to lack desire means to lack the primary ingredient for experiencing life's possibilities. Many people do not succeed because they do not know what they want or because they don't want it intensely enough.

There is a story about Paderewski and a woman he met at a reception who said, "Mr. Paderewski, I would give anything if I could play like you."

"No, Madame," he replied, "I don't believe you would, for I doubt that you want to badly enough to make the effort."

So the very first step in tapping our potential is the desire to be the best we can be.

•   •   •

With desire comes preparation. The desire to become a winner is important, but it isn't worth a nickel unless you also have the will to prepare. Preparation means yearning, learning, reading, listening, organizing, and expanding our thinking. It involves rigorous training of our minds and bodies to enjoy the privilege of success.

Anyone with the desire to grow and willingness to prepare must also accept the responsibility to take action. It is an established fact that the largest and most powerful locomotive in the world can be held in place by a one-inch block of wood. Placed in front of the eight drive wheels of a train, the block will hold it completely motionless. However, that same locomotive, with a "full head of steam," can crash through a steel-reinforced concrete wall with little resistance. That exemplifies the power of action.

Sir William Osler wrote, "To know just what has to be done, then do it, comprises the whole philosophy of practical life." Only in action do we learn and grow. And only through educated action will we achieve.

What is your TMP Quotient? TMP = Tapping My Potential

Consider the sage words of Abraham Maslow: "If you deliberately plan to be less than you are capable of being, then I warn you that you'll be unhappy for the rest of your lives. You'll be evading your own capacities, your own possibilities."

WHAT IF?

Toward the end of George Bernard Shaw's life, a reporter challenged him to play the "What If" game. "Mr. Shaw," he began, "you have been around some of the most famous people in the world. You are on a first-name basis with royalty, world-renowned authors, artists, teachers, and dignitaries from every part of this continent. If you had your life to live over and could be anybody you've ever known," the reporter asked, "who would you want to be?"

"I would choose," replied Shaw, "to be the man George Bernard Shaw could have been, but never was."

What would have been your answer? Who is it you want to be? What is it you want your life to become? If you had your life to live over, what would be different? Pursuing your potential is not found in attempting to be like someone else, or achieving what others have done but by pursuing the untapped reservoir within you.

Elie Wiesel tells of a rabbi who has said that when we cease to live and go before our creator, the question asked of us will not be why we did not become a messiah, a famous leader, or answer the great mysteries of life. The question will be simply why did you not become you, the fully active, realized person that only you had the potential of becoming.

"A rose only becomes beautiful and blesses others when it opens up and blooms," says Dale Galloway. "Its greatest tragedy is to stay in a tight-closed bud, never fulfilling its potential."

ONE SMALL DOT

Inventor and scientist Charles Kettering spoke to a group of prominent engineers. His audio-visuals included a large stainless steel backdrop. While addressing the engineers, he approached a corner of the sheet with a steel stylus. With a deliberate, almost slow-motion action, he carefully made a small, almost invisible dot. Turning to his audience, he said, "This small mark represents all that science has discovered up to this point. The remainder of the sheet represents that which has yet to be discovered."

That same small dot could very well reflect the portion of potential people tend to utilize. There is a vast amount yet to be discovered. Our job is to stake a claim on our discovery.

Take the case of James W. Marshall. He started the great Gold Rush of 1849 by discovering gold in Sutter's Creek. Sutter's Mill became a popular place as people came from all over America to seek their fortunes in California's gold fields. This massive migration to California produced fortunes for many. Then, late in the 1880s, the body of an itinerant gold miner was found in an abandoned gold-mining shaft. The body was that of James W. Marshall, the same man who set in force an economic revolution. However, Marshall died penniless. He had never taken the time to stake his own claim.

People have the potential to become infinitely more than they are now; in fact, the greatest limitations we will ever face will be those we place on ourselves by not staking claim to our potential.

MAKING A DIFFERENCE

Eleanor Roosevelt understood the importance of maximizing her potential to influence the world around her. Wife of president Franklin D. Roosevelt, she exercised her influence as a determined and indefatigable fighter. It has been said that Eleanor Roosevelt was a one-woman war on poverty during the Great Depression.

As Sheila Murray Bethel reports in *Making a Difference: 12 Qualities That Make You a Leader* (New York: Berkley Publishing, 1990, pp. 176–177), she traveled the nation, visiting hospitals, coal mines, and squatters' camps. She sat with kings, presidents, and the destitute around the world, proclaiming an empowering message filled with compassion and enthusiasm. Her one-woman dignity campaign succeeded despite crippling shyness.

When her husband died, Eleanor's zest for equality continued to live. In a variety of informal capacities, she continued to be a gallant spokesperson for dozens of causes. President Truman recognized her talents and breadth of expertise by appointing her to the League of Nations. She excelled! A seemingly unimportant committee assignment, arranged by Henry Cabot Lodge, gave Eleanor the public platform she needed to continue her fight for fairness and equality in human rights.

However, not everyone shared her opinions. She was ignored, her efforts minimized, and in some cases, Eleanor Roosevelt was ostracized. She continued to persuade, cajole, and at times, even compromise. But always the passionate and persevering activist, she stood firm to her commitments. Eleanor Roosevelt was determined to make a difference and her message that "no one can make you feel inferior unless you allow them to" affected countless lives.

A conversation with Eleanor Roosevelt always resulted in a clear understanding of her convictions. That may be a primary reason why, after four demanding years, Eleanor Roosevelt persuaded the newly formed United Nations to adopt the "Bill of Human Rights." This single document has been used as a basis for the constitutions of sixty nations.

One person, with an undying commitment to be and do all she could, made a major impact on our world. Providence, good luck, noble blood line, or being in the right place at the right time have little to do with the impact we can have. It is a recognition of what lies within us and what we are capable of becoming and doing that makes the difference.

Philip Adams says when people comment to him, "How do you do so many things?", he often answers them, without meaning to be cruel: "How do you do so little?" It seems to me that people have vast potential. Most people can do extraordinary things if they have the confidence or take the risks. Yet most people don't. They sit in front of the television and treat life as if it goes on forever.

DIGGING FOR MORE

Mel Fisher is a treasure hunter who searched for his pot of gold at the end of the rainbow and found it on the ocean floor. First it was an ocean floor covered with gold coins, but Mel Fisher believed there was more. He spent sixteen years looking for *Nuestra Señora de Atocha*. One day his dream became a reality. Divers salvaged millions of dollars' worth of treasures from the sunken ship—but not without paying a price. They worked long and hard with metal detectors, suffering from the adversities of their trade as they dove to investigate every metallic "hit." Their dreams, effort, and persistence paid off. The original find was only the tip of a treasure that made Mel Fisher a millionaire.

Don't shortchange your potential. Like Mel Fisher, you may have dreams of what can be, but beware of achieving only a part of the dream. Potential is an unlimited source of energy yet to be fully discovered. Why settle for gold coins when an entire treasure awaits you?

AN EXAMPLE OF MAXIMIZED POTENTIAL

People who maximize their potential stand out from the crowd. They possess the uncanny ability to make the most of themselves. Of one such woman Mark Twain said, "She will be as famous a thousand years from now as she is today." Consider this synopsis of the life and person of this remarkable woman:

She lost her sight and hearing in 1882, through illness. She was only nineteen months old.

She became a wild, rebellious, uncontrolled youngster until a nearly blind teacher was attracted to the challenge of teaching her. Under her teacher's direction, this little girl learned to read and write a language foreign to her.

She attended Radcliffe College. In addition to studying French and Greek, she learned to type her papers and assignments using a Braille-keyed typewriter.

At twenty-one she published her life's story and became a public phenomenon, yet misunderstood by the masses. Some believed she possessed mysterious powers, while others thought she was just mysterious. Yet, through it all, she remained dignified, excited about life, and compassionate toward the needs of others.

This incredible young woman became an activist who pushed for change. She promoted peace, raised funds for the American Foundation for the Blind, and developed a positive reputation as a lobbyist. During World War II, she and her companion Polly Thompson committed themselves to brightening the spirits of wounded soldiers in military hospitals.

Although living in a world of silence and darkness, Helen Keller refused to let a disability stand in the way of her potential. She altered people's views of individuals with disabilities, while making an impact on their own personal potential. It doesn't seem possible to reflect on Keller's life without getting excited about our own potential.

It has been said, "The more people develop their potential, the less they become like someone else." And, trying to be like someone else is self defeating. As long as you are trying to be like someone else, the best you can ever be is number two. That is what makes the story of Helen Keller so powerful. She never tried to be like anyone else. Rather, her efforts were directed toward being the best she could be.

PENSION FOR LIFE

The experiences of our pioneering forefathers and mothers teach us much about the potential of life today. Consider the poverty-stricken old man who found his way into a settlement on the western frontier. Out of food and life-sustaining supplies, he began visiting with other settlers and soliciting their wares. One settler noticed a small pouch attached to ribbon around the old man's neck and asked about its contents. The man explained that it had been a gift given to him years before but he had never looked at the contents. He carefully opened the pouch, removed a crumpled, stained paper and gave it to his inquirer. Upon examining it, the settler found it to be a discharge issued by the federal army. This discharge was signed by General George Washington and it entitled the man to a lifetime pension.

For all these years the man had been carrying around a personal guarantee that his physical needs would be met. Yet, they remained unexposed and unused, leaving him to wander through life a penniless man.

Abraham Maslow, the psychologist whose studies influenced our attitudes toward potential and self-actualization, referred to "capacities to be used which cease their clamor only when they are used sufficiently."

What unknown, clamoring resources might be waiting to be opened and used for the purposes for which they were intended . . . enriching your life?

A STORY ABOUT CHICKENS

A grandfather was attempting to impress upon his grandchildren that things were not always as they appeared. "When I was your age," he began, "my daddy raised a beautiful, large vegetable garden. We would sell the produce at a small roadside stand that we built ourselves. My parents always bought their chickens from Willy Scott. One day, while our family was working at the vegetable stand, Willy delivered chickens to our house in a crate and left them on our doorstep. When we returned home that evening we discovered the chickens had escaped and were running all over the yard. Each of us began chasing the chickens and putting them back in the crate. Dad was upset and decided to call Willy to express his unhappiness with the situation. I can still remember Dad telling Willy he didn't think it was a very good idea to leave the chickens in a crate unattended while we were gone. He told Willy how the family had to round-up chickens from all over the neighborhood and we were only able to find eleven. Then Willy shocked my dad."

"Eleven chickens isn't too bad," exclaimed Willy, "I only delivered six!"

How much could be accomplished if we had no idea what the limits were? The potential we possess is often restricted by self-imposed limits. Lord Chesterton, an eighteenth-century English diplomat, said that some people live all their lives and die without ever having their power released. Perform your next task, approach your next problem, or plan an upcoming project as if you had no idea how little or how much you can accomplish. You may find eleven chickens when you only needed six.

ELECTRIC FENCE SYNDROME

As a young boy, I enjoyed spending summer hours on my grandparents' farm. Not only did I have a great time with grandma and grandpa, I learned a lot about farming and life. On a walk to the pasture one morning, we came face to face with an electric fence. (For you nonfarming readers, electric fences are a single strand of wire strung around a piece of land usually containing livestock. It provides a powerful electric shock when a body comes in contact with it.)

Face-to-face with the wire, my grandfather looked around, then placed a hand on the wire to steady himself, and stepped over. It was a mysterious event for someone who had suffered the shocking effects of being zapped.

As we returned from the pasture I had a few questions for my wise grandfather. "Why did you look around before stepping over the wire? And for that matter, why have an electric fence if you're not going to turn on the power?"

Grandpa smiled and commented, "I was just looking to see if any cattle were watching me as I approached the fence. Never give them an idea of what they might be able to do. Electric fences don't need to be left on all the time. Once cattle learn that they will be shocked, they will graze right up to the fence and stop." Then he pointed to the different heights of grass on the two sides of the tiny wire.

What old limitations exist in your life that limit you from attempting to go further? Although it might have been a one-time experience, are there people, situations, or experiences that you have empowered to limit you? Step over the powerless fences and pursue new avenues with renewed energy and confidence.

PREPARATION

- I hated every minute of the training, but I said, "Don't quit. Suffer now and live the rest of your life as a champion."

  Muhammad Ali

- Luck is a matter of preparation meeting opportunity.

  Oprah Winfrey

- Practice does not make perfect; perfect practice makes perfect.

  Vince Lombardi

- In business or in football, it takes a lot of unspectacular preparation to produce spectacular results.

  Roger Staubach

- One of life's most painful moments comes when we must admit that we didn't do our homework, that we are not prepared.

  Merlin Olsen

- Even the best team, without a sound plan, can't score.

  Woody Hayes

- Don't do anything in practice that you wouldn't do in the game.

  George Halas

- Remember, it wasn't raining when Noah built the ark.

  Howard Ruff

- In all things, success depends upon previous preparation, and without such preparation, there is such to be failure.

  Confucius

- Unless a person has trained himself for his chance, the chance will only make him ridiculous. A great occasion is worth to man exactly what his preparation enables him to make of it.

  J. B. Matthews

THE WILL TO PREPARE

Indiana University's basketball team has made a habit of winning. In 1976, the Hoosiers were undefeated throughout the season and captured the NCAA National Championship under the leadership of Bobby Knight.

Shortly after this amazing feat, Coach Knight was interviewed on the television show "60 Minutes." The commentator asked him, "Why is it, Bobby, that your basketball teams at Indiana are always so successful? It is the will to succeed?"

"The will to succeed is important," replied Knight, "but I'll tell you what's more important—it's the will to prepare. It's the will to go out there every day, training and building those muscles and sharpening those skills."

"Spectacular achievement," believes Robert Schuller, "is always preceded by unspectacular preparation."

POSITIONED FOR SUCCESS

Someone once said, "You've got to be in a position for success to happen. Success doesn't go around looking for someone to stumble upon."

How do you get yourself into position to become a member of a world-championship basketball team? The answer may be different than you think. At least it was for Scottie Pippen.

As a 6-foot-2-inch, 145-pound point guard playing on his high school basketball team, his prospects for college ball were dim.

The state campus at Monticello failed to come through with an opportunity as Pippen had hoped. He ended up at the University of Central Arkansas, under head coach Donald Dyer, as a work-study "manager." But he was positioned to learn and prepare himself by working with the team and continuing his own skill-building practices.

Later at Central Arkansas he got a break. Pippen grew to 6 feet 8 inches and enjoyed an average of 23 points a game, earning him a full scholarship.

Scholar, basketball star, and senator Bill Bradley reminds us that, "When you are not practicing, remember, someone somewhere is practicing; and when you meet him, he will win."

Even though his chances were slim, Scottie Pippen didn't quit practicing. His constant preparation meant being ready when the opportunity arrived.

PROBLEMS

- Problems are not stop signs, they are guidelines.

Robert Schuller

- I am grateful for all my problems. After each one was overcome, I became stronger and more able to meet those that were still to come. I grew in all my difficulties.

J. C. Penney

- The basic problem most people have is that they are doing nothing to solve their basic problem.

Bob Richardson

- The world now has so many problems that if Moses had come down from Mount Sinai today, the two tablets he'd carry would be aspirin.

Robert Orben

- A man with fifty problems is twice as alive as a man with twenty-five. If you haven't got problems, you should get down on your knees and ask "Lord, don't you trust me anymore?"

John Bainbridge

- The best years of your life are the ones in which you decide your problems are your own. You don't blame them on your mother, the ecology or the president. You realize that you control your own destiny.

Albert Ellis

- Each problem has hidden in it an opportunity so powerful that it literally dwarfs the problem. The greatest success stories were created by people who recognized a problem and turned it into an opportunity.

Joseph Sugarman

- Find the essence of each situation, like a logger clearing a logjam. The pro climbs a tall tree and locates the key log, blows it, and lets the stream do the rest. An amateur would start at the edge of the jam and move all the logs, eventually moving the key log. Both approaches work, but the "essence" concept saves time and effort. Almost all problems have a "key" log if we learn to find it.

Fred Smith

■   Everybody has a problem, is a problem, or has to live with a problem.

Sam Shoemaker

VALUABLE INSIGHT

Psychologist Erich Fromm was fortunate to be able to flee from Nazi Germany to the United States. Although enjoying his freedom, he was puzzled by how the German people could let a man like Hitler come to power. In his book *Escape from Freedom* (Avon, 1982), Fromm shares a possible answer.

"Sometimes," he says, "the problems of life become so overwhelming that we despair of ever solving them. Should someone come along and say in a loud, confident voice, 'Follow me without question, do everything I tell you to, and I will lead you out of this,' many of us would find that a very tempting offer. When life becomes difficult, we want someone to say to us, 'Don't worry your little head about it. Let me do it for you, and all I want in return is your gratitude and total obedience.'"

Erich Fromm's insight remains applicable today, even for those of us living in freedom. It can be comforting to have a friend, spouse, clergyman, or colleague offer to carry our burden for us. Comforting, yes. Healthy, no! Taking responsibility for our problems is better for us and healthier for the relationship.

In *The Zen Way to the Martial Arts*, Taisen Deshimaru explains: "Life's problems are different for each of us, and each of us needs a different way of solving them. Therefore, each of us has to create his own method. If you imitate, you'll be wrong. You have to create for yourself."

THINK FRESH

In his book, *A Whack on the Side of the Head: How to Unlock Your Mind for Motivation* (Warner Books, 1988), Dr. Roger von Oech said, "It's no longer possible to solve today's problems with yesterday's solutions. Over and over again people are finding out that what worked two years ago won't work next week. This gives them a choice. They can either bemoan the fact that things aren't as easy as they used to be, or they can use their creative abilities to find new answers, new solutions, and new ideas."

Psychologist Abraham Maslow recognized the dangers of this phenomenon when he said, "People who are only good with hammers see every problem as a nail."

"In creative problem solving, it is frequently more important to look at a problem from different vantage points rather than run with the first solution that pops into your head," advises Eugene Raudsepp.

"There is nothing in this world more useless than answers you don't have problems for," says Don Snygg. That is an inevitable predicament when old solutions are being applied to new problems.

Mark Twain once said, "Periodically you need to take your brain out and dance on it." Based on our usual conditioned response to problems, this is probably the most important strategy for creative problem solving.

Chester Bowles, founder of an advertising agency, former governor of Connecticut, U.S. ambassador to India and Nepal, and best-selling author, suggests, "When you approach a problem, strip yourself of preconceived opinions and prejudice, assemble and learn the facts of the situation, make the decision which seems to you to be the most honest, and then stick to it."

DON'T SWEAT IT

Dr. Robert Eliot in his book *Is It Worth Dying For?* (Bantam, 1989) offers tremendous advice for those stressed by their nagging problems. "First," he says, "don't sweat the small stuff. And, second, it's all small stuff."

A CROWBAR APPROACH

A. B. Simpson related the story of an old farmer who for years had plowed around a large rock in his field. He had broken one cultivator and two plowshares by hitting it. Each time he approached the rock, he fretted about how much cropland he was losing around it and the damage it had done.

One day he decided he had enough and set out to dig it up and be done with it. Putting a large crowbar under one side, he found to his surprise (and probably dismay) that the rock was less than a foot thick. Soon he had it in his wagon and was carting it away. He smiled to think how that "big" old rock had caused him so many needless problems.

Not every problem is as easily removed as the farmer's stone. However, "Merely ignoring a problem will not make it go away," said Cullen Hightower, "nor will merely recognizing it." Get out your crowbar and use your leverage to remove those troubling stones.

YOU'RE NOT THE ONLY ONE

The next time you are convinced that you are the only person who has a problem, remember the story that Pope John XXIII told about himself. He admitted, "It often happens that I wake at night and begin to think about a serious problem and decide I must tell the Pope about it. Then I wake up completely and remember that I am the Pope."

Yes, even the Pope has his share of problems. Like the Pope, we may wish there was someone with a higher power we could talk to who would solve it for us. But guess what? We are responsible for finding answers to our own problems.

Keep in mind the word of Grenville Kaiser: "To every problem there is already a solution, whether you know what it is or not."

PURPOSE

- Purpose is the engine, the power that drives and directs our lives.

  John R. Noe

- Purpose, or mission, is determined by the development of values, balance, ethics, humor, morality, and sensitivities. It manifests itself in the way we look at life.

  Luci Swindoll

- Your purpose is what kind of business you are in as a person.

  Kenneth Blanchard and Norman Vincent Peale
  The Power of Ethical Management

- When you discover your mission, you will feel its demand. It will fill you with enthusiasm and a burning desire to get to work on it.

  W. Clement Stone

- A certain comfortable security, a certain profound inner peace, a kind of happy numbness, soothes the nerves of the human animal when absorbed in its allotted task.

  John Cowper Powys
  The Art of Forgetting the Unpleasant

- Miserable are the persons who do not have something beyond themselves to search for.

  Charles L. Allen

- More men fail through lack of purpose than through lack of talent.

  Billy Sunday

- A crusade is, simply put, something that's bigger than you are. It's a "cause" with an impact that reaches beyond your personal wants and needs.

  A. L. Williams
  Pushing Up People

- Anyone who values present comfort more highly than the attainment of a purpose is contributing to disillusionment and disappointment, because it is uncomfortably true that no person ever passes his self-imposed limitations.

  Royal Bank of Canada

■ Great minds have purposes, others have wishes. Little minds are tamed and subdued by misfortune, but great minds rise above them.

Washington Irving

■ Nothing is as necessary for success as the single-minded pursuit of an objective.

Fred Smith

■ The historic period in which we live is a period of reawakening to a commitment to higher values, a reawakening of individual purpose, and a reawakening of the longing to fulfill that purpose in life.

Robert Fritz
The Path of Least Resistance

■ Your first obligation is to carry out the mission you are meant for, not what your father, mother, mate, or friends say you should do. Your mission will manifest in you when you decide to listen to your heart's desire.

Naomi Stephan
Finding Your Life's Mission

■ My research offers impressive evidence that we feel better when we attempt to make our world better . . . to have a purpose beyond one's self lends to existence a meaning and direction—the most important characteristic of high well-being.

Gail Sheehy
Pathfinders

■ Each of our acts makes a statement as to our purpose.

Leo Buscaglia

■ As far as we can discern, the sole purpose of human existence is to kindle a light in the darkness of mere being.

Carl Jung

■ It is the paradox of life that the way to miss pleasure is to seek it first. The very first condition of lasting happiness is that a life should be full of purpose, aiming at something outside self.

Hugh Black

THE POWER OF PURPOSE

Standing on the snow-covered shores of Lake Michigan one wintry night, ready to jump into the freezing waters, a 32-year-old bankrupt dropout pondered the futility of his life. Gazing into the starry heavens, a chilling thought flashed through his mind: Do I have the right to end my life? The answer was clear, as clear as the majesty of that moonlit night. You have no right to eliminate yourself. You are responsible for grabbing hold of life.

R. Buckminster Fuller turned his back to the deathly waters and set out on a remarkable career. Bucky (as his friends referred to him) made a choice that later changed the lives of many people. Best known as the inventor of the geodesic dome, by the time of his natural death he held more than 170 patents and was world-famous as an engineer, mathematician, architect, philosopher, and poet.

Most of us will never achieve worldwide renown. Nor will we receive the big prizes like a Gold Medal, Emmy, Pulitzer, or *Who's Who in America* commendation. We can, however, choose the quality of the few years we spend on this fabulous earth. The key, of course, is to make choices that allow us to enjoy life's small yet valuable treasures.

Life is full of potential! It is meant to be lived to the fullest. Many people experience only a fraction of life's potential because they haven't decided what they want or where their life is going. "I just want to live day by day and see what happens" is a common approach people take to life.

Quality of life does not happen by chance. A fulfilling life begins with searching for and clarifying our reason for living . . . our life's purpose.

Imagine for a moment that today is your one-hundredth birthday. The local newspaper plans to print an extensive story outlining your personal and professional achievements. Prepare your story as you would like to have it printed. How would you want them to describe what you had achieved? What would you want people to say about you? What would you tell the reporter was your primary purpose in life? What was really important in your life? In other words, what gave meaning to your daily activities?

Turn that mental exercise into a statement expressing your supreme aim in life—your purpose. Don't make it complicated or theoretical. Purpose describes the kind of business our life is in and what we are living for. A meaningful purpose communicates what you want to accomplish and the contributions you want to make. In addition, your purpose will describe what you want to become—the person and character you desire to be.

"There is one quality which one must possess to win," said Napoleon Hill, "and that is definiteness of purpose, the knowledge of what one wants, and a burning desire to possess it."

Without a purpose, an understanding of what we want out of life, we become wandering generalities. Life's too short to squander it away just existing.

James Allen put it this way: "They who have no central purpose in life fall easy prey to petty worries, fears, troubles, and self-pitying, all of which lead to failure, unhappiness, and loss . . . for weakness cannot persist in a power-evolving universe."

If we do not develop our own personal mission and take responsibility for the quality of our lives, others will dictate it to us. Have you ever been overwhelmed by the demands of others? Do circumstances tend to control the direction and outcome of your day? Once you establish your purpose and determine that each day will be directed toward that purpose, then and only then can you be empowered to direct your own life. This valuable sense of direction, purpose, and meaning allows us to live above (not under) our circumstances.

Victor Frankl believed, "Everyone has their own specific vocation or mission in life . . . Therein, we cannot be replaced, nor can our lives be repeated. Thus, everyone's task is as unique as their specific opportunity to implement it."

What is your specific mission? "When you discover your mission, you will feel its demand," declared W. Clement Stone. "It will fill you with enthusiasm and a burning desire to get to work on it."

Fulfilled people have a strong sense of purpose. They know what they want, why they want it, and how they plan to achieve it. Purpose-driven people get in the habit of doing things they don't like to do in order to accomplish the purpose they have defined.

Decide what really matters in your life. Write it down, spell it out, and begin living beyond present limitations.

PEOPLE WITH A PURPOSE

Our lives are inspired by people who determined their life's purpose and then committed themselves to attaining it. These people unknowingly heeded the advice of Andrew Carnegie who said, "Put all your eggs in one basket and then watch the basket to see that no one kicks it over."

Bob Doss

Bob Doss was touched by his daughter's comment that many of the kids she knew were dropping out of high school. Doss remembered his own academic struggles and felt a tremendous desire to take charge and make something happen for these dropouts or potential dropouts. He began Upward Bound Academy in Bridgeport, Connecticut. Bob Doss recognized an urgent need to give these going-nowhere kids a new hope in life. Bob Doss made "giving kids a chance" his life purpose.

Shinichi Suzuki

Recognize the name Shinichi Suzuki? Maybe. Maybe not. Suzuki's purpose grew out of a vision that all children could learn to play the violin proficiently when taught creatively and with love. He realized his purpose through teaching 200,000 children to play the violin over a period of thirty years. His dogged determination resulted in some children, perceived as unteachable, mastering the violin. Suzuki's name became synonymous with successful violin instruction. However, his deepest sense of gratification came from watching his vision become a reality.

Alfred Nobel

Swedish chemist Alfred Nobel made a fortune inventing powerful explosives and marketing his inventions to governments for weapon development. The death of his brother changed all of that. One newspaper accidentally printed Alfred's obituary rather than his brother's. It was then he discovered how the world would remember him as the inventor of explosives that would enable armies around the world to destroy one another and innocent victims. It was unsettling to be identified as the man perfecting avenues for death and destruction. It was then he committed his life and fortune to a new purpose. Alfred Nobel established the Nobel Prizes, recognizing and rewarding accomplishments in the arts and sciences that would benefit humanity. Nobel's life purpose changed from amassing a fortune through destruction of life to investing a fortune in the enhancement of life.

Albert Schweitzer

Nobel prize-winner Albert Schweitzer visited Africa and fell in love with the land and its people. Schweitzer, a renowned physician, respected philosopher, brilliant biblical scholar, prolific author, accomplished organist, and crusader for world peace, was touched by the astounding need the African people had for medical help. His purpose became a one-man lifetime crusade to improve the health conditions and quality of life of African people. This honorable obsession won him a Nobel Peace Prize in 1952.

Mahatma Gandhi

Mahatma Gandhi, along with the people of India, wanted freedom from the rule of the British. He refused to engage in brutal battles where many lives would be lost. Instead, Gandhi organized nonviolent protests against British rule, which initially drew laughter and hesitancy from the masses. How could freedom be possible without bloodshed? His persistence to purpose paid off. Not only did India achieve independence, but his refusal to turn to violence set a standard of life for the Indian population. Gandhi demonstrated to his people—and the world—that change was possible through nonviolent means.

Moses

Then there was Moses. This meek, unassuming prophet encountered the burning bush and heard the angel of Jehovah. This life-changing experience transformed

Moses into a leader who led his people out of bondage in Egypt and through the wilderness, and who delivered the Ten Commandments. Instead of a wandering generality, Moses became a meaningful specific with a relentless determination to carry out his single-minded purpose: to free his people from slavery. So, Moses stood before Pharaoh and with a newfound confidence demanded, "Let my people go!"

Abraham Lincoln

Another person with freedom on his heart was Abraham Lincoln. Although shy and beset with marital difficulties and bouts of depression, Mr. Lincoln led the country through a devastating Civil War. His thoughts, actions, and decisions were anchored in a singleness of purpose, an undaunting desire to build "one nation, indivisible, with liberty and justice for all." Lincoln never saw his dream to completion. In fact, it took a hundred years after his death for America's leaders to finalize his purpose. Racial equality under the law was the result of Lincoln's dream, his life purpose.

Rosa Parks

Institutionalized injustice prompted a middle-aged woman in Montgomery, Alabama, to take a stand for personal dignity. Rosa Parks believed that having to give up her seat on the bus because she was black was not right. She took a stand for human rights that is recorded in history as the day equality for all people was put in a new perspective.

Apostle Paul

The radical anti-Christian tentmaker Saul of Tarsus literally saw the light one day on the road to Damascus. His conversion to Christianity transformed him from a persecutor of Christians to a charismatic proclaimer of the Gospel. Not only did his name change from Saul to Paul, but the apostle, along with his writings and works, became a dynamic force in the history of Christianity.

Winston Churchill

Winston Churchill, addressing the House of Commons in his first speech as Prime Minister on May 13, 1940, made his purpose clear: "You ask: 'What is our aim?' I can answer in one word: 'Victory!' Victory at all costs, victory in spite of terror, victory however long and hard the road may be; for without victory there is no survival."

Joe Frazier

Joe Frazier, when he was heavyweight champion of the world, made his purpose clear when asked by a reporter, "Why do you box?" Seeming irritated by the question, Frazier responded, "Because I'm a boxer."

Jan Scruggs

Vietnam veteran Jan Scruggs spent a sleepless night determining a plan for recognizing soldiers who had died in Vietnam. His wife thought he was crazy and the supervisor he worked for laughed him out of the office, but Jan Scruggs had a vision and commitment to a purpose. He would not allow others to steal it from him. Today, the Vietnam Veterans' Memorial, engraved with the names of over 58,000 Americans who lost their lives in that conflict, is the most visited monument in Washington. Jan Scruggs provided a long-overdue healing for thousands who suffered as a result of Vietnam.

•   •   •

Ralph Waldo Emerson once said that the power of the Gulf Stream will flow through an ordinary drinking straw, if the straw is placed parallel to the flow of the stream. The same is true of our lives. If we are lined up with a life purpose and dedicate our lives and actions toward its fruition, extraordinary achievements of lasting value can be attained.

GET MOISTENED

People are sometimes like the cryptobiotic tardigrade. This weird creature can exist for 100 years in a deathlike state, withdrawn in its spiny shell without water, oxygen or heat. But when it is moistened it immediately springs back to life, the legs and head poking out from its coffin-like shell.

People's lives can become dull, flat, and deathlike. Like the tardigrade, there is a tendency to withdraw from the adventure of living and just exist. Their perspectives, attitudes, and life can be refreshed when moistened with renewed purpose.

AN EXCUSE FOR LIVING

Dwight Hall, in his newsletter *Have a Good Day*, tells the story of a little fellow returning home from his first day of school. The teacher had asked the students to bring copies of their birth certificates so the school could be sure of accurate records. But *certificate* was a pretty big word for the boy to handle, although he had grasped the idea. Bounding into the house with his important message, he promptly called out, "Mom, tomorrow I have to take my excuse for being born."

Hall goes on to say, "That's an interesting way to put it—an excuse for living. Everyone should have one. What's your excuse? Anyone's life can be noble, free, and useful; or it can be slovenly, vile, and wasted. It all depends upon our choices. We can reach for the highest goals, or we can aim at nothing and hit it."

DRIFTING

Could it be said that without a purpose we exist in a world of nonspecifics? Daily activity is governed by hit-and-miss actions dependent on what comes our way. Consider the drifter on the street approached by a streetwise social worker:

Social Worker: Where do you live?

Drifter: Here and there.

Social Worker: What do you eat?

Drifter: This and that.

Social Worker: What do you do for a living?

Drifter: Anything and everything.

Social Worker: When do you bathe?

Drifter: Now and then.

Social Worker: You should sign up for government assistance.

Drifter: When would I get it?

Social Worker: Sooner or later.

"MADD" GAVE MEANING

On May 3, 1980, Cari Lightner's life was ended by a drunk driver. This tragic event changed the course and focus of her mother's life.

In the midst of the sorrow and stress of losing a child, Candy Lightner made a vow not to let this tragedy and others like it go unnoticed. Only four days after her daughter's death, Candy met with other friends to discuss what they could do to make an impact on drunken-driving fatalities. Her life took a whole new meaning that day as Mothers Against Drunk Driving (MADD) was born.

This handful of purpose-driven people grew to twenty as they demonstrated in California's capital, Sacramento. Then they went on to Washington D.C., where 100 people marched in front of the White House. They were committed to reducing drunk-driving disasters. Someone had to listen!

The efforts of this core group ultimately resulted in over 360 chapters throughout the world, a national commission against drunk driving, and more than 400 new laws in fifty states addressing drunk driving. In addition, young people concerned about losing friends formed Students Against Drunk Driving (SADD).

Amid the tears, cheers, and jeers, Candy Lightner believed that people who cared enough about their purpose could have an impact on the world around them. And she is right. Candy turned personal disaster into monumental achievement by setting her course and following it.

IT IS A MATTER OF LIFE AND DEATH

What is the correlation between being the owner of a successful metal manufacturing plant and confronting food manufacturers who use coconut and palm oils ("tropical oils") in their foods? For Phil Sokolof of Omaha, Nebraska, the former is a matter of livelihood while the latter is a matter of life and death.

Several years ago Phil had a heart attack. His cholesterol count exceeded 300, and the doctors told him to cut his cholesterol or count on another heart attack with the probable result being death. The doctors got his attention and Sokolof altered his eating habits dramatically. Although many foods cause the body to produce cholesterol, he decided to focus his efforts on helping to improve the American diet by eliminating the use of tropical oils by food manufacturers.

Eliminating tropical oils became Phil Sokolof's personal obsession. He became a one-man crusade to alter their use in the food we eat. His letters to manufacturers who use oils, newspaper and magazine ads warning the public of health issues related to tropical oils, as well as phone calls to food producers cost him $2 million of his personal income. These efforts also irritated a number of people.

However, his personal mission worked. Besides receiving national publicity, Phil Sokolof's commitment to purpose has altered the use of oils in our foods. Prior to his efforts, who really had given much thought to the topic? Nobody ever stepped forward to confront an issue affecting each of us. Although he could not eliminate cholesterol and heart disease, Phil Sokolof bit off what he could chew and formulated a personal purpose he was willing to stand behind.

A FINAL THOUGHT

You've heard it asked, "What would you do if you knew you only had six months to live?" Who says you have six months? What are you doing NOW to make the world a better place?

Martin Luther King, Jr. exclaimed, "Even if I knew the world would end tomorrow, I would plant a tree today." Consider Saint Augustine. While weeding his garden one morning, he was asked, "What would you do if you knew you were going to die before the sun went down?" Without a moment's hesitation Saint Augustine responded, "I would continue hoeing my garden." These two men were caught up in their purpose, and time, or the lack of it, would not alter their life's course.

In contrast, a person who possesses the best life has to offer can still be empty and directionless inside. Russian novelist Leo Tolstoy, who in his mid-forties was healthy, rich, famous, and happily married, testified that these outward signs of success were not indicators of inner fulfillment. He wrote, "A strange condition of mental terror began to grow upon me . . . The same questions continually presented themselves to me: 'Why?' and 'What afterward?' . . . My life had come to a sudden stop. I could breathe, eat, drink, sleep—indeed I couldn't help doing so. But there was no real life in me . . . Life had no meaning for me."

A line from the movie *Joe Versus the Volcano* fits perfectly here. Told that he had six months to live, Joe (played by Tom Hanks) marched up to his obnoxious, autocratic boss and proclaimed, "I was too chicken to live my life, so I sold it to you for $300 a week!"

Joe was communicating the same message as Tolstoy. The amount we earn or the success we achieve produces emptiness unless it is in line with a purpose beyond ourselves. As Charles Allen so aptly put it, "Miserable are the persons who do not have something beyond themselves to search for." We can sell our lives for so much a week or spend it on a valuable investment called purpose. The prospectus for either decision becomes self-fulfilling.

RELATIONSHIPS

- Getting people to like you is only the other side of liking them.

  Norman Vincent Peale

- A life without people, without the same people day after day, people who belong to us, people who will be there for us, people who need us and whom we need in return, may be very rich in other things, but in human terms, it is no life at all.

  Harold Kushner
  When All You've Ever Wanted Isn't Enough

- Those who distort the golden rule to say "those who have the gold, rule" eventually find that the only place they rule is in the kingdom of self.

  John R. Noe

- The basic cause of most inharmonious human relationships is the tendency to impose our values on other people.

  Robert Anthony

- I am going to be meeting people today who talk too much—people who are selfish, egotistical, ungrateful. But I won't be surprised or disturbed, for I can't imagine a world without such people.

  Marcus Aurelius Antoninus

- Human beings, like plants, grow in the soil of acceptance, not in the atmosphere of rejection.

  John Powell, S.J.

- Man wishes to be confirmed in his being by man and wishes to have a presence in the being of another. Secretly and bashfully he watches for a yes which can come to him from one human person to another.

  Martin Buber

- Human acceptance is the salvation of the world.

  Barbara Aiello

- When someone prizes us just as we are, he or she confirms our existence.

  Eugene Kennedy

317

■ At the heart of personality is the need to feel a sense of being lovable without having to qualify for that acceptance.

Maurice Wagner

■ Warmth, kindness, and friendship are the most yearned for commodities in the world. The person who can provide them will never be lonely.

Ann Landers

■ Those who hate you don't win unless you hate them—and then you destroy yourself.

Richard M. Nixon

■ I do unto others what they do unto me, only worse.

Jimmy Hoffa

■ We are not primarily put on this earth to see through one another, but to see one another through.

Peter DeVries

■ We should ever conduct ourselves towards our enemy as if he were one day to be our friend.

John Henry Newman

■ I like long walks, especially when they are taken by people who annoy me.

Fred Allen

■ Consider how hard it is to change yourself and you'll understand what little chance you have of trying to change others.

Jacob M. Braude

■ Do unto others as they do unto you. Plus 10 percent.

Henry Kissinger

■ If you do a good job for others, you heal yourself at the same time, because a dose of joy is a spiritual cure. It transcends all barriers.

Ed Sullivan

■ The easiest kind of relationship for me is with ten thousand people. The hardest is with one.

Joan Baez

A SURPRISING ACT OF KINDNESS

"How far you go in life," believed George Washington Carver, "depends on your being tender with the young, compassionate with the aged, sympathetic with the striving, and tolerant of the weak and strong. Because someday in your life you will have been all of these."

Fiorello H. La Guardia, New York City's mayor in 1935, must have held a comparable conviction. According to *Our Daily Bread* (April 4, 1992), he showed up in court one night in the poorest area of New York City and suggested the judge go home for the evening as he took over the bench.

La Guardia's first case involved an elderly woman arrested for stealing bread. When asked whether she was innocent or guilty, this soft reply was offered, "I needed the bread, Your Honor, to feed my grandchildren." "I've no option but to punish you," the mayor responded. "Ten dollars or ten days in jail."

Proclaiming the sentence, he simultaneously threw $10 into his hat. He then fined every person in the courtroom 50 cents for living in a city "where a grandmother has to steal food to feed her grandchildren." Imagine the surprise of those in the room, who probably thought this was a black-and-white, open-and-shut case. When all had contributed their 50 cents, the woman paid her fine and left the courtroom with an additional $47.50.

It has been said that kindness is the oil that takes the friction out of life. So often it is easy to be grit, rather than oil, by judging, condemning, or berating those going through trials and tribulations. Yet, an act or word of kindness can cool the friction and help someone keep pressing on. Look around you. To whom will you show a kindness like that experienced by the grandmother?

I LOVE HUMANKIND

Charlie Brown's young friend Linus made the mistake of confessing to his big sister Lucy that he wanted to be a doctor when he grew up. (Remember, it was Lucy who prompted her little brother to once remark that big sisters are "the crabgrass in the lawn of life.")

Lucy was astounded at her brother's declaration. "You, a doctor! That's a laugh! You could never be a doctor! You know why? Because you don't love humankind!"

Young Linus immediately responded, "I do too love humankind! It's people I can't stand!"

Linus was expressing a feeling shared by many. Humankind is easy to love. The difficulty and challenge comes in developing one-to-one relationships. Unfortunately, if we don't cultivate our relationships we'll end up fulfilling Dr. Albert Schweitzer's declaration that, "We are all so much together, but we are all dying of loneliness."

GIVING OTHERS A PUSH

Irene Sax, in a *Newsday* article, writes about the success of Jean Nidetch, founder of Weight Watchers. The organization has over one million members in twenty-four countries. Sax asked how Nidetch has been able to help so many people, and she shared how she began her passion for people as a teenager. Nidetch regularly walked through the park and watched mothers chatting while their toddlers sat on swings with no one to push them. "I'd give them a push," she said. "And you know what happens when you push a kid on a swing? Pretty soon he's pumping, doing it himself. That's what my role in life is—I'm there to give others a push."

Carl Rogers, writing in *Perceiving, Behaving, and Becoming*, says, "The degree to which I can create relationships which facilitate the growth of others as separate persons is a measure of the growth I have achieved in myself." Relationships provide a marvelous opportunity to give others a push, help them grow, provide encouragement, and enhance the quality of their lives. And in return, we will experience the same.

GETTING EVEN

Sir Winston Churchill and Lady Astor could have benefited from R. J. Rehwinkels advice that, "The only people you should try to get even with are those who have helped you." These two prominent British politicians experienced one of the most bitter relationships in history. Their interactions were constantly filled with sarcasm, conflict, and caustic remarks, each intending to get back at and outdo the other.

One day in Parliament, Lady Astor became upset with a Churchill decision and shouted, "Sir Winston, if you were my husband, I'd poison your tea."

Churchill quickly replied, "Lady Astor, if you were my wife, I'd drink it."

On another occasion Lady Astor encountered Churchill after he had spent the evening drinking. Seeing a marvelous opportunity to take advantage of the inebriated Churchill, she snapped, "Mr. Prime Minister, I perceive that you are drunk."

A wry smile appeared on Churchill's face as he retorted with, "Yes I am, Lady Astor, and I perceive you are ugly. But tomorrow I shall be sober."

As in Churchill and Astor's relationship, many people have traded building up one another for putting each other down. Positive, uplifting, and encouraging words have been traded for negative, piercing, and destructive ones.

Evaluate your relationships. Which direction have they taken? Be the first in your relationships to get even with only those who have helped you.

DOUBLE TALK

Gossipers cause undue contention and strife. The wise King Solomon said, "The words of a whisperer are like dainty morsels, and they go down into the innermost parts of the body." Both the gossiper and the one being talked about are injured by these "tiny morsels."

Consider the conversation where Mary says, "Ellen told me you told her the secret that I asked you not to tell her." Alice responds, "Well, I told her I wouldn't tell you that she told me, so please don't tell her I did." Confusing isn't it?

One thing is sure. Conversations like the one above result in damaged relationships. When trust is broken, so are friendships.

A CALCULATED RISK

"Trust is a calculated risk made with one's eyes open to the possibilities of failure," says Robert Levering, "but it is extended with the expectation of success."

This important relationship quality can be illustrated by the arrangement made between the shark and pilot fish. Sharks are renowned for their indiscriminate palates and will enjoy a meal of almost any ocean dweller—that is, except the pilot fish. Instead, sharks extend an invitation for the pilot fish to join them for lunch. Then, the smaller fish act as an automatic toothpick and eat the leftover food lodged between the sharks' teeth. It is a collaborative relationship: the shark gets clean teeth and the pilot fish gets nourished. Each fish is satisfied when the encounter is over.

Levering said trust is first of all a calculated risk. Second, it is extended with the expectation of success. So it is with the shark and pilot fish. The pilot fish trusts the shark will not eat it, and each fish knows that if it cooperates, its needs will be met.

RELIGION

■ Religious faith may very well be considered a science, for it responds invariably to certain formulae. Perform the technique of faith according to the laws which have been proved workable in human experience and you will always get a result of power.

Norman Vincent Peale

■ The God who made the world has no trouble being seen and heard by those who honestly want to know Him.

Martin R. De Haan II

■ Worship is the believer's response of all that he is—mind, emotion, will, and body—to all that God is and says and does.

Warren W. Wiersbe

■ The Bible does not provide a map for life—only a compass.

Haddon Robinson

■ The will of God is found in the Word of God. The more a person grows, the more he begins to think instinctively and habitually from a divine perspective.

Howard Hendricks

■ God is a verb.

R. Buckminster Fuller

■ The Bible is God's chart for you to steer by, to keep you from the bottom of the sea, and to show you where the harbor is, and how to reach it without running on rocks or bars.

Henry Ward Beecher

■ The deeds you do may be the only sermon some persons will hear today.

Saint Francis of Assisi

■ The world is all the richer for having the devil in it, so long as we keep our foot upon his neck.

William James

■ Someone has rather facetiously suggested that a pastor spends his time in two ways: 50 percent of it trying to comfort the agitated and the other 50 percent trying to agitate the comfortable.

Anonymous

■ Religion is like going to the dentist; if it is good for us, it is supposed to hurt.

Tom Mullen

■ I am ready to meet my Maker. Whether my Maker is prepared for the ordeal of meeting me is another matter.

Winston Churchill

■ I am certain that there will be three surprises in heaven. First of all, I will see some people there whom I never expected to see. Second, there will be a number whom I expect to be there who will not be there. And, even relying on His mercy, the biggest surprise of all may be that I will be there.

Archbishop Fulton J. Sheen

■ Sunday is the day many of us bow our heads. Some of us are praying and some of us are putting.

Glenn Wilson, Jr.

■ If the work of God could be comprehended by reason, it would be no longer wonderful, and faith would have no merit if reason provided proof.

Pope Gregory I

■ To believe in God is to know that all the rules will be fair—and that there will be many surprises!

Sister Corita

■ Don't be so heavenly minded you are of no earthly good. Don't be so earthly minded you are of no heavenly good.

Anonymous

■ The exercise of prayer, in those who habitually exert it, must be regarded by doctors as the most adequate and normal of all the pacifiers of the mind and calmers of the nerves.

William James
Essays on Faith and Morals

■ Faith is believing in things when common sense tells you not to.

George Seaton

■ Faith is building on what you know is here so you can reach what you know is there.

Cullen Hightower

■ Faith is not daydreaming, it is decision making!

Robert Schuller

■ Faith is not simply a patience which passively suffers until the storm is past. Rather, it is a spirit which bears things—with resignation, yes, but above all with blazing, serene hope.

Corazon Aquino

■ Faith is like radar that sees through the fog the reality of things at a distance that the human eye cannot see.

Corrie ten Boom
Tramp for the Lord

■ Faith is like a toothbrush. Every man should have one and use it regularly, but he shouldn't try to use someone else's.

J. G. Stipe

■ Faith is more than thinking something is true. Faith is thinking something is true to the extent that we act on it.

W. T. Purkiser

■ Faith is not trying to believe something regardless of the evidence. Faith is daring to do something regardless of the consequences.

Sherwood Eddy

■ Faith makes the uplook good, the outlook bright, the inlook favorable, and the future glorious.

V. Raymond Edman

■ Faith is to believe what we do not see, and the reward of this faith is to see what we believe.

Saint Augustine

OUR ACTIONS SPEAK LOUDLY

The finest testament of the Christian life is consistency between words and actions. This principle is beautifully illustrated by the humorous story of a self-righteous, boastful Sunday school teacher who was preaching to his class on the importance of exemplary living. With head held high and chest thrust outward, he strutted boldly back and forth across the room, while saying arrogantly, "Now, kids, why do people call me a Christian?" There was a momentary silence. Then one of the boys slowly raised his hand. "Yes?" boomed the teacher. The boy responded, "Probably because they don't know you."

Keep in mind:

> You are writing a gospel,
> A chapter each day,
> By deeds that you do,
> By words that you say.
>
> Men read what you write
> Whether faithless or true.
> Say! What is the gospel
> According to you?

Anonymous

PATTERNS OF PRAYER

According to a Poloma and Gallup Poll:

- 91 percent of women pray, as do 85 percent of men.
- 94 percent of blacks and 87 percent of whites pray.
- 32 percent regularly feel a deep sense of peace; 12 percent never experience this peace.
- 26 percent regularly sense the strong presence of God; 1 percent never sense God's presence.
- 15 percent regularly receive a definite answer to a specific prayer; 27 percent never receive a definite answer; and 25 percent have once or twice.
- 42 percent ask for material things when they pray; of this group, 59 percent are evangelicals, and 66 percent are black.
- Meditative prayer increases with age: 45 percent of 18- to 24-year-olds pray meditatively; 70 percent of 65-year-olds do so.

- Of those who say God exists, 70 percent pray daily, as do 10 percent of those who don't believe in God.

These statistics concerning prayer remind me of the father who took his small son with him to run errands. When lunchtime rolled around, the two of them stopped at a local restaurant for a sandwich. The server took their order and when lunch arrived, the father said, "Son, we'll just have a silent prayer." Dad finished praying first and waited for the boy to complete his prayer, but he just sat with his head bowed for an unusually long time. When he finally looked up, his father asked him, "What were you praying about all that time?" With the innocence and honesty of a child, he replied, "How do I know? It was a silent prayer."

Considering all the confusion about prayer, Ben Franklin, writing in *Poor Richard's Almanack*, offered wise advice: "Work as if you were to live a hundred years; pray as if you were to die tomorrow."

Yet, Abraham Lincoln's experience is undoubtedly the most common: "I have been driven many times to my knees by the overwhelming conviction that I had nowhere else to go."

With that realization, Kirkegaard reminds us: "Prayer doesn't change God, but changes him who prays."

NO LOOPHOLES

A recent poll conducted by *USA Today* showed that Americans are vitally interested in going to heaven, but their opinions about it are inconsistent. The randomly selected adults who were interviewed produced these results in the poll:

- 72 percent of the people polled rated their chances of getting to heaven as good to excellent.
- These same people said that only 60 percent of their friends will go to heaven.
- 80 percent said they believe in heaven, but only 67 percent said they believe in hell.

A SOURCE OF LIFE-CHANGING HELP

In 1929, J. C. Penney became critically ill and was hospitalized at the Kellogg Sanitarium in Battle Creek, Michigan for treatment. One night he reached the depths of despair and sat down to write farewell letters to his wife and son expressing doubt that he would see the sun rise.

J. C. Penney did, however, survive the night. The next morning provided an experience that changed his life. He wrote, "When I awoke the next morning, I was surprised to find that I was still alive. Going downstairs, I heard singing in a little chapel where devotional exercises were held each morning. I can still remember the hymn they were singing, 'God Will Take Care of You.' Going into the chapel, I listened with a weary heart to the singing, the reading of the Scripture lesson, and the prayer. Suddenly, something happened . . . I felt as if I had been instantly lifted out of the darkness of a dungeon into warm, brilliant sunlight. I felt as if I had been transported from hell to paradise. I felt the power of God as I never had felt it before. I realized that God with His love was there to help me."

J. C. Penney experienced the comfort of Gilbert Beenken's words that, "other men see only a hopeless end, but the Christian rejoices in an endless hope."

Likewise, Saint Augustine wrote centuries ago: "Thou hast made us for thyself, and the heart of man is restless until it finds its rest in thee."

A SOLUTION FOR EVERY EXCUSE GIVER

To make it possible for everyone to attend church next Sunday, we are going to have a special "No Excuse Sunday." Cots will be placed in the foyer for those who say, "Sunday is my only day to sleep in." There will be a special section with lounge chairs for those who feel that our pews are too hard. Eye drops will be available for those with tired eyes—from watching TV too late Saturday night. We will have steel helmets for those who say, "The roof would cave in if I ever came to church." Blankets will be furnished for those who think the church is too cold and fans for those who say it is too hot. Score cards will be available for those who wish to list the hypocrites present. Relatives and friends will be in attendance for those who like to go visiting on Sunday. There will be TV dinners for those who can't go to church and cook dinner, too. We will distribute "Stamp Out Stewardship" buttons for those who feel that the church is always asking for money.

One section will be devoted to trees and grass for those who like to seek God in nature. Doctors and nurses will be in attendance for those who plan to be sick on Sunday. The sanctuary will be decorated with both Christmas poinsettias and Easter lilies for those who never have seen the church without them. We will provide hearing aids for those who can't hear the preacher and cotton for those who can.

AN IMPRESSIVE RECORD

An anonymous author made this striking observation: Socrates taught for forty years, Plato for fifty, Aristotle for forty, and Jesus for only three. Yet the influence of Christ's three-year ministry infinitely transcends the impact left by the combined 130 years of teaching from these men who were among the greatest philosophers of all antiquity. Jesus painted no pictures; yet some of the finest paintings of Raphael, Michelangelo, and Leonardo da Vinci received their inspiration from Him. Jesus wrote no poetry; but Dante, Milton, and scores of the world's greatest poets were inspired by Him. Jesus composed no music; still Haydn, Handel, Beethoven,

Bach, and Mendelssohn reached their highest perfection of melody in the hymns, symphonies, and oratorios they composed in His praise. Every sphere of human greatness has been enriched by the humble Carpenter of Nazareth.

His unique contribution to the race of humans is the salvation of the soul! Philosophy could not accomplish that. Nor art. Nor literature. Nor music. Only Jesus Christ can break the enslaving chains of sin and Satan. He alone can speak peace to the human heart, strengthen the weak, and give life to those who are spiritually dead.

Jesus is a marvelous example and proven leader for Christians to emulate and serve.

RISK TAKING

- Even those who venture to dip a toe in the pond of risk never allow themselves to get used to the water.

  David Viscott

- By exposing yourself to risk, you're exposing yourself to heavy-duty learning, which gets you on all levels. It becomes a very emotional experience as well as an intellectual experience. Each time you make a mistake, you're learning from the school of hard knocks, which is the best education available.

  Gifford Pinchot

- You can measure opportunity with the same yardstick that measures the risk involved. They go together.

  Earl Nightingale

- The people who are playing it totally safe are never going to have either the fun or the reward of the people who decide to take some risk, stick out, do it differently.

  John Akers

- Behold the turtle. He makes progress only when he sticks his neck out.

  James B. Conant

- People who don't take risks generally make about two big mistakes a year. People who do take risks generally make about two big mistakes a year.

  Peter Drucker

- People who take risks are the people you'll lose against.

  John Sculley

- There are risks and costs to a program of action. But they are far less than the long-range risks and costs of comfortable inaction.

  John F. Kennedy

- There are seasons, in human affairs, when new depths seem to be broken up in the soul, when new wants are unfolded in multitudes, and a new and undefined good is thirsted for. There are periods when to dare, is the highest wisdom.

  William Ellery Channing

■   What is life, but one long risk?

Dorothy Canfield Fisher

OUT ON A LIMB

Some people are willing to risk the ridicule of the leaders in their industry while others risk starting a whole new industry. Risk takers embody Samuel Johnson's statement, "Nothing will ever be attempted if all possible objections must first be overcome," is certainly true.

King Camp Gillette dreamed of a cockeyed invention that caused investors, metal engineers, and experts at the Massachusetts Institute of Technology to snicker. No way could a razor be made sharp enough to provide a clean shave and yet cheap enough to be thrown away when it was dull. Gillette labored four years to produce the first disposable razor and another six years to place it on store shelves. Although only fifty-one blades sold the first year, 90,844 were purchased in the second year and Gillette's risk-taking innovation was on its way to revolutionizing the shaving industry.

Mary Kay Ash had the audacity to think beauty products would sell at home beauty shows. She believed her skin care products could be sold to small groups of women looking for ways to improve their image and potential for success. Her first home show produced $1.50 in sales. Mary Kay had risked her entire life's savings on this venture and $1.50 in sales was not a good return on her investment. She modified her selling techniques, refined the packaging, and adjusted her attitude to succeed. She did $34,000 in retail sales the first year. Fifteen years later, Mary Kay had 150,000 independent consultants and 3,000 directors producing gross sales of $200 million.

Charles House took what many would consider the ultimate risk. As head of corporate engineering at Hewlett-Packard, he ignored an order from co-founder David Packard to stop working on a high-quality, large screen video monitor. According to a *Time* magazine article, House pressed ahead anyway and the monitor has been used in heart transplant operations as well as for space travel. Seventeen thousand of the units were sold instead of the projected thirty, and Hewlett-Packard gave House a medal in 1982 for "extraordinary contempt and defiance beyond the normal call of engineering duty."

Anything worthwhile in life involves risk. As Will Rogers once said, "You've got to go out on a limb sometimes, because that's where the fruit is."

THE REWARD OF RISK

History depicts United States General George S. Patton, the spearhead of the Allied victory over Nazi Germany, as a reckless, impetuous hound of war—a gray-haired Rambo who shot from the hip.

But on D-Day, the sixth of June 1944, Patton wrote in a letter to his son, a West Point cadet, "Take calculated risks. That is far different from being rash."

That succinct but eloquent plea for good judgment helps explain the real reason for Patton's smashing success on the battlefield: Although he was decisive and quick to act, he looked before he leaped. Psychiatrists and psychologists say that is one of the characteristics of a good risk-taker.

Throughout most of recorded history, the worth of a man often was measured by his willingness to take risks. So it was that, as Pierre Corneille wrote in *Le Cid* in the seventeenth century, "To conquer without risk is to triumph without glory."

In the fifth century B.C., the Greek historian Herodotus set down eight words that are as timely today, in this age of space exploration, as they were when humankind was just beginning to explore the wonders of the world and mind: "Great deeds are usually wrought at great risks."

The sixteenth-century essayist Michel Eyquem de Montaigne, realizing that not all risks were worth taking—the romantic ideal of the times notwithstanding—was prompted to write: "The game is not worth the candle." (The risk is too great for the gain).

An old Telugu saying, echoed in the Bible, comments on the inadvisability of abandoning a risk-taking venture: "There is no greater folly than turning back after having once ventured to run a risk."

But the great Spanish writer Miguel de Cervantes urged prudence: "To retire is not to flee, and there is no wisdom in waiting, when danger outweighs hope, and it is the part of wise men to preserve themselves today for tomorrow, and not risk all in one day." In other words, he who fights and runs away will live to fight another day.

An old American proverb counsels against rashness: "Swift risks are often attended by precipitate falls."

But perhaps Englishman John Heywood best summed up risk taking when he wrote in 1546, "Nought venture nought have."

SELF

- The greatest single determinant of what you will be or do with your creative abilities is your perception of who you are. Self-esteem is central to the whole problem of securing any type of success in any endeavor.

  Michael LeBoeuf, Ph.D.

- An individual's self-concept is the core of his personality. It affects every aspect of human behavior: the ability to learn, the capacity to grow and change, the choice of friends, mates, and careers. It is no exaggeration to say that a strong, positive self-image is the best possible preparation for success in life.

  Dr. Joyce Brothers

- We must be trying to learn who we really are rather than trying to tell ourselves who we should be.

  John Powell, S. J.

- Until you make peace with who you are, you'll never be content with what you have.

  Doris Mortman

- Know yourself. Don't accept your dog's admiration as conclusive evidence that you are wonderful.

  Ann Landers

- Whenever I get full of myself, I remember the nice, elderly couple who approached me with a camera on a street in Honolulu one day. When I struck a pose for them, the man said, "No, no, we want you to take a picture of US."

  Tom Selleck

- When a man no longer feels he must be remarkable, he is more free to be himself and work according to his own wishes and talents.

  Dr. Daniel Levinson
  Seasons of a Man's Life

- To be a champ, you have to believe in yourself when nobody else will.

  Sugar Ray Robinson

■ Confidence isn't something you hype yourself into. A person going "I'm the greatest" is really thinking "I can't," or he wouldn't be saying that. Confidence is what's left when doubt is removed.

W. Timothy Gallwey
The Inner Game of Tennis

■ Confidence is simply that quiet, assured feeling you have before you fall flat on your face.

Anonymous

■ Man's self-concept is enhanced when he takes responsibility for himself.

William C. Shutz

■ I yam what I yam and that's all that I yam.

Popeye the Sailor Man

■ Until I accept my faults I will most certainly doubt my virtues.

Hugh Prather

■ The first basic of successful living is self-acceptance.

Art Linkletter

■ You can never be better than your own self-esteem; that is, how you feel about yourself in relation to others, based on your sense of self-acceptance.

Robert Anthony

■ People travel to wonder at the height of mountains, at the huge waves of the sea, at the long courses of rivers, at the vast compass of the ocean, at the circular motion of the stars, and they pass by themselves without wondering.

Saint Augustine

■ You are embarking on the greatest adventure of your life, to improve your self-image, to create more meaning in your life and in the lives of others.

Dr. Maxwell Maltz

■ What a man is is the basis of what he dreams and thinks, accepts and rejects, feels and perceives.

John Mason Brown

■ The more self-awareness a person has the more alive he is.

Rollo May

■ It is not an easy world to live in. It is not an easy world to be decent in. It is not an easy world to understand oneself in, nor to like oneself in. But it must be lived in, and in the living there is one person you absolutely have to be with.

Jo Coudert
Advice from a Failure

■ You better not compromise yourself . . . it's all you got.

Janis Joplin

■ We can change our whole life and the attitude of people around us simply by changing ourselves.

Rudolf Dreidurs

■ The very purpose of existence is to reconcile that glowing opinion we hold of ourselves with the appalling things that other people think about us.

Quentin Crisp

■ The more you are like yourself, the less you are like anyone else. This is what makes you unique.

Walt Disney

■ While one person hesitates because he feels inferior, the other is busy making mistakes and becoming superior.

Henry C. Link

■ A human being's first responsibility is to shake hands with himself.

Henry Winkler

■ To feel valued, to know, even if only once in a while, that you can do a job well, is an absolutely marvelous feeling.

Barbara Walters

■ The basic purpose of all human activity is the protection, the maintenance, and the enhancement, not of the self, but of the self-concept of self.

Samuel I. Hayakuwa

■ There is no value judgment more important to man—no factor more decisive in his psychological development and motivation—than the estimate he passes on himself.

Nathaniel Branden
The Psychology of Self-Esteem

■ I am somebody! I may be poor—but I am somebody! I may be in prison—but I am somebody. I may be uneducated—but I am somebody!

Rev. Jesse Jackson

■ Positive self-esteem is a realistic appraisal of self, and when we look at ourselves this way, we can see we are like other people. Pride is an unrealistic appraisal of self. We think we are better than others. Low self-esteem is an unrealistic appraisal of self. We think we are not as good as others, and these two things—pride and low self-esteem— stifle God's best for us.

Ray Burwick
You're Better Than You Think

YOU ARE AN ORIGINAL

A famous musician announced before a concert that he would be playing one of the world's most expensive violins. His first selection was beautifully and flawlessly played. The audience erupted in appreciative applause.

The violinist bowed graciously and then proceeded to smash the instrument over his knee. The horrified audience fell deathly silent. "Never fear," the man said assuredly, "this was only a cheap counterfeit."

Then he proceeded to position the expensive violin and draw the bow across its strings. The sound once again captivated the audience, but most people could not tell the difference between the music from the expensive violin and the low-cost one. The quality of the instrument was only secondary to the skill of the performer.

Whether you realize it or not, you are an expensive, individually designed, absolutely unique instrument.

Most people are the product of twenty-three chromosomes from our mother and twenty-three chromosomes from our father. Geneticists have determined the odds of our parents having another child like us (not an identical twin) are one in 10 to the 2,000,000,000th power. The combination of attributes that constitutes us will never be duplicated.

When God made you, He threw the mold away. There never has been or ever will be another person just like you. So, you are an original, a meticulously designed instrument. That's great! But you will never perform, live, or achieve above the value you attribute to yourself.

It is impossible to perform consistently in a manner inconsistent with the way we see ourselves. In short, we usually act in direct proportion to our self-image. How you see yourself will determine how you think, feel, act, and react to others. In order to change outward actions it is necessary to change the inward perception of self.

The image or perception you have of yourself today exists because of past experiences. Those experiences have influenced the way you are and the way you believe you are.

Parade magazine featured an interview with comedian Steve Allen and his wife, Jayne Meadows, on their many years together in marriage. Much of the article focuses on Steve's unstable and dysfunctional family background. In a final comment about his childhood, Jayne said, "We are who we are because of where we've been."

Somerset Maugham suggested, "Men and women are not only themselves; they are the region in which they were born, the city apartment in which they learned to walk, the games they played as children, the old wives' tales they overheard, the food they ate, the schools they attended, the sports they followed, the poems they read, and the God they believed in."

Psychologists tell us that by the time we reach age two, 50 percent of what we ever believed about ourselves had been formed; by the age of six, 60 percent of our self-belief had been established, and by the age of eight, about 80 percent. By the time we reached the age of fourteen, over 99 percent of us had a well-developed sense of inferiority.

Some of us may feel like the man who went to see a counselor because he was feeling inferior. After the third session, the counselor announced he had good news and bad news. "First the good news: You don't have an inferiority complex. The bad news is, you are inferior."

In Victor Hugo's story, *Ninety-Three*, a ship is caught in a raging storm. The frightened crew hears a terrible crashing sound below. Immediately, the sailors know what it is: a cannon has broken loose and is crashing into the ship's side with every smashing blow of the sea! Two men, risking their lives, go into the inner hull and manage to fasten it down again. The men were well aware that the unfastened cannon was more dangerous than the raging storm.

So it is with people. Their greatest danger is not the external conditions but what lies within.

Sir Edmund Hillary of New Zealand, the first person to set foot on the top of the world's highest mountain, Mount Everest, said, "It's not the mountain we conquer, but ourselves."

So, how do we overcome the barriers to beautifully playing the instrument with which we've been blessed?

A marvelous piece of literature is *The Great Stone Face* by Nathaniel Hawthorne. On the side of a mountain was a face. It was a strong, kind, and honorable face. Living in a nearby village was a boy named Ernest. Day by day he would look at that face, and he was thrilled by what he saw. Throughout his young life and even into adulthood Ernest spent countless hours gazing upon the face on the mountain. Legend had it that someday a man would appear in the community who would look exactly like the face. For years the legend lived on. One day, when the people were discussing the legend, someone exclaimed, "Behold, behold, Ernest is himself the likeness of the Great Stone Face." Indeed, it happened. Ernest had become that which he visualized.

Hawthorne's story doesn't suggest we should try to become something we are not. In fact, being and accepting yourself is the first step to becoming your best. Emerson said, "Man surrounds himself with the image of himself." What he surrounds himself with he becomes. Therein, rests the value of Hawthorne's story. Seeing oneself as already having value, worth and dignity increases our ability to behave in such a manner.

Listen to Norman Vincent Peale's encouragement: "Believe in yourself. Have faith in your abilities! Without a humble but reasonable confidence in your own powers, you cannot be successful or happy."

John Denver, giving a commencement speech at his old high school, offered this encouragement: "The best thing you have to offer the world is yourself. You don't have to copy anyone else. If you do, you're second best. To achieve success is to be first, and that's being yourself."

One of the qualities people admire in former First Lady Barbara Bush is her acceptance of herself as she is. Comparing herself to her predecessor, Mrs. Bush said: "Nancy Reagan adores her husband; I adore mine. She fights drugs; I fight illiteracy. She wears a size 3; so's my leg."

That healthy, non-apologetic attitude has allowed Mrs. Bush to make the most of who she is. She doesn't spend her time trying to be like someone else or acting in a manner inconsistent with the way she sees herself. People who accept themselves for who they are can effectively perform with the instrument they've been given.

. . .

Thousands of years ago, a slave named Aesop wrote some simple fables that illustrated certain principles of thought and behavior. They continue to affect people's lives because the applications remain relevant. One such fable is that of the deer and the hunter. The deer was admiring his reflection in the pool.

"Ah," said he, "where can you see such noble horns as these, with such antlers? I wish I had legs worthy to bear such a glorious crown. It is a pity they are so slim and unsightly." At that moment, a hunter appeared and sent an arrow flying towards the deer. The deer bounded off and by means of his nimble legs that he was just complaining about was quickly out of range of the hunter.

Prize yourself. Stop tearing yourself down. Build on your strengths. Don't dwell on your weaknesses. Act and think in ways that make you like yourself. Don't compare yourself to other people or compare what you are to what you think you should be. Celebrate who you are and be the best you can be.

WHAT A PITCHER!

My son is interested in any activity that involves a ball. His favorite sport is solely dependent on the time of year. During his stint in T-Ball, he became bored with hitting a baseball off a tee and wanted to play baseball like the big boys. One bright Saturday morning he stood in an empty lot by our home practicing his batting.

Throwing the ball into the air, Matthew took a healthy swing with his new aluminum bat and missed. "Steee-rike one," he screamed. Tossing the ball in the air once again, he swung and missed. "Steee-rike two," his young voice declared. Repeating the action one more time, Matthew once again, failed to make contact. "Steee-rike three, you're out."

I anxiously waited to see how my son would handle the disappointment. He dropped his bat to the ground, wiped his forehead, and then proudly declared, "What a pitcher!"

Ever had a strikeout experience? There is a tendency to tear ourselves down, get hard on ourselves, or give up when the final strike has been called.

Take a lesson from Matthew. Focus on the good. Even in the worst situation, we still have value. Find it!

LOOSEN UP!

Abe Lincoln laughed at himself, and especially at his appearance. He once shared this story about himself:

"Sometimes I feel like the ugly man who met an old woman traveling through a forest.

"The old woman said, 'You're the ugliest man I ever saw.'

" 'I can't help it,' the ugly man said.

" 'No, I guess not,' the woman admitted, 'but the least you could do is stay at home.'"

Whenever I begin taking myself or life too seriously, I reflect on Abraham Lincoln's ability to laugh at himself. I'm convinced if more people could loosen up and laugh at themselves, life wouldn't seem so difficult.

Try it . . . You might like it.

DAILY REMINDER

This is a daily reminder
That I have made for me;
To make the most of life

And to be the best I can be.
To treat others with the respect
That I would like myself
To face upcoming goals
Rather than put them on a shelf.
This is a daily reminder that
I have made for me.

Amy Martinez
(Seminar Participant)

HELP WANTED: ONE FAIRY GODMOTHER

Robert Schuller has a catchy saying that's worth thinking about: "You are not what you think you are, you are not what I think you are, you are what you think I think you are."

This principle is illustrated in the message of storybook heroine Cinderella. This lonely young woman was trapped in a life of backbreaking drudgery and daily belittling by her stepsisters and stepmother. As a servant to this humiliating family, Cinderella existed in a lifestyle dictated by what her sisters told her. For example, they laughed at the thought of Cinderella going to the ball and eventually even Cinderella considered it a ludicrous dream.

Even when the fairy godmother appeared, Cinderella opposed the suggestion that she too might attend the dance. She was ugly. Her clothes were second-rate and soiled. Her hands were stained and callused. She didn't possess the proper social mannerisms and would most likely be the laughing stock of this gala affair. Surely, the fairy godmother must be joking.

Then, with a swish of her magic wand, the fairy godmother changed Cinderella into a beautiful maiden who stole the heart of the handsome prince. Suddenly she was beautiful no matter what her stepsisters said. What an amazing transformation.

Like Cinderella, we often receive our self-image from those around us. It is not necessarily what they think of us but what we think they think of us that impacts our personal view of our value. The facts have little to do with reality. Whoever is the most convincing seems to have the greatest impact on how we see ourselves.

Find yourself a fairy godmother; someone who loves, values, and respects you for who you are. Seek out relationships where people are interested in helping you bring out the best in yourself.

LIKE YOURSELF

Sometimes the messages we receive from others can be confusing and frustrating. You may feel like Alice of *Alice in Wonderland* when the Duchess said to her, "Be what you would seem to be—or, if you'd like it put more simply—never imagine yourself not to be otherwise than what it might appear to others that what you were or might have been was not otherwise than what you had been would have appeared to them to be otherwise."

Did you catch that? Simply stated, the Duchess could have said, "Like yourself . . . just the way you are. Realize how special you are."

My daughter spells her name *Katy*. On her first day of school the teacher asked her to spell her name. "*K-A-T-Y*." "That's interesting," responded the teacher. "Most girls I know spell it *K-A-T-I-E*. I wonder why yours is different."

"I don't know," responded Katy, "I guess I'm just special." And she is.

Katy may not always see herself as being everything she wants to be, but I hope she will always be able to say, "I guess I'm just special."

HOW EXCITING!

According to Bill Farmer's newspaper column, J. Upton Dickson was a fun-loving person who announced he was writing a book entitled *Cower Power*. He also was forming a group for insecure, submissive people called the *Doormats*. It's an acronym for Dependent Order Of Really Meek And Timid Souls. Their motto was: "The meek shall inherit the earth—if that's okay with everybody." The national symbol was the yellow traffic light.

I AIN'T NO DUMBBELL

When the football coach screamed out, "Now all of you dumbbells go take a shower!" all but one player did so. Angered by what he thought was disobedience, the coach charged up to the player and growled, "Well?" But the young man just stood there smiling and chuckled as he replied, "There certainly were a lot of them coach, weren't there?"

It is great to be able to affirm yourself even in the face of demeaning comments. Socrates said, "The greatest way to live with honor in this world is to be what we pretend to be—to be, in reality, what we want others to think we are."

THE VALUE OF A HUG

In 1983, Kathleen Keating introduced us to the value of hugging. Her excellent work, *The Hug Therapy Book* (Comcare Publications), beautifully addresses the question, "What's so good about a hug?" Keating explains: "Hugging is healthy; it helps the body's immunity system. It keeps you healthier, it cures depression, it reduces stress, it induces sleep, it's invigorating, it's rejuvenating, it has no unpleasant side effects, and hugging is nothing less than a miracle drug. Hugging is all natural. It is organic, naturally sweet, has no pesticides, no preservatives, no artificial ingredients, and is 100 percent wholesome. Hugging is practically perfect. There are no movable parts, no batteries to wear out, no periodic check-ups, low energy consumption, high energy yield, inflation-proof, non-fattening, no monthly payments, no insurance requirements, theft-proof, non-taxable, non-polluting, and, of course, fully returnable."

Hugging is no doubt one of the most naturally therapeutic actions we can engage in. It seems to me we owe it to ourselves and those we love to frequently share this mutually beneficial gift.

SERVANTHOOD

- There is no more noble occupation in the world than to assist another human being—to help someone succeed.

    Alan Loy McGinnis

- Everybody can be great . . . because anybody can serve. You don't have to have a college degree to serve. You don't have to make your subject and verb agree to serve . . . You only need a heart full of grace, a soul generated by love.

    Martin Luther King, Jr.

- The service we render to others is really the rent we pay for our room on this earth. It is obvious that man is himself a traveler; that the purpose of this world is not "to have and to hold" but "to give and serve." There can be no other meaning.

    Sir Wilfred T. Grenfell

- Try to forget yourself in the service of others. For when we think too much of ourselves and our own interests, we easily become despondent. But when we work for others, our efforts return to bless us.

    Sidney Powell

- Half of the world is on the wrong scent in the pursuit of happiness. They think it consists in having and getting, and in being served by others. It consists in giving and serving others.

    Henry Drummond

- From now on, any definition of a successful life must include serving others.

    George Bush

- When people are serving, life is no longer meaningless.

    John Gardner

- I don't know what your destiny will be but one thing I do know, the only ones among you who will be really happy are those who have sought and found how to serve.

    Albert Schweitzer

■ One need not be a servant to be able to serve.

Victor Frankl

■ Dedicate some of your life to others. Your dedication will not be a sacrifice. It will be an exhilarating experience because it is intense effort applied toward a meaningful end.

Dr. Thomas Dooley

A SELFISH SERVANT

In her book *The Corn of Wheat*, Gladys Nash relates an experience when her car broke down in the middle of nowhere. After a lengthy wait, she noticed a service vehicle approaching and motioned for the driver to stop. When he inspected her stalled car, he quickly discovered the problem. It needed a new water hose. He said he would get to town for a replacement, then return and install it for her.

Relieved, Gladys waited and waited and waited, but the man didn't return. "He's surely forgotten all about me," she muttered to herself. Finally, however, he showed up. Thoroughly exasperated, she asked, "Where have you been all this time?" He replied, "Well, I had to go home and have my dinner." Recalling the incident, Gladys exclaimed, "My dinner! I ask you, what service!'"

The actions of this mechanic illustrate how we tend to serve each other. When our personal desires, comforts and needs are taken care of, we then might find the time and energy to reach out to someone else. Servanthood is marked by unselfish giving rather than "What's in it for me" living.

A PASSION FOR SERVING

Joan Rawlusyk states in "Reach Out and Touch Someone" (*The PEO Record*, Vol. 98, No. 5, May, 1985), "There is a great paradox in reaching out to touch someone— and that is, the more you reach out to others, the more you will be touched yourself. Joy and happiness in great measure are waiting for us if we will reach just a little further. In the reaching, we become God's own hand. He is touching through us. Somebody today needs to be touched—by you and by me. Someone today is in great need of something only we can give."

Mother Teresa would offer a resounding "amen" to these thoughts. "Unless life is lived for others," she said, "it is not worthwhile." As a young nun she developed a burning desire to work with the homeless and hopeless. Although she was convinced of this calling, her superiors suggested her youth and inexperience would surely cause her to fail in such an endeavor. Mother Teresa was, therefore, assigned to teach at a convent in India.

Mother Teresa's mission to serve others unable to meet their own needs burned deep in her heart. Finally, at age thirty-nine, she was allowed to pursue her passion in poverty stricken Calcutta. On her first day, she encountered a man lying in the gutter, so covered with disease and insects that everyone avoided him. Mother Teresa knelt down next to him and began cleaning his infested body. He was so astounded at her caring, he asked her, "Why are you helping me?" Mother Teresa smiled and replied, "Because I love you."

Mother Teresa and her Sisters of Charity continue to serve worldwide without request for funds or special assistance. Their passion to serve is an extension of God's hand reaching out to touch the untouchable.

WHICH DO YOU WISH TO BE?

Twenty-five centuries ago, Lao-tse, a Chinese sage, offered this profound insight:
"The reason why rivers and seas receive the homage of a hundred mountain streams is that they keep below them. Thus they are able to reign over all the mountain streams. So the sage, wishing to be above men, putteth himself below them; wishing to be before them, he putteth himself behind them. Thus, though his place be above men, they do not feel his weight; though his place be before them, they do not count it an injury."

So it is with humankind. Those who wish to yield the greatest influence will unselfishly position themselves below others, so as to serve them better.

Bruce Barton told a parable of two seas in Palestine that expounds on the wisdom of Lao-tse. One sea is fresh. Fish live in it. Trees and bushes grow near it. Children splash and play in it. The river Jordan flows into this sea with sparkling water from the hills. People build their homes near it. Every kind of life is happier because it is there. The same river Jordan flows south into another sea. Here there are no fish, no green things, no children playing, no homes a-building. Stale air hangs above its waters, and neither man nor beast will drink of it. What makes the difference between these neighbor seas? Not the Jordan River. It empties the same good water into both. Nor is it the soil or the countryside.

The difference is that the Sea of Galilee receives water but does not keep it. For every drop that flows in, another drop flows out. The giving and the receiving go on in equal measure. The other sea hoards its income. Every drop it gets it keeps. The Sea of Galilee lives and lives. The other sea gives nothing. It is called the Dead Sea.

There are also two kinds of people in this world—those Dead Sea people who take without giving back, and the givers who remain fresh and vibrant by freely sharing of themselves.

STRESS

- In most cases, stress itself does not cause disease. A certain amount of stress is a necessary and an important part of daily life.

  Dr. S. I. McMillen

- I've tried relaxing, but—I don't know—I feel more comfortable tense.

  Caption for Hamilton Cartoon

- Most stress is caused by people who overestimate the importance of their problems.

  Michael LeBoeuf, Ph.D.

- Stress is a state of fatigue or frustration brought about by devotion to a cause, way of life, or relationship that failed to produce the expected reward.

  Herbert J. Freudenberger

- Burnout is all in the mind, primarily the lack of stretching and exciting goals and expectations, fueled by a growing awareness of one's strengths and possibilities.

  Joe Batten

- Managing stress is tuning it down when it's too much, and increasing it when it's too little.

  Dr. Donald Tubesing

- Stress is defined as an inability, or the perception that you are unable, to take control of your life. If you feel in control—even if you're not but perceive that you are—you won't feel the stress. And stress leads to burnout.

  Dr. Gary Grody

- Unless we come apart and rest a while, we may just plain come apart.

  Vance Havner

- In most incidences, it's not the individual or the job that causes burnout; rather, burnout is the result of a mismatch between the personality or the goals of the worker and the job description or the expectations of the workplace. Realize that stress is an unavoidable consequence of life.

  Dr. Paul Rosch

■   The point is that those who feel a sense of purpose and commitment, who view
     change as a challenge instead of a threat, aren't affected by stress in a negative
     way.

                                                                           Success, *May 1986*

■   Find what things you can have some control over, and come up with creative
     ways to take control.

                                                                           Dr. Paul Rosch

HOW TO KEEP FROM BEING WIRED AND TIRED

When was the last time you woke up totally refreshed, ready for the day? How
long did you remain energized, excited, and exuberant about the day's activities?

For far too many people, the stressors of life have zapped their ability to do their
best, be their best, and enjoy their daily activities. Consider for a moment that:

- 1 million Americans have a heart attack each year,
- 13 billion doses of tranquilizers, barbiturates, and amphetamines are
  prescribed yearly,
- 8 million Americans have stomach ulcers,
- there are an estimated 50,000 stress-related suicides each year (only
  "one" in "eight" attempts are successful); and
- we have 12 million alcoholics in this country.

This is only the tip of the iceberg concerning stress-related statistics. In fact, Dr.
David Schwartz believes that 80 percent of the illnesses treated in this country are
emotionally induced illnesses (EII).

Stress is a used, misused, abused, and overused word in our daily conversations.
What is stress really? Dr. Hans Seyle, the father of Stress Management Research,
says, "Stress is the wear and tear on your body caused by life's events." It is the
body's physical, mental, and chemical reactions to circumstances that frighten,
excite, confuse, endanger, and irritate.

Hundreds of experiences in life cause stress. These stressors create *eustress* (good
stress) or *distress* (negative stress). Our bodies are designed to meet these stressors.
However, each person must determine what is just the right amount of stress for
them to function at their optimum level. Experiencing too little stress causes
irritability, boredom, dullness, and apathy. Too much stress can produce comparable results, along with feelings of being overwhelmed.

Defining stress is relatively simple compared to the task of developing effective
stress-management tools. One thing is certain: eliminating the destructive effects of
stress requires an individual, concentrated effort.

Dr. Seyle believed the most frequent causes of stress are an inability to adapt and not having an established code of behavior to guide our actions.

Adapt? Millions of years ago, this planet was populated by dinosaurs the size of which we have not seen on this earth. Then something happened. Scientists have indicated that although dinosaurs existed for millions of years, their ultimate inability to adapt to a changing world resulted in extinction.

Another kind of creature lived during the dinosaur age. That species remains in existence today because of its ability to adapt. Any guesses?

Frogs. Yes, those amphibious, adaptable creatures survived the changes.

Before we get too gung-ho about adapting, don't forget the second cause of stress: not having an established code of behavior to guide actions.

In a laboratory experiment, frogs were placed in a shallow pan of room temperature water. They were free to jump out of the pan at will. Under each pan was a bunsen burner, which heated the water very gradually. As the temperature rose, the frogs adapted. Unfortunately, regardless of how hot the water became, the frogs never became uncomfortable enough to jump out of the pan.

So what happened? The frogs died because they did not have a code of behavior that told them to jump.

We, too, need to learn when enough is enough. Adapting is fine but not without a code of behavior that warns us when it is time to jump.

Dr. Paul Rosch at the American Institute of Stress says, "The answer to stress management is to realize that stress is an unavoidable consequence of life." And I would add: Practice strategies that keep this consequence from becoming overwhelming.

STRESS-MANAGEMENT STRATEGIES

1. Get in the driver's seat.

Emotionally healthy people tend to maintain a high degree of control over their life. Feeling in control helps reduce feelings of stress.

2. Passionately pursue your purpose.

An article in *Success* magazine commented, "Those who feel a sense of purpose and commitment, who view change as a challenge instead of a threat, aren't affected by stress in a negative way."

3. Work your plan.

Take one thing at a time. Refrain from procrastinating. Choose how you spend your time.

4. Put problems in perspective.

Dr. Michael LeBoeuf believes, "Most stress is caused by people who overestimate the importance of their problems."

5. Become a kookaburra.

A what? Kookaburras are Australian birds known for their deep laughing sound. When was the last time you had a good, belly-wrenching laugh?

6. Don't strangle yourself.

Worry comes from the Anglo-Saxon word meaning to strangle or choke. Worry restricts your ability to think and act effectively. As the old saying goes, "It ain't no use putting up your umbrella until it rains."

7. Listen to what you are saying.

Our self-talk and perceptions of events cause undue stress. We become what we think, and our perception of any event will determine our reaction to it.

8. Are we having fun yet?

So you live to be "seventy," which amounts to 613,200 hours. That is far too much time not to have fun. Fun is a diversion from the norm that gets us out of the rut the stressors of life create.

9. Build a buddy system.

Focus on building quality relationships. Give up judging, criticizing, holding grudges, unnecessary competition, and the like. Earn your neighbor's love.

10. Change your oil.

Most people take better care of their cars than they do of themselves.

—Relax: it's cheaper than therapy.

—Recess: exercise rejuvenates our system.

—Reserve: build an energy reserve through smart nutrition.

—Recognize your limits.

—Release: find a non-judgmental person you can talk to.

11. See streams in the desert.

Keep life in perspective. Concentrate on the positive. Keep failure and mistakes in perspective. Develop enthusiasm. See something good in every experience you have.

Leo Buscaglia suggests, "When you get to the end of your rope, tie a knot, hang on, and swing."

Remember to adapt and create a code of behavior to guide your actions toward a healthy lifestyle.

SUCCESS

- Six essential qualities that are keys to success: sincerity, personal integrity, humility, courtesy, wisdom, charity.

  Dr. William Menninger

- Success can make you go one of two ways. It can make you a prima donna, or it can smooth the edges, take away the insecurities, let the nice things come out.

  Barbara Walters

- The person who has discovered the pleasures of truly human living, the person whose life is rich in friendships and caring people, the person who enjoys daily the pleasures of good food and sunshine, will not need to wear herself out in pursuit of some other kind of success.

  Harold Kushner

- Success is not a harbor but a voyage with its own perils to the spirit. The game of life is to come up a winner, to be a success, or to achieve what we set out to do. Yet there is always a danger of failing as a human being. The lesson that most of us on this voyage never learn, but can never quite forget, is that to win is sometimes to lose.

  Richard M. Nixon

- Success comes from knowing that you did your best to become the best that you are capable of becoming.

  John Wooden

- In order to succeed, at times you have to make something from nothing.

  Ruth Mickleby-Land

- What is success in this world? I would say it consists of four simple things—to live a lot, to love a lot, to laugh a lot, and from it all, to learn a lot.

  Richard J. Needham

- Success has a price tag on it, and the tag reads COURAGE, DETERMINATION, DISCIPLINE, RISK TAKING, PERSEVERANCE and CONSISTENCY—doing the RIGHT THINGS for the RIGHT REASONS and not just when we feel like it.

  James M. Meston

■   Success is failure with the dirt brushed off.

Mamie McCullough

■   Most people think of success and failure as opposites, but they are actually both products of the same process.

Roger von Oech

■   There is only one other lesson that success should teach us: Be as amazed by your own success as your friends are.

Harvey Mackay

■   The elevator to success is out of order. You'll have to use the stairs . . . one step at a time.

Joe Girard

■   The price of success is hard work, dedication to the job at hand, and the determination that whether we win or lose, we have applied the best of ourselves to the task at hand.

Vince Lombardi

■   Success is not a reward to be enjoyed, but a trust to be administered.

Charles "Tremendous" Jones

■   All of us are born for a reason, but all of us don't discover why. Success in life has nothing to do with what you gain in life or accomplish for yourself. It's what you do for others.

Danny Thomas

■   A man is a success if he gets up in the morning and gets to bed at night and in between does what he wants to do.

Bob Dylan

■   Sometimes I worry about being a success in a mediocre world.

Lily Tomlin

■   To me, the model of progress is not linear. Success is completing the full circle of yourself.

Gloria Steinem

■ You must listen to your own heart. You can't be successful if you aren't happy with what you're doing.

Curtis Carlson

■ The person who succeeds is not the one who holds back, fearing failure, nor the one who never fails . . . but rather the one who moves on in spite of failure.

Charles Swindoll

■ Success is courageously living each moment as fully as possible. Success means the courage to flow, struggle, change, grow, and all other contradictions of the human condition. Success means being true to you.

Dr. Tom Rusk and Dr. Randy Read
I Want to Change, But I Don't Know How

■ I attribute my success to this: I never gave or took an excuse.

Florence Nightingale

DON'T SIT THERE DROOPY-EYED . . . MAKE SOMETHING HAPPEN

Snoopy, the cherished "Peanuts" cartoon pet, sat droopy-eyed at the entrance of his dog house. He lamented, "Yesterday I was a dog. Today I'm a dog. Tomorrow I'll probably still be a dog. SIGH. There's so little hope for advancement!"

Perhaps you feel like Snoopy—hopeless with very little expectation of any advancement or success in your life. There's an old saying that suggests "if you keep doing what you're doing, you'll keep getting what you've got." And if, like Snoopy, we continue lamenting our demise without doing something different, the future will be a repeat of the present.

Aristotle, the Greek philosopher, once devised a formula for success and happiness. "First," he wrote, "have a definite, clear, practical idea—a goal, an objective." Second, he recommended attaining it by whatever means available, whether "wisdom, money, materials, or methods. Third, adjust all your means to that end."

According to Aristotle, there is no success without applying our resources toward a specific aim and then going for it. In so doing, most people come to the conclusion that success is a process more than a realization.

The dictionary definition of *success* is, "The favorable termination of a venture." Earl Nightingale defines success this way: "Success is the progressive realization of a worthy ideal." Denis Waitley says in his book, *Seeds of Greatness* (Fleming H. Revell, 1983), "It's when you are working and moving toward an accomplishment that brings you respect and dignity that you are succeeding." He says, "It's not what you get that makes you successful, it's what you are continuing to do with what you've got."

•   •   •

A worthy ideal along with continuing to do with what you've got are solid foundations for success. For example, baking cookies was always just a hobby for Debbi Sivyer, the youngest of five girls in a working-class family from Oakland, California. That is, until she decided to go into business for herself using a chocolate chip cookie recipe she had perfected.

According to a *USA Weekend* report, Debbi never knew she would be going into the cookie business. "I was really struggling with what I wanted to do with my life. I wanted to be married and have children, but I needed something for me. Baking cookies is something I love. It was my way of having fun."

Friends and family discouraged her, saying starting a business "was a stupid idea." But they all agreed she made wonderful cookies. "I really believed in my product."

Her husband, Randy Fields, and her local Small Business Administration gave her the encouragement and support she needed. Randy, then an investment advisor and economist, helped her get a $50,000 bank loan, and the first "Mrs. Fields" store opened in 1977 in Palo Alto, California.

The secret to her early success: When people wouldn't buy, she marched into the streets of Palo Alto and gave her cookies away. Customers soon beat a path to her store. Fields and her husband, the firm's chairperson, now oversee a company with 600 stores worldwide. Her latest concoction: oat bran cookies, now available in Mrs. Fields stores across the USA.

Debbi Sivyer believes in using what she has toward a worthy ideal.

•   •   •

So does Bill Gates. He's been called everything from a billionaire whiz kid to a brilliant entrepreneur. Gates got in on the ground floor of both the IBM and Macintosh markets to create a software dynasty. Microsoft became one of the fastest growing companies of the 1980's with $590 million in revenues after just thirteen years in business. In eight years the company mushroomed from eighty to eighteen hundred employees.

Bill Gates epitomizes the reality that successful people capitalize on what they have to set out on a journey of success. Like Gates, they are passionate about what they do and relentless in their pursuit of every possibility.

Malcolm Forbes said people often asked him how to become successful. Forbes simply replied, "Whatever you like to do, just find a way to do it. The biggest mistake people make in life is not trying to make a living at doing what they most enjoy."

That's dynamite advice. First, decide what you like to do. Then, determine how to be successful doing it.

. . .

Movie great Clark Gable enjoyed big-screen success, but life was a success for him before stardom. Gable always enjoyed a new challenge or adventure. Prior to riches and fame, he was a water boy in a mine and a timekeeping clerk in a steel products plant. After World War I, he worked part-time in a clothing store. At age twenty, he went to work as a garage mechanic and later invested long hours learning to become a tool dresser. He then acted for a stock company, spending two years with a tent show at $10 a week. Later he tested his skill as a lumberjack. Clark Gable's unquenchable zest for life at whatever job he was doing made him successful, not the fact that he became a movie star.

Football coach Joe Kapp suggests, "Success is living up to your potential. That's all. Wake up with a smile and go after life. Don't just show up at the game—or at the office. Live it, enjoy it, taste it, smell it, feel it."

"Success," says Nido Qubein, "is finding and doing to the best of your ability, in each moment of your life, what you enjoy most doing, what you can do best, and what has the greatest possibility of providing the means to live as you would like to live in the relation to yourself and all persons you value."

So, to the "Snoopies" of this world, Buck Rogers offered this bit of advice in *Getting the Best Out of Yourself and Others* (Harper & Row, 1988): "To be successful, you have to believe you can change the conditions in your life. You have to get out of the back seat of someone else's car and get behind your own steering wheel. You can't wish away the things in your life that make you unhappy and you can't daydream your hopes into reality. You have to consider options, reach decisions, take steps, make moves. Make things happen."

In other words, don't just sit there droopy-eyed. Go out and make something happen.

A HORATIO ALGER STORY WITHOUT A HAPPY ENDING

"Only in America, can the rugged individual, however poor and uneducated, rise to riches and position through his own efforts and in his own lifetime." This is one of the momentous truths written by Horatio Alger. Alger wrote many rags-to-riches stories and in so doing, his name became synonymous with success. A lifetime of sixty-five years produced over 100 novels with stirring stories and emotional endings. His characters were the epitomy of the American Dream come true.

Ironically, Horatio Alger's life did not have the same happy ending. Disillusioned with writing, he dabbled in various jobs, eventually suffering a nervous breakdown and dying broke.

There is a significant difference between recording the virtues of hard work, perseverance, and determination and living them. Thinking, writing, or talking about success does not a successful person make.

REDEFINING SUCCESS

There is a tendency at times to equate happiness and success. There are those who believe that if only they could be successful, happiness would follow. Not so. To be happy is to be successful, but being successful does not guarantee happiness. Louis Binstock began his book *The Road to Successful Living* with these words:

> "The most conspicuous failure in our time is success. No age in man's history has been so feverishly occupied with success; no age has been so noisily boastful of it. The reality or the promise of 'good things' pervades our view of the world; almost everywhere plenty has replaced or has begun to replace poverty. This age has beheld one of humanity's recurrent disillusionments, one of the great unlearned lessons of history. Success does not create happiness . . . For half a century it has been taught by both precept and example that material success—distinction in the acquisition of fame and money, position, and power—is the most important goal in life . . . Material success is what a man has; spiritual success is what he is; and we had tended to lump them together, to assume that happiness was the product of wealth. We had been proved wrong."

Berry Gordy, President of Motown Industries, echoes Binstock's statement in a 1979 *New York Times* article (January 14, 1979):

> "One of the most important problems in being an entrepreneur is the problem of happiness after success. Many people might say, 'Hey, Baby, give me the success, and I'll worry about the happiness afterwards.' Unfortunately, it doesn't happen that way. Unless you consider happiness before you consider success, then the manner in which you achieve your success will be something that will destroy you at some later date. Many people, in their rise to success, are so busy running to the top, stepping on their competitors, stepping on their enemies, and saddest of all, stepping on their friends and loved ones, that when they get to the top, they look around and discover that they are extremely lonely and unhappy. They'll ask me, 'Where did I go wrong?' My answer has always been, 'Probably at the beginning.'"

John D. Rockefeller was a marvelous example of the devastation success brings when we assume happiness will follow. By the time Rockefeller was fifty-three his life was a wreck. Throughout his business career he said, "I never placed my head upon the pillow at night without reminding myself that my success might be only temporary." He was the richest man in the world and yet he was miserable in every sense of the word. He was sick physically, mentally, and emotionally. There was no humor, balance, or joy in his life.

Then a transformation occurred. He determined to become a giver rather than an accumulator. He began to give his millions away. He founded the Rockefeller Foundation, dedicated to fighting disease and ignorance around the world. He lived to be ninety-eight years old and was a happy man in those years because of his new and revitalized definition of *success*.

Without a healthy, happy, hopeful life, success is elusive. Maybe it's time that we, like Rockefeller, redefine the meaning of success.

MASTER OF MUSIC TRIVIA

A young disc jockey in Oakland, California was asked to give up his on-the-air humor by the station manager, who, to put it nicely, wasn't impressed.

Contemplating what to do, the disappointed disc jockey pulled a discarded magazine from a waste basket. In it he noticed biographies, record-sales statistics, and interesting facts about pop singers and musicians. That night, before playing a song, he entertained listeners with interesting anecdotes and obscure information about the artist. Then he would identify the singer after playing one of their songs.

Listeners responded, the station manager was pleased, and Casey Kasem was off and running. His nationally syndicated "American Top 40" radio show became a resounding success.

Casey Kasem definitely matches Andrew Carnegie's definition of success. "I believe the true road to preeminent success in any line," he said, "is to make yourself master of that line!" Casey Kasem is the Master of Music Trivia.

FORMULA FOR SUCCESS

As reported in the *Little Gazette*, a former president of the General Motors Corporation started out as a stock boy and had a career that would have delighted Horatio Alger. At the time of his retirement, a reporter asked him whether it was still possible for a young man nowadays to start at the bottom and get to the top—and if so, how?

"Indeed, it is," was his answer. "The sad fact, however, is that so few young people realize it." Then he outlined a formula for success that will prove out not only in the auto industry but in any business.

"Keep thinking ahead of your job! Do it better than it needs to be done. Next time, doing it well will be child's play. Let no one, or anything, stand between you and a difficult task. Let nothing deny you the rich opportunity to gain strength in adversity, confidence in mastery. Do each task better each time. Do it better than anyone else can do it. Do these things, and nothing can keep the job ahead from reaching out after you!"

THE COOKIE KID

The names Markita Andrews and Girl Scout Cookies are synonymous with success.

Markita grew up in difficult circumstances. Her father left home, leaving Markita and her mother to fend for themselves. Although Mrs. Andrews had a dream to travel, the money she earned as a waitress was being saved for her daughter's college education. Traveling around the world would have to wait.

Markita had other plans. As a Girl Scout, she read that selling enough Girl Scout cookies would win a trip around the world for herself and her mom. There was one catch: she had to sell more cookies than any Girl Scout ever had. She wasn't excited about selling cookies but was determined to win that trip around the world.

Markita followed the advice of an aunt who told her to "go where the people with money are and ask them to buy cookies." She approached prospective buyers with her polite yet direct sales pitch, saying, "I'm earning a trip to camp. Would you like to invest in one dozen Girl Scout cookies or two dozen?" Five years and 39,000 sold boxes of cookies later, Markita and her mother enjoyed that trip around the world.

Markita's story doesn't end here. Her selling success prompted IBM to invite Markita to speak to their salespeople. She also addressed the insurance business's "Million Dollar Round Table." While there, she enthusiastically sold each of the 5,000 people a box of Girl Scout cookies.

Walt Disney productions made a movie about her called *The Cookie Kid*. Her book, *How to Sell More Cookies, Condos, Cadillacs or Anything*, quickly became a nationwide bestseller.

Amazing results occur when people set a course, pursue it with relentless passion and keep their mind focused on the desired result. Markita Andrews apparently subscribed to Denis Waitley's observation, "Success is not reserved for the talented. It is not in the high I.Q., not in the gifted birth. Not in the best equipment. Not even in ability. Success is almost totally dependent upon drive, focus, and persistence!"

TIME

- Time is the scarcest resource and unless it is managed nothing else can be managed.

  Peter Drucker

- Aside from Velcro, time is the most mysterious substance in the universe. You can't see it or touch it, yet a plumber can charge you upwards of seventy-five dollars per hour for it, without necessarily fixing anything.

  Dave Barry

- Time is neither our friend nor our enemy; it is something that gets measured out to us, to see what we will make of it.

  Richard Gaylord Briley

- Control your own time. Don't let it be done for you. If you are working off the in-box that is fed you, you are probably working on the priority of others.

  Donald Rumsfeld

- If you want to make good use of your time, you've got to know what's most important and then give it all you've got.

  Lee Iacocca

- People who make the worst use of their time are the same ones who complain that there is never enough time.

  Anonymous

- Time is everything. Anything you want, anything you accomplish—pleasure, success, fortune—is measured in time.

  Joyce C. Hall

- Time is the inexplicable raw material of everything.

  Arnold Bennett

- The great dividing line between success and failure can be expressed in five words: "I did not have time."

  Robert J. Hastings

■   Good time management means making the time to do the things that are most
     important to you.

Michael LeBoeuf, Ph.D.

■   There can't be a crisis next week. My schedule is already full.

Henry Kissinger

■   I resolve to live with all my might while I do live. I resolve never to lose one
     moment of time and to improve my use of time in the most profitable way I
     possibly can. I resolve never to do anything I wouldn't do, if it were the last
     hour of my life.

Jonathan Edwards

■   Time is a fixed income, and as with any income, the real problem facing us is
     how to work successfully with our daily allotment. Plan each day down to the
     moment because once time is wasted, you can never get it back.

Percy Whiting

■   Let anyone try, I will not say to arrest, but to notice or to attend to, the present
     moment of time. One of the most baffling experiences occurs. Where is it, this
     present? It has melted in our grasp, fled ere we could touch it, gone in the instant
     of becoming.

William James

THE GIFT OF TIME

Reflect on these words from *Christ Church Unity Church Bulletin*, Brookline,
Massachusetts:

What will you do with the rich gift of time? Will you take it and fill it or will you
simply stumble through it like a bleak and empty desert to be crossed? Oh listen!
Take heed of God's enjoinder, TAKE TIME . . .

Take time to look. It is the price of **beauty**. God has bestrewn your road with
boundless beauty. Take time to stop . . . not merely to glance but to really look at
His wonders.

Take time to work. It is the price of true **fulfillment**. Resolve that you will not
simply labour with head and hands, you will work with head, hands, heart, and
soul. Thus each and every task will bring its own glory of fulfillment.

Take time to play. It is the price of **perennial youth**. "All work and no play . . .
" leads to premature aging of the body and a withering of the spirit.

Take time to read. It is the price of **distilled wisdom**. Within the covers of good
books men have left behind a rich legacy of wisdom that is yours for the reading.

Take time to laugh. It is the **music of the soul.** Let your joy ring out in trills and cadenzas of lilting laughter.

Take time for prayer. It is the secret of **ever-renewing power.** Set aside your private time with your own in-dwelling Lord every day. Recharge your spiritual batteries and revitalize your every cell in quiet prayer.

Take time for a love that will outlast you. Give your soul to some activity that will ring for you down the corridors of endless time, an everlasting footprint in the sands of perfect love.

ONE GRAIN AT A TIME

James Gordon Gilkey shares his insights into time and life:

> Most of us think of ourselves as standing wearily and helplessly at the center of a circle bristling with tasks, burdens, problems, annoyances, and responsibilities which are rushing in upon us. At every moment we have a dozen different things to do, a dozen problems to solve, a dozen strains to endure. We see ourselves as overdriven, overburdened, overtired.
>
> This is a common mental picture—and it is totally false. No one of us, however crowded his life, has such an existence.
>
> What is the true picture of your life? Imagine that there is an hourglass on your desk. Connecting the bowl at the top with the bowl at the bottom is a tube so thin that only one grain of sand can pass through it at a time.
>
> That is the true picture of your life, even on a super-busy day. The crowded hours come to you always one moment at a time. That is the only way they can come. The day may bring many tasks, many problems, strains, but invariably they come in single file.
>
> You want to gain emotional poise? Remember the hourglass, the grains of sand dropping one by one.

THE CUMULATIVE VALUE OF A MINUTE

Benjamin Franklin said, "If we take care of the minutes, the years will take care of themselves." One minute. It doesn't seem like much. However, never underestimate the cumulative effect of each minute we live.

Let's suppose, for example, a minute is worth one penny. You see a penny lying on the street but pass it by because it is hardly worth the effort of leaning over to pick it up. But suppose you began to double that penny each day for a month. At the end of a week, you would only have sixty-four pennies. I know that's not much but at the end of a month you would have 536,870,912 pennies. Translated into dollars, that's $5,368,709.12.

The value we place on each minute of every day will have a cumulative impact on the remainder of our lives.

UNDERSTANDING

- To understand others you should get behind their eyes and walk down their spines.

  Rod McKuen

- If I can listen to what he tells me, if I can understand how it seems to him, if I can sense the emotional flavor which it has for him, then I will be releasing potent forces of change within him.

  Carl Rogers

- Sometimes I think that the main obstacle to empathy is our persistent belief that everybody is exactly like us.

  John Powell, S. J.

- Empathy is the ability to share other people's feelings, to see things, even if you don't agree with them, from their point of view. This is important in virtually all phases of human interaction, and extremely important in any large organization. You can't underestimate the need to handle interpersonal relations well, and empathy is the quality that counts most in that.

  G. J. Tankersley

- No one can develop freely in this world and find a full life without feeling understood by at least one person.

  Paul Tournier

- What a pity human beings can't exchange problems. Everyone knows exactly how to solve the other fellow's.

  Olin Miller

- To love you as I love myself is to seek to hear you as I want to be heard and understand you as I long to be understood.

  David Augsburger

- The man who can put himself in place of the other man, who can understand the workings of other minds, need never worry about what the future has in store for him.

  Owen D. Young

- Everything that irritates us about others can lead us to an understanding of ourselves.

Carl Jung

- We may not always see eye to eye, but we can try to see heart to heart.

Sam Levenson

A SIMPLE MISUNDERSTANDING

The following story is well known. Unfortunately its origin is uncertain. It is an exaggerated and comical illustration of what can happen when our words are misunderstood.

An English woman looking for a room in Switzerland asked for help from the schoolmaster of the village where she wanted to live. After finding a place that suited her, she returned to London for her baggage. Once there, however, she remembered that she hadn't asked about a bathroom, or "water closet," as she called it. So she wrote the village schoolmaster with her question, referring to these facilities in her letter as a "WC."

The schoolmaster, puzzled by these initials, sought the help of a parish priest. The priest decided the woman must be asking about a wayside chapel.

Now imagine being this woman and receiving the following response to your request.

Dear Madam:

I regret very much the delay in answering your letter. But I now take the pleasure in informing you that a "WC" is located about 9 miles from the house, in the center of a beautiful grove of trees. It is capable of seating 250 people at a time. It is open Tuesday, Thursday, and Sunday each week. I admit it is quite a distance away if you are in the habit of going regularly, but no doubt you will be pleased to know that a great number of people take their lunches along and make a day of it. They usually arrive early and stay late. The last time my wife and I went was six years ago. It was so crowded we had to stand the whole time we were there. It may interest you to know that there is a supper being planned to raise money to buy more seats. Likewise, it may interest you to know that my daughter met her husband the first time in the WC, and they were later married in the WC. I would like to say it pains me very much not to be able to go more regularly, but it is surely no lack of desire on my part. As we grow older, it seems to be more of an effort, particularly in cold weather. If you should decide to come for a visit, perhaps I could go with you the first time you go, sit with you, and introduce you to all the other folks. Remember, this is a friendly community.

Yours truly,
The Schoolmaster

SHE WORE THEIR SHOES

A *Business Week* article tells how designer Patricia Moore, moved by her arthritic grandfather's challenges, was prompted to do an unusual experiment (Joan Hamilton, "Gray Expectations: A New Force in Design," April 11, 1988). Then only twenty-five, she reconstructed herself into an elderly woman with bound joints. She padded her back into a hump and wore contact lenses smeared with vaseline. To complete her make-over, she wore support panty hose and a fuzzy wool coat.

Moore found herself being ignored in stores, struggling to complete simple tasks, too slow to cross the street before the light changed and encountering people apathetic to her circumstances. As a result of her experiences, several companies became more sensitive to the needs of the elderly.

Moore challenges people to try their own experiment. "Play tennis until your muscles ache; put on gloves with a couple of fingers sewn together; wear sunglasses with scratched lenses; then go and make yourself a bowl of soup. It won't be easy but you'll learn what life often is like for people with arthritis and cataracts."

Step back a few years to relive a scene from Harper Lee's *To Kill a Mockingbird* (Lippincott, 1961).

"First of all," he said, "if you can learn a simple trick, Scout, you'll get along a lot better with all kinds of folks. You never really understand a person until you consider things from his point of view . . . "

"Sir?"

" . . . until you climb into his skin and walk around in it."

That's exactly what Patricia Moore did, and it enhanced her compassion for the circumstances elderly people face. There's a whole world of people out there hoping we will step into their shoes . . . even if it's only an experiment.

SHARE THE PAIN

John Dreschler offers a superb illustration of the yearning for understanding in his touching book, *If I Were to Raise My Family Again*. A little boy was trying desperately to get the attention of his father, who was engrossed in the newspaper. The little fellow was trying to tell his daddy about falling and cutting his knee and how it hurt him so. After several such interruptions, the father impatiently and angrily scowls at the boy and asks, "What can I do about it?" The little fellow puts his head down and shuffles away saying, "You could say 'Ouch.'"

It's easy to be so self-absorbed we fail to say "ouch" and share the pain of those we love.

HAVE A LITTLE EMPATHY, LUCY

Charles Schulz's "Peanuts" comic strip has entertained readers with sarcastic conversations, heart-warming experiences, real-to-life scenarios, and lessons to be learned.

I recall one encounter between Lucy and Linus that touches close to home. It begins with Lucy (who else) shouting at Linus, "You blockhead!"

Linus counters, "Why did you call me a dumbbell?"

"I didn't say dumbbell, I said blockhead," Lucy sarcastically replies. With chin in hand, elbows resting on the top of the wall, Lucy says to herself, "That's what causes so much trouble between people today, there is no real understanding."

Of course if we had to listen to somebody like Lucy all day, who would want to understand? Perhaps if Lucy could feel what Linus feels, she wouldn't say half of the things she says.

I wonder if the same could be said of us?

MIXED MESSAGE

Gloria Hoffman and Pauline Graivier, in their book *Speak the Language of Success* (Berkley Books, 1987), share an entertaining story about mixed messages. A fellow walked into a department store and asked the first salesperson he met, "Excuse me, could you tell me where the restrooms are?" Misunderstanding him, she thought he had asked for the restaurants and replied, "There's one on the top floor if you want to sit down, and one on the ground floor, under the stairs, if you want to stand up."

Such misunderstandings could certainly be painful . . . or at least uncomfortable.

We're human. We're imperfect. Even in the simplest interactions there will be misunderstanding. Let's strive to understand as well as we can with what we have.

HASTY CONCLUSIONS

Our Daily Bread (July 10, 1990) retells the old story of the Persian king who wanted to teach his four sons never to make rash judgments. So he told the eldest to go in winter to see a mango tree, the next to go in spring, the third in summer, and the youngest in the fall.

After the last son had returned from his autumn visit, the king called them together to describe what they had observed. "It looks like a burnt old stump," said the eldest. "No," said the second, "it is lacy green." The third described it as "beautiful as a rose." The youngest said, "No, its fruit is like a pear." "Each is right," said the king, "for each of you saw the tree in a different season."

The lesson is obvious: Take time to understand, get the facts, learn the background, and place yourself where others are.

WHO'S THE AUTHORITY?

In his book *Witness Is Withness*, David Augsburger told a story about a man who had just arrived in heaven. Attracted by a large crowd, he inquired what was going on. "Oh, it's 'show-and-tell' time," came the answer. He was asked if he had anything he'd like to share. "Why sure," the new arrival quickly responded. "I'll tell about the big flood we had back in 1889, when I was a boy in Pennsylvania." "That will be fine," he was told, "but remember, Noah will be in the audience."

•

VALUES

- The intergenerational poverty that troubles us so much today is predominantly a poverty of values.

  Dan Quayle

- Values determine our needs. Needs determine our goals.

  Earl Nightingale

- A corporation's values are its life's blood. Without effective communication, actively practiced, without the art of scrutiny, those values will disappear in a sea of trivial memos and impertinent reports.

  Max DePree

- Know what your values are and live in a way consistent with your values.

  Danny Cox

- Our value is the sum of our values.

  Joe Batten

- Values are guiding devices to enhance our ability to achieve our purposes.

  Allan Cox

- Values are the foundation of our character and of our confidence. A person who does not know what he stands for or what he should stand for will never enjoy true happiness and success.

  Lionel Kendrick

- I believe that a person ought to know what he believes, why he believes it, and then believe it.

  Charles "Tremendous" Jones

- You will like yourself better when you have the approval of your conscience.

  Orison Swett Marden

- If you don't stand for something, you'll fall for anything.

  Steve Bartkowski

■ Cultivate optimism by committing yourself to a cause, a plan, or a value system. You'll feel that you are growing in a meaningful direction which will help you rise above day-to-day setbacks.

Dr. Robert Conroy

■ There can be no happiness if the things we believe in are different from the things we do.

Freya Stark

■ Keep true, never be ashamed of doing right; decide on what you think is right and stick to it.

George Eliot

■ Don't compromise yourself. You are all you've got.

Betty Ford

■ Be bold in what you stand for and careful what you fall for.

Ruth Boorstin

■ Let us suppose that we were asked for one all-purpose bit of advice for management, one truth that we were able to distill from the excellent companies' research. We might be tempted to reply, "figure out your value system."

Thomas Peters and Robert Waterman
In Search of Excellence

KNOW WHAT YOU VALUE AND LIVE IT

The mighty and majestic *Queen Mary* was the largest ship to cross the oceans when it was launched in 1936. She enjoyed a distinguished career through four decades and a world war. After retirement, the *Queen Mary* was anchored in Long Beach, California and converted into a hotel and museum. Restoration crews removed three massive smoke stacks slated to be scraped and painted. However, once detached from their supported location, the smoke stacks crumbled. All that remained of the three-quarter-inch steel plate from which they had been constructed were several layers of paint that had been applied over the years. The steel had disintegrated.

The *Queen Mary* suffered a condition common to humankind. Polished and attractive exteriors crumble over time if not supported by internal substance. Our lives break down, get out of balance, deteriorate or even collapse without a solid set of values.

Our thinking produces attitudes resulting in values that are reflected in our personality. They serve as guidelines for how we behave and see the world. We speak our values through our possessions, personal appearance, gestures, and facial expressions. Our actions and the words we use are primary indicators of the values we possess.

Defining your values is not just an academic exercise. Rather, it is a down-to-earth step toward realizing fulfillment in life. Carl Rogers said, "Clarifying your values is the essential first step toward a richer, fuller, more productive life."

To clarify your values, ask yourself:

- "What do I believe in?"
- "In what guiding principles can I become constructively obsessed?"
- "What governs my life?"
- "What do I stand for?"
- "What puts meaning into my life?"
- "What qualities are important for my life to be complete?"

This is not a simple exercise. Grappling for the right words is normal. Values are not contrived on the spur of the moment, given to vacillating, or negotiable principles that come and go with each passing day. Rather, they are ingrained in the fiber of a person's heart and soul. As Joe Batten said, "Our value is the sum of our values." It is impossible to separate personal value from personally held values.

Take the time to determine exactly what values are important to you. Your personal convictions, not those of others, will determine how you live. Whatever your list of value words, make them a living testament. Transform those words into guiding principles for everything you do.

• • •

Some groups of Native Americans pictured the conscience in the form of a triangle, a three-cornered stone located deep within. Whenever values were violated the stone would revolve or turn. With each turn the corners cut you, but the corner wore off a little, too. If the conscience continued to be violated, sooner or later the sharp corners of the stone would be rounded off, and the conscience could no longer "cut" as it should.

Once established, envision your values becoming directly connected to the nerve endings of your conscience. The concept of the conscience being worn down whenever values were violated provides an encompassing explanation of world events. Racism, negativism, jealousy, deceit, greed, sexual harrassment, promiscuity and the like will gradually grind down the corners of a nation's moral integrity.

Equality, optimism, dignity, hope, empathy, and love are a few of the values personal, corporate and national greatness are made of.

• • •

The story is told of a motorist driving through a dense fog following the taillights ahead of her. The driver in front did all the squinting, worrying, and navigating. Suddenly the car in front stopped and the two cars collided.

"Hey, why didn't you signal when you stopped?" yelled the woman behind.

"Why should I?" came the reply. "I'm in my own garage."

People's lives can follow a comparable scenario. Without sharpened and clear values we travel through the fog of life following someone else. Rather than establishing a clear path for ourselves, we follow blindly and end up in someone else's garage, blaming them for our being there.

Confucius, the Chinese philosopher who lived in fifth century B.C., wrote many maxims, including his "Rules of Life." In them he said: "The rule of life is to be found within yourself. Ask yourself constantly, 'What is the right thing to do?' Beware of doing that which you are likely, sooner or later, to repent of having done."

Found within yourself are the rules of life—values. Rather than waiting for someone else to offer direction, decide what principles and values you will live by. In the process, you will take responsibility for your feelings and attitudes, thoughts and actions. Your decisions will be based on your inner-directed value system, not the emotional influence of others. Life's challenges are transformed into ammunition for adventurous living.

Values are the glue that hold life's demanding details in place. Peace, harmony, and direction are harvested in people who know what they value and live it.

LIVING HIS CONVICTIONS

Dr. C. Everett Koop never viewed his job as surgeon general as a popularity contest. Koop's mandates aroused the anger and rattled the cages of many. He spoke out against tobacco products, declaring nicotine an addictive drug. Koop's anti-abortion, pro-sex-education, and condemnation of child abuse stances were non-negotiable. He promoted the exploration of free needle programs for drug addicts to avert the spread of AIDS and advocated the medical rights of babies with disabilities.

Dr. Koop maintained a compassionate approach to AIDS as a health issue. One hundred and seven million AIDS information booklets were printed and distributed to every home in America. Protection against and elimination of the deadly virus received equal attention.

Koop condemned TV violence, smoking in public places, and addressed organ donor programs. His views were inharmonious with those endorsing euthanasia or mandatory AIDS testing.

Dr. C. Everett Koop's career is an expression of his intense values. He saw himself as the surgeon general of all the people and attempted to implement programs consistent with his values that would benefit the American public.

Koop's directives were not always politically expedient or universally accepted, but they were consistent with his internal value system.

FOXY ADVICE

In the famous French story, *The Little Prince,* by Antoine de Saint Exupery, the best friend the little guy makes on the fictitious planet to which he has been banished is a fox. When the fox must depart from the prince forever, he offers to tell him the most wonderful secret in the world if the prince meets certain conditions. The little prince agrees, does what is expected, and then asks to be told the greatest secret. "Only that which is invisible is essential," the fox replies.

Values—You can't see them, touch them, taste them, or smell them. They are critical, intangible essentials that bring continuity and meaning to life.

MORE THAN AN IMPROMPTU SPEECH

William Safire in "Bush's Cabinet: Who's Up, Who's Down" (*New York Times Magazine,* March 25, 1990), reports that one week before assuming his responsibilities as President of the United States, George Bush was asked what he would tell his cabinet appointees. We received a glimpse of Bush's personal and presidential values as he reached into his pocket, pulled out a hand-written note and responded:

"Think big, challenge the system . . . adhere to the highest ethical standards."

"I don't like kiss-and-tell books."

"I'd rather see their name on the record than insidiously leaked to somebody. Be on the record as much as possible."

Several months after his inauguration, Bush was infuriated by published reports that his aides were trashing former President Reagan. The furious president chewed out his White House staff for verbalizing their criticisms and threatened to fire anyone caught doing it again.

Moral of the story: Don't mess with the president's values.

MAKINGS OF A CHAMPION TEAM

Do you remember the 1989 Fiesta Bowl when Notre Dame took on West Virginia? Notre Dame walked away with a national championship that day, but the players also learned a lesson about Lou Holtz's coaching values.

Late in the game, Notre Dame was assessed penalties on two consecutive plays for "taunting" the opposition. Lou Holtz quickly stormed out onto the field, knowing his actions would bring on another penalty, and asked the officials which of his players were doing the taunting. Then Coach Holtz—in front of a national TV audience, no less—went directly to the player and gave him a piece of his mind.

Lou Holtz coached at five colleges and succeeded in taking all of them to a bowl game. He is a vibrant believer in his players but also demands they adhere to his philosophy consisting of three simple rules:

1. Do what is right. Be on time, polite, honest, remain free from drugs, and if you have any questions, get out your Bible.

2. Do your best. Mediocrity is unacceptable when you are capable of doing better.

3. Treat others as you would like to be treated (the Golden Rule). Practice love and understanding.

Back to the Fiesta Bowl. It is probably fair to say that "taunting" violated Holtz's values.

WALK THE TALK

Values are those closely held beliefs people support with thoughts, words, feelings, and most importantly, action. What we do reflects what we believe. Each person's fundamental beliefs will ultimately have the final say over actions. Here are a few examples of people who walked the talk.

I read about a high school basketball coach who, a few years ago, relinquished his state championship after he had unknowingly used an ineligible player. Integrity meant more to this coach than the achievement of a lifetime dream, the trophy, glory, and the pride.

William Lloyd Garrison lived in nineteenth-century America, a nation where slavery was an accepted way of life. Garrison saw it differently. To him, slavery was a hideous crime against God and people. The masses jeered and laughed at his efforts to eliminate what he opposed. But Garrison continued to preach his message until a headstone was placed on the grave of slavery.

Albert Schweitzer forfeited a prestigious medical and possibly even music career and went to Africa to build hospitals providing services for the poor. Schweitzer's life was driven by a desire to meet the medical needs of people who were unable to do so themselves. He maintained his zest for living up to his death at age ninety, in 1965. His whole life was a powerful message to humankind.

In 1776, during the Revolutionary War, a young man was captured while spying on the British. His solid patriotic conviction prompted a response to his captors that will be forever recorded in history. Nathan Hale said, "I only regret that I have but one life to give for my country." That's the response of one committed to his beliefs.

J. C. Penney founded his retailing empire on the Golden Rule. Simply treating customers and employees as he would want to be treated earned J. C. Penney the respect and admiration of employees, as well as loyal customers.

Milton S. Hershey started the Hershey Corporation on the same values that governed his personal life. Integrity, industry, benefit to others, as well as family and community involvement were the supporting pillars of his company. Eighty years later, they remain a trademark of the Hershey Corporation.

As a young lawyer arriving in South Africa, Mahandas K. Gandhi was overwhelmed by the treatment non-whites received. How could people in their own country be required to carry identification papers or be refused travel on the same train as whites? Gandhi began a value-based campaign that is now known worldwide as "passive resistance." He later extended his crusade into India, attempting to free them from British colonial rule. Enduring considerable mental and physical anguish, Gandhi remained focused on truth and justice through passive resistance.

It is always dangerous to put people in the spotlight. In these examples, however, time has tested their credibility. Will the same be said of us?

ENTERTAINMENT . . . BURGERS . . . MEDICINE

The Walt Disney Company is the epitome of an organization driven by values. Disney is in business to provide an intangible product called happiness. Their "Disney courtesy" concept is based on four key values—safety, courtesy, show, and efficiency. Every performance standard is encompassed by these deeply held beliefs. Customer service is more than a token experience, it is a lifestyle for all Disney employees.

Disney cast members are indoctrinated with the philosophy and standards of "guest service." No cast member begins his or her role without substantial orientation to Walt Disney's concept of service. Employees think, walk, talk, and breathe safety, courtesy, show, and efficiency. It is a way of life. This lifestyle creates happiness for guests.

•   •   •

Consider McDonald's. Ray Kroc created an organizational culture reflecting quality, service, cleanliness, and value. Every employee is indoctrinated with these values, and rare is the McDonald's restaurant that doesn't espouse them. In fact, the story is told that Ray Kroc visited a Canadian franchise and found a single dead fly. Two weeks later, Kroc stripped them of their McDonald's franchise.

Another McDonald's franchise is located on the eastbound side of the Connecticut Turnpike (Interstate 95) in Darien. Prior to 1985, this was the location of an inconceivably filthy roadside restaurant. Three years later McDonald's had succeeded in making this site one of its most profitable franchises. In fact, this site produced an all-time monthly domestic record of $604,000 in sales. Whoever thought quality, service, cleanliness, and value could produce such a turnaround?

•   •   •

It's difficult to discuss organizational values without mentioning Johnson & Johnson. The first line of their company's credo reads: "Our first responsibility is to the doctors, nurses, and patients, to mothers, and all others who use our products." These are not just empty words, but the values by which this corporation lives and makes decisions.

Consider this scenario. Several people died after using Tylenol™ capsules (manufactured by Johnson & Johnson). Cyanide had been inserted to poison the medication, and testing indicated the tampering had taken place after the products reached the retail shelves. However, the safety of people was at stake and the company had a disaster on its hands.

Johnson & Johnson managers immediately decided to recall 31 million bottles of Tylenol™. Let me repeat that. They recalled 31 million bottles. Why? It was later determined that only seventy-five capsules in eight bottles had been injected, but the reality was Tylenol™ customers' safety and health were in jeopardy. Driven by their values, Johnson & Johnson responded to a critical situation in a timely manner and this heightened their reputation. The bottom line was at stake and their values tested. Johnson & Johnson proved that values would govern decision-making.

These companies no doubt ascribe to Max De Pree's conviction that, "A corporation's values are its life blood."

IBM'S FOUNDATION

In 1914, a young, aggressive entrepreneur set out on a new business venture. He was determined to make the company financially successful, but he also wanted the operation to reflect his personal values. The man's name was Thomas Watson, Senior. His business? International Business Machines (IBM).

From the conception of IBM, Watson recorded his values on paper and preached those beliefs to every employee. Each customer he served knew Watson was a living testament of his profound yet simple values. Here's what he believed:

1. The individual must be respected.

2. The customer must be given the best possible service.

3. Excellence and superior performance must be pursued.

Every action, decision, and policy was directly influenced by these values. They become (and remain) the foundation for the company's operation. Thomas Watson, Senior subscribed to a personal value system that set IBM apart from the crowd.

Thomas Watson, Jr. reaffirmed the importance of his father's commitment to a governing code of behavior. He wrote:

> Consider any great organization that has lasted over the years, and I think you
> will find that it owed its resilience not to its form of organization or administrative

skill, but to the power of what we call beliefs and the appeal these beliefs provide. This, then, is my thesis: I firmly believe that any organization, in order to survive and achieve success, must have a sound set of beliefs on which it premises all its policies and actions. Next, I believe that the most important single factor in the corporate success is faithful adherence to those beliefs. And finally, I believe that if an organization is to meet the challenges of a changing world, it must be prepared to change everything about itself except those beliefs as it moves through corporate life.

VISION

- Exercising vision is developing an understanding of where you are and where you're headed—both as an individual and as an organization.

  Allan Cox

- Vision without action is merely a dream. Action without vision just passes the time. Vision with action can change the world.

  Joel Arthur Barker

- Good business leaders create a vision, articulate the vision, passionately own the vision, and relentlessly drive it to completion.

  Jack Welch

- I've always believed in the art of the possible. I believe there's a difference between brave-heartedness and foolishness and I believe in whatever I'm going to do, if I don't see success somewhere through the tunnel of that vision, I don't even bother with it.

  Governor Douglas Wilder

- See things as you would have them be instead of as they are.

  Robert Collier

- One essential ingredient for being an original in the day of copies is courageous vision.

  Charles Swindoll

- Vision is a process that allows you to think ahead to where you want to be and what you want to be doing, and to create workable plans to lead you there.

  Fred Pryor

- In the absence of a vision, there can be no clear and consistent focus. In the absence of a dream, there can be no renewal of hope. In the absence of a philosophy, there is no real meaning to work and to life itself.

  Joe Batten

- A vision is a point on the horizon that will be reached only at some date in the future, a statement of what will be created years or decades ahead. To create visions, leaders must become preoccupied with the future. They must be able to project themselves ahead in time.

  James M. Kouzes and Barry Z. Posner
  The Leadership Challenge

- The world of tomorrow belongs to the person who has the vision today.

  Robert Schuller

- Ideals are like stars. You will not succeed in touching them with your hands. But like the seafaring man on the desert of waters, you choose them as your guides and following them you will reach your destiny.

  Carl Schurz

- The bravest are surely those who have the clearest vision of what is before them, glory and danger alike, and yet not withstanding, go out to meet it.

  Thucydides

- If you don't have a vision for your life, then you probably haven't focused in on anything.

  Dr. David Burns

- Vision is not so much what you think as how you think. Vision is less a matter of content than process. Vision is moving away from micromanagement, from "flyspeck management" to macroleadership.

  Anonymous

- Vision is not necessarily having a plan, but having a mind that always plans. In sum, vision means to be in touch with the unlimited potential and expanse of this marvelous instrument called the human mind.

  Peter Koestenbaum

- A vision is not a vision unless it says yes to some ideas and no to others, inspires people and is a reason to get out of bed in the morning and come to work.

  Gifford Pinchot

- Cherish your visions and your dreams, as they are the children of your soul, the blueprints of your ultimate achievements.

  Napoleon Hill

■ The vision of things to be done may come a long time before the way of doing them becomes clear, but woe to him who distrusts the vision.

Jenkin L. Jones

■ The people who shape our lives and our cultures have the ability to communicate a vision or a quest or a joy or a mission.

Anthony Robbins

■ The willingness to create a new vision is a statement of your belief in your potential.

David McNally

■ Vision without action is merely a dream. Action without vision just passes the time. Vision with action can change the world.

Joel Arthur Barker

■ A vision without a task is but a dream; a task without a vision is drudgery; a vision with a task is the hope of the world.

Anonymous

■ The very essence of leadership is you have to have a vision. It's got to be a vision you articulate clearly and forcefully on every occasion. You can't blow an uncertain trumpet.

Father Theodore Hesburgh

■ Vision is composed of one part foresight, one part insight, plenty of imagination and judgment, and often, a healthy dose of chutzpah.

Burt Nanus

VISION: THE ART OF CREATING WHAT'S "JUST RIGHT"

As a young boy, I was fascinated by fairy tales. One of my favorites was "Goldilocks and the Three Bears." You remember the story line. The three bears lived in a small suburb on the city's outskirts. On one bright sunny morning, the bear family journeyed into the city to do a little shopping at the mall. (O.K., I admit it—the story has changed slightly to keep up with the times.)

While away, a young girl named Goldilocks rode up to the bears' suburban home on her ten-speed bike. She peeked through each paned glass window and rang the chiming door bell. Unable to arouse anyone's attention, Goldilocks easily entered through the back door and into the family's kitchen.

Noticing three bowls neatly set at the country-style table, Goldilocks tasted the contents of the first bowl. It was far too hot! The cereal in the second bowl was too cold! However, the third bowl's cereal was *just right*. Goldilocks devoured its contents.

Making her way to the living room, Goldilocks noticed three beautifully stuffed chairs. Testing the largest overstuffed chair, Goldilocks didn't feel comfortable. The medium-sized wing-backed chair was not much better. However, the third, smaller chair was *just right* ... until it collapsed. Frightened by the sound of snapping pine, Goldilocks quickly ran up the stairs.

The upstairs was a spacious sleeping loft containing three neatly made beds in varying sizes. Goldilocks stretched her small frame on the largest bed. It was far too hard to suit her liking. The medium-sized bed was cushiony soft but sagged in the middle. The third and smallest bed provided adequate support, was the perfect size and the bedspread colors matched Goldilocks' sundress. In fact, this bed was *just right*, and Goldilocks fell fast asleep.

Visionary people, like Goldilocks, are willing to experiment to find out what's *just right*. They are commited to break through the status quo, create a new way of life and live on the cutting edge of fresh and exciting prospects. Visionaries, *unlike* Goldilocks, refuse to become so comfortable they fall asleep and get trapped by their contentment.

Charles Swindoll, in *Living Beyond Mediocrity* (Word Books, 1987), writes,

> "I have in mind the ability to see above and beyond the majority. I am reminded of the eagle, which has eight times as many visual cells per cubic centimeter than does a human. This translates into rather astounding abilities. For example, flying at 600 feet elevation, an eagle can spot an object the size of a dime moving through six-inch grass. The same creature can see three-inch fish jumping in a lake five miles away. Eaglelike people can envision what most would miss. Visionary people see beyond the hum-drum of everyday activities into future possibilities."

Thomas Watson, Sr. was forty when he took over as general manager of a little firm that manufactured meat slicers, time clocks, and simple tabulators. He had a vision for a machine that could process and store information long before the computer was a commercial reality. To match his lofty vision, Watson soon renamed his company International Business Machines Corporation. Toward the end of his life, Watson was asked at what point he envisioned IBM becoming so successful. His reply was simply, "At the very beginning."

Success is no surprise to visionary people. They know what they want, determine a plan to achieve it and expect positive results.

In his book, *Hey, Wait a Minute* (Ballantine, 1985), John Madden writes about a conversation with Vince Lombardi about good and bad coaches. Lombardi said, "The best coaches know what the end result looks like, whether it's an offensive play, a defensive play, a defensive coverage, or just some area of the organization.

If you don't know what the end result is supposed to look like, you can't get there. All the teams basically do the same things. We all have drafts, we all have training camps, we all have practices. But the bad coaches don't know what they want. The good coaches do."

Knowing what you want and where you are going is the stuff vision is made of. "If you plan, you can greatly influence your own future," said Roger Smith in a 1989 *Fortune* article. "I think everybody needs a vision. A lot of people just wander mindlessly through this world, thinking one or maybe two days ahead. They don't have a vision for themselves of where and what they want to be. My vision always has been to make General Motors the world's premier automotive corporation."

•   •   •

Vision seems to be an elusive yet important life principle. Your vision describes the ideal future for you to attain. It provides meaning and direction while forcing you to break through present limitations. Holding a clear picture in your mind of the desired future will mobilize your creative efforts and generate the desire and energy to perform.

Vision then is quite simply a mental picture of what tomorrow will look like. Sometime ago, I read an advertisement placed by Shearson/Lehman Brothers that beautifully, yet simply, defined vision and its impact. The ad read: "Vision is having an acute sense of the possible. It is seeing what others don't see. And when those with similar vision are drawn together, something extraordinary occurs."

John F. Kennedy knew the power of vision. Consider his goal, set in 1960, to place a man on the moon by 1970. That seemingly outrageous ideal kindled the imagination of an entire nation. Millions of people set about concentrating their time and effort toward achieving this lofty ideal. Ideas were generated and the wheels set in motion to make this dream a reality. The result is now history. That was *vision*.

John F. Kennedy was a living example of Mitchell Kapor's belief that, "If you can genuinely present a picture that makes sense to people, that unifies the seemingly disparate elements of their experience, if you can give people something they can resonate with because it's meaningful, then they'll be immensely responsive to it." JFK presented that picture and America responded.

•   •   •

Tom Fatjo knew where he wanted to go. By the time he was thirty-six years old, he had turned $500 and a used garbage truck into the country's biggest solid-waste-disposal company. Fatjo credits his success to "creative dreaming." For instance, he says, "In the beginning stages of developing our first garbage company in Houston, I used to imagine trucks, a whole fleet of blue trucks, running out of our lot onto the streets of Houston in the early morning mist. In my imagination I could 'see' the trucks and the men as they wound their way around the streets of our town." That is *vision*.

Fatjo explained that these times of dreaming were not spent planning or figuring out how to implement his vision. Instead, he held a clear picture in his mind of his incredible dream as already being a reality.

• • •

Fred Smith has eagle vision. In the early 1970s, he was writing a term paper for his economics class at Yale University. Smith envisioned an overnight, nationwide, air express delivery system for urgent packages. Unfortunately, his professor didn't share in the excitement of Smith's idea and gave him a "C" on the term paper. Smith, however, took the ideas from this "average" paper and created an exceptional company known as Federal Express.

Today Federal Express enjoys a reputation as one of the finest companies in the world and has captured a healthy percentage of the air express market in the United States. In addition, Federal Express is consistently ranked in the top ten of the best places to work in America.

Fred Smith saw an opportunity others were missing. He didn't allow the discouragement of a college professor to thwart his vision. Rather, he used the setback as a springboard to make his idea a "flying" success. Fred Smith has *vision*.

• • •

Curt Carlson began his career selling soap for Proctor and Gamble. During his tenure, he became intrigued with the idea of using a trading stamp promotion. Carlson left his position and set out to introduce Gold Bond trading stamps in 1938. After fourteen years of selling, he landed the Super Valu account, placing his stamps in stores across the country.

Today, Curt Carlson is board chair and sole owner of the $9.3 billion-a-year Carlson Companies. This international business conglomerate includes more than seventy-five different companies employing more than 70,000 people in thirty-eight countries. The Carlson Companies is one of the nation's largest privately-held companies.

Carlson attributes his success to his "ability to see, to imagine how things can be. I'm not distracted," he says, "by how things are."

At the risk of reaching "vision" overload, consider these historical visionaries. Billy Graham prayed, "God let me do something, anything for you." Henry Royce was unwilling to accept anything but automobile perfection. Orville and Wilbur Wright were inspired at a children's birthday party when they saw a toy with a wound-up rubberband take to the air. Marie Curie held high her commitment to scientific excellence in spite of doubters and made important contributions until the day she died. Mohandas K. Gandhi and Martin Luther King, Jr. held a dream of a better life for all people. Lee Iacocca preaches "I have one, and only one, ambition for Chrysler; to be the best. What else is there?" These people had *vision*.

These people were able to see above and beyond the majority to a condition that was *just right*. They taught us that a vision begins with imagination coupled with a belief that dreams can one day be made real.

"Look at things not as they are, but as they can be," encourages David J. Schwartz. "Visualization adds value to everything. A big thinker always visualized what can be done in the future. He isn't stuck with the present."

What is your vision of the future? What have you envisioned to be *just right* for you? How do you plan to make next year different from the past or for that matter, how will you be better tomorrow than you are today?

I like the story of the little girl who was drawing with her new set of 64 crayons. Her mother asked what the picture was about and the little girl quickly answered, "I'm drawing God." The mother, questioning her daughter's artistic direction, responded with, "But honey, nobody knows what God looks like." The child continued drawing and then said confidently, "They'll know when I'm finished."

People with vision already know what the *just right* outcome will be even if no one has ever seen it before.

Remember the words of James Allen: "Your vision is the promise of what you shall one day be; your ideal is the prophecy of what you shall at last unveil."

(Portions of this section were excerpted from Glenn Van Ekeren's *The Art of Visionary Leadership* and used with permission.)

PERISH OR PROSPER

The Bible says that "Without a vision, the people perish." And, we might add, life gets complicated.

You've no doubt heard that Biblical quotation before. For an applicable story, turn to Numbers 13. God sent Moses to deliver the Israelites from captivity in Egypt. Now Moses wasn't excited about the idea but agreed, with God's help, to lead His people into the Promised Land. A well-orchestrated escape plan worked beautifully, and as the people approached the Promised Land, spies were sent ahead to check out the situation. One man from each of the twelve tribes was chosen for the scouting exhibition.

The Israelites anxiously awaited their return and report. The scouting summary prompted chaos. Ten spies saw giants who would crush them like grasshoppers. Jacob and Caleb, on the other hand, saw a land "flowing with milk and honey." "Let's do it," they encouraged. "You're crazy," said the others. The majority won and because of their fear, the people died in the wilderness—except two. Joshua and Caleb entered the Promised Land.

God had already promised the Israelites safe entry. Yet, with a guaranteed vision clearly before them, the Israelites chose to follow their self-imposed limitations. How sad! Such opportunities are also overlooked today because people lack the faith and determination to pursue a vision—and they are slowly perishing.

WEALTH

- All money represents to me is pride of accomplishment.

  Ray Kroc
  Founder, McDonald's

- There's no reason to be the richest man in the cemetery. You can't do any business from there.

  Colonel Harlan Sanders

- Wealth was originally perceived as a state of mind, not a condition of purse.

  Richard Gaylord Briley
  Are You Positive?

- If you can actually count your money, then you're not rich.

  Joseph P. Kennedy

- I learned growing up that there were two very important things that money couldn't buy—love and poverty. And my family had as much of both as no money could buy.

  Tommy Lasorda
  Manager, L.A. Dodgers

- Most of us aren't that interested in getting rich—we just don't want to get poor.

  Andy Rooney

- Bank accounts give a person a good feeling ... until he realizes they are insured by an agency of a Federal Government that's two trillion dollars in debt.

  The Indianapolis News

- Money won't buy happiness, but it will pay the salaries of a large research staff to study the problem.

  Bill Vaughan

- Money doesn't always bring happiness. People with $10 million are no happier than people with $9 million.

  Hobart Brown

- One of the weaknesses of our age is our apparent inability to distinguish our needs from our greeds.

  Dan Robinson

- Actually, I have no regard for money. Aside from its purchasing power, it's completely useless as far as I'm concerned.

  Alfred Hitchcock

- The chief value of money lies in the fact that one lives in a world in which it is overestimated.

  H. L. Mencken

- Wealth is enjoying what we already have, not getting more of what we think will make us happy.

  John Rogers and Peter McWilliams
  Wealth 101

- Before I had a lot of money, I was really quite happy. And, I will tell you this—you may not believe it—I never would have gotten the money if I wasn't happy to begin with. I never would have gotten it.

  Oprah Winfrey

- Money doesn't buy happiness, but that's not the reason so many people are poor.

  Laurence J. Peters

- I started out with nothing. I still have most of it.

  Michael Davis

- After a certain point, money is meaningless. It ceases to be the goal. The game is what counts.

  Aristotle Onassis

HOW MUCH MORE?

Someone once said, "What is considered a living wage depends on whether you pay it or get it." An employee entered her supervisor's office and exclaimed, "I can't live on the weekly salary you are paying me!"

Startled, yet able to compose herself, the supervisor responded, "I'm sorry to hear that. How much more do you need?"

"If only I could make $20 a week more, I would be comfortable."

The supervisor thought it over and agreed to the request. As the employee exited the office she was heard to say, "If only I had asked for $40."

Although a living wage may depend on whether we are getting or giving it, humankind has a tendency to never be satsified very long with what they get. Lee Iacocca's father once told him, "Be careful about money. When you have five thousand, you'll want ten. And when you have ten, you'll want twenty." "He was right," Lee reflected. "No matter what you have, it's never enough."

SPEND IT CAREFULLY

It is reported that when Chrysler was experiencing its darkest financial condition, balancing on the edge of bankruptcy, CEO Lee Iacocca announced that to control costs, he would reduce his annual salary to $1 per year. When one of the stockholders questioned the wisdom of his decision, Iacocca replied, "Don't worry . . . I'll spend it carefully."

SIMPLE ACCOUNTING

A Hungarian immigrant to the United States started out modestly with a wayside vegetable stand. The quality of his products and reasonable prices soon launched him into expanding. He opened a small grocery store, which turned into a dozen chain outlets.

When his son became a CPA, he returned to work in the family business and was appalled by his father's seat-of-the-pants accounting system. He noticed that on the right-hand side of the cash register was a cigar box containing his accounts payable. His daily cash sales were placed in the cash register, and a box on the left-hand side contained the receipts for paid bills. "It's not possible to run a business with this crude system! How do you know what your profits are?"

"Well, son," the father replied, "when I came to the United States, I had nothing but the shirt on my back. I started from scratch and today your brother is an engineer. Your sister is a doctor, and you are a CPA. We have a nice home, a decent car, and a home on the lake. Our business is booming and everything is paid for . . . Now add all of that together, subtract the shirt, and that is your profit."

ANXIOUS FOR MONEY

Did you know that French philosopher Voltaire acquired enough wealth to retire by age forty? It wasn't his prolific writing that produced such wealth, but the investment in nobility's future fortune. Voltaire lent money to young nobles who had not yet received their inheritance. Anxious to enjoy the "good life," these young people borrowed money from Voltaire at 10 percent a year—for life. Their satisfaction of present desires without consideration of the long-term cost made Voltaire a rich man.

WISDOM FROM A SAVVY INVESTOR

Mark Twain was quoted as believing, "There are two times in a man's life when he should not speculate in stocks: when he can't afford it, and when he can."

Warren Buffet might disagree. He is not only one of the richest people in the United States but a much revered investor. Buffet searches for safe established companies whose stocks are selling cheaply, then he researches the company, buys the stock, and waits for the market to value his purchase. It works! Had you given Mr. Buffet ten thousand dollars to play with in 1956, you would now have around thirty million.

He says this about Wall Street, "It is the only place that people ride to in a Rolls Royce to get advice from those who take the subway."

Of course, he is often asked for his secrets of investing. Buffet's most quoted advice is this: "The first rule is not to lose money. The second rule is not to forget the first rule." For those who believe the stock market is their ticket to riches, Buffet warns: "You shouldn't own common stocks if a 50 percent decrease in their market value in a short period of time would cause you acute distress."

WHY YOU MAKE WHAT YOU MAKE

If you have been wondering how to increase your personal wealth, Earl Nightingale suggested, "The amount of money we receive will always be in direct ratio to the demand for what we do; our ability to do it; and the difficulty in replacing us."

JUST THINK

Methusaleh of Biblical times lived to the ripe old age of 969 years. Just think how rich he would have been if he'd opened an IRA account!

IN SEARCH OF WEALTH

According to a 1987 survey conducted by the American Council on Education, 75 percent of the 200,000 incoming freshmen who were polled felt that being well-off financially is either an "essential" or a "very important" end to achieve. Seventy-one percent of the students said the primary reason they were in college was so they could attain high-paying jobs upon graduation.

Unfortunately, only 29 percent of these aspiring young people believed it was necessary to develop a meaningful philosophy of life.

In Srully Blotnick's research reflected in *Getting Rich Your Own Way* (Playboy Paperbacks, 1982), 1,500 people were divided into two groups and followed for twenty years: Group A made up 83 percent of the sample. These people were embarking on a career chosen for the reason of making money now in order to do what they wanted later. Group B, the other 17 percent, chose their career based on what they wanted to do now and worry about the money later.

The data revealed some startling discoveries:

- At the end of the twenty years, 101 of the 1,500 had become millionaires.
- Of the millionaires, all but one—100 out of 101—were from Group B, the group that had chosen to pursue what they loved!

According to this research, people who set out to make their million without serious consideration of their philosophy of life or what career would bring meaning and fulfillment are apt to be disappointed.

Henry Ward Beecher had a point: "Very few people acquire wealth in such a manner as to receive pleasure from it. As long as there is the enthusiasm of the chase, they enjoy it. But when they begin to look around and think of settling down, they find that the part by which joy enters in is dead to them. They have spent their lives in heaping up colossal piles of treasure, which stand at the end, like pyramids in the desert, holding only the dust of things."

WINNERS

- Whoever said, "It's not whether you win or lose that counts," probably lost.

  Martina Navratilova

- Winning is assessed simply by how you feel about life, and how you feel about life is determined by what your life is about.

  David McNally

- You don't have just one chance to win, but you don't have unlimited opportunities either.

  A. L. Williams

- The will to win is not nearly as important as the will to prepare to win.

  Bobby Knight

- Let's try winning and see what it feels like. If we don't like it, we can go back to our traditions.

  Paul Tsongas

- If football taught me anything about business, it is that you win the game one play at a time.

  Fran Tarkenton

- Part of being a winner is knowing when enough is enough. Sometimes you have to give up the fight and walk away, and move on to something that's more productive.

  Donald Trump

- Always imitate the behavior of the winners when you lose.

  George Meredith

- Winning is a reflex action. If you've been there in your mind, you'll go there in your body.

  Denis Waitley

- Winners make their goals; losers make excuses.

  Nido Qubein

■ The lesson that most of us on this voyage never learn, but can never quite forget, is that to win is sometimes to lose.

John Wooden

■ Anyone can win—unless there happens to be a second entry.

George Ade

■ You gotta lose 'em sometime. When you do, lose 'em right.

Casey Stengel

I AM A WINNER

. . . because I think like a winner, prepare like a winner, and perform like a winner.

. . . because I set high but attainable goals, work toward those goals with determination and persistence, and never stop until I reach them.

. . . because I am strong enough to say "No!" to those things that would make me less than my best, and to say "Yes!" to the challenges and opportunities that will make me grow and improve my life.

. . . because total commitment is my constant companion, and personal integrity is my life-time mentor.

. . . because I am learning to avoid the tempting shortcuts that can lead to disappointment, and the unhealthy habits that could result in defeat.

. . . because I have a well-earned confidence in myself, a high regard for my teammates and co-workers, and a healthy respect for those in authority over me.

. . . because I have learned to accept criticism, not as a threat, but as an opportunity to examine my attitudes and to improve my skills.

. . . because I persevere in the midst of obstacles and fight on in the face of defeat.

. . . because I am made in the image and likeness of my Creator, who gave me a burning desire, a measure of talent, and a strong faith to attempt the difficult and to overcome the seemingly impossible.

. . . because of my enthusiasm for life, my enjoyment of the present, and my trust in the future.

William Arthur Ward

ACT LIKE A WINNER

Denis Waitley teaches that "winners believe in their worth in advance of their performance." Winners prepare to win, think like winners, act like winners, and look like winners.

Minnesota Vikings football coach Bud Grant ingrained this philosophy in his players through demonstration. Newcomers were no doubt surprised with Grant's first drill at the first session of training camp. Grant lined up the entire team and demonstrated how he wanted them to properly stand for the national anthem. "You're winners," he would say, "so look and act like winners every second you're part of this team."

Winners believe they are winners because they've learned to act like winners— right down to the smallest detail.

QUITE A CONTRIBUTION

Bob Uecker, the former major league catcher turned broadcaster and actor, made periodic appearances on Johnny Carson's "Tonight Show." During one interview he told Carson, "You know, I made a major contribution to the St. Louis Cardinals' pennant drive in 1964." "What did you do?" asked Carson. "I came down with hepatitis and had to be taken out of the lineup." "How did you catch hepatitis?" asked Carson. "The Cardinals trainer injected me with it."

WINNING WOULD BE NICE

The will to win is expressed in a "Peanuts" cartoon in which Charlie Brown, after striking out, is consoled by Lucy. "That's all right, Charlie Brown. You win some, you lose some." Charlie Brown replies, "That would be wonderful!"

Not every situation is a winning endeavor, and at times it seems more are not than are. "Remember you will not always win," Maxwell Maltz reminds us. Some day, the most resourceful individual will taste defeat. But there is, in this case, always tomorrow—after you have done your best to achieve success today.

FANS WANT VICTORIES

A football coach, speaking at his college's booster club fund raiser, was having a difficult time avoiding the subject of his team's losing season. (The coach was no doubt feeling like Casey Stengel after joining the expansion team New York Mets. As he watched the team get beat game after game, Stengel remarked, "I've been in this game a hundred years, but I see new ways to lose I never knew existed before.") He finally decided to make light of his predicament. "As you all know, we're not doing too well in our conference," he began. "We're not winning any ball games, but you must admit, we are exciting to watch." With that he proceeded to expound on the virtues of playing the game with enthusiasm versus the need to win.

At the program's conclusion, a faithful supporter approached the coach and offered this suggestion: "Why don't you play with a little less hype and win a few games."

Avid sports fans agree with "Bear" Bryant that, "Winning isn't everything, but it beats anything that comes in second."

STRONG TO THE FINISH

In the late 1950s Bobby Unser was pumping gas in his father's service station, fixing up cars to race and struggling to save enough to buy more cars.

Unser was determined to become a winning race car driver. His daily pursuit of success resulted in winning multiple accolades in the race car industry including a two-time victory at the Indianapolis 500. Unser went from meager means to achieving considerable wealth, owning a ranch, airplane, racing cars, and Bobby Unser Enterprises that promoted everything from food products to auto tires.

After one of his victories, Unser was asked, "Bobby, what makes you a winner? Your cars are not that much better, are they?"

"I found out years ago that winning pays more than losing," Unser replied. Then he added this profound thought, "It takes very little more to be successful than to fail."

Mickey Thompson, another race car driver, would agree. His racing team built the fastest cars around, yet ironically, not one of those cars ever produced a checkered flag. His cars were hot out of the gates but couldn't finish. The little more Thompson needed were cars built to endure the entire race. Engines blew. Carburators failed. Gearboxes stripped. Thompson's cars were fast starters but couldn't hold up through to the finish line.

Winning is more than quick starts or periodic bursts of energy. From the point of preparation to the thrill of victory, winners are intent to win throughout the race.

"When you are in any contest, you should work as if there were—to the very last minute—a chance to lose it. This is battle, this is politics, this is anything," advised Dwight D. Eisenhower.

The little bit more—determination, preparation, skill refining, guts, perseverance—produces winners who are strong to the finish.

WORK

- A professional is one who does his best work when he feels the least like working.

  Frank Lloyd Wright

- As soon as people hear you say "business," they know you're not talking about "fun."

  John Madden

- Give me a stock clerk who wants to work and I will give you a person who will make history. Give me a person who does not want to work, and I will give you a stock clerk.

  J. C. Penney

- Work is love made visible. And if you cannot work with love but only with distaste, it is better that you should leave your work and sit at the gate of the temple and take alms of those who work with joy.

  Kahlil Gibran

- When we do more than we are paid to do, eventually we will be paid more for what we do.

  Zig Ziglar

- I don't have anything against work. I just figure, why deprive somebody who really loves it?

  Dobie Gillis, TV character

- Some of us will do our jobs well and some will not, but we will all be judged by only one thing—the result.

  Vince Lombardi

- Anyone can do any amount of work provided it isn't the work he is supposed to be doing at that moment.

  Robert Benchley

- The thing most of us don't like about work is that it's so daily.

  Anonymous

■ We need to stop looking at work as simply a means of earning a living and start realizing it is one of the elemental ingredients of making a life.

Luci Swindoll

■ You may have the loftiest goals, the highest ideals, the noblest dreams, but remember this, nothing works unless you do.

Nido Qubein

■ Meaning should be bound up in the work we do. If we cannot find meaning in work, we spend our eight hours every week-day in quiet desperation. If we can find meaning in work, we can keep ourselves recharged, and the organizations we work for stand a chance of staying renewed themselves.

Robert H. Waterman

■ Work is who we are. Our work is key to our "belonging" in contemporary society. It's the label by which others quickly identify us and by which we present ourselves to the world.

Jay Rohrlich
Work and Love: The Crucial Balance

■ Most people look at work as a necessary drag. I don't. I think it's great fun.

Ralph Nader

■ If you are called to be a street sweeper, sweep streets even as Michelangelo painted, or Beethoven composed music, or Shakespeare wrote poetry. Sweep streets so well that all the hosts of heaven and earth will pause to say, here lived a great street sweeper who did his job well.

Martin Luther King, Jr.

■ Fall in love with what you are going to do for a living. To be able to get out of bed and do what you love to do for the rest of the day is beyond words. I'd rather be a failure in something that I love than be successful in something that I hate.

George Burns

■ Folks who never do any more than they get paid for never get paid for any more than they do.

Elbert Hubbard

TAKE YOUR JOB AND LOVE IT!

Work. The satisfaction, fun, and fulfillment you experience are benefits you can give yourself.

In a national survey of 180,000 American workers, 80 percent indicated a dislike for their jobs. That is a sad reflection on an activity that absorbs a major portion of our lives. To make matters worse, few people who dislike their vocation will ever be a success at it. It's a double wammy!

Maybe it's time for a conscious renovation of our thoughts about work. It seems to me we can choose one of two approaches:

First, consider Thomas Edison's view of work: "I never did a day's work in my life. It was all fun." Edison believed the purpose of work was joy and fulfillment. Kahlil Gibran suggested, "If you cannot work with love but only with distaste, it is better that you should leave your work."

Our second choice can be compared to the experience of a foolish king in Greek mythology. Because of his evil lifestyle, King Sisyphus was condemned to Hades forever. His daily duty was pushing a large rock up a mountain. At the end of each day, the rock rolled down again. Each day was a repeat of the last.

Hordes of people view their daily responsibilities as replicating the uninspired, fruitless experience of King Sisyphus. There is an estimated 37,000 ways to make a living in the United States. Whatever our chosen career, it is imperative we stop looking at work as simply a means of making a living and realize it is an essential ingredient in making a quality life.

So how do we get beyond feeling our only work enjoyment is morning break, lunch, afternoon break, five o'clock, and payday?

Will Rogers believed that, "in order to succeed, you must know what you are doing, like what you are doing, and believe in what you are doing." Roger's suggestions deserve a closer look.

1. **Know what you are doing.** Winners in life are willing to do the things losers refuse to do. This principle is ingrained in the employees who know what they are doing. Steve Allen suggests, "Nobody should think they can coast their way through life on the basis of gifts that they have nothing to do with in the first place. You have to pay your dues and do your homework." Winners prepare, study, train, apply themselves, and work to become the best at what they do. Choose one part of your job. Apply your talents. Become the expert. Excel.

Some people approach their jobs like a mosquito in a nudist camp—they see lots of opportunity but can't decide where to start.

2. **Like what you are doing.** One of my favorite questions to ask applicants I'm interviewing is: "What prompted you to apply here?" Over and over again, I've heard, "I thought you might have something available I would like." Our organization doesn't have positions people automatically like. However, we have committed people who love what they do.

I'm baffled by the number of people who spend five-sevenths of their week doing something they don't like so they can spend the other two-sevenths doing what they enjoy. "Whether we find pleasure in work or whether we find it a bore," said B.C. Forbes, "depends entirely on our mental attitude." Sister Mary Lauretta adds, "To be successful, the first thing to do is fall in love with your work." In other words, the secret to happiness, success, satisfaction, and fulfillment in our work is not doing what one likes, but in liking what one does.

When all else fails, listen to the advice of the seven dwarfs: "Whistle while you work."

3. **Believe in what you do.** Successful people are not in a job *for something to do* . . . they are in their work *to do something*. This requisite is difficult to explain to those poor souls struggling through their work day. But those fortunate people who work for a cause rather than so much an hour know exactly what it means.

Get beyond the job description, title, paycheck, or "to do" list. See the end result. Become absorbed with your organization's purpose and mission.

• • •

Many people with a B.S., M.A., or even Ph.D. haven't yet learned what it means to believe in their J.O.B. Now they wonder what they went to school for. Education won't do it! Experience won't do it! A raise won't do it and neither will a promotion. The self-esteem, satisfaction, and fulfillment you experience at work depends on you.

The philosophy of Art Linkletter summarizes what it takes to turn good into better, boredom into stimulating activity, and discontent into commitment:

> Do a little more than you're paid to;
> Give a little more than you have to;
> Try a little harder than you want to;
> Aim a little higher than you think possible;
> And give a lot of thanks to God for health, family, and friends.

To transform your daily "have-to's" into a lifestyle of "want-to's," consider these two questions: What do I want out of my life's work? What am I willing to do to make it happen?

Therein rests the self-fulfilling information you need to love your job and never have to work another day in your life.

Take your job and love it . . . one of life's seldom experienced pleasures.

AN INCOMPLETE MASTERPIECE

Today's workforce can learn from the experience of the renowned English painter and engraver William Hogarth, who was hired to paint a representation of the Destruction of Pharaoh's Host in the Red Sea. The miser who engaged Hogarth's services wanted the painting for his staircase done at a reduced price.

Hogarth plastered the entire canvas with red paint and pronounced the project finished. When the astonished purchaser asked, "Where are the Israelites?" Hogarth answered, "They've all crossed over."

"Then where are all the Egyptians?" sputtered the man.

"They've all drowned," the painter calmly replied.

Anyone who decides to be stingy with their output may very well find a minimal return on their investment. The real benefit comes when 100 percent of time, effort, and energy is applied to any task. Don't let your masterpiece be incomplete.

NOW THAT'S FAST

Three boys were comparing notes about their fathers' abilities. With an air of arrogance and pride, the first boy said, "My dad is so fast he can shoot an arrow at a target and catch the arrow before it reaches the target."

"That's pretty good," the second boy responded, "but my dad is so fast he can shoot at a deer and tackle the deer before the bullet gets there."

Listening quietly, the third lad could restrain himself no longer. "My dad is faster than both of yours. He can get off work at 4:30 and be home by 4:15."

AN ENTERTAINING FLIGHT ATTENDANT

"Good morning, ladies and gentlemen! Welcome aboard United Airlines flight 548, direct from Palm Springs to Chicago." (Wait a minute! My mind starts racing. I know it's early in the morning, 6:50 A.M. to be exact, but I was sure this flight went to Denver.)

"Now that I have your attention, my name is Annamarie and I'll be your first flight attendant today. Actually, we will be en route to Denver so if you were not planning to go there, now would be a good time to get off the plane.

"In the event that we mistakenly land in a body of water, a decision must be made. You can either pray and swim like crazy or use your seat as a flotation device.

"We will be serving breakfast in flight this morning. On the menu I have eggs benedict and fruit crepes . . . not really but they sound good to me. However, the flight attendants will be offering your choice of an omelette or cold cereal."

William Faulkner once lamented that "the saddest thing in life is that the only thing we can do for eight hours a day, day after day, is work. We can't eat for eight hours a day, or drink for eight hours a day, or make love for eight hours a day. All that we can do for that long a period," he said, "is work, which is the reason man makes himself and everybody else so miserable and unhappy."

I'm thankful the flight attendant on flight 548 didn't possess Faulkner's attitude about work. It was evident she enjoyed what she did. Her entertaining approach to a normally routine, boring take-off procedure endeared the passengers to her. Think of the benefits people would experience were they to add this positive approach to their normal routine.

JUST WORK HALF DAYS

Kemmons Wilson, the founder of Holiday Inns, never received his high school diploma. Nevertheless, the school he attended invited him to deliver the commencement address to a graduating class. Wilson began his speech with, "I really don't know why I'm here. I never got a degree and I've only worked half days my entire life. My advice to you is to do the same. Work half days every day. It doesn't matter which half you work . . . the first twelve hours or the second twelve hours."

Wilson's advice may seem a bit demanding. In fact, there are people desperately seeking ways to minimize the hours they work and maximize leisure time. Therein lies a conflict.

A student once wrote to the famous preacher, Henry Ward Beecher, asking him how to obtain "an easy job." Mr. Beecher replied, "If that's your attitude, you'll never amount to anything. You cannot be an editor or become a lawyer or think of entering the ministry. None of these professions is easy. You will have to forget the fields of merchandising and shipping, abhor the practice of politics, and forget about the difficult field of medicine. To be a farmer or even a good soldier, you must study and think. My son, you have come into a hard world. I know of only one easy place in it, and that is in the grave."

What do you want from your work? What level of success do you desire to achieve? And finally, what are you willing to do to make it happen? Now, consider working half-days to make it a reality.

NO REGRETS

Abraham Maslow, at age sixty-nine and nearing death, voiced his regret for so short a life: "I'd conservatively estimate that I have two hundred years of good work in me."

Curtiss Carlson, now in his seventies, is making certain he has no comparable regrets by using all available energy. Carlson is the Chief Executive Officer of the privately held Carlson Companies, which includes the Radisson Hotels, the world's largest travel agency, and the Country Kitchens restaurant chain. Not bad for someone who began by selling Gold Bond stamps out of the trunk of his car and went on to build a business empire.

Carlson has a simple approach to work. "I work Monday through Friday," says Carlson, "to keep up with the competition. Saturday and Sunday give me the edge over the competition."

Is Carlson a workaholic? He doesn't think so. To him, work is not work. It is an enjoyable way of life. In the end, it is not having the money, but making it, that stimulates Curt Carlson. He would no doubt agree with H. L. Mencken who declared in 1932, "I go on working for the same reason that a hen goes on laying eggs."

I'm also convinced Carlson and the prolific author, Louis L'Amour, could have swapped a few notes. His ability to produce book after book no doubt was an extension of his belief that, "the things I would do for fun are the things necessary to my work anyway. My work is also my hobby. I am happiest when working."

ARE YOU A HALL-OF-FAME CANDIDATE?

Roy Campanella is a member of the baseball Hall of Fame. Despite a tragic accident that shortened his career and left him paralyzed in a wheelchair for the rest of his life, Roy Campanella made his mark in professional baseball as a catcher for the Brooklyn Dodgers.

The road to becoming a professional catcher began when Roy was in high school. While trying out for the team, his coach began identifying players for various positions. Roy noticed that the catching position was open, so he volunteered. (As a former catcher, I can report first-hand that it is a dirty, dangerous, and difficult position.)

Roy gave himself totally to becoming the best player on the team from a thankless and unglamorous position. The rest is history.

"Personally, I have never received a promotion in my life," Ralph Waldo Emerson reflected, "that I could not trace directly to recognition that I had gained by rendering more service and better service than that for which I was paid."

How many tough jobs have you volunteered for lately? Are you willing to commit yourself to becoming the best in positions where appreciation is limited? When was the last time you tackled a task no one else wanted to do? Your willingness in these areas may not win you a spot in the Organizational Hall of Fame, but they are necessities on the road to success.

WISDOM OF THE AGES

The president of a management consultant firm summoned her staff together and gave them a commission. "Our job is to ensure increased organizational and personal effectiveness for our clients. For many years, we've done just that. Now, I want you to compile the best of your wisdom and experience on work success so that we might be able to pass it down through the ages."

The consultant team left the conference room excited about their task. They worked long and hard to record their insights. Twelve months later, the finished product was delivered to the president (all 1,427 pages). The president looked in astonishment at this massive masterpiece. "I'm sure this is an accurate accumulation of your knowledge," began the president, "but who is going to sit down and read all of this? Take it with you and revise it."

Again the team went to work condensing their material and with a sense of accomplishment delivered the revised version to the president. "How many pages?" she asked.

"Only 324."

"I still fear people will not read it. Condense it further."

With sluggish discipline, the team condensed their findings to fewer than a hundred pages, then ten pages, and finally down to one single page. Figuring they had come this far, they diligently sought one statement that would reflect the wisdom they had accumulated concerning work success.

When the president read the one sentence, a smile crossed her face and she congratulated the team. "You have truly captured the essence of our work and research findings. As soon as employees and employers everywhere learn this simple truth, work effectiveness will be substantially improved."

What was the sentence? Simply this:

"There ain't no free lunch."

... and there ain't.

ADDICTION OR DRUDGERY?

Dr. Denton Cooley, the world-famous heart surgeon, once confessed to being addicted to work. "I am most relaxed and have the most mental peace when I'm working," he said. "One characteristic of an addict is that he has withdrawal symptoms when he is unable to indulge his addiction. I feel the same way when I'm not at my work. This is particularly true when I go on vacation. I feel uneasy—

almost frantic—to get back on the job." Is it any wonder Dr. Cooley is recognized as one of the world's greatest surgeons?

In contrast, an April, 1990 *Boardroom Report* indicated that substantial research shows upward of 70 percent of all white-collar workers are dissatisfied with their jobs. Of those people, 40 percent say that "they would be happier working someplace else." Over one third of 1,100 middle managers surveyed had been in touch with a job-search company in the past six months. More than half said they had recently updated their résumés.

A survey of 500 salespeople found that one third of sales reps surveyed were on the verge of quitting their jobs! Another 40 percent said they were only moderately happy with their positions. Furthermore, the American Bar Association found that one fourth of the 3,000 lawyers it surveyed planned to change jobs in the next two years.

In addition, in a survey conducted by the Wilson Learning Corporation, 1,500 people were asked, "If you had enough money to live comfortably for the rest of your life, would you continue to work?" Seventy percent said that they would continue to work, but 60 percent of those said they would change jobs and seek "more satisfying work."

Why the discrepancy? How can one person find total fulfillment and even relaxation in their work while the next person finds it drudgery? Could B. C. Forbes be on to something when he says that "whether we find pleasure in our work or whether we find it a bore depends entirely upon our mental attitude towards it, not upon the task itself."

WORRY

- Thinking about what you don't want to happen increases the odds that it will.

  Robert Kriegel
  If It Ain't Broke . . . Break It

- Ain't no use putting up your umbrella till it rains.

  Alice Caldwell Rice

- Every evening I turn worries over to God. He's going to be up all night anyway.

  Mary C. Crowley

- Worry is like a rocking chair: it gives you something to do but it doesn't get you anywhere.

  Evan Esar

- You can't start worrying about what's going to happen. You can get spastic enough worrying about what's happening now.

  Lauren Bacall

- Worry affects circulation, the heart and the glands, the whole nervous system, and profoundly affects the heart. I have never known a man who died from overwork, but many who died from doubt.

  Dr. Charles Mayo

- We experience moments absolutely free from worry. These brief respites are called panic.

  Cullen Hightower

- When I don't have anything to worry about, I begin to worry about that.

  Walter Kelly

- Worry is nothing less than the misuse of your imagination.

  Ed Foreman

- Worry is a thin stream of fear trickling through the mind. If encouraged, it cuts a channel into which all other thoughts are drained.

  Arthur Somers Roche

KEEP YOUR TICKER TICKING

It's a rare occasion that a clock experiences a nervous breakdown. But one little ticker worked himself into a frenzy thinking about how often it would have to tick in the coming year. "I'll have to tick two times per second," he muttered. "Oh my, that means 120 ticks a minute, 7,200 each hour, 172,800 a day." Continuing to calculate his responsibilities, the little clock worried it would not be able to complete the necessary 1,209,600 ticks every week. The clock suddenly realized it would have to tick nearly 63 million times during the next 12 months. The more he thought about it, the more worried he became. Finally the little clock became so anxious his little ticker went on the blink.

Realizing he needed help, the clock sought the counsel of a psychiatrist. "I just don't have what it takes to tick that often," he lamented. The counselor responded, "How many ticks must you tick at a time?" The clock answered, "Just one." "How about using your energies to tick just one tick at a time," suggested the counselor, "and I think you will be just fine."

So, the little clock wound himself up, concerned himself with one tick at a time and ticked happily ever after.

Take life one tick at a time. Although your problems, upcoming challenges, or ongoing burdens seem insurmountable, you'll find renewed strength by taking life one step at a time.

BEST OF BOTH WORLDS

In *Success Is Never Ending, Failure Is Never Final* (Thomas Nelson Publishers, 1989), Dr. Robert Schuller says people often get caught up in a web of anxiety like a poor widow who lived in Asia. According to Schuller, she had two sons and depended entirely on their meager little business to support them. Every day she worried about their business, fretting and hoping they would do well.

One son sold umbrellas. So when the mother awakened in the morning she would look to see if the sun was shining or if it looked like rain. If it was dark and cloudy she would gleefully say, "Oh, he will surely sell umbrellas today."

If the sun was shining, she would be miserable and anxious all day because she feared that nobody would buy her son's umbrellas.

The widow's other son sold fans. Every morning when the poor old widow looked to the skies, if the sun was hidden and it looked like a rainy day, she would get very depressed and moan, "Nobody's going to buy my son's fans today."

No matter what the weather was, this poor woman had something to fret about. With such an attitude she was bound to lose.

One day she ran into a friend who said, "You've got it all wrong, my dear. The truth is that you can't help but win. You live off both of your sons. If the sun is shining, people will buy fans; it it rains, they'll buy umbrellas. Either way—sun or rain—you win!"

From then on, according to the parable, she was a happy and peaceful woman.

IS IT WORTH THE WORRY?

Barbara was an aspiring junior executive who had just been assigned a major project that could enhance her career. At night she tossed and turned, worrying about getting the final report completed in time. Her husband, who had also been kept awake, became annoyed with the sleepless night and asked his wife what was worrying her so much. "My entire future rests on successfully completing this report by noon tomorrow," she said, "and there is no way I can have it done."

Her husband got out of bed, went to the phone and called her boss. "Barbara is a fantastic employee who deserves any promotion you might consider her for. However, this one report will not be in to you by noon tomorrow. Good night."

"What do you think you are doing?" Barbara asked her husband as he returned to bed.

"You have a report due at noon tomorrow. It is not going to be done so I let your boss know, and now she can worry about it."

YOUTH

- There's nothing wrong with teenagers that reasoning with them won't aggravate.

  Anonymous

- Every school morning some 42 million American children gulp their breakfast, grab their books, slam the front door, and dash off to class. Among them go not one but several future presidents of the United States, a handful of future Supreme Court justices and dozens of future cabinet members.

  John Gardner

- A boy becomes an adult about three years before his parents think he does and about two years after he thinks he does.

  Lewis B. Hershe

- You know children are growing up when they start asking questions that have answers.

  John J. Plomp

- The greatest natural resource that any country can have is its children.

  Danny Kaye

- We've speeded up the clock without being very helpful to adolescents. We teach them about fallopian tubes but very little about the meaning of relationships and responsibility toward others.

  Dr. Betty Hamburg

DON'T UNDERESTIMATE YOUTH

How quickly we say, "You're too young for that." Before thwarting youthful efforts, we might do well to remember that Macaulay was a historian at eight. Byron wrote verses at ten. Benjamin Franklin was publishing at sixteen. Six-year-old Wolfgang Amadeus Mozart showed astounding musical ability while his friends were learning do-re-me. He actually published violin sonatas in Paris and London before the age of ten. Douglas Jerrold scored a success on stage when he was only fourteen.

Rudyard Kipling wrote, "I speak to youth which can accomplish everything, precisely because it accepts no past, obeys no present and fears no future."

CHILDHOOD INGENUITY

When Johnny arrived home from downtown with an ice cream cone in each hand, his mother queried, "Did you spend all of your allowance?"

"Nope, I didn't spend anything," he responded.

"Did someone buy the ice cream for you?"

The little boy shook his head.

"You didn't steal them, did you?"

"Oh, no, I wouldn't steal," said Johnny. "I just put a chocolate cone in one hand, vanilla in the other. Then I told the clerk she could get the money from my pocket, but please be careful for Franky my pet frog."

A CHILD'S POINT OF VIEW

It no doubt goes without saying that children see the world a little differently than adults. Their innocence allows them to see life and accept events at face value. Their confusion with the actions and verbiage of adults provides endearing moments.

During the first day of kindergarten, the teacher was explaining the classroom rules to her new students. "Now, when you have to go to the restroom," she began, "please raise your hand."

Sally immediately raised her hand and asked, "How will that help?"

. . .

Children possess an incomparable zest for living. Their ability to enjoy life with all its goodness and adventure is admirable, although sometimes misunderstood.

A Bible school teacher was telling her class about the beauties and excitement of Heaven. She concluded by asking, "How many of you are glad to be going to Heaven?" Every hand immediately shot up—except Billy's. "Billy, why don't you want to go to Heaven?"

"Well," he replied, "I have a baseball game this afternoon."

A child's point of view is honest, sometimes naive, and delightfully innocent.

. . .

One Saturday evening, my nine-year-old son and I were watching a sporting event on ESPN. During a commercial break, *Sports Illustrated* advertised a special subscription offer. Thirteen issues of their magazine along with other amenities, including the recent swimsuit edition, were all available for one special price. As the toll-free number appeared on the screen, my son innocently asked, "Dad, why would I even want the swimsuit edition? It doesn't even have boy's suits."

Oh, the fresh innocence of a child.

•   •   •

Finally, a Sunday School teacher asked his class of 6-year-olds to each name one of the ten commandments. Matthew hesitated a moment and then declared, "Don't drink and drive."

Maybe adults would do themselves a favor to see life from a child's point of view.

YOUTHFUL HONESTY

Iowa's governer Terry Branstad tells a funny story about his first year in office when he took his family around the state to demonstrate all the things to do in Iowa. He and his wife, Chris, along with their eight-year-old son, Eric, were at a crafts fair near Cedar Rapids. As planned, television cameras turned out to hear the governor extoll the virtues of tourism in Iowa.

Unexpectedly, a television reporter thrust the microphone into little Eric Branstad's face. "What do you think about all of this?" he was asked.

The boy looked into the camera and said, "I'm hot and I'm bored and I want to go home."

IT'S O.K. TO BE DIFFERENT

It hurts on the outside to be called different when you are being yourself from the inside. It hurts to be teased. Kids can be cruel. It seems not to matter who you are, where you are, or what you are doing. Someone will be jealous or angry or full of spite, and try to be awful to other people. Be calm, be yourself. Try to remember the person who is teasing must feel bad inside. Try to think why that person is feeling bad. Maybe you can help yourself too! Too often we react with anger when someone is attacking us with words. Maybe there are other ways—dare to be different—think about it!

Being different is like:

Tying your shoe with your left hand.

Starting to bowl with your left hand when you are really right-handed.

Not being fast when everyone else seems to be.

Holding your pencil with two fingers instead of your finger and thumb.

Stumbling over your size thirteen shoes.

Being able to disco when your classmates think you can't.

It's hard to be a teenager—hard to find what is inside. Keep trying, don't stop. There's a you inside that's important to your outside.

Set your own goals. Find what you are inside, be confident as a person. Know what you can do and cannot do. No one can take that away from you.

Know your faults, recognize you have time—work with them. Keep them under control.

Sometimes daring to be different can be like each and every day being a terrible, horrible, awful experience. Take it from Alexander in the story, "It was a terrible, horrible, very bad day."

There was a man born at the turn of the century. As a boy, he was shy and dreamy. While his schoolmates were busy playing, he was off by himself. At school even his teachers considered him a misfit. At the age of twenty-six, this man contributed to mankind the theory of relativity. Yes, Albert Einstein was different but it pays to be different.

It's O.K. to not like drugs and not to want to smoke.

It's O.K. to be your own person.

It's O.K. to make and keep your own goals.

It's O.K. to be different.

This story was given to me by Ardell Conner, the mother of the young boy who wrote the story. Bill Conner not only endured the challenge of youth but as a young boy wrestled with the additional complexities of being mentally retarded. Bill Conner is an example to young and old alike that "it's O.K. to be different."

GLENN VAN EKEREN

Keynote speaker and seminar leader Glenn Van Ekeren is director of People Building Institute. Glenn's presentations, which he has given for national and state associations, companies, education, and nonprofit organizations, are known for their high content, enthusiasm, and down home presentation style.

For further information about Glenn Van Ekeren's programs and other products available through People Building Institute, contact:

Glenn Van Ekeren
People Building Institute
330 Village Circle
Sheldon, Iowa 51201
(712) 324-4873

INDEX